Resisting Dictatorship

Vince Boudreau's book compares the relationship between state repression and social resistance under the dictatorships of Burma's Ne Win, Indonesia's Suharto and the Philippines' Ferdinand Marcos. In each case the dictator faced distinct social challenges and responded with specifically tailored repressive strategies. These strategies shaped dissidents' resources, social bases and opposition cultures, and so influenced the entire pattern and effectiveness of dissent and political contention. The author considers his first-hand research in the countries in question in light of the social movements literature to analyse the long-term interactions between the regimes and their societies in the wake of repression, and during the democracy movements that followed. This thought-provoking book offers one of the first truly comparative studies of dictatorship, resistance and democratization in Southeast Asia. As such, it will be invaluable to students, policy makers and commentators on the region.

VINCE BOUDREAU is Associate Professor of Political Science at City College of New York. His publications include *Grassroots and Cadre in the Protest Movement* (2001).

T0384724

Resisting Dictatorship

Repression and Protest in Southeast Asia

Vince Boudreau

The City College of New York

CAMBRIDGE
UNIVERSITY PRESS

CAMBRIDGE UNIVERSITY PRESS
Cambridge, New York, Melbourne, Madrid, Cape Town, Singapore, São Paulo, Delhi

Cambridge University Press
The Edinburgh Building, Cambridge CB2 8RU, UK

Published in the United States of America by Cambridge University Press, New York

www.cambridge.org
Information on this title: www.cambridge.org/9780521109611

First published 2004
This digitally printed version 2009

A catalogue record for this publication is available from the British Library

Library of Congress Cataloguing in Publication data

Boudreau, Vincent.
    Resisting dictatorship: repression and protest in Southeast Asia/Vince Boudreau.
        p.   cm.
    Includes bibliographical references and index.
    ISBN 0 521 83989 0
    1. Burma – Politics and government – 1962–1988.   2. Indonesia – Politics
    and government – 1966–1998.   3. Philippines – Politics and government –
    1973–1986.   4. Dictatorship.   I. Title.
    DS530.6.B68   2004
    321.9′0959 – dc22
                                                                        2004041852

ISBN 978-0-521-83989-1 hardback
ISBN 978-0-521-10961-1 paperback

To my first teachers: Grace and Gordon.

Contents

Maps

Acknowledgments

It would be hard to imagine a single country specialist, as I have been, undertaking a comparative work of this nature without generous and substantial help from many people. I have been fortunate to receive such assistance, in more ways than I can detail here. A great many of my debts to individuals stem from a larger and more fundamental debt I have to George McT Kahin, and Benedict Anderson, under whose direct influence a cohort of remarkable young scholars formed at Cornell University in the early 1990s. These people thought new thoughts about places like Indonesia, Burma and The Philippines, and, more important, had been taught to treat one another as colleagues, collaborators, and friends. Many of this number helped teach me about Indonesia and Burma with grace, kindness, and more than a little indulgence. I am grateful to this group of colleagues, but also understand that such a group does not form by itself. We all benefited from the generous shadow cast by Professors Anderson and Kahin.

Some of my deepest debts are almost certainly to those who helped me in the field. In Indonesia, I would have been lost without the hospitality of Sarah Maxim and Nobertus Nuranto, the great support of Benny Subianto, and the deep insights of the wild and wonderful Douglas Kammen. Others helped as well: Laksono, Father Budi, Made Tony Supriatma, Joel Tesoro, Daniel Dhakidae, Amrih Widodo and Andrew Abalahin. I spoke to many people in Indonesia, some quoted or referenced in what follows, and some who provided me with background information, insight, contacts of encouragement. Thank you all.

In the Philippines, I have more experience and a more varied list of creditors. I married into a family replete with activists, many of whom helped shape my ideas about Philippine protest, which were my initial foundation for these comparisons. Marivic Raquiza and Fidel Nemenzo, Dodong and Princess Nemenzo, and my own Toinette have been teaching me about Philippine politics for years, with no sign of letting up. Others at and around the University of the Philippines also helped shape this work: Maricris Valte, the scholars, at different times, in the

Third World Studies Center (where I first presented my ideas about these cases) and at the Center for Integrated Development Studies come most immediately to mind. My Philippine family – brothers and sisters-in-law, nieces, nephews, my astounding mother-in-law, and an extensive and wonderful barkada – helped make my two years of field work a walk in the park.

My most poignant debts are to Burmese people, who spoke to me at length though they knew me not at all – and who risked more than I can calculate in those discussions. I cannot acknowledge you here, for obvious reasons – and that is a bitter thing. Some day, I will be able to say that the remarkable poet or activist or lawyer quoted in this passage, or that, was named X. I have not forgotten any of you, and will be grateful forever. The reason these people did talk to me – besides their great kindness – was that the story of 1988, in the details they revealed, weighed heavy on them. To carry this sort of news is an important and sacred charge. I hope I have been up to the task. I did have one kind and capable interlocutor outside of Burma, who I am able to name, though never repay: Kyaw Yin Hlaing, my brother and friend, has done so much to help me, I wouldn't know where to start thanking him.

Many American academics helped me refine and sharpen this work, but I owe particularly great debts to two people, who read this work at just the right time, offering encouragement and criticism in just the right mix to help me along. Mary Callahan helped me with her exceptional knack for comparative thinking and her deep insights into Burmese politics. She has been a net stretched beneath the high-wire act of my foray into Burmese politics. I wonder if any acrobat was ever so grateful for a net. Elizabeth Wood shared her generous insights about repression, protest and clear thinking.

I have others to thank. Charles Tilly played innkeeper as the usual patrons of his Contentious Politics Workshop stomped and stroked various sections of this work over the past few years. John Krinsky, Jeff Goodwin, Linda Gordon, Roy Licklider, Elizabeth Remmick, David Meyer, Francis Piven, Benedict Anderson, Christian Davenport, Mary Katzenstein, Sidney Tarrow, Carol Mueller and Hank Johnston all looked at some portion of this work at some stage, to my great benefit. Three graduate students, Yujin Ha, Begi Hersutanto and Miriam Jimenez helped me with data analysis crucial to developing the Indonesian section of this work – much of it during an exhausting home stretch run.

And every day, Toinette has been prepared to encourage, criticize or scold me, depending on what I deserved.

Thank you, one and all.

Abbreviations

A6LM	April 6th Liberation Movement (Philippines)
ABRI	*Angkatan Bersenjata Republik Indonesia* (Armed Forces of the Republic of Indonesia)
AFL-CIO	American Federation of Labor-Congress of Industrial Organizations
AFO	Anti-Fascist Organization (Burma)
AFP	Armed Forces of the Philippines
AFPFL	Anti-Fascist People's Freedom League (Burma)
AMRSP	Association of Major Religious Superiors of the Philippines
ASEAN	Association of Southeast Asian Nations
BANDILLA	*Bansang Nagkaisa sa Diwa at Layunin* (The Nation, Unified in Spirit and Purpose)
BAYAN	*Bagong Alyansa Makabayan* (New Nationalist Alliance, Philippines)
BBC	British Broadcasting Corporation
BCP	Burma Communist Party
BIA	Burma Independence Army
BISIG	*Bukluran sa Ikauunlad ng Soyalistang Isip at Gawa* (Federation for the Advancement of Socialist Theory and Praxis, Philippines)
BMP	*Bukluran ng mga Mangagawang Pilipino* (Association of Filipino Workers)
BNA	Burmese National Army
BSPP	Burma Socialist Program Party
BTUC	Burma Trade Union Congress
BWPP	Burma Workers and Peasants Party
CBCP	Catholic Bishops' Conference of the Philippines
CGSC	Command and General Staff College (Philippines)
CIA	Central Intelligence Agency (USA)
CIDES	Center for Information and Development Studies
CNL	Christians for National Liberation (Philippines)

CORD	Coalition of Organizations for the Restoration of Democracy (Philippines)
CPB	Communist Party of Burma
CPP	Communist Party of the Philippines
DA	Democratic Alliance (Philippines)
DM	*Dewan Mahasiswa* (Student Council, Indonesia)
DPR	*Dewan Perwakilan Rakyat* (People's Representative Council)
DSO	Democratic Students Organization (Burma)
EDSA	Epifanio delos Santos Avenue
FBIS	Foreign Broadcast Information Service
FBSI	*Federasi Buruh Seluruh Indonesia* (All-Indonesia Workers' Federation)
FFF	Federation of Free Farmers (Philippines)
FFW	Federation of Free Workers (Philippines)
FLAG	Free Legal Assistance Group
GABRIELA	General Assembly Binding Women for Reforms, Integrity, Equality, Leadership and Action (Philippines)
GAPUR	*Gerakan Pemyimpkan Uang Rakyat* (Movement to Save the People's Money, Indonesia)
GOLKAR	*Golongan Karya* (Functional Groups, Indonesia)
Golput	*Golongan Puti* (White Group, Indonesia)
HMI	*Himpunan Mahhasiswa Islam* (Association of Islamic Students)
IBP	*Interim Batasaan Pambansa* (Interim National Legislature)
IIRB	the Indonesian Islamic Revolutionary Board
IMF	International Monetary Fund
IPMI	*Ikatan Pers Mashasiswa Indonesia* (Indonesian Student Press Union)
JAJA	Justice for Aquino, Justice for All (Philipines)
KAK	Komite Anti-Korupsi (Anti-Corruption Committee)
KAMI	*Kesatuan Aksi Mahasiswa Indonesia* (Indonesian United Student Action)
KAP	*Katipunan ng mga Anak-Pawis* (Proletarian Labor Congress, Philippines)
KAPPI	*Kesatuan Aksi Pelajar Pelajar Indonesia* (Indonesian Students' Action Front)
KASAPI	*Kapulungan ng Mga Sandigan ng Pilipinas* (Organization of Defenders of the Philippines)
KEPARAD	*Komite Perjuangan Rakyat anti Dwi Fungsi* (Committee for the Struggle Against Armed Forces Dual Function)

KIPP	*Komiti Independen Pemantau Pemilu* (Independent Election Monitoring Committee)
KKN	*Komite Kabanggaan Nasional* (Committee for National Development)
KM	*Kabataan Makabayan* (Nationalist Youth, Philippines)
KMP	*Kilusang Magbubukid ng Pilipinas* (Movement of Philippine Peasants)
KMT	Kuomintang
KMU	*Kilusang Mayo Uno*
KNPI	*Kesatuan Nasional Pemuda Indonesia*
KOMPIL	*Kongresso ng Mamamayan Pilipino* (Congress of the Filipino People)
KOSTRAD	*Komando Cadangan Strategis Angkatan Darat* (Army Strategic Reserve Command, Indonesia)
LABAN	*Lakas ng Bayan* (Strength of the Nation)
LAFM	Light a Fire Movement (Philippines)
LBH	*Lembaga Bantuan Hukum* (Legal Aid Foundation, Indonesia)
LDC	Least Developed Country
LSM	*Lembaga Swadaya Masyarakat* (Private Social Organizations – the Indonesian equivalent of the NGO).
Malari	*Malapetaka Januari* (January Disaster, Indonesia)
MNLF	Moro National Liberation Front
MPR	*Majelis Permusyawaratan Rakyat* (People's Consultative Assembly, Indonesia)
MR	*Manila Rizal* (Regional Branch of the CPP)
NAMFREL	National Movement for Free Elections
NCHR	National Committee on Human Rights
ND	National Democratic (Philippines)
NDCP	National Defense College of the Philippines
NDF	National Democratic Front (Philippines)
NGO	Non-Governmental Organization
NII	*Negera Islam Indonesia* (Indonesian Islamic State)
NKK/BKK	*Normalasisi Kahidupan Kampus/Baden Koordinisisi Kamahahsiswaan* (Normalization of Campus Life/ Body to Coordinate Students, Indonesia)
NMFJP	National Movement for Freedom Justice and Democracy, Philippines
NPA	New People's Army (Philippines)
NU	*Nataduul Ulama* (Indonesia)
NUF	National United Front (Burma)
NUSP	National Union of Student of the Philippines

Ormas	Mass Organization (Indonesia)
PD	Presidential Decree (Philippines)
PDI	*Partai Demokrasi Indonesia* (Indonesian Democratic Party)
PDP	Parliamentary Democracy Party (Burma)
PDP-LABAN	*Partido Demikratiko ng Pilipina-Lakas ng Bayan* (Philippine Democratic Party-Strength of the Nation)
PDSP	Philippine Democratic Socialist Party
PETA	*Pembela Tanah Air* Defenders of the Fatherland (Indonesia)
Petrus	*Penembakan Misterius* (Mysterious Shootings, Indonesia)
PI	*Perhimpuan Indonesia* (Indonesian Association)
PKI	*Partai Komunis Indonesia* (Indonesian Communist Party)
PKI	*Perserikatan Kamunis di India* (India Communist Party)
PKP	*Partido Komunista ng Pilipinas* (Communist Party of the Philippines)
PMII	*Pergerakan Mahasiswa Islam Indonesia* (Movement of Islamic Students of Indonesia)
PNI	*Partai Nasionalis Indonesia* (Indonesian Nationalist Party)
PPBI	*Pusat Perjuangan Buruh Indonesia* (Indonesian Center for Labor Struggle)
PPP	*Partai Persatuan Pembangunan* (United Development Party)
PRD	*Partai Rakyat Demokrasi* (People's Democratic Party, Indonesia)
PRP	The People's Revolutionary Party (Burma)
PRRI	*Pemerintahan Revolusioner Republik Indonesia* (Revolutionary Government Of The Republic of Indonesia)
PUDI	*Partai Uni Demokrasi Indonesia* (United Democratic Party of Indonesia)
PVO	People's Volunteer Organization (Burma)
RAM	Reform Armed Forces Movement (Philippines)
RC	Revolutionary Council (Burma)
RIT	Rangoon Institute of Technology (Burma)
ROTC	Reserve Officer Training Corps
RPKAD	*Resimen Para Komando Angkatan Darat* (Indonesian Special Forces)
RU	Rangoon University (Burma)
SAC	Security and Administration Committee (Burma)

SAMAKANA	*Samahan ng mga Malayang Kababaihan na Nagkakaisa* (The Movement of Free and Unified Women, Philippines)
SBSI	*Sejahtera Buru Seriket Indonesia* (Prosperous Workers' Union of Indonesia)
SD	Social Democratic (Philippines)
SI	*Seriket Islam* (Islamic Union, Indonesia)
SLORC	State Law and Order Restoration Committee (Burma)
SMID	*Solidaritas Mahasiswa Indonesia untuk Demokrasi* (Student Solidarity for Indonesian Democracy)
SMPT	*Senat Mahasiswa Perguruan Tinggi* (University Student Senate)
SOKSI	*Seriket Organisasi Karyawan Socialis Indonesia* (Union of Indonesian Socialist Karaywan Organizations)
SPSI	*Seriket Pekerja Seluruh Indonesia* (The All Indonesia Workers' Union)
STI	*Seriket Tani Nasional* (National Peasants Union, Indonesia)
SUF	Student United Front (Burma)
TGPF	*Tim Gabungan Pencari Fakta* (Consolidated Fact-Finding Team)
TFD	Task Force Detainees (Philippines)
TPC	Township Peasant Councils (Burma)
UG	Underground
UNDP	United Nations Development Program
UNIDO	United Nationalist Democratic Organization
UR	University of Rangoon
VOA	Voice of America
VOC	Village Organizing Councils
WOMB	Women Against Marcos Boycott (Philippines)

1   Introduction

There are times and places about which nothing seems more significant than the sheer energy and violence that states direct against basic freedoms. The snippets of information that filter from these dictatorial seasons – tales of furtive hiding and tragic discovery: hard times and uneasy sleep – describe lives utterly structured by state repression. Authoritarians bent on taking power, consolidating their rule or seizing resources frequently silence opponents with bludgeons, bullets and shallow graves, and those who find themselves in the path of the state juggernaut probably have trouble even imagining protest or resistance without also calculating the severity or likelihood of state repression. Such considerations surely influence whether individuals take action or maintain a frustrated silence, and will over time broadly shape protest and resistance. They also influence what modes of democracy struggle will emerge or succeed in a given setting. Democracy movements arise against established patterns of contention: their timing, base, and outcome reflect state-movement interactions begun at the dictatorship's outset and reproduced (with adjustments) thereafter, in interactions between repression and contention. Institutions and repertoires of contention that survive, or are ignored by, state repression inform important aspects of anti-dictatorship movements, and influence the role that protest plays in transitions to democracy.

Analysts, however, have seldom attempted to understand *modes* of protest in authoritarian settings – or indeed elsewhere – via its relationship to *styles* of state repression. More often, we have been concerned with quantitative associations between the degree of repression and the extent of protest.[1] Such associations, however, may miss the strategic heart of political contention, in which authorities try to undermine or capture movement activists, discredit their lines of argument, interdict their connection to supporters, and eliminate opportunities for mobilization,

---

[1] Duff and McCamant 1976; Duvall and Shamir 1980; Rummel 1984; Opp 1989.

1

while movement leaders build on whatever opportunities they have, and endeavor to fit activity to specific sets of constraints. To grasp how authoritarian states influence protest requires distinctions *among* repressive strategies, and explanations of how these differences influence political contention.

But how should one distinguish among repressive regimes? How does one gauge authoritarian rule's influences on social protest and dissent? Quantitative answers imagine a more or less linear continuum from utter dictatorship to pure democracy, and locate repression at some point along this range. To fix a regime's character, one gathers information about its degree of openness or brutality. It makes sense, in this view, to ask whether Nigeria or Cambodia is more repressive, and to develop answers based on how often elections, political murders, or press closings take place. In this approach, one can define repression independently of its political consequences, and include physical violence, arrest, preventing assembly and expression, and perhaps even threats to do any of these things. For those compelled to live under a *specific* repressive regime, however, repression's *form* may be as important as its *extent*. A formally democratic state that periodically kills ethnic minorities profoundly affects members of that group. Authorities who tolerate student demonstrations but shoot up picket lines will encourage different contentious forms than those that allow labor a freer hand but clamp down on campus activism. Those who challenge authoritarians – particularly consolidating authoritarians – face off against active, calculating and often cruel adversaries. Citizens cannot plan a strike, a demonstration, a boycott or often even a poetry reading without concern for state reaction, and it makes sense that labor leaders, activists and poets will seek to anticipate, and somehow outflank, state repression.

Authorities facing actual or likely social challenge may attempt to prevent, interrupt or punish dissident expressions in acts we call repression. Following others, we define repression functionally, as coercive acts or threats that weaken resistance to authorities' will.[2] Defined in these terms, repression runs a broad gamut from physically harming members of society (i.e. summary execution and torture) to limiting activity (i.e. close surveillance, threats, warnings). Our definition regards repression contingently: we will see, for instance, that Indonesian officials often issued threats to dissidents that were expressed in terms of outward support or at least permission. On some universal scale of repression based on quanta of violence or overt menace, such supporting remarks

---

[2] Stohl and Lopez 1984: 7; Henderson 1991: 121.

would likely not qualify. Viewed in relation to the Indonesian historical context of punishment and threat, however, they certainly do.

This work explores how particular modes of state attack encourage specific patterns of political contention. Regime opponents anticipate state activity, search out its pattern, and in light of that pattern, calibrate movement practice to navigate between the innocuous and the suicidal. Some movements abandon activist forms crushed by surveillance and violence, others challenge prohibitions, or act evasively. Impending or recollected repression warns protesters away from some acts, and pushes them toward others, either because of the collective memory or more direct menace. Some dissidents are schooled by older comrades; others are haunted by their elimination. Apart from activists' explicit perceptions and intentions, moreover, state repression influences protest and resistance by changing movement organizations and oppositional cultures. Repressive patterns sometimes emerge with relative clarity, and I examine how and why this might be so. But even where state activity is more erratic, dissidents will have little choice but to forecast and adjust to state repression, because heedless mobilization carries such high costs in authoritarian settings.

I compare the Burmese, Indonesian and Philippine cases to illustrate the variety of repressive strategies available to states, and the connection between each strategy and modes of collective action and resistance. In defining the universe of cases in this way, I hope to persuade readers that repression does not operate in similar ways across settings, nor does it vary systematically between more and less democratic or developed settings. Careful comparison among these countries persuades me that case-specific interaction between authorities and challengers, identified most starkly by different patterns of political repression, initiate path-dependent sequences of contention. Naturally, contention in the cases will respond to some common triggers. Philippine, Indonesian and Burmese democracy movements, for instance, display some similar elements, which may help to explain the occurrence of anti-regime mobilization. A charismatic female leader led each, each unfolded during periods of acute economic crisis, and each opposed a regime under increasing international pressure. Still, important variations in the process and outcome of struggle in each case reflect deeper and historically established contentious patterns, patterns essential to understanding how economic or political crisis play out.

The accounts begin with the rise of men who would become their country's most important post-war dictators – Ne Win, Suharto and Ferdinand Marcos. Each developed initial strategies of attack to secure and consolidate power, and these strategies provided templates for later state activity, although this activity also developed and evolved over time for each. Repression in the cases sorts into three simple models. Ne Win moved with swift and deadly violence against any open protest or dissent in lowland Burma, driving resistance underground or to the country's frontier-based insurgencies. Suharto murdered an astounding number of Indonesian communists in the PKI (*Partia Komunis Indonesia*, Indonesian Communist Party) then rooted out or constrained other opposition *organizations*, but less regularly had authorities attack demonstrations, particularly in urban, or central areas. Ferdinand Marcos's contradictory efforts to terrorize opponents and legitimize his regime required that he divide insurgents from moderate, less-organized and semi-legal activists. From these beginnings, regimes and movements tried to thwart one another by adjusting to new threats and opportunities, learning from mistakes, adapting to new conditions.

Interactions between state repression and movement response (what I will refer to as patterns of political contention) establish broader themes in mobilization and demobilization by underwriting context-specific ideas about what constitutes a political opportunity, what movement goals will attract support, and what modes of struggle will likely prosper. Roughly similar events in different settings – elections, newly restrictive press laws, and economic downturns – produce radically different modes of political contention. Over time, a relational logic emerges in the state and social sides of political struggle that informs authorities' views about the difference between harmless and subversive mobilization, governs what challenges provoke state attacks, and structures consequent political contention. I work from these patterned relations toward a perspective on the confrontations between state and democracy movement that ended each dictator's reign.

Three state attacks and movement legacies

A dictatorship may impose itself on society most powerfully in grinding daily encounters between authority and subjects. Nevertheless, authorities often etch the lessons, threats and warnings fundamental to the regime in extraordinary moments of confrontation and repression. At such times, the state wades into society to emphasize or rewrite its rules, often via attacks that crush some opponents and eliminate some modes of activism. Across time and space, moreover, authorities often choose between clearly distinct patterns of repression. Human rights advocates and journalists may dwell on regime brutality as unreasoning and inhuman. Yet something *more* menacing than lapses in rationality or compassion probably guides many attacks: a cold logic and methodology geared

Southeast Asia

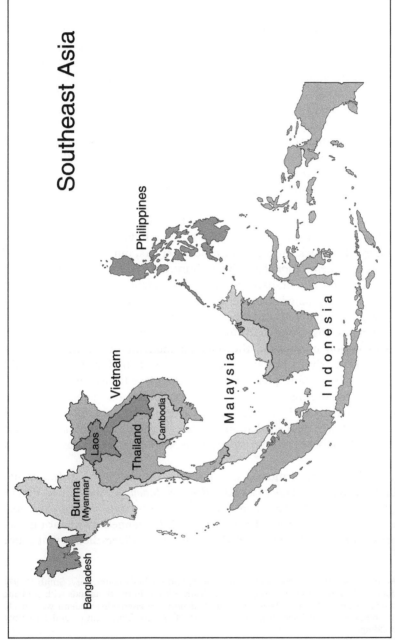

Map 1 Southeast Asia

to specific objectives that constitute clear political lessons and more veiled threats to generations of dissidents. State attacks leave legacies of fear and caution that realign authoritarian rule and social resistance for years. Consider, the rough outline of three political and military coups.

Just over three months after seizing power in March 1962, members of the Burmese military, or *Tatmadaw*, arrived at Rangoon University's campus to confront student protests. On that day, demonstrators stood near the university's student union-building, from where they denounced military rule and protested General Ne Win's coup. Several uncertain minutes after the soldiers surrounded the building, students shook off their initial apprehension, and some even shouted insults at the soldiers. A uniformed figure separated from the uniformed ranks, gave a signaling wave, and the troops opened fire. Many students were wounded, killed, or arrested, while others took shelter within the union building. Hours later, military personnel padlocked the building and dynamited it to the ground – killing a still undetermined number hiding within.[3] According to many, the attack shocked Burmese observers, but so did the status of the target in their national pantheon. Burmese students in the anti-British nationalist movement had erected that student union, under British auspices, after pitched struggle. It figured centrally in the independence struggle, had sheltered students in the first nationalist organizations, had been a nationalist womb and shrine for over thirty years.[4] The shootings and explosion constituted the opening moment in the new regime's campaign utterly to prevent protest in post-coup Burma; there could not have been a more pointed or dramatic place to deliver the opening salvo. In its aftermath, student activists one by one slipped into the countryside to join insurgent and underground forces. Between 1962 and 1988, fewer than six demonstrations, clustered in 1968 and around 1974 to 1975, disturbed the *urban* peace Ne Win built that day; all ended in bloodshed.[5]

A different sort of murder began in late October 1965 in Indonesia. There, ABRI (*Angkatan Bersenjata Republik Indonesia*, the Armed Forces of the Republic of Indonesia) set out to consolidate power after out-maneuvering an attempted coup, most likely planned by junior officers from Central Java. Seven of ABRI's most senior officers died in that coup,

---

[3] Accounts on the exact character of the attack, and the body count, vary. Smith (1997) quotes *The Times* (July 9, 1962) that the death toll was in the thousands with students inside the union. Lintner (1994, 1990) quite definitively asserts that students were inside the building, while Silverstein and Wohl (1964) report fewer deaths, and an empty building.

[4] Moscotti 1974.

[5] Lintner 1994.

and only General Suharto, then commanding the KOSTRAD *(Komando Cadangan Strategis Angkatan Darat,* or Army Strategic Reserve Command) seemed positioned to turn back the challenge. In this moment (or perhaps sometime earlier) Suharto glimpsed an opportunity to eliminate ABRI's arch-rival for national power, the PKI; under his leadership, the army stirred the flames of suspicion surrounding the PKI's role in the coup to full-throated outrage. By the end of October, soldiers led a campaign to murder and arrest Indonesian communists, for which they found willing allies in some rural, largely Islamic groups.[6] Six months later, between 300,000 and 1,000,000 people were dead, mainly on Java, Bali and Sumatra.[7] Soldiers carried out a great many of these killings, but also provided logistical and intelligence support, as well as ideological encouragement to civilian groups. It bears mention that the American CIA *also* contributed intelligence to the operation.[8] When the killings stopped, no organized opposition to Suharto existed. Except for separatist movements in Aceh, Irian Jaya and East Timor, the New Order state virtually prevented organized opposition to its rule from that point forward.[9]

Philippine President Ferdinand Marcos, elected once by popular vote and once by massive fraud, decided in mid-1972 that he was through with constitutional restraints on his power, and declared martial law. To that point, his regime had already done much to concentrate traditionally decentralized power in the national executive. Under martial law, Marcos suspended civil institutions like the Supreme Court and Legislature, and thereafter ruled via unilateral presidential decree. In the days following the September 23 public declaration of martial law, moreover, he imprisoned his parliamentary rivals and a broad range of activists from campuses, labor unions and the recently organized Communist Party of the Philippines (CPP). Four months later, according to an Amnesty International report, some 30,000 people had been detained.[10] For a time, under state pressure, the urban sites of protest – the Plaza Miranda, Mendiola Bridge, and the Liwasang Bonifacio – were becalmed. In the countryside, invigorated military pursuit dealt heavy setbacks to the armed CPP/NPA (New People's Army) insurgency.

[6] Anderson and McVey 1971; Crouch 1978: Schulte-Nordholdt 1987.
[7] Collin Cribb provides a sensitive account of the difficulties surrounding any effort definitively to count the number of people killed in the massacre. His survey of different efforts to arrive at a final tally includes more than twenty attempts, which range from low estimates of 150,000 killed to a high of 1,000,000, Cribb 1990: 12.
[8] See Simmons 2000: 179–181; and Robinson 1984; Scott 1985.
[9] Cribb 1990; Fein 1993; Robinson 1995.
[10] Amnesty International 1977.

However, Marcos was more dependent on US support than either Ne Win or Suharto, and from the first he tried to legitimize martial law to placate American policymakers. This effort gave elite oppositionists, many of whom were soon released from jail, opportunities to position themselves against the regime. Meanwhile, Marcos's heavy-handed counterinsurgency in the countryside was undermined by the dictates of fighting the Muslim insurgency in the South, and by Marcos's greater attention to state building. Hence by 1975, both the urban protest movement and the organized rural insurgency had rebounded, and remained active (sometimes operating in tandem, often separately) through Marcos's remaining years as president.[11]

How should one think comparatively about these cases? The social movements literature has often treated Third World cases mainly as contrasts to industrial society.[12] If we think along these lines, we may well consider it appropriate to describe the three as similar: generic Third World, authoritarian or even Southeast Asian examples of state crackdowns on social opposition. Each state attempted to expand and consolidate strong central power, and to that end threw off earlier post-colonial regimes. We might note authorities' apparently easy resort to violence, or recognize that in the Cold War's descending darkness, each attack (even in *socialist* Burma) hoisted the pennant of anti-communism, and used it for decades to justify some of the region's most horrific abuses.

Yet perhaps more interesting comparative gains await those willing to explore *differences* among Indonesia, Burma and the Philippines, and to consider broad possibilities for how states may respond to opposition. If we think about repression as strategic, we might ask where and how it occurs, and with what legacies. We would soon discover important diversity across the three cases, hints of larger comparative issues. The Burmese military killed students engaged in urban protest, and then devoted its greatest attention to eliminating any visible sign of dissent from their society. After the 1962 student-union massacre shocked Burmese society into silence, the government set to work eliminating protest from Burmese society, and particularly from the cities. Most activists evaded detection by taking great care and few risks. Some students withdrew into an underground existence, and in 1964 joined BCP (Burma Communist Party) cadres in their countryside bases. Authorities made little effort to stop the student exodus, and seemed content to police urban territory and quash the threat of new mass protest. The regime

---

[11] Wurfel 1988; Thompson 1995.
[12] Boudreau 1996; Ponna 1993.

was then also busy eliminating structures and institutions that supported student protest (at first), and broader dissent thereafter. Throughout, the shock of the campus murders underscored the deadly consequences of renewed protest or open dissent.

Indonesian state violence eliminated the PKI's entire organization – first killing many of its members and then driving others into hiding or silence. The slaughter reached the greatest heights in rural areas where the communist party had strong support from rural farmers – which hints at an important strategic decision. Forces working to seize and consolidate national power may first build countryside bases in preparation for larger and more central battles – a classic guerilla strategy. But why would a powerfully central institution like ABRI so strongly focus on provincial struggles, and not concentrate most on wresting control from civil authority in the cities (as the *Tatmadaw* had done in Burma)? Indeed, in the midst of the struggle between an increasingly weakened Sukarno and a rising Suharto, the General took an instructive gamble: he allowed and encouraged Indonesian students to protest against the president. Admittedly, these protests allied themselves with the military leadership. Yet mass demonstrations are risky and unpredictable affairs, less congenial tools than others a hierarchical military might take up.

Here, then, we find two contrasts between the Indonesian and the Burmese assaults: first, and most clearly, while the *Tatmadaw* eliminated protest but allowed protesters to escape into the underground, ABRI killed members of the communist organization, but allowed protest to occur in the cities, even after those protests began to turn against his rule. Second, the Burmese fought the students in the cities to claim that strategic territory, but Suharto eliminated a rival organization – and devoted most attention to areas where the PKI was strongest – even if this meant taking the struggle to places like Bali and Northern Sumatra with comparatively less strategic value. Indeed, in Java's largest and most central cities, he allowed the largest and most organized protests.

In contrast, Marcos's martial law struck at both opposition organizations and protest, but with considerably less vigor or focus. Campaigns against insurgent organizations and more moderate protesters betrayed some equivocation on the new dictator's part. Under US pressure, and more a politician himself than either Suharto or Ne Win, Marcos was unable to keep most parliamentary opponents jailed for more than several months. Many had advance warning and slipped away to the United States or into the countryside before or during the clampdown. The military's efforts against the insurgency never achieved the energy or ruthlessness that Suharto mustered against the PKI, nor did Marcos have existing anti-communist antagonisms in his society such as those that accelerated the Indonesian slaughter, for communism had shallow roots in Philippine experience. Marcos, in fact, devoted less of his initial attention to specific opponents than to reworking the Philippine state's legal and institutional foundations to expand his power. In contrast, Suharto wiped out the PKI before constructing the New Order's apparatus, and Burma waited twelve years for its socialist constitution.

What lessons do these comparisons yield? The scope of state violence differs sharply among the cases. The Indonesian massacre far outstrips anything in Burma or the Philippines, and Burma's crackdown was more violent than Philippine events. These differences do influence subsequent patterns of contention, particularly in Indonesia, where the specter of mass murder haunts all forms of dissent. But more than levels of violence, sharper and more significant differences in the *logics* of violence and repression distinguish the cases from one another. Burmese authorities drove all dissent far underground, where it was preserved but encapsulated in the form of armed insurgencies or secret cells. The Indonesian campaign against the PKI began a consistent state effort to draw an uncompromising line this side of organization: dissidents could protest, but protesters could not organize. Hence the Burmese and Indonesian state strategies exactly reversed one another. The Philippine effort fell somewhere in between, for Marcos was able neither decisively to eliminate the armed insurgent organization or its underground party, nor long silence less-organized, more moderate and open protest. After their authoritarian onsets, actors in each state developed new plans to defeat resistance and extend power, but generally built on and refreshed the politico-institutional legacies of the original attack.

Of these legacies, which are most important? I concentrate on three. The first is institutional and material. State repression killed, bruised, imprisoned and terrified citizens, but seldom indiscriminately. Most focused on specific targets, and so shaped the material and organizational resources that survived, promoting political forms that escaped the state's most direct proscription. Often, forms that authorities judge least threatening survived – as with student protests in 1970s Indonesia. Elsewhere, forms survived because authorities had neither the capacity nor will to defeat them – as with insurgencies in both the Philippines and Burma. Activist forms and organizations, however, do not exist independently of activists. Repression shapes the duration, direction and intensity of activist careers in ways that profoundly influence political contention. Where activist forms and organizations survive state attack, generations of experienced dissidents bring their accumulated wisdom and leadership to the struggle, and provide a thicker and more complex network of support for new protest. Elsewhere, authorities may eliminate entire activist generations, and deprive new claim makers of experienced leaders. Activists in well-elaborated movement structures that include an insurgent army and overseas solidarity branches may sustain a lifetime of struggle. Where repression crushed supporting institutions, activist careers will be shorter, and either more precarious or less committed. Deprived of activist organizations, for example, Burmese and Indonesian dissidents could muster only short bursts of activity and ultimately had little choice, as individuals, but to join the authoritarian mainstream.

The second legacy is tactical and interpretive. Although state attacks target specific adversaries and challengers, they place entire societies on notice, establishing patterns and expectations against which dissidents assess any activity's probable consequences. Here one finds an important contrast with protest in industrial democracies. Activists under more moderate regimes can focus on concerns about recruitment, publicity and movement outcomes, for regime moderation narrows the general possibility of direct repression. The observation, of course, is empirical rather that categorical, and even liberal states sometimes attack demonstrations.[13] In contrast, movements under authoritarian regimes must always anticipate state repression, and explicitly incorporate this anticipation into their plans. Movements that seriously challenge highly regarded state interests may find themselves facing tear gas, gunfire, arrest and summary execution. Some activists deliberately, or at least with resignation, draw fire from the state – as we will see, Burmese protests were cataclysmic and prone to violent escalation precisely because most participants reasonably expected devastating repression. Others plan to negotiate a line between utterly routine activity with little effect and acts that will surely provoke repression. Sufficiently strong movement capacities may allow activists to challenge state proscriptions, while weaker movements may comply with them. Activist plans reflect interpretations of past state responses to social challenges, and these interpretations help establish which events constitute mobilizing opportunities.

Third, historically patterned modes of contention create distinct movement cultures in each setting. Often, the culture represents little more than the combined effect of repression's institutional/material and tactical/political legacies. Yet operating within the constraints of these first two legacies, activists work out ways of thinking politically, engaging society and contesting authority. Even substantively moderate movements in the Philippines adopted revolutionary forms and expressions,

---

[13] Davenport 1999.

while all Indonesian protest, including deeply repressed Marxist perspectives, relied on circumspect and intellectualized assertions of moral suasion. To describe such differences as inherently Filipino, Indonesian, or Javanese, I argue, is less compelling than demonstrating how political contention, and particularly the weight of state repression, worked to change and shape activist cultures. In making the case, I look particularly at how florid state violence at the dictator's rise upset established patterns and cultural expressions. Why do Filipino activists cherish ideological debate, while Burmese protesters follow the flow of mass sentiment? What accounts for the legalism of Indonesian movement discourse, or the exalted place that public intellectuals hold in Jakarta's reform movement? The reckless violence of Burmese students, the obliqueness of New Order intellectuals, the organization-minded radicalism of the Philippine left, all emerged from the historical interplay of states and societies.

These three legacies combine to produce different *patterns* of political contention, going forward, in the three countries. In Burma, protest was a relatively rare but cataclysmic phenomenon. Cycles of rising, increasingly organized protest occur at roughly decade-long intervals, triggered by massive economic dislocation, marked by increasing organization and coordination, and ending with escalating violence. Indonesian protest was on the whole less rare, less violent, and more localized than Burmese contention. Occasionally, protest produced massive rioting, and authorities who responded to dissent with deadly force. Typically, however, dissidents were tentative enough to avoid the starkest repression, and unorganized enough for contention to remain atomized and sporadic. Activist organizations dominated Philippine contention, sometimes steering activity into electoral campaigns, sometimes directing efforts toward the anti-state insurgency, but always in substantial control of when or where protest would rise. These longer-term patterns of political contention, moreover, shaped explosive democracy movements in each case, molding both patterns of struggle, likely patterns of defection from the regime, and movement outcomes. In each phase of the study, therefore, I am attempting to identify and explain not mere repertoires of contentious forms, but repertoires of contentious *interaction*.

The consequence of authoritarian regimes for political contention requires such careful and individualized attention for several reasons. First, they remain woefully understudied and under-theorized. It is difficult to begin making broad generalizations about authoritarian states and social movements without first attempting focused analysis with firm empirical foundations. My instinct in this endeavor brings me to carefully focused comparison among these cases. Second, the authoritarian state's range of options may in fact be broader than those available to democratic states. The openness of democratic societies, the relative ease with which international media, organization and business penetrate liberal countries render them perhaps more similar and modular in their responses to social movements. Secrecy and autonomy, however, the very lifeblood of authoritarianism and cloistered states like those in Burma and Indonesia, allow the coercive apparatus more leeway in repressive forms, producing more varied patterns of contention. The expectation of variety encourages a more open-ended approach to efforts at developing new structural explanations for social protest under authoritarian rule. Where clear patterns emerge from the comparison among careful case studies, they may enable more certain and deft generalization. Finally, efforts to develop connections between established theory and new cases often encounter problems when analysts attempt a too literal transfer of indicators and variables from one setting to another. Rather than mechanical application, we need to reinterpret and sometimes translate theories for application in new settings, in ways that preserve the original spirit of the analysis.

On method and data

It does not take much field work in Burma, Indonesia or even the Philippines before one is almost tempted to give up on social science methodology. The problem is not simply that complete information on protest is seldom available. Data are unavailable in different degrees across cases, and similar collection methods seldom yield comparable information. Even during martial law, Philippine demonstrations were regularly recorded in national dailies, but the Burmese state entirely controls the media and substitutes European football news for any information about internal politics. Indonesian press restrictions wax and wane in response to state pressure, and the media is often *most* devoid of political stories when protest and strikes increase. Nor can one conduct fieldwork in the similar ways in these countries. By the 1990s, Filipino activists were quite willing to grant interviews with foreign researchers, but Burmese who consented to be interviewed hazarded arrest and prison terms. Most of the brave men and women I interviewed in Burma only consented to talk provided that I did not record our conversations, and even then risked so very much. (Yet many were also exceptionally eager to reflect on 1988. I had the good fortune to arrive at Burma at a time when movement participants were less interested in the polemics of the struggle than in attempting to understand it, and that orientation enabled me to have some remarkable conversations.) In Indonesia, I taped interviews with activists and used press archives, but it was often, for reasons that directly bear on my argument, easier to find information on political *ideas* than on *events*. Not surprisingly, then, interviews are perhaps least necessary where they are most freely given. It is, of course, possible to get more comparable data from external and secondary sources. Beginning in 1984, for example, wire reports became available via electronic Nexus/Lexus services. For decades, the BBC and the US government's Foreign Broadcast Information Service (FBIS) have provided external data bases for comparing protest across countries. Yet such sources surely labor under the same constraints that hamper researchers, and so one again expects the most complete information about Philippine protest and the least complete and reliable on Burma.

At the work's heart, perhaps unavoidably, lie differences in the empirical foundations for each case: I hope to make amends for that inconsistency with my comparative strategy, looking to uncover big patterns and trends, rather than minute details of struggle in each setting. Even where it may be impossible to reconstruct all details of any one struggle (or counterproductive to recount only one case in detail) the broad comparisons among them help to build an argument about how analysts might approach the study of protest in similar settings. In this objective, I am encouraged by personal experience: in a decade's study of Philippine protest, I never understood how the armed and rural insurrection influenced urban, legal and organizationally independent protest movements fully until I examined first the Indonesian and then the Burmese cases, both devoid of such interaction. Because the comparative objectives are so central to this project, I make liberal use of secondary sources, and often use my own fieldwork more to answer questions suggested by comparisons among secondary accounts. Such narratives establish the backdrop for my interview and archival research, and allow me to focus on moments of new or heightened activity or state repression – asking why things may have changed when and how they did – or why they did not. It is in the comparative evaluations of answers to such questions that I hope to make my biggest contribution.

Chapter outline

After this introduction, chapter 2 develops this work's theoretical perspective, particularly how institutional/material, tactical/political, and cultural legacies of authoritarian state repression shape protest. In that chapter I distinguish my framework from the structural approaches developed in relation to advanced industrial societies on which I still deeply depend, and consider how analysis of post-colonial states requires adjustments in these approaches. The chapter concludes with a discussion of social movements theory and democratic transitions, arguing that democracy protest represents a particular kind of collective contention.

Chapter 3 sets forth, and attempts to explain the differences in state repression at each dictator's rise. The discussion traces social and political legacies of colonialism and decolonialization to patterns of contestation, threat and fear between rising dictators and other social forces. Discussion then moves to the political and authoritarian norms manifest in the state attack consolidated in the new authoritarian regime. The chapter ends by considering the three cases comparatively.

The rest of the book is organized as two distinct clusters of chapters, each beginning with three case-study chapters that consider Burma, Indonesia and the Philippines in turn, followed by a comparative chapter that reviews themes from the case studies, and develops comparisons between them. Chapters 4, 5 and 6 each describe protest and contention under one of the three dictatorships, beginning with sporadic and cataclysmic Burmese protest, the more constant but scattered, localized and circumspect Indonesian protest, and the Philippine model of steadily accumulating and increasingly mainstream revolutionary, and revolution-*esque* opposition. Each discusses modes of state repression and social resistance, noting the ways in which interactions between the two change over time. Chapter 7 compares and integrates the cases. The final four chapters examine the democracy movements in each case. Working chronologically, chapter 8 discusses Philippine democracy protests, chapter 9 concentrates on the Burmese uprising of 1988, and chapter 10 details the movement against Suharto in 1998. Chapter 11 compares the three democracy movements, and also serves as a general conclusion and summary.

This mode of presenting the material hopefully emphasizes my two central objectives. First I wish to make broad argument about contentious politics in these settings. The repressive activities of an active authoritarian state represent important and indispensable aspects of the movement's political context and broadly shape political contention. A larger point looms beyond this argument: in the contentious and often violent struggles between Southern states and societies, the terms of interaction between state and society often come down to more particular fights. Figuring out how movements work demands sensitivity to context and history. Of necessity, the work I present stays fairly close to the interesting ground of political contention in Burma, Indonesia and the Philippines. But I also hope to demonstrate how one must approach these questions in places like those I study.

Second, regarding Southeast Asia, I hope in each case, and among the comparative set, more accurately to indicate the elements of the state–society struggle that have influenced protest and resistance. By stepping back somewhat from the details of any individual history and contrasting events across settings, I try to single out the influences that shaped protest, and describe more general patterns of state attack and movement response. I think that this context-specific and comparative interpretation of contention provides a useful antidote to generic interpretations of democratization that pay little heed to individual country histories, and concentrate instead on external pressures and inducements. State repression, social resistance and democracy struggle are intimately associated with, and indebted to, contentious patterns worked out between dictators and their oppositions over the years.

2 Protest, repression and transition in Southeast Asia

Ideas about social conflict underwent a curious change over the twentieth century's last decades. At the height of the Cold War, contentious domestic politics seemed always pregnant with broader conflagration. People on both sides of the ideological fence associated social unrest with worldwide subversion (or proletarian victory), falling dominoes (or a triumphant line of march), and the descent into anarchy (or world historical progress). Middle-class American college students in the 1960s joined "the revolution" while US intelligence officers viewed peasants scrambling to subsist as communist operatives. Many then had difficulty recognizing that social movements often pursued limited objectives from autonomous positions rather than as parts of a larger revolutionary process. Decades after Saigon's "fall," however, we face an almost complete reversal: as theories about social movements gain credibility and explanatory power, the fears and hopes about revolutionary challenges to state power have quietly yielded to broader assumptions that struggle seeks more modulated influence and access *within* prevailing systems.[1] Increasingly, analysts examine movement radicalization and violence as signs that participants have become frustrated or disappointed in originally more civil programs of struggle, rather than as inherent aspects of the struggle itself.[2] Of course, attachments to either revolutionary or social movement images have important empirical foundations: for decades world communist organizations *did* often support revolutions, even where these revolutions remained grounded in local conditions, and the Soviet Union's dissolution, combined with a spate of apparent transitions to democracy, encourage more reform-oriented, less revolutionary protest.[3]

Something important fell into the space between these two approaches, however. For decades, movements in Africa, Asia and Latin America

---

[1] Van Aelst and Walgrave 2000.
[2] Tarrow 1998; White 1989; Zimmermann 1998.
[3] Hipscher 1998; Lee 1998; Giugni, McAdam, and Tilly 1998; Garreton and Antonio 1996.

struggled against dictatorships. In the interval, we could look on these contests with a sort of analytical patience, for each at least held the potential for eventual state crisis and social polarization to render them intelligible as preludes to a revolutionary climax. Yet as revolutionary explosions failed to occur and scholarship moved from the anticipation of revolution toward a social movement perspective,[4] analysts also imported assumptions and expectations culled from Northern protest, including domesticating perspectives about the extent of movement demands (they are limited), the methodology of change (movements seek influence *within* existing arrangements), or the likely influence of state repression (repression demobilizes protest).[5] In Ne Win's Burma, Suharto's Indonesia, Marcos's Philippines and many other places, these assumptions impair analysis. Regimes in each country resort to repressive strategies far outside any reasonable civil parameter, and repression's extent and nature greatly shape other aspects of political contention. Movement objectives in each case depend on wider and more variable patterns of state and social power: state repression shaped institutional and political options available to movements, and so some activists operated primarily through armed and underground struggle, others through civil associations, still others via unpredictable waves of popular unrest. Indonesian activists prevented from building large opposition organizations often demonstrated to influence or support particular state actors judged sympathetic to their demands. Filipino activist organizations could draw on both civil and insurgent formations, and pursued objectives ranging from acquiring patronage resources, through promoting reform to pursuing a state-replacing revolutionary program. Burmese dissidents could only frame demands (when they could) in state-replacing terms. These differences, I argue, reflect the distinct influences of violent and repressive regimes working according to particular strategies to control their societies.

The political process model, with its careful attention to the conditions that trigger and shape mobilization provides important signposts for our analysis, but we must still rethink how this processes unfolds in the different contexts of the global South. In many cases, we would be particularly misled by assumptions and indicators designed to account for civil demonstrations in prosperous liberal societies. In what follows, I retheorize elements of the political process model for application to the Southeast Asian context, both to further my own thinking about these

---

[4] Smith and Haas 1997; Opp 1989; Kitschelt 1986; Kriesi *et al.* 1992; McAdam 1982; Tarrow 1998.
[5] Boudreau 1996.

three cases, and as a model for those who wish to undertake similar efforts in relation to other areas of the world. Scholars of state repression in post-Soviet successor states will naturally need to figure out unique puzzles in that area of the world, as would any comparativist or area specialist. While state activity depends on context-specific contests for power, I hope to demonstrate that basic elements of political contention in many places plausibly emerge from the interaction of repression and resistance.[6] The usefulness of these Southeast Asian cases is not, therefore, in their utter uniqueness, but rather that state repression and social resistance in Southeast Asia interacted to produce particularly salient patterns that may have broader theory building and comparative utility.

The post-colonial state and social challenges

Processes of state and social formation in Africa and Southeast Asia were in significant ways unique.[7] In many post-colonial countries, including at least two under consideration here, successor states at independence were barely distinct from other groups striving to control government. Decolonization often so drained state resources that apparent national leaders and challengers stood on relatively equal footing.[8] Southeast Asian independence struggles and World War Two mobilized social demand and reduced central state capacities. In Indonesia, this process created myriad local and autonomous militia; in Burma, it produced a single but ideologically diverse national leadership, and sharpened ethnic antagonisms. In the Philippines (where, among these three cases, the most unified and institutionally coherent apparatus existed) it still produced leftist challenges and fiscal crisis. Over time, from the jumble of mobilized nationalist movements, post-colonial authorities consolidated power. It is tempting to read history backward, as if one band of robbers or heroes had from the outset been destined to rule. In truth, however, the outcome of these power struggles was seldom evident beforehand, and early post-colonial politics were often more contests among rival social networks than between states and societies.

The prior emergence, under colonial auspices, of social networks capable of mounting advanced forms of national or proto-national struggles posed particular problems for post-colonial states, problems absent from the global North. Consider the more familiar sequence of European state

---

[6] This interactive approach picks up principles laid out in McAdam, Tarrow and Tilly 2001 (see especially pp. 44–63).
[7] Young 1994.
[8] Randall 1998; Alatas 1997; Migdal 1988.

and social emergence. Much of the literature argues that styles of protest and collective tactics (commonly, the *collective repertoire*) develop in relation to opportunities and ideas enabled or endorsed by emerging state institutions and expanding social networks. Under such influences, people invent new forms of collective activity, which are then reproduced and diffused. Charles Tilly describes how Britain's evolving national parliament encouraged citizens to demonstrate in the national capital rather than make local and unilateral attacks on tax collectors, landlords and the like.[9] Emerging national institutions both opened new venues for political contention, and more obviously linked grievances to national policy. Broader social connections allowed populations to synchronize claims and form common cause, thereby encouraging national social movements.[10] Still, the new state institutions pre-dated, and could settle in before these modes of challenge gathered steam – and so authorities could develop a politics of scale while society remained localized and fragmented.[11]

Consider a contrasting post-colonial experience, where the imperial state's centralized institutions and processes provided a prominent target for national protest rather early in the game. Indigenous elite networks germinated within the colonial regime, seeded by contacts in schools, the local bureaucracy, and (sometimes) representative assemblies. Colonial institutions, although nationalist targets, also helped colonial elites and other members of local society develop the ideas, power and networks to challenge foreign rule.[12] The subsequent collapse of colonial regimes, and the labored attempts of local successors to resuscitate its remnants on indigenous foundations (with vastly diminished resources) rendered post-colonial states far more vulnerable to, and less distinct from, other social contenders.[13] *Each* of the three new states we are concerned with, moreover, gained independence after profoundly damaging World War Two fighting – both under the initial Japanese occupation and at the allies' return. In some cases, the damage mainly crippled the infrastructure and economy, as in the Philippines. In Burma, the fighting also shattered the last possibility of coherent and civil relations among different ethnic groups. War-ravaged and cut off from metropolitan resources, astride perhaps precociously mobilized societies, and attempting to

---

[9] Tilly 1995.
[10] Tarrow 1998.
[11] Badie and Birnbaum 1983.
[12] Anderson 1983a; Lockman 1988.
[13] Migdal 1988.

measure up to colonial standards for administrative scope, each needed to reconsolidate central state power.

The project often faced threats absent from Europe centuries earlier, for the anti-colonial struggle had politicized social networks within which post-war Southeast Asian leaders jostled one another for power – and the post-colonial state's initial social base reflects that struggle's character and extent. The prolonged, mobilizing Indonesian revolution produced an energetic and diverse social base, while the managed transition to independence in the Philippines allowed a narrow colonial elite to maintain power.[14] In Burma, when the nationalist struggle moved to the final, more negotiated settlement phase, nationalist elites narrowed their social base, and important divisions among leaders emerged more clearly. Weakened or divided independence coalitions proved volatile. In case after case, some coalition faction seized the upper hand and drove erstwhile comrades to insurgent and revolutionary challenges. The relatively equal capacities of new states and non-state challengers produced more balanced, and so particularly dangerous struggles among them. For all these reasons, the new Burmese, Indonesian and Philippine states first spread their independent wings during perilous seasons. Confronting comparatively daunting social challengers, authorities never developed the prior political hegemony in advance of social mobilization that allowed European states to face national social movements from a position of comparative strength, because the *colonial* state (rather than conditions at independence) had already called forth and shaped these social challenges.

The juxtaposition of embryonic states and mobilized social networks produced peculiar contentious dynamics. Institutionally weak and resource poor, post-colonial states had comparatively little prestige or authority with which to meet opponents. The institutions of emergent rule may have looked amateurish and flimsy;[15] the state's ideological ramparts may still have been under construction and easily breached. New political personages could seem under-whelming and unsettled, particularly in relation to nationalism's sweeping promises.[16] Authorities facing social challenges found themselves hard pressed and beleaguered, and often fell back on sheer fire power.[17] In this inhospitable

---

[14] Anderson 1988.
[15] Tarling 1998.
[16] This also reflects modes of transition. Anderson calls attention to contrasts between the opulence of Philippine assembly members and the simplicity of Indonesian nationalists. Anderson 1998: 279.
[17] Dinnen 1999; Linz and Chahabi 1998.

climate, post-colonial state leaders probably did not think about protest and resistance as votes won or lost, as friction dragging on a favored policy, or even as redistributive threats to property. Rather, they had reason to fear the loss of power, the anger of adversaries, death and retribution. This fear motivated a more strategic way of engaging political protest and social movements. In the comparatively high-stakes struggle for national power, state actors laid plans to disperse their most formidable opponents.[18] Officials, moreover, probably did not equally fear all opponents. Some dissidents exercised restraint, had limited resources, or resources that did not threaten the regime's particular purchase on power. Other challengers, however, may have wielded sufficient power, in precisely the most dangerous currency, to upset officials. Perhaps they possessed a strong organization, key links to international backers, or a powerful popular base. Depending on the foundations of state power – which naturally vary from case to case – one or another such opposition movement may loom particularly large and inspire special modes of repression. Authorities needed to decide whom to fear, to what extent, and with what consequences.

The active state and social movements theory

Structural models of political contention concentrate on how both stable and volatile environmental conditions influence social mobilization.[19] Some analysts examine how the institutional legacies of long-term processes like state building influence collective repertoires;[20] others note how volatile structural changes increase or decrease political opportunities for mobilization.[21] Discussions on either side of this divide, however, depict the state as oddly passive and dominated by institutional features, rather than by strategy.[22] Centralized states funnel protest in national directions as a deep ravine forces water into narrow cascades, and decentralized states encourage local and diffused expressions of claim making, the way a delta dissipates a slow river. Even more dynamic state programs and interests emerge in the language of architecture and geography: a president's sympathy may open new doors for a movement; a woman's promotion to the justice department may improve the terrain for women's struggles. Under some conditions, of course, this image may

---

[18] Brown 1996.
[19] Gamson and Meyer 1996; Tilly 1995.
[20] Eisinger 1973; Tilly 1978; Kitschelt 1986; Tilly 1986; Tilly 1995.
[21] McAdam 1982; Tarrow 1998; McAdam, Tarrow and Tilly 2001.
[22] Hoover and Kowalewski 1991: 151.

make sense: where officials are relatively secure, they may meet claim making with lethargy and organizational routines, and not fret over their hold on power. Even so, research on state repression in advanced industrial democracies is replete with examples of exceptionally active states taking explicit aim at dissidents.[23]

But even if descriptions of state lethargy appropriately capture institutionalized and secure states' responses to protest, they fail in connection to more besieged Southeast Asian state actors in the immediate postcolonial period. The Burmese and Indonesian states were particularly fluid, composed of politicians, soldiers, revolutionaries and clerks all trying to grasp the new roles into which they had been thrust. Especially in the decades following independence, Southeast Asian states were every bit as much in motion as their societies. How should we adjust our analytic approach to explain how calculating authorities operating in fluid state organizations respond to pressure from powerful social forces? First, we anticipate that state survival, rather than mere police practice, biases or cultures, drives repression. In strategic interplays between authorities and dissidents (involving state leaders' ideas about their vulnerability and peril relative to social challengers) security force orientations (or the state's degree of centralization, strength or openness) will not explain patterns of repression.[24] Those in power will probably think about dissidents as people or organizations with track records for reliability, treachery, power or weakness, and calculate repression accordingly. Hence, analysts might profitably analyze repression as a response to specific social challenges to specific authorities.[25]

Second, modes of repression and social resistance will perhaps be more important than mere levels of either – a point not entirely embraced by the literature to date. Some of the most established debates about repression and social movements concern themselves entirely with relations between *levels* of repression and *levels* of mobilization,[26] or between levels of state and social violence.[27] But quantitative measures of state violence, democracy, or strength sometimes describe incomplete pictures, for a generally violent state may use force selectively, and a democratic regime may still discriminate against certain social forces.[28] We need, instead, a more strategic reading of violence, democracy and strength cognizant of larger

---

[23] Davenport 1999; della Porta and Reiter 1998; Koopmans 1997; Davenport 1996; Davenport 1995; Francisco 1996.
[24] Escobar 1993.
[25] Jacobs 1979; Gartner and Regan 1996.
[26] Mason and Krane 1989; Khawaja 1993.
[27] White 1989; Lichbach 1987.
[28] For an especially nuanced typology of different modes of repression, see Earl 2003.

state–society relationships: if the state is violent, in relation to what challenges is it particularly so? If the state is undemocratic, to what sort of voices is it most determinedly deaf? If the state is strong or weak, in relation to which social forces is this strength or weakness most manifest? Authorities' ability to shut off some modes of dissent or favor others – or a movement's ability to ignore or maneuver around such proscriptions – may set the political table for years to come.

Even work that accounts for repressive modalities often seeks to explain when and why different repressive modes produce variable levels of protest. Both Francisco's predator–prey model (which argues that authorities and movements adapt to one another) and Loveman's fine work on strategies of repression and embedded social networks ultimately explain potentials for sustained collective action.[29] The strategic logic so important to each argument, however, suggests that interactions between state and society loom largest when fundamental issues of power (on both sides of the contest) hang in the balance, and mobilization levels may only partially help us understand these issues. Questions about how state and movement interactions shape modes of contention and contestant power should be more central to the analysis. Such a relational logic more closely informs DeNardo's work, which recognizes that state and social strategies evolve in light of perceived advantage and vulnerabilities during struggle.[30] Similarly, Beissinger's analysis of the Soviet Union's collapse describes both how state repression shaped and marginalized nationalism in long "quiet" phases, and how "noisy," active nationalist mobilization transformed collective identities and strategies – and ultimately the state. If the distinction between quiet and noisy politics is still described in partly quantitative terms, Beissinger understands that "[M]uch of what occurs in the 'quiet' phases of nationalism conditions what takes place within the 'noisy' stages."[31] The reverse, of course, is also true, particularly when regimes begin with periods of noisy repression: patterns of repression and resistance *both* provide an essential context for interpreting what political contention, ultimately, will mean.

I begin my analysis with three critical moments of state attack on their societies. Such attacks suggest whom authorities feared, and on which flank they felt most vulnerable. Each attack helped a rising dictator hurdle barriers to power erected by social and political rivals, but also indicated which of these rivals seemed most dangerous to the new regimes, none of which indiscriminately attacked its society. I regard these attacks as

---

[29] Francisco 1996; Loveman 1998.
[30] DeNardo 1985.
[31] Beissinger 2002: 26.

chilling applications of a calculus gauged to reinforce and extend emerging state power, and explain them by examining the balance of forces and histories of animosity transmitted from the colonial period through independence. These attacks wiped some historical slates clean, but also left new marks: a record of state actors' anxiety, inscribed in a fresh reordering of social and political relations.

Strategic interactions and four principles of analysis

The logic of conquest frequently sprouts into a logic of rule. Repressive programs, enacted by authorities facing regime-endangering threats or nurturing regime-building plans reveal ambitions and fears, and also provide a foundation for new political arrangements. Subsequent policy both institutionally reproduces and adapts initial repressive programs, suggesting how and against whom authorities will use force and violence.[32] As we will see, adaptation is not always perfect, and differences between what a situation demands and what officials are accustomed to do often opens opportunities for anti-regime mobilization. State attacks also reshape social forces. Some do not survive authoritarian murders, arrests, or intimidation campaigns. Repression may eliminate the media, close university campuses and even constrain informal gatherings that support or encourage movements. Political activists and dissidents develop strategies based on how they understand repressive frameworks and use surviving institutions; analysts should pay heed as well, and attempt to discern the strategic dimension in early regime attacks, and recognize both modification in that strategy that respond to unfolding political events, and institutional mechanisms that extend established modes of repression.[33] These considerations prompt me to suggest a four-fold adjustment in how we investigate state repression and its influence over social movements.

Principle 1: Authorities uncertain of their grasp on power will more likely engage social movements strategically, to identify and neutralize their most dangerous opponents. Analysis should search out this pattern. It remains important to tally people imprisoned, killed or tortured, and many have undertaken the task of examining what general conditions likely encourage such violence.[34] Still, this accounting cannot substitute for efforts to understand repression in terms of the targets and tactics that authorities most insistently proscribe. Movement efforts to mobilize populations

---

[32] Worby 1998; Hoover and Kowalewsky 1991: 152; Jenkins 1985.
[33] Fatton 1991; Coronil and Skurski 1991; White 1989.
[34] See, for example, Mitchell and McCormick 1988; Poe and Tate 1994.

likely respond to these patterns of repression, and by understanding authorities' orientation toward collective action, we can begin to figure out the latitude available for different contentious forms. Claim makers likely plan or adopt activity in the light of expected state responses. Under auspicious material or political conditions, they may risk expressly prohibited and repeatedly repressed forms of struggle. Burmese activists, for instance, sometimes undertook such risks when widespread economic crisis had already mobilized broad social discontent. Short of these rare frontal assaults, claim makers may seek to avoid state repression by adjusting their strategies, reorganizing their formations, or seeking shelter and support from civic institutions or powerful allies.[35] Movement leaders, activists and cadres not only anticipate how a state might respond to one mode of collective action or another (the attribution of threats and opportunities)[36] they also gauge the level of popular support that any campaign or mode of struggle will attract.

To date, social movements' literatures have tended toward two important explanations of movement strategy: new contentious repertoires often emerge in relationship to long-term shifts in social and state structures, and subsequently diffuse across populations and time.[37] The concept of the repertoire and its evolution, however, says more about possible tactics at any moment than about those actually selected by a given movement. *Within* protest cycles, scholars have linked changes in collective tactics to the different stages in the struggle: activists may use more mass mobilizing and moderate tactics during contention's ascending curve, and radicalize or institutionalize as protest peaks and then declines.[38] McCammon has argued that defeats are particularly important in motivating movements to change tactics, while others link tactical change to efforts to sustain their political initiative or retain their mass base.[39] Some examine how different levels of repression influence collective forms.[40] Important clues to movement strategy, however, may be connected to how movement participants respond to the forms of state repression they encounter or expect. States that squeeze off particularly threatening modes of resistance frequently leave room for other

---

[35] McAdam (1983) speaks of similar tactical innovations in the US black insurgency, as civil rights activists adjusted to segregationist opponents' moves to undercut them. I am here more interested in a state–movement nexus, mainly because of the overwhelmingly statist character of the movements I examine.

[36] McAdam, Tarrow and Tilly 2001: 46–47.

[37] Tilly 1995.

[38] Tarrow 1998.

[39] McCammon 2003; Gibson 1989.

[40] White 1989.

expressions – and this opens a new range of questions. How do patterns of repression influence the resources and plans available to activists and claim-makers? What imprints do different repressive forms leave on social movements? Given actual and expected patterns of state repression, can we begin to develop more nuanced concepts of political opportunity that is contingent on repression-shaped notions of possible movement strategy? Even in the less strategic or purposive realm of movement culture and activist orientation, we can ask about the legacy of state repression.[41]

Such questions divide into three categories that together constitute the remaining three principles of analysis. *Principle 2: The range of legal and illegal organizations that survive repression shapes the modes of struggle within range of claim makers under authoritarian rule.* Are legal urban organizations destroyed? Are underground organizations eliminated? How do surviving organizations shape modes of struggle? An array of armed insurgent organizations may accumulate capacities to displace a state, but few faculties for urban-based reform campaigns. Prohibitions on movement organization may only allow claim makers to mobilize limited and immediately affected constituencies. Where both underground insurgent organizations and legal protest organizations exist, a kind of cooperation may evolve between the two, wherein combat victories force regime concessions that encourage protest, and legal struggles secretly recruit for the armed movement.

Principle 3: Movement participants' selection of contentious forms occur against larger issues of power, informed by risk hierarchies associated with different modes of repression. Activists and claim makers, no less than authorities, assess threats and opportunities.[42] State acts that imprison, kill or intimidate social challengers, also serve warning to future activists. Authorities that routinely fire on urban demonstrations will likely do so in the future; a military that hunted one party to extinction will not likely tolerate a similar group's emergence. A student march in one setting may risk little; in another, it may risk all. Past contention provides a context that defines which forms of struggle are routine and which more directly challenge authorities. Because idiosyncratic and context-specific hierarchies of risk exist among contentious forms, structural changes *acquire significance* as political opportunities by changing a regime's ability to proscribe modes of collective action or claim makers' willingness to defy those proscriptions.[43] Hence it may be more interesting to ask under what

---

[41] See Tilly 1999.
[42] Fatton 1991; White 1989; McAdam 1983.
[43] Lichbach 1995; Moodie 2003.

conditions people mobilize in *particularly subversive ways* than merely to ask why they mobilize.

Principle 4: Opposition cultures are at least partial consequences of inter-action between authorities and society, and may serve to reproduce authoritarian proscriptions even as state power weakens. Whether movements "typically" burn down police stations, give democracy speeches or recruit urban workers to the armed struggle largely depend, I have so far argued, on state activity, its legacies, and movement responses. Over time, these possibilities become encoded into larger ideas about what is politically possible, how one must live under a particular regime, and what kinds of acts might change things. Tactical considerations may move from the realm of explicit calculation to pre-strategic ideas about what one might or should do. In the Philippines, many people of all classes came to believe that the dictatorship would fall when organized and revolutionary forces grew sufficiently strong, and ideas about coordinated opposition struggle lurked behind most anti-regime efforts; in Burma, some regime critics paid as much attention to auspicious cosmic alignments as to insurgent plans, and even underground activists seldom imagined that they could "make" the anti-Ne Win revolution. In defining large sweeps of opposition imagination, cultural patterns go beyond mere accumula-tions of institutional possibilities and cautionary tales learned, and instead influence how citizens think about politics and their roles in it. Repression often sharply rewrites some of these patterns, and subsequent opposition cultures may prolong and reproduce repression's influence.[44]

These principles suggest a strategy for contextualizing broadly useful structural arguments. I have argued elsewhere that political opportunity is contingent on movement demands and forms of struggle.[45] Collective action modes have particular political logics: some aim at a broader voice within the state, some aim to amass power to displace the state, and some combine the two. Since all structural shifts do not encourage all conten-tious forms, we cannot define opportunity independent of a movement's tactics or objectives;[46] a state land-reform campaign may encourage demonstrations but undercut a revolution's ties to its mass base. Movements angling for international support against an abusive regime may only respond to opportunities that promise a significant foreign audience. Efforts to identify opportunity structures *outside* places where reform-oriented movements typically seek broader voice in liberal

---

[44] See the essays collected in Meyer, Whittier and Robnet 2002.
[45] Boudreau 1996.
[46] See Moodie 2002: 49–51.

regimes require that we rethink the relationship between structural change, established patterns of state activity, and movement objectives.

Moreover, opportunity is not merely contingent on the form of collective struggle, but also on the political meaning of specific collective acts in the power balance between an authoritarian state and its society. For long stretches, politics in Burma, Indonesia and the Philippines operated under conditions that differ from those in the global North, and political opportunities in each reflect assumptions about what contention might achieve under those specific conditions. Different forms of state repression *also* promote case-specific logics of opportunity. Modes of repression menace some expressions and accommodate others; authorities stake their reputations in some realms, but not elsewhere. Real political opportunities undercut the state's dominant strategy of control and intimidation: to identify such opportunities, one must figure out repression's over-arching logic and also distinguish routine from subversive collective acts. Authorities may allow, encourage, or even compel some collective tactics, channeling them in directions that neither threaten authorities nor especially jeopardize participants – but in what ways should we consider exogenous triggers for anemic activism true "opportunities?"[47] Other conditions, other triggers, may encourage claim makers to mount forbidden modes of activity in the very teeth of state repression. Identifying the especially important opportunities that encourage such acts, and the circumstances under which these opportunities can occur, requires careful attention to context, and a willingness to bring interpretive skills to the effort.

This work follows the prescriptions of this perspective. Proceeding via comparisons among the case narratives, I first attempt to discern and describe patterns of state repression, and the contentious politics to which they give rise. Working with what organizations and allies they can, burdened by the shadow of state repression, movements were not merely encouraged or inhibited by repression: they were sculpted by it. Activists in each setting, moreover, needed to decide whether to work within state prohibitions or to challenge them – each needed to decide how unfolding conditions might alter the political balance sheet inscribed since the dictator's rise. Most approached these problems with some understanding of how the state dealt with activists in the past; virtually all worked from within oppositional cultures greatly changed by dictatorship. Together, interpretations of how repression, surviving institutions, activist

---

[47] Earl 2003. Earl relies on Oberschall's (1973) concept of "channeling" in her exposition.

calculation, and oppositional cultures interact help explain patterns of protest and resistance in these three Southeast Asian dictatorships.

Democracy struggle and social movements theory

This work culminates by comparing democracy movements in the three cases from a social movements' perspective: a logical theoretical pairing which nevertheless remains in its infancy. By far, most scholars who are interested in transitions to democracy have focused on long-term developments in the class and social structure,[48] short-term realignments in the authoritarian regime's coalition,[49] or international pressures, demonstration effects and diffusion.[50] Few investigators focus on the collective struggle itself, save descriptively, and this struggle may be an essential influence on the decisions so central to many explanations of regime transition.[51] Admittedly, democracy movements rarely *themselves* bring down governments, and we should be wary of claims that equate democratization with strong pro-democratic mobilization.[52] More commonly, pro-democracy activists influence regime transitions by paralleling or accelerating initiatives originating within the regime, or by sparking defections from the regime by acts of protest and dissent. Still, where protest movements are most involved in the process, as in the Philippines, we should perhaps ask why this is so.[53] In what remains of this chapter, I will clarify my understanding of the democracy movements' particularity *qua* movement by situating them in established contentious patterns.

In what follows, I argue that protest and struggle exercise an independent influence on regime transitions. Established patterns of contention help us anticipate when, how and with what consequences regimes are likely to break down and change. In some ways, the effort runs parallel to recent arguments about the political and economic basis for regime transition. In a telling critique of the choice-based literature of regime realignment, Haggard and Kaufman strive to explain actor preferences, rather than taking them as exogenous, as others commonly do.[54] Their corrective concentrates on political economic conditions, arguing in part

[48] Lipset, Seong and Torres 1993.
[49] O'Donnell and Schmitter 1986; Snyder 1992; Przeworski 1991; Karl 1990.
[50] Huntington 1991; Pye 1990; Hill and Rothchild 1986; Haggard and Kaufman 1997; Pion-Berlin 1997; Lee 2001; Becky 2001.
[51] For exceptions, see Collier and Mahoney 1997; Bormeo 1997; and Adler and Webster 1995.
[52] Glenn 1999.
[53] Geddes 1999.
[54] Haggard and Kaufman 1997.

that economic performance and need shape political opportunities and structure actor preferences. Elizabeth Wood's explication of an insurgent path to democracy argues that the escalating costs of protracted insurgent struggle in El Salvador and South Africa divide the regime's political and economic elite from its security forces, making the former interested in negotiated settlements even though the latter prefer to continue to fight. Wood places contention at the center of her explanation by demonstrating that patterns of insurgency encouraged the regime crisis and divisions (which others have analyzed in isolation from social challenges).[55] Bratton and van de Walle examine regime leaders' decisions to reform in light of the breadth, power and viability of opposition coalitions that emerge in struggle.[56] Histories of struggle also influence other aspects of the transition process, shaping the possibility of alliances between former regime members and activists, the possibility of defections from the regime, and the politics of the transition itself.

To understand how repression may shape transitions to democracy, we must first ask how contemporary democracy movements have often worked. An important clue lies in their rather peculiar combination of goals and tactics. For much of this century, rather clear associations existed between a movement's goals and its level of violence. Movements with broader, state-replacing objectives more regularly adopted armed struggle, while reform-oriented movements sought non-routine but generally less violent tactics. Mao famously wrote that political power came from the barrel of a gun; the Russian anarchist Kropotkin and the Algerian revolutionary Fanon both associated direct challenges to the state with violence.[57] In contrast, movements that have sought to instigate some change *within* a political arrangement or regime have adopted peaceful, and sometimes explicitly non-violent modes of activity.[58] Less commonly, essentially unarmed protests adopted regime-displacing goals, as did the Indian struggle for independence, but until recently, these were atypical events that required special understanding.[59] Moreover, Gandhi's non-violent methods have most widely been adopted by more programmatically limited movements, such as the

---

[55] Wood 2000.
[56] Bratton and van de Walle 1992: 436–438.
[57] Kropotkin 1995; Fanon 1963.
[58] Pollatta (2002) eloquently demonstrates the connection between movement objectives and modes of activity.
[59] Barrington Moore, for instance, explains the Indian movement's non-violence in terms of legacies left by British commercial practices, which destroyed an indigenous stratum of entrepreneurs and drove them into the anti-colonial movement that reflected their bourgeois orientations. Moore 1966.

moderate wing of the American civil-rights movement; self-styled revo-lutionaries in that same movement gravitated toward more violent modes of struggle.[60] Since the middle 1980s, however, several democracy move-ments have used primarily *non-violent tactics* like massed demonstrations, boycotts and hunger strikes to support *state-replacing objectives*, and this is puzzling.

In examining the question of how transitions to democracy work, several analysts direct our attention toward the defection of officials from the authoritarian regime to the opposition camp, for emergent alliance between regime defectors and a democracy movement may shake a dictatorship to its very foundations.[61] Some analysts have pro-ceeded as if inherent political affinities between reformers inside the regime and without underpin defections and alliances.[62] Others reject such an essentialist reading of things, and adopt a more contingent approach, asking how interactions between regime officials and democ-racy advocates may dissolve old coalitions and produce newer, more democratic arrangements.[63] Accordingly, new political coalitions emerge on a rather short time horizon, in response to eroding state positions or particularly compelling protest.[64] I am interested here in uncovering the deeper roots of defection and pro-democracy alliance, which I suspect lie buried in established patterns of regime repression and social response. Accepting the importance of contingent influences on emerging alliances during democracy movements, can we still theorize conditions that make regime defectors and dissidents more or less available to one another? I think that we can, on both ideological and existential levels.

Unlike revolutionary movements that thrive on regime weakness and pose comprehensive alternatives to ruling arrangements, democracy movements often do not juxtapose new ideas about governance with those state actors *espouse* – a word I use in a strictly limited way. Often, authoritarian regimes advocate democratic principles but fail to act democratically: some present authoritarian rule as merely transitional, while others redefine democracy as (*faux*) consensus, (enforced) social harmony, or (alleged) equity while retaining authoritarian practices. Attempts to package non-democratic programs as democracy suggest that contemporary regimes are less able *explicitly* to invoke authoritarian

---

[60] Zald 1988. Hipscher (1996) tells this story in reverse in her account of how the increasingly moderate goals of Chilean social movements after 1990 led to increasingly moderate tactics.
[61] Beissinger 2002; Przeworski 1986: 56.
[62] O'Donnell and Schmitter 1986.
[63] Karl 1990; Tilly 2000.
[64] Glenn 1999; Younes 2000: 122.

principles than was previously the case. Deeply enmeshed in international organization and business networks, governments must at least pay lip service to increasingly universal principles of political democracy and economic liberalism – even when they do so with reservations or violate these principles in practice.[65] The similarity between what democracy movements *demand* and what established regimes *profess* suggests that democracy movements may differ from other state-replacing movements in their ability to use the dictatorship's public ideological foundations as political resources, particularly to build bridges to regime members and to indoctrinated populations.[66] That alliances can exist between activists outside the regime and disaffected regime sectors based on *shared* ideas marks these movements as significantly different from other regime-displacing contention. Even divided authoritarian states may close ranks in the presence of a strong communist challenge, and a socialist revolutionary force will have trouble recruiting even unhappy members of a state built on capitalist foundations. But when an authoritarian regime acknowledges principles of democratic participation and economic liberalism – as even repressive states in the increasingly globalized world have – weakening central authority may embolden disaffected regime actors to take reforming action, and even to justify defection as defending regime principles against leaders who have slipped the rails.[67]

The point may grow clearer if we consider a comparison between Eastern European socialist states and at least some fascist regimes. Avineri argues that socialism's ideological framework shapes anti-regime movements. State socialism has difficulty justifying itself without reference to citizens' social and economic circumstances, and this inadvertently provides resources for people mistreated or disappointed by the socialist apparatus, and helps economic dissatisfaction accelerate into demands for regime replacement.[68] In comparison, classical fascism offered virtually no promise of citizen prosperity or social equity, and depended on conquest and racialist strivings for ideological legitimacy.[69] Having pledged so little, however, the fascist regime provides a correspondingly slim internal framework for anti-regime mobilization. Contemporary and internationally nested authoritarian regimes, in contrast, participate in a global capitalist system where admittedly minimal

[65] Diamond 1999: 58.
[66] Noonan offers an interesting parallel in her discussion of the relationship between Pinochet's ideological appropriation of women's issues and the anti-regime women's movement (1995: 98).
[67] Abrahamsen 1997: 147–151.
[68] Avineri 1991.
[69] Moore 1966.

promises of procedural justice still provide resources against corrupt, brutal or patrimonial regimes.[70] Regimes that guarantee equal protection before the law and denounce corruption, but still plunder their own societies, violate narrow principles of capitalist justice. Those that stage elections to legitimize their rule, but prevent free participation in those elections, violate narrow principles of procedural democracy. Either way, the regime provides normative resources to anti-regime movements.

But why have reforming or dissident members of authoritarian states frequently allied with or encouraged democracy movements over the last several decades? In part, the answer can be found in the democratization literature itself, which expects diversifying states with increased international linkages to be more open to democratizing impulses.[71] Another part of the answer rests in a historically particular conjunction of factors: over the last century's first half, as modern bureaucracies and armies emerged outside Europe, dissidents inside these institutions seldom had strong mass societies to support reforming positions, and often acted through internal coups, or not at all. During the Cold War, ideas about mass susceptibility to communist subversion made alliances between social dissidents and state reformers unattractive to officials who were not themselves leftist – unless they could rely on non- or anti-communist constituencies (as Suharto would in 1965 to 1966). Only in the late 1980s was mass society both available and judged free enough of communist subversion for non-revolutionary reformers inside the state to consider working in tandem with popular coalitions demanding democratic reform, "at the very moment when (for the movement) notions of alternative societies have vanished."[72] Needless to say, the post-1989 climate also made capitalist governments freer in supporting these alliances.[73]

In combination, these factors help contemporary democratization movements imagine that a successful campaign to replace the regime can consist largely in moderate protest, rather than in armed revolution or insurrection – and explain how in some situations that campaign succeeds. It also indicates the direction of a possible synthesis between different theoretical approaches to democracy protests. Transitions do not occur merely from realignments in the political coalition that supported authoritarian rule. Political mobilization can constitute a central factor in forcing that realignment into areas the old order can no longer

[70] Meyer 2000, Abrahamsen 1997.
[71] Franck 1992: 59.
[72] Adler and Webster 1995: 86.
[73] Bratton and van de Walle 1992: 435; Chipman 1982.

contain,[74] and can provide opportunities for one faction of the state against competitors.[75] Cracks in the authoritarian armor also provide political opportunities to counter-hegemonic movements, precisely as political process models in the social movements' literature predict. Still, this presentation of how democracy movements *may* work says little about *when* they will most likely occur, and with what outcomes. To make these more precise judgments, we revisit considerations of established, patterned relations between authoritarian states and their societies.

Historical (as well as proximate) conditions (particularly, I hope to demonstrate, long histories of repression) influence the extent to which state and movement reformers will be politically and existentially available to one another.[76] Do prominent dissident movements exist to receive and protect defectors from the state, or have these been wiped out or driven underground by state violence? Will alliances between erstwhile regime members and activists require improbable political adjustments (to, for instance, armed struggle) or has dissent evolved to within range of regime members' imaginations? By shaping the contours of political dissent, I argue, repression also influences the nature of alliances that are possible or likely between opposition movements and potential defectors from the regime (and so the timing and character of pro-democracy mobilization).

Conditions most likely to produce successfully democratizing protest often permit some connection between isolated, disgruntled, or concerned members of the ruling coalition and social reformers and activists. Patterns of state repression affect the potential for, and terms of, these alliances. By shaping the institutions, practices and culture of the political opposition, repression helps determine whether the disenchanted or disgruntled regime official, in turning away from the state, finds plausible allies in society. Repression also influences whether movement activists, in grappling with the possibilities of regime change, view officials as unambiguous enemies, or as at least potential confederates. As we will see, Burmese state repression utterly marginalized social reformers, who readily mobilized mass society, but could build no bridge to state actors. Indonesian state attacks on activist organization *divided* social reformers from mass society: constrained from building dissident organizations, pro-democracy actors instead solicited support from elements of the state – even if this meant foregoing the initiative in the realm of mass politics. Bourgeois reformers in the Philippines built and controlled larger

[74] Collier and Mahoney 1997; Adler and Webster 1995; Stepan 2001: 123–125.
[75] Amenta and Zylan 1995.
[76] Younes 2000.

and more institutionalized movement organizations, and used those resources to position themselves as senior partners in the transition. Different patterns of regime repression shape social institutions and political practice in ways that both enable or forestall cooperation between society and reforming state actors, and also dictate the relative balance between state and society in the transition.

In this treatment, the social movements' and democratic transitions' literatures become indispensable to one another. Those seeking to explain and predict when and how disenchanted members of the regime's ruling coalition finally move against the state must interpret established patterns of political contention and relationships between dissidents and authorities. Students of social movements may only be able to understand how the process of anti-regime mobilization influence a democratic transition by examining how the activity of divided regimes helps accelerate a period of protest into a full-fledged democratic attack on state power; social movements scholars may also need to examine this shift in uncustomary ways: i.e., not merely as mobilization opportunities, but as a central element of the attack on the authoritarian citadel.

3   Authoritarian attack and dictatorial rise

The first puzzles en route to understanding how state repression influenced contention concern each dictatorship's inaugural violence. I hope to demonstrate that these attacks were strategic (not merely passionate) responses to social opposition. Each undercut the most formidable or apparent challenge to the new regime and established rules that played to each dictator's advantage. Authorities who faced specific, powerful adversaries set out decisively to defeat that force – leading, for instance, Suharto's murderous anti-PKI campaign. Authorities with preferential access to particular resources attacked those with access to different resources – as when the Burmese military (*Tatmadaw*) eliminated public politics. In either case, we understand the dictator's attack within the geography of power in the post-colonial regime. The discussion that follows traces the social foundations of colonial rule and nationalism in each case, asks how different transitions to independence influenced those social forces, and then examines the engines of upward political mobility in the post-colonial period. These three lines of inquiry bring the terrain of contestation surrounding each dictator's rise into sharper focus. We begin with brief narrative descriptions of each case, and then move to a comparative discussion.

Burma

In several ways, the Burmese *Tatmadaw*'s attack against student protesters on July 7, 1962 is puzzling. Only months before, Ne Win's new military regime had used comparative restraint against initial, scattered protests (in Mandalay, demonstrators blocked university entrances; in Rangoon, they rallied at the Student Union building): soldiers arrested activists, closed campuses for three months, and in several places fired teargas at

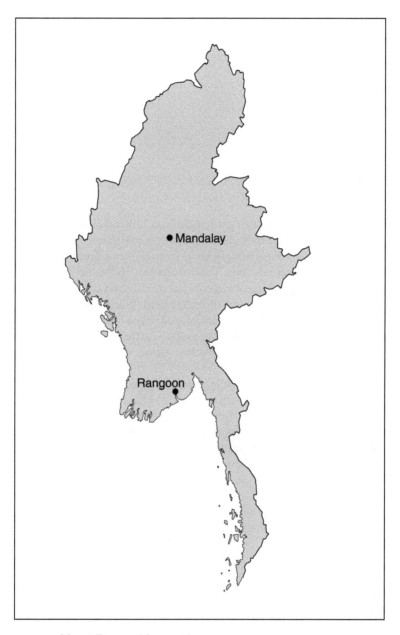

Map 2 Burma (Myanmar)

demonstrators.[1] Before reopening schools in June, the new Revolutionary Council (RC) avowed leftist principles and issued the "Burmese Way to Socialism," an eclectic and in some way peculiar document that attracted broad activist support.[2] Many members of the large, leftist coalition that had opposed the old government (the National United Front, or NUF and its related Student United Front, the SUF) pledged to support the new Burma Socialist Program Party (BSPP), isolating the Burmese Communist Party (BCP), and more conservative opposition groups like the Democratic Students Organization (DSO).[3]

This period of shifting alliances explains why student protesters in July were mainly BCP members, and perhaps also why the regime decided to act against them. But the ruthless and extraneous detonation of the hallowed union building remains confusing. The BCP in 1962 was too weak to pose any imminent threat of substance to the regime. From 1955 onward, it passed through a difficult period of internal conflict, military loss and defections that significantly undercut its power and rendered its urban sympathizers extremely vulnerable. Moreover, events following the explosion make it hard to argue that communism *per se* provoked the regime's ire, for shortly thereafter, authorities initiated peace talks with BCP insurgents, and when those talks broke down, allowed insurgent leaders to return to their bases: unimaginable behavior, for example, in Indonesia, circa 1965.[4] What explains the explosion?

The answer, I think, is that students came under fire because they pursued the mobilizing politics so central to the old regime. The 1962 attack only incidentally killed BCP supporters. It was *aimed* at a kind of politics that the military had come to despise. Several important factors pushed the *Tatmadaw* in this direction. British colonialism in lowland Burma destroyed potential connections between local elites and mass society. The path to independence, moreover, did not produce strong

---

[1] According to a Mandalay activist from that time, "There was no front gate at the entrance to the campus, so we felled some trees and made a barricade. The military surrounded the campus, and talked to the students through megaphones from the other side of the barricades, asking us to remove the trees. Eventually, we were dispersed with teargas. There were some arrests, and then the campus was closed for three months." (Interview B–4).

[2] Critics often ridicule this paper, but one can't understand the unfolding relationship between Burmese society and Ne Win's government without acknowledging its initial popularity. See, Mya Maung 1991.

[3] The NUF contained different socialist organizations, designated as Red and White Socialists, as well as the Burmese Workers and Peasants Party. Smith 1999: 164.

[4] Burmese authorities also worried that strong anti-communist moves might provoke Chinese interference in domestic affairs. I am indebted, for this idea, to discussions with Mary Callahan.

organizations linking leaders and soldiers, national elites and mass members. Achieving Burmese independence required that anti-colonial elites build nationalist associations and even armies, but never required concerted and extended struggle that would have eliminated groups without strong, functioning organizations. In ways that foreshadow Burmese parliamentary politics, largely urban elites with weak connections to mass supporters controlled the nationalist struggle. After independence, competing urban politicians mobilized social support through patronage to mass organizations and to provincial strong men, efforts that freed officials from the need to meet constituent demands through national policy: most achieved sufficient support through segmented deals with clients, and poor performance in office *manifestly* did not bar one from re-election. This system allowed ethnic Burman[5] elites, concentrated in large central cities, to focus exclusively on parochial lowland politics. In this system, the military's growing organizational capacity and national perspective were of little political use, and officers developed deep antagonisms toward an open, mobilizing style of politics for which they had no feel. After the 1962 coup, they first encountered these politics in the Rangoon student protests.

British rule and the social base of Burmese nationalism

Ultimately, British colonial rule interacted with Burmese society to produce an anti-colonial elite based in Central Burma's urban areas and only loosely connected to mass society, particularly outside the cities. The British approached Burma as an *ad hoc* adjunct to its more defined Indian colony, acquiring first lower and then upper Burma in the Anglo-Burmese wars (1825–1826, 1852, and 1885–1886). After these wars, the British ended the Burmese monarchy and eliminated hereditary local authorities, the *Myothugyis* (literally, town big man/person). These moves took out a geographically dispersed elite stratum, positioned between mass society and central authority, and left only monks systematically connected to mass society. To manage the state apparatus, the British extended the Indian administration, with its Indian functionaries, into the new territory, and founded Indian-style colonial schools to train non-elite Burmese for low-level service.[6] Outside central Burma, the British installed indirect, flexible patterns of rule that worked through indigenous leaders. Christian missionaries exerted the strongest colonial influence in these

---

[5] Following Silverstein (1977) *Burman* will denote the ethnic/language group and *Burmese* to denote the multi-ethnic population of the Burmese nation–state.

[6] Furnivall 1941.

parts, and their efforts produced recruits for the colonial militia.[7] In the main, however, the British had little ambition to rule Burma, and valued the territory first for its strategic location between China and India, and later for the food resources its fertile deltas could provide India.

Unlike Dutch or American colonial policy (or British policy in frontier regions beyond central Burma) the British never used Burmese elites to buffer other social forces – and indeed Indian troops that put down pockets of resistance after the Anglo-Burmese wars sharply alienated local populations.[8] By abolishing the monarchy and other local elites, colonists inadvertently placed local graduates in immediately leading nationalist roles. Particularly once educational reforms 1917 and 1920 produced powerful student bodies, graduates were caught between the colonial perspectives they were made to study and the nationalist mantle they would inherit.[9] Before those reforms, Buddhist monks and religio-civic associations like the (British-sponsored) Young Men's Buddhist Association were better situated to spearhead anti-colonial resistance. Religious leaders, however, missed the now-absent elite support, and particularly after the British began reorganizing agrarian life to boost production in the late 1920s, local populations were also provided fewer resources to the Sangha. Rural resentment fueled by these new agricultural policies exploded in the *Hsaya San* Rebellion, which tore across fertile Irrawaddy Delta in 1930 (partly because no coopted rural elites existed to moderate things as Malay Sultans or Javanese aristocrats had done[10]). However, that rebellion was Burma's last great explosion of rural-based nationalist resistance.[11]

As religious mobilization lost steam, students and lawyers produced a second, more secular nationalist surge. Local school graduates had begun to compete with, and resent, Indians dominating the bureaucracy, particularly given their role in colonial suppression and the proliferation also of usurious Indian moneylenders.[12] After World War One, moreover, the British separated Burma from India to keep reforms promised to Indian nationalists from spreading to Burma. This division reinforced nationalist distinctions between Burman and Indian bureaucrats, and raised contentious questions about the terms of the separation from India.[13] This

---

[7] Smith 1999: 41–44.
[8] Cady 1958; Furnivall 1956.
[9] Moscotti 1974.
[10] Taylor 1974.
[11] Herbert 1982: 5–13. Herbert, however, also stresses the importance of new associations and organizations in the *Hsaya San* Rebellion.
[12] Furnivall 1956: 116–121, 157–158.
[13] Moscotti 1974.

second nationalist movement won new concessions like the Rangoon University, the important Student Union, and generally strong provisions for home rule in the 1935 constitution. Within this secular movement, however, important differences existed. The lawyers were quite interested in obtaining positions in the new governmental structure, and were naturally most qualified among nationalists for those positions. Students leaned toward radical anti-colonial expressions like protest, the martial display of paramilitary groups (*tats*) and the nativist "We Belong" (*Dohbama Asyiayone*) movement.[14]

Two things distinguish this period in Burmese nationalism from the pre-war ferment in Indonesia and the Philippines. First, provisions for Burmese political participation (as distinct from the recruitment of ethnic minorities into colonial armies) came so late that they encountered full blown demands for self-rule, and could only divide some sections of the nationalist movement (often lawyers) from their younger and more radical comrades; they did not, however, establish committed collaborators similar to powerful and wealthy Philippine Assembly members under American (1907) or the aristocratic colonial bureaucracy in Indonesia. Facing this Burmese nationalism by 1936, Assembly elections carried a stain from the start, and voter turnout never surpassed 18 percent.[15] Second, students, bureaucrats and lawyers leading the Burmese nationalist movement were creations of an urban administrative and educational structure, with relatively few ties to rural society or to any mass base. Even the formidable *Hsaya San* Rebellion was mainly the last gasp of subsiding religious nationalism – the newer secular battles were led by urban elites with no natural mass constituencies.[16] The People's Revolutionary Party (PRP) the Sinyetha, and the Burmese Communist Party formed in the 1930s and backed more frequent and sustained strikes by 1938. As Linter notes, these associations drew from the same small, urban membership pool of student and ex-student nationalists, likely to join any (and so belonging to many) anti-colonial organization.[17] Hence, at least until World War Two, formal structures mattered less than the network of students, lawyers, and leaders from the *Dohbama Asiayone* (the *Thakins*) present in most nationalist organizations. The paramilitary *tats* mentioned above, for example, depended on prominent

[14] See Khin 1988 and Donnison 1970.
[15] In Fact, Khin describes *Dohbama* electoral participation as being designed all along to subvert the constitution (1988: 38–40); see also Taylor 1981.
[16] Moscotti 1974.
[17] Linter 1990.

individuals, often *thakins* involved in other nationalist organizations, but remained local groups, without any larger, more formal structure.

World War Two moved Burmese nationalists toward firmer political and organizational positions. By 1939, Marxism's growing appeal among nationalists, evident both in earlier associations and in study groups (Rangoon's Nagani Book Club, for instance, provided students with Marxist and Fabian socialist literature) produced the BCP. The global anti-colonial discourse had by then moved sharply left. Chinese and Indian communist advances impressed the young nationalists, and convinced some of communism's *particular* anti-imperialist power. Across South and Southeast Asia, local communist parties (but particularly those linked to the Comintern as the BCP was not) participated in anti-fascist United Front coalitions to force colonists into post-war concessions, or at least to build anti-colonial organizations in the struggle. But the BCP and other nationalists also needed to consider Japan's potential dynamism as well. Some had argued for association with the rightist *Kuomintang* (KMT), and deemed an alliance with Japan an expedient way to throw off the colonial yoke.[18] These different opinions had for a time coexisted in the nationalist movement, but the war's steady advance soon required that nationalists choose sides.

Given this background, some questions remain about the cadre of young nationalists (called the *30 Comrades*) who led the Burmese fight in World War Two.[19] Some believe that they decided to accept Japanese support against the British, but it seems more likely that Aung San, the clear leader, was seeking support from Chinese communists in Amoy, but hadn't heard that the city had fallen to the Japanese, into whose hands he promptly stumbled. The captured leader soon found himself in Tokyo, entertaining alliance proposals.[20] Whatever his original intent, Aung San sent for other top nationalists, who joined him in Hainan to train under the Japanese. Over the next several months, they founded the Burma Independence Army (BIA) under Aung San's command, and in 1942 thay accompanied Japan's imperial campaign back into Burma. It was, then, *Japanese* power that set the British colonial administration to flight and gave an initially small BIA the opportunity to recruit without either fending off British attack or worrying about its own battle readiness. In the calm behind Japan's military breakwater, the BIA incorporated *tats*,

---

[18] Moscotti 1974.
[19] See for instance the official handbook of the World War Two colonial government in exile (the Sinla government) which John Furnivall quotes at length in Furnivall 1956: 8–9.
[20] Taylor 1987: 232–233.

dacoits, and rebels, and took over administrative positions vacated in Britain's flight, but the BIA soon outstripped its leaders' managerial capacities. Many local units used their new power to settle scores with Karen or Kachin collaborators. Japanese officers, moreover, began to treat Burma as a larder for campaigns elsewhere in Southeast Asia, and their tightening grip aroused Burmese impatience for independence.[21]

As resentment in the BIA mounted, Japanese officers reorganized Burmese forces in ways that gave younger nationalists a decisive upper hand while establishing firmer, central control. Within these centralized units, a sense of institutional coherence and capacity began to germinate: Callahan describes how marches through newly "national" Burmese territory and rigorous training created cohesion among soldiers that set them apart from civilian supporters.[22] Of these supporters, some of the older generation, including many lawyers, took top positions in village administrations and in the central government (where they could claim to build power and gather intelligence). Younger civilian nationalists undertook insurgent activity (sometimes within Japan-sponsored organizations like the East Asia Youth League)[23] and assumed secondary administrative positions. When Burmese nationalists eventually grew tired of their subordination to Japanese authority, and formed the Anti-Fascist Organization (AFO) and its Burmese National Army (BNA) in July and August 1944, the movement was therefore importantly heterogeneous.[24] As things developed, older nationalists snapped up comfortable, urban positions that grew less important as resistance to the Japanese progressed, and younger war fighters behind Aung San seized unambiguous control of the movement.

The importance of political struggle and external events (rather than war-fighting) in the anti-colonial campaign made nationalist parties, and not the nationalist army, the new regime's leading organ. Over the next few years, the AFO fought the Japanese, sometimes cooperating with, sometimes harassing returning colonial troops, but never putting together coordinated, complex campaigns.[25] Disagreements inside the British administration, rather than battlefield accomplishments, were probably most responsible for improving the nationalists' standing. Lord Louis Mountbatten, Supreme Commander of the Allied Forces, regarded the AFO as the strongest ally against Japan in the larger struggle, while Governor Dorman-Smith was more interested in re-establishing British

---

[21] U Nu 1975: 102–113.
[22] Callahan 1996: 159–163.
[23] Guyod 1966: 296–298.
[24] Callahan 1996: 228.
[25] Dupuy 1985; and Lebra 1969.

colonialism and punishing wayward subjects like Aung San. Mountbatten's defeat of Dorman-Smith on these issues paved the way for a negotiated settlement, although when talks stalled, the AFO (renamed the Anti-Fascist People's Freedom League or AFPFL) organized disciplined and largely non-violent demonstrations. Actual independence in 1947 followed a negotiated agreement, and the strikes and protests that hastened that agreement were all AFPFL actions.[26]Aung San ensured nationalists an independent military capacity by regrouping some BNA forces (slated for incorporation into British-organized forces) into a "veteran's organization" under AFPFL control called the People's Volunteer Organization (PVO), and ordering some of his followers to re-enlist in the army. But political, rather than military developments dominated the transition.

Though ascendant, the AFPFL also had significant weaknesses, each a direct consequence of this pattern of struggle. First, because international involvement was decisive in achieving Burmese independence, no nationalist organ had ever fought the British or the Japanese across Burma's entire domain, or built a truly strong or nationally integrated anti-colonial organization. It is not clear, of course, that had the young urban Burmese nationalists *needed* to build such an apparatus, they could have – but conditions they actually faced allowed success via rather insular political vehicles. In consequence, the AFPFL built only weak links to mass society, and rural forces in the resistance often stubbornly guarded their autonomy.[27] Post-war Burma was also armed to the teeth, and various gangs used those arms to carve out areas of authority and power. Independent forces established a variety of relations with the state – they fought it, bribed it, threatened it, supported or ignored it – sometimes all at once. Eventually central politicians needed to find ways of either clearing out or accommodating these local pockets of power.[28] Second, and despite Aung San's efforts to build minority AFPFL chapters, nationalists had little support in minority communities. What ethnic support the new regime had came largely from colonial military levies. Even in the army, however, ethnic relations remained brittle and Karen-unit defections in 1948 were clear signs of a nationalities' problem that still haunts Burma. Finally the AFPFL was a coalition among Socialists, the BCP, the Communist Party of Burma (CPB, or "red flag" communists) and the PVO. Aung San and the anti-Britain struggle, generated sufficient bonds among these groups to hold the coalition together. When Aung San was assassinated in July 1947, however, unities unraveled. The

---

[26] Muscotti 1974.
[27] Selth 1986.
[28] Callahan 1996.

BCP rebelled against the AFPFL in 1948, triggering crippling military defections from a variety of groups.[29]

The nationalist struggle, then, left power in the hands of an insular and divided AFPFL. While the military had more organizational coherence, it was peripheral to the final, negotiated settlement, and weakened by the PVO's formation and insurgent defections. Outside large Central Burmese cities, autonomous organizations, pocket armies and warlords resisted integration into national political parties, and needed to be courted, conquered or mollified, often by side deals with national politicians. Under these conditions, central Burman elites needed only to compete among themselves for political power.

Post-colonial pressures

In 1948 alone, communist, Karen and Kachin troop rebellions diminished *Tatmadaw* troop strength to less than 2,000 soldiers, and by 1949, vast areas of the Irrawaddy Delta and suburbs of Rangoon fell to BCP or Karen hands.[30] Crime rates climbed precipitously.[31] Amidst this chaos, former PRP members inside the AFPFL formed the Socialist Party to consolidate control over the coalition. They convinced upcountry strongmen not to support or feed BCP and Karen rebels, and in this way slowed the insurgents' progress. But socialists could not bully local leaders, and needed instead to woo their compliance by offering arms and the recognition of local authority. Unable to establish strong central control, Rangoon politicians rode out conflict among local groups by remaining aloof, an arrangement that substituted for the more extended organization-building that groups like white and red flag communists carried out.[32]

It also set larger state–society patterns for the period. Electoral contests between the AFPFL and other contenders remained insular, urban, sectarian, and dependent upon patronage-driven connections with mass associations.[33] Labor associations for instance, were linked to electoral parties (the Trade Union Congress of Burma, for instance, was an AFPFL organ, while the Burma Trade Union Congress, or BTUC, was connected to the Burmese Workers and Peasants Party or BWPP).[34] One factory worker outside Mandalay recalls how his organizing committee switched

---

[29] Smith 1999.
[30] U Nu 1975: 147–161.
[31] Guyod 1966: 212.
[32] Callahan 1996.
[33] Taylor 1987: 244.
[34] "Red Socialists," who broke with the Socialist Party in 1950, organized the BWPP. See Badgley 1958: 339–340.

from the AFPFL to the BWPP because the factory manager belonged to the AFPFL, which in consequence would not pressure the manager to meet worker demands. Still, the new relationship with the more activist BWPP was, in instructive ways, limited:

At that time, the BWPP was sifting through the different labor organizing committee to find promising leaders they could recruit as party activists. This wouldn't necessarily mean that the labor leader's organizing committee would join the BWPP, but in fact, if the leader was a party cadre, the workers would follow the BTUC line. In general, the organizing committees raised money for the BWPP election funds and assisted in BWPP-called general strikes.[35]

Similarly, local farmers' associations could expect patronage in exchange for political support.

Student groups were also linked to electoral parties, and available for party-related mobilization. College associations also organized high-school branches (one former BWPP member recalls beating up high-school classmates affiliated with the DSO at the suggestion of party activists in college). Student politics were so integral to elections and other mainstream political activities that state practice accommodated protest. Consider, for example, how arrested student activists were treated in the 1950s:

To be arrested wasn't a big deal. Students were considered B prisoners. C prisoners were common criminals – crammed into cells, eating brown rice with the husks mostly on, and vegetable curry. They were sometimes tortured and could not receive regular visitors. For us, things were different. First, we got meat, white rice, and brown bread. We had regular access to newspapers and books . . . We even had butter and jam for our bread. It got to the point where we joked that we lived better in jail than outside, because as students, of course, we were always broke.[36]

Students continued their studies from prison, and sat for university exams in their cells, so protest was sustainable.[37] In fact, some of the strongest campus protests in the 1950s occurred when authorities

---

[35] Interview B–5. More than either Philippine or Indonesian informants, Burmese who agreed to talk to me took great risks. Many would not have our conversations taped, and I made certain to transcribe taped interviews before leaving the country, and destroyed all tapes. To capture untapped interviews, I always took notes during the discussions and immediately, with the assistance of others who took part in the talks, reconstructed the conversation in notes. I have developed a code system to help me identify and keep separate these interviews. Because of the extreme danger discovery would pose to these sources I only identify informants by a code, and will provide only sketchy descriptions of these people.

[36] Interview B–10.

[37] Several informants (B–4, B–10, B–11) reported prolonging their studies in this manner. As informant B–10 remarked: "Activists who wanted to work politically on the campuses would fail on purpose – so they could repeat that year. This was never a problem, and did not reflect badly on your record."

attempted to set rules expelling those who thrice failed a subject, for this would remove many activists from college. Participation in campus politics, even if it earned one indifferent grades and a police record, often improved student prospects in subsequent political life.[38]

Student groups sympathetic to the BCP also remained active on campus.[39] When schisms in the socialist party (nationally) produced parallel rifts among student groups, BCP sympathizers recruited some of the new groups into the SUF. From the mid-1950s onward, SUF groups criticized the government and held frequent demonstrations – often denouncing warfare against rural insurgent force or criticizing officials who seemed uninterested in resolving major social problems. More radical student groups were often accused of communist affiliations, but activism was important enough to the conduct of politics that such charges seldom produced sustained penalties, repression or prohibition.

The *Tatmadaw* handled the insurgencies, and countered Chinese KMT incursions, suffering great hardship at first.[40] These efforts spurred the military to reorganize itself in ways that shook off civilian oversight and strengthened the *Tatmadaw*'s Rangoon war office. Structures of command and control improved, and by the middle 1950s the *Tatmadaw* had finally fulfilled the wartime BIA's promise: to be independent Burma's first centralized but national institution.[41]

State crises and authoritarian response

Burma's movement from political crisis to authoritarian response in the late 1950s partly reflects the balance between civilian and military institutions. Inside the AFPFL, working within the socialist party, Prime Minister U Nu recklessly juggled commitments and compromise, and seemed willing to trade grants of autonomy for minority support. By 1956, such moves contributed to his faction's image as corrupt and unprincipled, and further fragmented a deeply divided AFPFL. The crisis for U Nu's government came in 1958, when he tried to turn the AFPFL coalition into a unified party. When the party split in response to these moves, U Nu temporarily stepped down as Prime Minister, and turned power over to a military caretaker government under General Ne Win,

---

[38] Informant B–4: "DSO members received money from the government and were supported by U Nu. When DSO students graduated, they always had positions waiting for them, and had logistical support from the government when they mobilized."

[39] Shwe Lu Maung 1989; see also Aye Saung 1989.

[40] Taylor 1973. For a more narrative account see Maung Maung 1953.

[41] On military efforts against the KMT see Taylor 1973; for the *Tatmadaw* reorganization, see Callahan 1996.

which stressed non-sectarian policies reflecting the *Tatmadaw*'s new institutional cohesiveness.[42] Six scheduled months of military rule stretched to eighteen, but the *Tatmadaw* did stem lawlessness and corruption, although urban elites despised the sweat brigades that made manual public service mandatory.[43] Civilian government returned to power after elections in 1960, during which one AFPFL faction, U Nu's Union Party (formerly, the AFPFL's "Clean" faction) roundly defeated the AFPFL's military-backed "Stable" faction.

Given U Nu's record in the late 1950s and the army's comparative success, these electoral results surprised many, and raised *Tatmadaw* resentment. The military's anti-insurgent mission placed a premium on national unity and sovereignty – and U Nu's style of rule (as well as apparent popular support for that rule) offended both values.[44] The military caretaker period (1958–1960) provided soldiers the opportunity to assess their capacities against those of a bungling civil administration, and discussions of parliamentary rule's failures circulated within the *Tatmadaw*.[45] Having restored some order to Burma's political and social scene, the army clearly hoped that the "stable" AFPFL faction would defeat U Nu's Union party.

But U Nu's Union Party faced virtually insurmountable problems. Squabbling broke out between three of its internal groups, and the new government resumed patterns of corrupt, inefficient and parochial rule.[46] Students and other popular organizations denounced socialists' failings and the civil war, and strengthened alliances with BCP activists. Mass organizations, even those that had worked to support the AFPFL, grew impatient with the pace of socialist transformation, and anti-regime demonstrations escalated during 1961. Rumors also circulated that Shan leaders would exercise their constitutional right to demand independence. By the end of 1961, the "Shan Principles Paper" was making the rounds – reputed to confirm this intent, but more likely representing a minority position. Such rumors probably originated among military personnel seeking to promote a new crisis, but U Nu's Nationalities Seminar, called to settle the matter in February 1962, highlighted the contrast between sectarian political perspectives and the military's vision of unity and sovereignty. By early 1962, frustrated soldiers would therefore have

---

[42] Smith 1999: chapter 10.
[43] These "sweat brigades"are described in Dupuy 1961: 428–440.
[44] Steinberg 1982: 71–72.
[45] Callahan 1996: 478 cites "Some Reflections on our Constitution" read at the *Tatmadaw* conference on October 20–21, 1958. See also Steinberg 1982: 71–72.
[46] Maung Maung 1999: 21–22.

perceived that civilian rule had neither the capacity nor the will for efficient, unified policy making, and as long as brokerage and patronage were central to electoral competition (and populations resented sacrifices like the caretaker-era "sweat brigades") elections would not favor military interests or power. Soldiers probably also knew that the *Tatmadaw* was unrivaled in its institutional reach or capacity.

In their March 2 coup, military officers arrested fifty-two participants in the Nationalities Conference (including the president, Premier U Nu, his cabinet and eleven parliament members) and then formed a Revolutionary Council (RC) to wield power. The military did encounter some early protest, but responded with relative leniency while recruiting popular support among leftist groups. As one university student council leader recalls:

> In 1962, when the revolutionary council took power, we thoroughly supported it, as did many of the other student groups, because the original moves toward the Burmese Way to Socialism were so interesting. Only the BCP did not support the new government – and, of course the rightist group.[47]

Ties between the military and urban activist groups isolated BCP activists, who also represented something generally odious to military eyes: the programmatically flexible and mass mobilizing politics of the parliamentary period.

As we discuss in chapter 5, RC efforts to build mass support were but the first steps in a process that soon narrowed, and then eliminated, participation in government. Between March and July, however, the RC ensured that the initial clash with political participation engaged a narrow and isolated group, rather than broader fronts or coalitions. When campuses reopened under new curfews and dormitory regulations, BCP supporters among the students had prepared more organized demonstrations.[48] In Rangoon, these centered on the Student Union building; in Mandalay activists drifted toward Buddhist monasteries, where monks on the political right and left also mistrusted military rule. In both cities, however, the opposition's base had so narrowed that the *Tatmadaw* could directly move against BCP protesters. When soldiers blew up the student union building in Rangoon, it sent shock waves across the country, scattering student activists. Mandalay students took refuge in monasteries – especially after the military dismantled their union building, as they did every other free-standing Burmese student

---

[47] Interview B-5.

[48] It is curious that most sources disagree on what, exactly provoked the demonstrations. Maung Maung (1999) says that students were compelled to retake exams, and for that reason protested. Silverstein and Wohl (1964) attribute the protests to new dormitory regulations. Others argue that activists were denouncing the coup (Lintner 1990).

union. In Rangoon, activists hid on campus. Everywhere, the explosion irredeemably changed politics.

Indonesia

ABRI's response to the September 30, 1965 coup attempt, launched by mid-level Indonesian officers from Central Java to protect Sukarno against a rumored rightist plot, was to exterminate the PKI and a significant part of its membership. The murders began in October 1965, and lasted for some six months, during which time members of ABRI and Islamic groups affiliated with the *Nahdlatul Ulama* (NU) executed somewhere between 300,000 and 1,000,000 communists (and some Chinese). The New Order's own account suggests around 1,000,000 deaths.[49] Never did anyone seriously discuss rehabilitating individual communists during the massacres. Prison camps separated deeply committed PKI members from sympathizers, but nobody seems to have doubted that the latter must die. Where local authorities were reluctant to get on with the slaughter, ABRI officers often chided them into more vigorous action.[50] The apparatus assembled around these murders (concentration camps, membership lists, informants, interviews, mass assemblies and executions) suggest foresight, planning and commitment. Questions still persist about how the slaughter got underway, and how many it consumed; but apart from these questions, we might also ask why the anti-communist massacre was designed so relentlessly to eliminate the PKI. If the killings were mainly tools to established ABRI's political control, why did the military mobilize popular, often unruly, participation in them? Given that the PKI was on the defensive from the first, and made only scattered, futile attempts at counterattack, why did the butchery move relentlessly past mere victory to extermination? The New Order's corporatist structure absorbed parties like the PNI. Why not the PKI?

The answer, I think, lies in the certifying role that *organization* played in ABRI's drive for power. Indonesia's nationalist revolution triggered broad and deep social mobilization across the archipelago, and enough sustained fighting to spawn armies and militia nationwide, but produced fundamentally weak political institutions. Since independence, but particularly in the early 1960s, the military regarded itself as uniquely qualified for national leadership because of its organizational capacity, and the modernizing echoes that capacity stirred. Given the balance

---

[49] For a compelling essay describing difficulties determining the actual casualty figures, as well as a survey of different estimates, consult Cribb 1990.
[50] Robinson 1995.

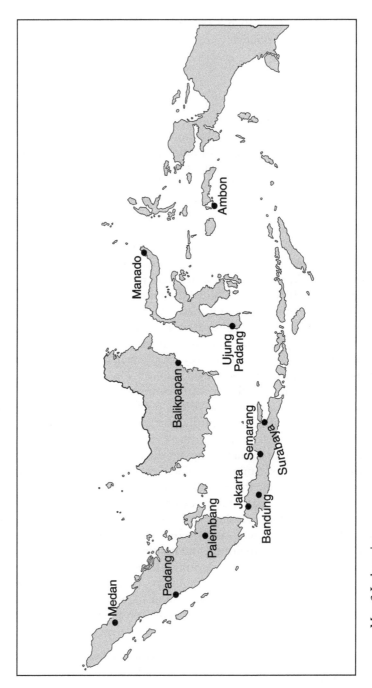

Map 3 Indonesia

between institutionally strong military and weaker civilian institutions, McVey argues that perhaps the principal question about Sukarno's Indonesia is how the president thwarted military ambitions for so long.[51] He did so partly because his charismatic hold on the idiom of revolution allowed him to mobilize direct popular support, and partly because he often played central and regional commands off against one another. However, during Sukarno's latter authoritarian period (called Guided Democracy, and stretching from 1958 to 1965) he increasingly maintained power by balancing ABRI against the PKI – the *only* force apart from ABRI with a strong organizational machinery – or the reputation of one. ABRI's approach to the PKI certainly had ideological and historical roots, but it thrived as competition between the only two potential sources of *organized* political power. Despite its mistrust of political Islam, ABRI could unleash more scattered Muslim groups against the communists, and would not rest until the communist *network* was annihilated.[52] As with Burma, clues to this rivalry's origin lie in the structure of colonialism, and in the process of liberation.

Dutch rule and the social base of Indonesian nationalism

In the early twentieth century, important events changed colonial administration and society in the Dutch East Indies. Until then, the Dutch ruled indirectly, with European officials working alongside local aristocrats. Administrative positions provided local elites with economic security and an explicitly ennobled niche in the colonial structure,[53] while elites mediated between Dutch rule and local society. By the end of the nineteenth century, however, changes in cultivation regulations, designed to boost production, placed Dutch managers and overseers in more directly supervisory roles over plantation labor.[54] This change, plus increased civil servant arrivals from the Netherlands, reduced the colonial state's need for local intermediaries. As available administrative positions diminished, however, local school graduates expecting civil service positions increased. Colonial officials, Kahin explains, feared the spread of pan-Islamic thought into the colony after the Suez Canal's opening in 1869 eased travel to the Middle East for study. To counteract this perceived threat, the Dutch opened First Class Native Schools in 1893, and local

---

[51] McVey 1971; and McVey 1972.
[52] For the role of Muslim groups in the killing, see Cribb 1990: 26–29.
[53] Sutherland. 1979.
[54] In particular, the state-mandated Cultivation System ended at the end of the nineteenth century. Kahin 1952: 41–42; see also Stoler 1985.

education rapidly expanded thereafter.[55] Soon local Islamic movements like the *Muhammadiyah* (1912) and the *Taman Siswa* movements (1922) established vocational schools and more tradition-based institutions. By the 1920s, jobs did not exist for all school graduates, who began to compete with aristocrats and Dutch migrants. Education placed non-aristocrats in line for positions similar to those that aristocrats held, and created initial tension between the groups.[56] As university degrees became the standard for professional capacity, however, these divisions blurred[57] and dissatisfaction at declining job opportunities acquired a broader social base in Indonesia than in Burma or (as we will see) the Philippines.

Increasingly direct Dutch economic and political control, therefore, diminished the aristocracy's capacity to buffer mass resentment precisely as elite dissatisfaction itself rose. This combination allowed nationalism to develop important bases at all social strata. When in 1917 the Dutch organized a local representative assembly (the *Volksraad*) it provided an institutional foundation for elite nationalists, particularly when parties eventually formed in the 1920s.[58] Still, *Volksraad* politics remained relatively moderate, in contrast to developments outside the assembly.[59] In that realm, changing economic and social relations prompted the organization of Islamic and increasingly nationalist organizations. The end of the Cultivation System in the early 1900s altered relations between indigenous traders (including some of society's most orthodox Muslims) and Chinese competitors, prompting Muslims to found trading associations to counter what they viewed as a new pro-Chinese bias.[60] New associations like *Muhammadiyah* (1912), concentrated on essentially religious debates, but by 1917 the *Seriket Islam* (Islamic Union) formed behind more powerful nationalist positions. The *Perhimpuan Indonesia* (Indonesian Association or PI) emerged in 1922 from the more nationally ambiguous *Indies* Association, formed in 1908; in 1926 under Mohammad Hatta, the PI merged into the PKI (*Perserikatan Komunis di India*, the Indian Communist Party) itself forced out of the *Seriket Islam* in 1921.

Such nationalist expressions integrated elements of the local society in ways that contrast with the Burmese experience. The Burmese struggle

---

[55] Kahin 1952; van der Veur 1969.
[56] Van Niel 1950.
[57] Legge 1988: 16–19.
[58] Van Niel 1950.
[59] Ingleson 1979.
[60] Peltzer 1979.

included (on its under-card) a contest between ethnic Burmans – anti-colonial school graduates – and educated, non-Burman groups serving the colonial state. With battle lines drawn in this manner, and reinforced by inter-ethnic clashes from the 1930s through World War Two, the contest narrowed nationalism's integrative power. The anti-colonial movement became a sometimes-dual struggle against the British and against non-Burmans – hence the nativist specificity of movements like the *Dohbama Asyiayone*. In Indonesia, the Dutch parallel administration preserved antagonisms between the Dutch and all of the colony's different societies, and assured that even collaborators would mainly operate in relation to members of their own regional and language groups. Tension between the Dutch and portions of all local societies permitted an integrating, supranational formulation of local nationalist aspirations: Indonesia. This broad way of setting out the anti-imperialist opposition, moreover, resonated with anti-colonial currents encountered by Indonesian students in Europe.[61]

Yet Indonesia's vastness made coordination between the movement's different centers difficult, and rendered its institutions vulnerable to Dutch repression. Dutch proscriptions on the *Seriket Islam*'s central organs, for instance, dissipated the movement by setting local chapters adrift. Local and rural Indonesian religious and intellectual leaders, particularly those based at Islamic schools or *Pesantren*, were not integrated into a larger national structure, and did not produce a national network.[62] The communist party, possessed of perhaps the most capable organizational network in the 1920s, fell to Dutch attack after an aborted uprising between 1926 and 1927.[63] Later, when nationalism became a stronger current in the *Volksraad*, the Dutch periodically banned groups that demanded or organized behind independence, and stalled the nationalist movement by arresting leaders like Sjahrir, Sukarno and Hatta.[64] By the advent of the Pacific War, the Dutch had imposed such control that nationalism's most visible expressions came in the cautious demands of the older, *diplomasi* nationalists.[65] Nowhere, however, could nationalists construct effective movement organizations asserting their supra-national vision of Indonesia.

---

[61] See for example, the account of life in exile in Rose 1987.
[62] This is suggested in a telling comparison in Harvey 1998: 71.
[63] Kahin 1952: 85–87.
[64] For a description of the exiled life of these nationalist leaders and their relationship to the nationalist struggle, see Mrazek 1996: 41–65; Legge 1988.
[65] Shiraishi 2003, Kahin 1952, Reid 1974.

The organizations of Indonesian nationalism and World War Two

As we saw earlier, Japan recruited and trained Burmese nationalist youths already controlling their movement, and then set the British colonial state to flight. In contrast, the Japanese met a far flatter nationalist organization in the Dutch East Indies, with different local groups across the archipelago, but no accepted central hierarchy. Early in their occupation, the Japanese returned arrested and exiled nationalists Sukarno and Hatta from exile – partly because they found *diplomasi* nationalists in the bureaucracy politically suspect – and provided them broadcast facilities that allowed direct appeal to the population, without mediating organizations.[66] Nominally supporting Japan, Sukarno and Hatta spent most of their effort encouraging a supranational idea of Indonesia, but built no strong central organizations. Rather, the Japanese organized local mass organizations and youth-based militia (*Pembela Tanah Air*,[67] PETA). Under Japanese tutelage, the impetuous *pemuda* (youth) activists, long isolated by older *diplomasi* nationalists, advanced an emotional and dynamic nationalism of struggle (*perjuangan*). As in Burma (although less decisively) the Japanese forced cautious, older nationalists to make way for younger activists. Unlike in Burma, Indonesian nationalists had few central mechanisms, but many local organizations ready for struggle.[68]

The entire nationalist structure depended on Japanese support and shelter against colonial adversaries. Despite heavy Japanese impositions, their relations with the Indonesians never deteriorated into open conflict, and no anti-fascist alliance with the Dutch ever materialized, though the colonial government did reject a nationalist–proposed anti-fascist alliance in the late 1930s. The end of Japanese rule also came suddenly, in August 1945, and was entirely unrelated to losses inflicted on Japanese forces in Indonesia. Hence significant time passed before colonial powers would attempt to retake the archipelago, during which the Indonesian Republic (founded on August 17) set down precarious and shallow roots (assisted somewhat by Japanese soldiers marking time before their departure). The new Republic had barely a month before British troops landed in Jogjakarta on September 29.

From then until December 27, 1949, Indonesian nationalists fought returning Dutch rule in a revolution that widened divisions between central political leaders and local armed groups. The war

---

[66] Reid 1974.
[67] "Defenders of the Fatherland."
[68] Anderson 1974; see also Anderson 1966.

began with the fierce local resistance of the *baden perjuangan* (militia) and PETA units, barely coordinated by the weak and skeletal civilian Republican apparatus that *diplomasi* nationalists controlled. These politicians, however, were utterly out of step with the militias' revolutionary thrust. Nine Republican governments resigned in rapid succession after each negotiated concessions with the Dutch that enraged revolutionary fighters.[69] In the countryside, militia shared wartime experiences that provided a foundation on which the national army would emerge, and set war fighters apart from civilian leaders. But through the parade of governments, Sukarno and Hatta retained control of the revolution's political voice, severing any necessary connection between them and any *one* government. Both stood between the faltering structures of central rule and the growing power of the armed revolution. The Dutch met defeat after they arrested the civilian leadership's most important figures, and freed the dynamic and violent *baden perjuangan* from Republican restraints.[70] The furious fighting that followed combined with international pressure on the Dutch compelled the colonists to relinquish all territory except West Papua.

The war left powerful political legacies. First, the Japanese occupation forces had provided support and training for a fairly significant range of local organizations, from the PETA to a collection of important Muslim organizations (the Masjumi) to different sections of the PKI.[71] Each of these groups would play important roles in Independent Indonesia. Second, guerilla warfare forged several political forces crucial to the post-war environment. Although decentralized, the army produced strong personages atop heroic mythologies – and with civilian leaders in jail, *soldiers* forced the final Dutch defeat. But the PKI also figured prominently in the battles, and used wartime exploits to rebuild its organization and prestige (although it badly overplayed its hand in a 1948 Madiun uprising *before* the revolution's end, seeking to seize control over other revolutionary forces).[72] Third, civilian leaders had established but the barest outline of a governing structure, depended on Sukarno's dazzling rhetoric to mobilize mass support, and exercised notably thin control over the army.

---

[69] Kahin 1952; Reid 1974. A lot of this becomes more clear in retrospect, particularly in how ABRI subsequently represents the revolution, and its role in it (see Bourchier 1992a).

[70] Anderson 1974.

[71] Anderson 1966; Reid 1980.

[72] Swift 1989; McVey 1965; and Wertheim 1987: 115–116.

Post-colonial pressures, guided democracy and the contest of organizations

Interactions among three important factors governed politics in newly independent Indonesia. First, strong rivalries developed between governing institutions, primarily between the army and parliamentary forces. Second, political competition within the new national framework heightened rivalries between political Islam and communism, or between the outer Islands and the Javanese centers, and undercut institution-building processes like parliament's efforts to stabilize its rule or military endeavors to build an effective chain of command. Both institutional and factional politics, however, receded in the face of a third factor: the charismatic figure of Sukarno, at the revolutionary government's heart, masterfully wielding its mobilizing politics and symbols.

From independence until the late 1950s, the civilian government strove to maintain power with weak institutions, a bureaucracy rife with remnants of a collaborating elite, and flimsy revolutionary credentials – a tall order, when one considers the vast territory over which the revolution had mobilized an often demanding population. In this effort, Sukarno faced challenges from both state agencies and society. Several military attempts to grab power occurred soon after independence. In 1952, Java-based leaders of the newly named ABRI, under General Nasution, sought to force Sukarno to dismiss parliament, rule more directly and rein in persistently autonomous outer-island security forces. In 1956, field commands (given stronger operational and financial capacities to defeat Nasution in 1952) and supported by more orthodox Masjumi chapters and local militia remnants, rose (in the *Pemerintahan Revolusioner Republik Indonesia* rebellion[PRRI, Revolutionary Government of the Indonesian Republic]) against the crippled parliamentary system and the central military command. Sukarno rode out both challenges, partly by playing the military's internal divisions against one another, but partly by keeping Indonesian society astir with revolutionary invocations.[73] In 1952, he appealed for popular support for the revolution, decried selfish and counter-revolutionary military ambitions in Java, and enlisted outer-island commands chaffing under ABRI's centralizing efforts. In 1957, Sukarno took the first steps toward building a more authoritarian and centralized system by empowering ABRI's central command under a rehabilitated Nasution, and declaring martial law on March 14.[74]

---

[73] McVey 1971; McVey 1972.
[74] Feith 1962.

That declaration empowered ABRI's central command, but Sukarno simultaneously encouraged outer-island lower echelon officers to displace commanding officers.

Social tensions also grew during this same period. Daniel Lev describes a tension at the revolution's heart: its leaders needed to mobilize a poor population without opening the floodgates of class conflict that would sweep aside elite prerogatives.[75] Sukarno attempted to solve this puzzle by directing social energies against targets inside or outside Indonesia, turning revolutionary enthusiasm away from frontal attacks on elite privilege. In this effort, he soon adopted his most sharply anti-imperialist rhetoric, withdrew from the United Nations, and eventually launched two confrontation campaigns – against remnants of Dutch colonialism in West Papua, and against the British in Malaya – to direct domestic energies into foreign policy objectives. Before those efforts however (mainly in the 1960s) Sukarno deflected mass unrest by accusing electoral parties and political Islam of subverting the revolution. Demonstrations supporting these accusations renewed support for Sukarno, despite economic decline, without moving against Indonesian elites.

Still, the twin pressures of a restive society and ambitious institutions compelled Sukarno in 1957 to acquiesce to General Nasution's design for a more authoritarian and corporatist arrangement that was called "Guided Democracy." The new system built on the idea that organizational power was the best, perhaps only, way to control Indonesia's vast and often unruly society, and began by undercutting most political parties and Muslim groups, and replacing these with a Working Cabinet. Unlike former governmental arrangements, however, this cabinet did not favor urban parties, but gave pride of place to institutions and organizations that could control territory and populations. Accordingly, two organizations with the greatest capacity and reach, ABRI and the PKI, became centrally important. ABRI's power, formerly constrained only by divisions among officers, expanded after Sukarno declared martial law, re-centralized ABRI, and placed military officials in charge of nationalized Dutch firms (responsibilities institutionalized in the military's doctrine of dual political and security responsibilities, or *dwifungsi*). Since 1948, the PKI steadily organized a mass machinery, but remained largely apart from national electoral politics. It had worked in the (mainly Javanese) countryside to build large organizations and would soon claim 25 million members across a fairly broad social spectrum.[76]

[75] Lev 1966b.
[76] Mortimer 1974.

Had either force *alone* provided Guided Democracy's organizational power, it might well have overwhelmed Sukarno. With both on board, however, their rivalry kept each in check, and Sukarno in charge. By basing Guided Democracy on two organizations eager to outdo one another, Sukarno navigated past organizationally powerful groups without *himself* building any strong political machinery. Nevertheless, it was an unstable balance, for both ABRI and the PKI undercut one another in ways that destabilized the entire arrangement.[77]

The military contrasted with the PKI along two dimensions: the communists' relatively greater hold over mass society, and ABRI's monopoly of armed force. (ABRI also had a geographically broader reach, but the centralizing resolution of the 1956 coup attempt emphasized its Java-based machinery, and made the two groups more similar.) To undercut communist advantage, ABRI began building its own mass groupings that explicitly – even in their names – rivaled PKI associations: the *Seriket Organisasi Karyawan Socialis Indonesia* (Union of Indonesian Socialist Karaywan Organizations, SOKSI) countered PKI labor unions, for instance.[78] These measures matched PKI strengths and helped the military establish positions within Guided Democracy's corporatist structures.[79]

The communists at first engaged the rivalry cautiously, for party leaders were caught between impoverished, restive constituencies and a precarious national environment. For years, the PKI had been excluded from parliamentary cabinets despite frequently winning electoral pluralities, and they consequently cultivated a compensating image as reliable, moderate politicians. Their mass actions avoided explicit class confrontation, and emphasized cooperative ventures, education drives, and the party's transforming modernity.[80] The PKI also contained conservative rural elites attracted by the party's strong electoral performances, and willing to ignore a class struggle line that seemed largely rhetorical.[81] By 1963, however, these constraints began to loosen. The party had virtually exhausted its ability to mobilize its mass base without challenging elites. As social and economic conditions deteriorated and ABRI grew impatient with Sukarno, the president drew closer to the PKI, and depended more on its mobilizing power. This dependence provided opportunities for the party, but also triggered more antagonistic relations with ABRI and other social forces. The PKI's campaign unilaterally to implement agrarian

[77] Anderson 1983b; Lev 1963–1964.
[78] Reeve 1992: 165–167.
[79] Suryadinata 1989: 9–12.
[80] McVey 1996.
[81] Mortimer 1974.

reform laws through land occupations in 1963 angered conservative Muslims landowners (with their own history of friction with the communists and Sukarno) and also military officers who had also begun acquiring and developing lands.[82]

Still, the development that probably most aroused ABRI anxiety came in 1965, when the PKI began to organize, with Sukarno's approval, a civilian militia. With this so-called "fifth force" the PKI set out to acquire the single institutional capacity that was ABRI's alone.[83] From the announcement of the militia's formation until September 30, 1965, relations between ABRI and the PKI rapidly deteriorated. In that interval, the communists launched more active protests and demonstrations, and more aggressively challenged property rights and elite privilege. By September, rumors were rife of both a communist and a military putsch, and the junior officers that attempted to take control in the original coup d'état seemed mainly interested in blocking a power-grab from more conservative quarters in ABRI.

In an important sense, Guided Democracy contributed to the bloodshed in 1965. When Sukarno staked his authority upon mobilizing revolutionary idioms, he virtually assured that at some point, these forms would turn against elements of the state's central alliance. Repeated mobilization to defend Indonesia acclimatised people to the contention that enemies (counter-revolutionaries, imperialists, colonial sympathizers, and political Muslims) had slipped through the revolution's skein, lodged themselves in post-revolutionary society, and worked enough mischief to jeopardize the whole project. This rhetoric legitimized internal witch-hunts, and sanctioned the idea of popular and heroic risings to preserve the revolution and its leader. Yet the unanimity with which Indonesians affirmed the revolution meant that its particular stewardship – and hence the definition of its enemies and heroes – was open to contest. *Both* the September 30 coup attempt to protect Sukarno from rightist Generals, and the rightist reaction to that coup, presented themselves as preserving the revolution.

The main question, however, is not why either the PKI or the military would move against one another in 1965, but why the counter-coup completely eliminated the PKI, and established a regime that prevented the organization of dissent, but not its expression. We will soon examine this question in greater and more comparative detail. For now, I will reiterate the short answer that this chronology suggests: as political

---

[82] Lev 1966b; Feith 1963.
[83] Anderson 1983b: 485.

power came increasingly to be contested between the only two forces with significant organizational capacities, the principle of organization – both in Guided Democracy and the New Order's corporatist structures – became the accepted means of establishing domestic control. Political forces with weak organizational resources could not really threaten ABRI, and did not call forth great violence. (The military could thus mobilize *Nahdlatul Ulama* participation in the slaughter because Muslim groups did not possess strong organizational resources.) The PKI, however, had such organizational capacities that when Suharto thwarted the September 30 coup attempt, he directly set out to eradicate the communists altogether.

The Philippines

Marcos declared martial law on September 21, 1972, after almost two years of toying with the possibility, closing the legislature, the Constitutional Commission and important media outlets. Soldiers swept through the streets to arrest activists and prevent demonstrations – the very communists (apparently) against whom Marcos had warned for months. First, however, security forces arrested opposition senator Benigno Aquino, and then pursued other prominent politicians like Senators Jose Diokno and Jovito Salonga.[84] Seizing dictatorial powers was, of course, easier for Marcos than for either Suharto or Ne Win because Marcos already held executive office. Perhaps in part for this reason – but for others that we will explore – the martial law regime exercised comparative restraint, and for longer than Ne Win could manage in Burma. There were no massive initial killings, and many activists escaped relatively unhindered into the countryside. Martial law, to use David Wurfel's phrase, did not eliminate activists, but disbursed them.[85] Most politicians imprisoned in those first days soon found themselves released, and some of Marcos's strongest opponents (the Lopez family, Raul Manglapus, Heherson Alvarez) left the Philippines before martial law – a strikingly different fate than that suffered by those Ne Win and Suharto struck down. Marcos in some ways seemed preoccupied with other matters – including drafting a new constitution and building a strong state machinery.

Down the line, Marcos's distracted pursuit of regime opponents hurt his regime. Repression drove legal and moderate groups toward radical positions, and many approached the Communist Party of the

---

[84] Wurfel 1988: 114–153; see also Thompson 1995: 57–63; and Staff Report 1973: 1–4; van der Kroef provides a list of those detained (1973b: 45).
[85] Wurfel 1988: 226.

Map 4 The Philippines

Philippines (CPP). Politicians freed from jail, and many that avoided arrest altogether, found enough leeway in the new authoritarian dispensation – particularly at the beginning, when Marcos seemed confident of his power – to begin criticizing the dictatorship. The survival of both underground armed groups and more open political resistance provided a beginning for anti-dictatorship resistance that blossomed in the late 1970s and early 1980s. By underestimating these opponents when they were small and scattered, Marcos allowed them to survive, and his pattern of repressive policies assured that they would grow. Before they became formidable opponents, however, these forces had become impossible to eradicate.

The opposition's growth from 1972 onward will concern us shortly; for now, we concentrate on explaining the comparatively gentle onset of martial law – at least compared to Indonesian and Burmese events. The short explanation, I think, is that unlike Suharto or Ne Win, Marcos seized dictatorial powers without needing to defeat any specific adversary. Suharto set out to eliminate the PKI while Ne Win struck against parliamentarians who had just won a new mandate. Marcos, however, had mastered the electoral system, and was in his second presidential term. Unlike Suharto, he did not face an immediately threatening (specific) opponent. Movement and insurgent challenges, on the other hand which sought power in the different coin of mass mobilization, remained weak, and so unlike Ne Win, Marcos faced no opponent with skills and capacities he could not match. Rather, Marcos set out to overturn constitutional constraints that limited his presidency's duration and power, and so needed less to cut down opponents than to hold them at bay. In this way, the Philippine passage into dictatorship preserved an elite political opposition, a radical underground, and civil institutions, and this preservation shaped anti-Marcos resistance in fundamental ways. To examine why, we must review the structure of American colonial rule, and the process by which Filipinos acquired independence.

American rule and the social base of Philippine nationalism

The United States did not acquire its Philippine colony in consequence of any clear expansionist plan, and its first decades of Philippine rule demonstrate some ambivalence on the question of rule. Its greatest colonial presence occurred during the Philippine–American war, and sharply fell from a 1901 high of 71,528 to only 12,748 in 1903.[86] Responsibility for maintaining law and order passed to a new constabulary, in which by

---

[86] Jose 1992: 15.

1904, only 345 American officers led 7,000 Filipinos.[87] As troop strengths declined, the real colonial shock troops arrived in robust numbers: American newspapermen, entrepreneurs, bankers and lawyers flooded Manila and streamed into the provinces. Taking advantage of the conversion of Catholic Friar lands to private control, they sought to meet global demand for sugar, copra and abaca, established the great sugar centrals, mapped out strategies for broader export-oriented fruit production, and accelerated timber and mining operations. In these efforts, Americans worked with landed provincial elites – an alliance rendered essential by restrictions on US participation in the Philippine plantation economy.[88] For Philippine elites, it was a time of plenty: credit was abundant, new production strategies energized industry, and formerly tight Spanish export controls yielded to preferential access to the large American market and a generally more open orientation toward global trade.[89] By taking over niches previously dominated by the Spanish and rapidly adapting to the more freewheeling and liberal American system of trade and production, local businessmen made a killing.

The political system supporting this activity depended on two alliances between American colonialism and Philippine society. First, American-sponsored primary education (far more broadly available in the Philippines than in Burma or the Netherlands East Indies) produced a cadre of relatively poor but skilled administrators to work in the colonial state. Most came from middle or lower class families, for whom knowledge and skill provided important (if limited) avenues for social mobility.[90] Second, landed elites, benefiting from the American-driven economic boom, gained election to the new Philippine Assembly, from where they protected their economic interests and soon fused into an identifiable national elite.[91] Nascent tension existed between these groups. In some part, the strain resided in considerations of class and privilege, for

---

[87] Jose 1992: 18.

[88] As Rivera reports, "During (the American colonial period) a significant portion of the assets and investments in major agro-mineral export industries (particularly sugar milling and cordage, mining and logging/saw milling) had already come under the ownership and control of a privileged landlord and merchant class. Further, commercial agricultural export production was largely controlled by Filipino landlords and compradores since earlier legislation limiting the size of land holdings for corporate plantation agriculture dampened US capital investment in large scale agriculture" (1994: 25–26).

[89] Doeppers 1984: 9.

[90] Doeppers 1984: 59–68.

[91] The electoral system's literacy *and* property requirements initially restricted the franchise to roughly 2 percent of the population. Municipal elections in 1902 helped establish patronage machines for the first lower house elections in 1907, and broader bicameral contests in 1916. Catilo and Tapales 1988: 139.

nouveau aristocrats in the Assembly had little interest in sharing power or prestige with poorer, upwardly striving functionaries.[92] But tensions divided elected politicians from the state's new employees. Assembly elites typically did not use national positions to accumulate power, but to preserve their standing in local arenas and against change or external challenge; Assembly members were animated about regulations governing tariffs, market quotas and monetary policy – but beyond that, wanted to be left alone. Virtually everyone with a chance to win office also wanted to keep the national apparatus weak, and this led to considerable suspicion toward members of the state apparatus. Hence, unlike Burma or Indonesia, where administrative postings provided opportunities for both established elites and new (even poor) school graduates, land remained a stronger and more excluding avenue to power and wealth in the Philippines.

This division helped prevent strong nationalist expressions. Landed elites, of course, were largely happy with their fortunes under American rule, and their tepid appetite for independence was sated by gradual negotiations with the United States. The Assembly also attracted student support and admiration, and provided such clear career paths for politically ambitious students that few attempted to organize more radical nationalist associations.[93] Nor, at first, was there much to fear from the civil service, for career opportunities had never been better.

By the early 1920s, however, the administration was fully staffed and a surplus of qualified college graduates existed. Officials began to pick and choose among job applicants, and were better positioned to construct patronage networks that would assure their dominance over the bureaucracy.[94] It was among those who had been rejected by, or purged from the bureaucracy that mass-mobilizing nationalism found its strongest leaders – but they had reason to focus on criticizing Filipino politicians (their most immediate antagonists) rather than American colonists. As the electoral franchise expanded, independence debates became largely domesticated campaign fare, guiding nationalism in directions that colonists could accommodate. On the American model, for instance, Philippine labor groups linked themselves to electoral machines through ties of patronage and so politicians did not rely on their political *programs* to win over supporters.[95]

[92] Catilo and Tapales 1988.
[93] For an example of this, see Tolentino's (1990) account of the relationship that evolved between student activists like himself and Commonwealth politicians like Quezon and Roxas.
[94] Friend 1965.
[95] Scott 1983; Kerkvliet 1982; and Doeppers 1984: 124.

Educational patterns under US rule placed students in national, rather than international networks. While young Indonesians and Burmese could acquire a passable administrative education in their home countries, those who studied further typically traveled to Europe. With the liberalization of local Philippine education under American rule, established and new universities provided Filipinos with broader local opportunities for study, and so fewer students were exposed to Marxist anti-colonialism moving through Europe than other Southeast Asian nationalists.[96] University life in the Philippines helped solidify ties among these future elites, and also built ties between bankable pools of future leaders and the parties. Such party–campus links were also available to some of the non-elite students who began to arrive on campus in significant numbers, diverting some of the most dynamic and potentially radical candidates for the state bureaucracy into electoral politics. Hence, despite periodic protests in the late 1920s, students directed their most fervent attention toward electoral politics, and campus protests often served the parties – in this sense resembling Burmese student politics in the parliamentary period rather than other Southeast Asian nationalist movements.

In combination, these factors allowed nationalism to become a safe rhetorical position for Philippine political elites. Across Southeast Asia, more pitched independence struggles required nationalist elites to seek broad social support, and anti-colonialism's main proponents commonly found Marxism's class line either attractive or necessary. Philippine national elites engaged in independence negotiations didn't need mass support (for they had already been promised independence) and had no reason to jeopardize their social and economic standing by forming radical alliances with workers, peasants or students.[97] The bureaucracy as an institution thrived under American rule and suffered under Philippine elite restrictions; when a nationalist did emerge from the state machinery, he was likely to reserve his fire for Filipino targets. Associations that former bureaucrats organized usually had weak leaderships, willing to drop radical posturing in exchange for a new job in government. More resilient mass organizations (for example, the Socialist party founded by Pedro Abad-Santos, and in the urban *Katipunan ng mga Anak-Pawis* [KAP, the

[96] As I suggest elsewhere these differences are also a matter of world time. Philippine nationalists working against Spanish rule in the late nineteenth century traveled to Europe in significant numbers. Yet the nationalism they learned in these travels was the Creole nationalism that mainly demanded representation within European arrangements, not the independence that would dominate anti-colonial demands in the following decades. Boudreau 2003.
[97] McCoy 1988; Corpuz 1989.

Proletarian Labor Congress]) were more entirely working-class expressions, and weak for that very reason.[98]

World War Two, independence, and the organized left

The Philippine independence movement's particular timing rendered the Pacific War a different influence here than elsewhere. Most Southeast Asian Marxist-nationalists favored the Comintern's anti-fascist United Front, which called for politically ticklish alliances with colonial powers. Other nationalists saw opportunities to use Japanese support against colonial regimes, and in Burma and Indonesia, even leftists rejected the anti-fascist front to secure some Japanese help against European colonialism. In the Philippines, nationalists had already received assurances of full independence after the war, and the question for elites was not how to use the Japanese occupation in the nationalist cause, but how to survive it.[99] This puzzle produced extensive collaboration among elites, and it was mainly groups with ambitious programs against entrenched or recalcitrant adversaries, such as the *Partido Komunista ng Pilipinas* (PKP, Communist Party of the Philippines) or working in league with American forces that initially formed substantial anti-Japan formations.[100]

After the war, as independence struggles across Southeast Asia entered their critical phases, Philippine elites could concentrate on consolidating their positions against local challenges to property and privilege, and so they closed ranks. Nobody much objected when US-led troops disarmed Huk soldiers, for the guerillas were viewed as threats to local property, rather than as nationalist allies.[101] When the Senate and Congress refused to allow six winning candidates from the leftist Democratic Alliance (DA) to assume posts they won in 1946 elections, the courts upheld the move, and few voices outside the DA protested very strongly. Under some American prodding, local elites agreed to view wartime divisions among themselves as different strategies to power, rather than as patriotism or treason.[102] The military defeat of the PKP-led Huk rebellion in the early 1950s decisively marginalized the PKP, and turned many potential revolutionaries into bandits and extortionists.[103]

---

[98] Kerkvliet 1992: 71–91.
[99] Setsuho 1999.
[100] Tolentino 1990. As in Burma, however, the often-brutal conduct of the Japanese occupation also encouraged more and more Filipinos to join anti-fascist alliances.
[101] Kerkvliet 1986; Constantino and Constantino 1978.
[102] Steinberg 1960.
[103] Kerkvliet 1986.

On the other hand, the negotiated transfer of colonial institutions to local control never required the political movements so central to Indonesian and Burmese independence, or the national army so important to Indonesia. The Philippine constabulary was never a national fighting force, and its officers were subordinate to provincial politicians. The bureaucracy was similarly weak, and expanded in the 1940s and 1950s through political patronage rather than coherent state building. The thicket of patronage ties prevented state institutions from developing autonomous power or interests.[104] In fact, wasteful patronage drove the government to virtual collapse in 1949, and only a last ditch infusion of US resources stemmed the crisis. Even then, however, elites viewed constraints on state capacity as a generally good thing – and no state institution had the standing effectively to disagree.

The constitutional regime

An emerging orthodoxy about the Philippine state emphasizes the oligarchy's rent-seeking activity in relations between the weak state and the strong society. Hutchcroft argues that families plundered the weak state precisely because Americans supported the landed oligarchs and neglected to build a coherent central administration.[105] McCoy associates accelerating rent-seeking with independence, when elected officials became more dependent on provincial elites to deliver votes.[106] Both advance compelling descriptions of a weak central apparatus, captured and divided by powerful social forces. Yet to explain the rise of the Marcos dictatorship, we need also to acknowledge significant changes in rent-seeking patterns promoting new class interests.

After the war, the Philippines entered a new era of import substitution, fueled by a reconstruction boom. Landed elites, however, accustomed under American colonialism to accumulating wealth by using their local dominance to exploit local opportunities, showed little interest in these newer industrial and manufacturing propects. The state, therefore, initially took a direct hand running new industrial concerns. Officials' corruption and ineptitude,[107] however, soon spurred privatization that involved new entrepreneurs, largely outside the landed elite (Chinese traders and moneylenders, Filipino management professionals, lawyers and bureaucrats)[108]

---

[104] For a discussion of this, see Hutchcroft 1993: 39–41; Anderson 1998.
[105] Hutchcroft 1998; Anderson 1988.
[106] McCoy 1993.
[107] Golay 1971.
[108] Kunio 1985.

and changing patronage and rent-seeking practices. Gary Hawes explains:

What was vital to all entrepreneurs in import-substituting manufacture was access to both capital and political favor, for the government controlled the licensing of new import-substitution ventures, the granting of import permits, the right to exchange pesos for the dollars needed to import, and the amount of hard currency exporters would get after turning their export receipts over to the Central Bank.[109]

New entrepreneurs often came to manufacturing with little besides administrative skills, connections, and a taste for something new. Many got initial capital, licensing and contacts from state sponsors. As licensing became crucial to enterprise success, political and administrative professionals (as distinct from landed elites) acquired more influence.[110]

In time, some provincial elites invested in real estate and banking, but most attempted to prevent or reverse the trend toward protectionist policies that encouraged local manufacturing. By the late 1950s, import-substituting manufacturing entrepreneurs openly competed with landed elites favoring export-oriented policies.[111] Elections produced periodic swings between these two blocs, and so the state could commit to neither an export-oriented strategy nor to import substitution: each required more policy continuity than the patronage-riddled apparatus could deliver.[112] Marcos rose to power in the context of this competition: a creature of neither camp (despite his initial base in the former) but of the impasse between them.

Marcos thrived on his ability to work the state. He began public life as a lawyer with a flair for public relations, and a facility with political organization and coalition building.[113] As a young congressman in the 1950s, he accumulated power by securing state license, resources, and especially foreign exchange for entrepreneurs. His ascent marked a reversal in established paths to power, when economic activity required little state support, and bureaucrats were firmly subordinate to landed politicians.[114] As manufacturing grew more important, business required more of the state, and those skilled in statecraft grew formidable. Marcos was among the most prominent of these new politicians, enriched

---

[109] Hawes 1992: 150.
[110] Hawes 1992. (Hawes relies on Kunio 1985; and Baldwin 1975), see also Doronila 1992: 83–98.
[111] See Boyce 1993: 7; Ofreneo 1984: 469.
[112] Hawes 1992.
[113] McCoy 1994: 16.
[114] Anderson 1988.

directly by state power,[115] and in his first presidential term (1966–1970) he consolidated that power by centralizing state institutions on a scale unseen since Manuel Quezon's Commonwealth presidency (1935–1944).[116]

Much of this effort concentrated on the military. Marcos initially retained the Minister of National Defense portfolio and reorganized the dispersed military structure to form Regional Unified Commands that broke landed politicians' ties to soldiers. He replaced officers' old provincial loyalties with ties to himself, and built a national structure that included police forces and constabulary under the Armed Forces of the Philippines (AFP) command in 1967. At around that time, Marcos formed Manila's Metrocom anti-riot squad, entrusting it (and the expanded Presidential Security Force) to his cousin and former driver, Fabian Ver (a man who soon controlled the entire AFP).[117] Through promotions, salary raises and other incentives, Marcos constructed a loyal security force with broad powers and substantial autonomy from Philippine society.[118] He also mobilized civilian graduates of leading Philippine universities – men with only rudimentary ROTC training (Reserve Officer Training Corps), but the skills to carry out new political and surveillance tasks. Officers from the middle AFP hierarchy began to study management and related fields in two new schools. The National Defense College of the Philippines (NDCP) held its first regular class in 1966 (for senior military officers) and the Command and General Staff College (CGSC) opened in 1969 (for lower echelon officers).[119]

Mass mobilizations and the central state

Apart from government inefficiency, Marcos's main justification for martial law in 1972 was an overblown allegation of communist threat. As we have seen, the mode and timing of Philippine independence meant that the PKP could never strongly establish itself in the post-colonial arrangement – particularly in comparison to the Indonesian PKI or even the Burmese BCP. In 1968, young student activists broke away from the PKP's stagnant old guard to form the Maoist CPP. The new group would prove far more dynamic, but remained small and weak in the early 1970s.[120] Its really dramatic expansion occurred *after* martial law

---

[115] Macado 1971; Gary Hawes 1992: 148; Valdepenas 1970; and Manapat 1991.
[116] The centralization process had begun in 1962, under President Macapagal. Hawes 1992: 159; McCoy 1988.
[117] For a discussion of Ver's political rise, see McCoy 1999: 224–230.
[118] Thompson 1995: 55; McCoy 1999.
[119] Miranda 1990: 31–39.
[120] Jones 1989; Weekley 1996.

foreclosed legal avenues for dissent. Some even suggest that Marcos supported militant demonstrations on the sly in 1972 to create the impression of leftist menace.[121]

Nevertheless, mass (if not communist) politics was on the rise in those days, taking on new national and urban expressions. An expanding student population launched the first protests around 1966 to denounce a Manila meeting between US President Johnson and Southeast Asian leaders. The protest echoed US demonstrations against the Vietnam War, but had important local foundations. Some student activity began in established campus organizations, like University Student Councils and the National Union of Students of the Philippines (NUSP), but youth sections of the new CPP, such as the *Kabataan Makabayan* (KM, Nationalist Youth) were also exceptionally active. Students were perfect antagonists to the new interventionist state, for many traveled from the provinces to the national center, bringing local grievances into an integrated national focus. A proliferation of "university belt" campuses – lower quality schools established as businesses to provide diplomas for middle- and working-class students – injected a more easily radicalized element into the mix. Social ties between these students and expanding urban laboring communities (tied to the cash economy and deeply affected by currency and commodity price regulations) were closer than ever, and oil price hikes and fare increases hurt both groups. Vatican II's message of social activism inspired labor and peasant organizations, and Church-supported groups like the Federation of Free Farmers (FFF) and the Federation of Free Workers (FFW) put together national networks that featured Manila headquarters and provincial chapters.[122]

Expanding urban society also enabled activists to imagine an audience apart from the state. Protest increasingly adopted symbolic expressions designed to generate support from society: at violent Lyceum University protests on January 28, 1969, students heaped grass into a grave-shaped mound, knelt before it like penitents, and intoned grievances against the Marcoses; at Congress's 1970 opening, activists thrust a cardboard crocodile and coffin at Marcos as he left the Legislature.[123] Supreme Court pronouncements or Congress's annual opening became demonstration venues, and in 1970, the FFF camped on the Senate steps for weeks to protest against the government's agrarian policy.[124] Such contention departed from earlier modes of more direct and localized struggle –

[121] Rosenberg 1974–1975: 479; van der Kroef 1973b: 30–34.
[122] Youngblood 1981.
[123] De Dios 1988.
[124] Wurfel 1988.

rebellion, land occupations and theft. By the late 1960s, mass politics played to larger and more attentive national audiences, and benefited from parliamentary support and press coverage.

Hence, Marcos's efforts to extend his rule encountered more broadly mobilized resistance. Demonstrations demanded a fair Constitutional Commission in 1971, and then broadly denounced the Marcos regime. Three days after Marcos received his cardboard crocodile, students clashed with police outside Malacañang, leaving six activists dead. By February, protests raged at all the capital's universities, and new activist organizations ran teach-ins at public plazas. In March, transportation workers struck, and a combined force of students and laborers staged a "People's March" that ended in violence. These events formed the flash-points of the First Quarter Storm: the Philippines' first *urban* movement to make national, integrated demands. Even after protests receded, they left residues in Philippine society: Jose Lacaba, for example, recalls arriving at the Pinaglabanan Church for Independence Day celebrations on June 12 to find middle- and upper-class university students singing leftist songs in an open public ceremony.[125] Yet these new leftists were distinct from others across Southeast Asia. New radicals in the late 1960s were not recruited into a strong, established party with a long insurgent history. Rather, they sprang from the same modern, centralizing and urban forces that produced Marcos himself. Some came from the new, restless middle class, others from expanding bureaucratic and educational elites. They might never have adopted insurgency had martial law not criminalized acts of formerly legal dissent.

Marcos would not declare martial law for a year and a half after those March 1971 demonstrations. Between 1971 and September 1972, the most decisive changes in Philippine politics did not involve, as he claimed, communist menace, but constitutional limits on his presidency. The judiciary remained independent, and had since the late 1960s issued decisions diminishing American standing in the Philippine economy – and Marcos depended on American support. In 1972, the 320 Constitutional Convention delegates (chosen in a November 1970 popular election) were favoring a parliamentary system in which Marcos and his wife could not hold executive office. The press, moreover, printed stories alleging that Marcos bribed or pressured delegates to influence the draft.[126] Fueled partly by the broader protest movement, and partly by specific demonstrations demanding electoral reform, the Liberal Party

[125] Lacaba 1970.
[126] Pineda-Ofreneo 1988.

defeated Marcos's *Nacionalistas* in 1972 elections, making him the first post-war president to lose such a contest. With his opponents apparently poised to take the presidency, Marcos needed to prepare either to leave office, or to circumvent constitutional regulations.

The 1971 to1972 political crisis was hence not a crisis for state institutions, but for their incumbents.[127] With the language and methods of anti-communist authoritarianism globally accessible, Marcos saw that he would gain international support for authoritarian rule by claiming a life and death struggle against leftist insurgency; he abetted the impression by faking attacks on his officials, and staging explosions around Manila.[128] In an incident that captured the spirit of those days, two grenades exploded at the Liberal Party's August 21, 1971 *Meeting de Advance* at the Plaza Miranda, wounding several senators and killing at least six onlookers. Following that attack, Marcos suspended the writ of habeas corpus for one month, in what may have been a dry run for martial law. Starting in March 1972 small bombs periodically exploded across Manila. In July, the government intercepted an arms shipment from North Korea, unloaded from the ship *Karagatan* and intended for the small but growing New People's Army (NPA) insurgency. Through August, the explosions occurred more frequently, and in September, an alleged attempt on Defense Minister Juan Ponce Enrile's life (in reality a clumsy affair staged by the government) provided the final excuse for martial law.[129]

Still, Philippine left did not inspire some version of the killing blows that fell in Indonesia and Burma – although thousands were arrested in martial law's first weeks. The CPP was, as we have seen, organizationally weak, and not entirely responsible for the growing unrest. Marcos was cut from the same sociological cloth as many movement leaders, and valued the same educational and social institutions that shaped many radicals. Ne Win and Suharto moved strongly against communist opponents sharply different from themselves; Marcos, were he thirty years younger, might have joined student radicals on the streets. Indeed, Marcos's main trepidation seems to have focused on America's possible reaction, and he sent an envoy ahead of time to allay US anxiety, and then took pains to proceed in ways that wouldn't disturb liberal America.[130]

---

[127] Hawes 1992.
[128] Staff Report 1973: 32; van der Kroef 1973b: 40.
[129] Goodno 1991: 65; Wurfel 1977: 7.
[130] Bonner 1988.

Comparisons

In their rise, Ne Win, Suharto, and Ferdinand Marcos wove shrouds of domination that overcame rivals and reconfigured the terms of future rivalry. Repression in each country molded society and citizens to favor each dictator's power resources and shield his vulnerabilities – and would thenceforth draw social challengers into fights the dictator anticipated winning. Four main points structure our analysis of these processes. First, differences among the social foundations of colonialism and nationalism influenced who had capacity for or interest in state power, and so shaped the array of rivals a dictator had to best. Second, transitions from colonialism influenced state institutions' orientations, interests and strength – all fundamental factors in post-independence conflict. Third, rising dictators in each case challenged initial post-colonial arrangements from specific institutional or class positions, and their senses of vulnerability and opportunity reflect these foundations. Finally, the character of power embodied in the dictator's challenge to post-colonial arrangements influenced the shape and ferocity of state repression.

The social base of colonialism and resistance

Colonial states in the three cases recruited and trained their local collaborators according to different models, producing variations in imperial relationships to local society. In deposing Burma's monarchy and geographically diffused aristocracy, the British pre-empted alliances between rural elites and agrarian society, leaving only insular and city-bound graduates of colonial schools to pick up the anti-imperialist thread. Nationalism therefore eventually emerged as an urban, cosmopolitan force, led by lawyers and students (the important *rural Hsaya San* Rebellion notwithstanding). Burmese nationalists, like the British, concentrated in the cities where different sorts of people (British, Burman, Indian, Karen, Communist) strove to control state power. Britain's divide and rule policies exacerbated competition among these groups, and so nationalism's demand for local rule touched off immediate disputes about who (among the diverse local inhabitants) would rule.

The Indonesian situation produced a more broad-based and mass mobilizing nationalism. Colonial interactions with local society brought forth a multi-layered leadership structure that incorporated the old aristocracy, newly educated bureaucrats, some *Pesantren* clerics, their students and PKI cadres. Dutch-run plantations made imperial domination a tangible target of attack from the working class up. *Pemuda* nationalists, fortified by Japanese support, pursued their struggle in local formations, militia-style, on a grid already marked by Indonesian bureaucrats and aristocrats making their own nationalist efforts. Hence as Sukarno and Hatta's electrifying wartime radio broadcasts instilled the idea of Indonesia across the archipelago, the movement developed local roots – quite in contrast to Burmese events. Local nationalism arose as syncretic, rather than divisive parts of the whole, and one would never think of the movement as a limited circle in any one city.

Like the Dutch, US colonists in the Philippines recruited provincial collaborators, landed Filipino elites who were expected to assume national political roles, received significant economic incentives, and promised independence early on. Under American tutelage, Filipinos embarked on a slow, negotiated transition to independence, mainly designed (in elite minds at least) to preserve existing status hierarchies and avoid dangerous, unnecessary mass mobilization. Within elite political parties, therefore, nationalism was a tepid, mainly rhetorical device for bounded electoral competition. Non-elites periodically mounted more militant nationalist protests, but had difficulty attaining any significant scope precisely because they lacked cosmopolitan, integrating leadership. Hence, no Philippine nationalist movement since the *Katipunan* had either Burma's committed cosmopolitan cadre or Indonesia's broad reach – and the structure of powerful class privilege survived the transition intact.

With no local economic elite, political power in Indonesia and Burma grew within institutional arenas, reflecting the power and resources that office or experience provided. Burmese school graduates, whatever their backgrounds, could establish standing in the nationalist movement, while an Indonesian clerk had a level shot at revolutionary heroism. In the long run, the colonial state's dispersal in Indonesia and concentration in Burma produced important differences between the two cases – but in both, power reflected institutional positioning. In the Philippines, the institutional terrain was *itself* less important than class positions. Even the most skilled colonial bureaucrat had limited power, and electoral office was effectively closed to non-elites. Not surprisingly, challenges to postcolonial government in Burma and Indonesia emerged from disgruntled members of state institutions, but from new social forces in the Philippines.

Modes of struggle, paths to independence, and post-colonial change

The mystique of revolutionary struggle pervades post-colonial Indonesia and Burma. Two decades along, Sukarno could tap its legacy to summon mass support, while Burmese still gild the *30 comrades'* memory with near-religious reverence. Nevertheless, of the two, only Indonesian forces actually *fought* a sustained war against colonialism, and this difference influenced the balance between their respective post-independence militaries and civilian governments. More obviously, both Indonesian and Burmese transitions contrast with Philippine events, where elites needed no leverage against a departing American state. These paths to independence influenced the character of post-colonial states and societies, and the fault lines within each.

Burmese nationalist advance against the British depended initially on Japanese military support and subsequently on the Pacific War's shifting fortunes. Hence, at independence the *Tatmadaw* had rather thin fighting experience, rudimentary command and control structures, and an urban organization that was a secondary player to the political movement. In Indonesia, militia engaged returning Dutch forces in a decentralized war that lasted five years, and soldiers could regard victory as mainly their achievement. Wartime fighting experience might have set up the armed forces as Indonesia's dominant institution at independence, but the revolution wore Marxist, nationalist, Islamic and Republican masks: while everyone struggled for an independent and free Indonesia, that struggle produced a military that was more divided and heterogeneous than the *Tatmadaw*. Consequently, both Burmese and Indonesian militaries began independence subordinate to *weak* civilian regimes.

Soon after independence, however, each developed new strengths. Faced with insurgencies, defections and KMT incursions in the north, the *Tatmadaw* undertook self-triage and determined institution building that produced more clearly national and territorial orientations, as well as more robust logistical and institutional capacities. Hence it was a stronger, more capable and self-consciously national army that looked with dismay upon the civilian regime's descent into corruption and chaos in the 1950s. By the caretaker period, political parties could defeat the *Tatmadaw* in urban, electoral arenas, but perhaps *only* there. Isolated from political squabbling and demographically and experientially coherent, the military was more capable of powerful united action than any other political force. In 1962, therefore, the army needed merely to quash cosmopolitan (but insular) urban opponents to win state power.

Revolution shook all of Indonesia awake and prevented any purely central force from controlling state power, for dominant Jakarta was as potentially insular as anywhere else. Over the first independent decade, Sukarno mastered the situation with direct mobilizing appeals to the population that ABRI could not successfully challenge (despite several attempts). When the military did reach for state power, Sukarno reshuffled its command structure, playing on ABRI's internal diversity to isolate aggressive forces and strengthen those that seemed at least momentarily loyal. Nevertheless, and despite its internal differences, ABRI alone had the organizational reach to stretch across all of Indonesia. Hence, when the Guided Democracy regime strove to build state power and control social unrest in part by granting ABRI new power and resources, which in part it used to build a stronger internal hierarchy, the military's self-image as the Revolution's beating heart and foremost heir began casting a more substantial shadow. But by then, Sukarno had found a new counterbalance to military ambition: the PKI.

The two militaries, then, developed appetites and capacities for power within different contexts, and eventually set out against very different rivals. As the only substantial national institution with any reach, the *Tatmadaw* competed with urban political rivals that were very different from itself. The coup and its immediate aftermath therefore make most sense as an effort to subdue an urban political arena in which party capacity exceeded the military's. Under Guided Democracy, ABRI's rivalry with most parties was rendered unnecessary long before 1965 by weak parliamentary governments, Guided Democracy, and the parties' own parochialism. Organizational capacity and access to central author- ity mattered most under Guided Democracy, and in both respects, the PKI constituted ABRI's only serious rival. Ideological factors, of course, increased ABRI-PKI animosity, but so did Sukarno's explicit reliance on both ABRI and the PKI. Hence, while Burmese soldiers needed to neutralize the urban political arena, ABRI set out to eliminate a specific rival which, like the military itself, could claim to control a national network.

Differences between Burma and Indonesia, on the one hand, and the Philippines, on the other, are less subtle. Neither negotiated indepen- dence nor the Pacific War much disturbed the formidable class hierar- chies that US rule built in the Philippines. Approaching independence (and new US Cold-War policies) encouraged elites divided by the war to smooth over their differences, and made them disinterested in sponsoring the social mobilization that undercut old status hierarchies in Indonesia and Burma. Without any substantial mass mobilizing anti-colonial strug- gle, communism remained relatively remote from Philippine mass experi- ence, except in Central Luzon, until the Marcos regime itself. Nor, of course, did many political radicals win state posts or elected office. In contrast, socially mobilizing recruitment into Burmese and Indonesian nationalist formations reworked the social basis of political power, and focused later competition on institutions. Even where subsequent insti- tutional consolidation reasserted older class-based prerogatives (as McVey argues occurred in ABRI's post-independence rationalization) institutional positioning remained central to political competition. In the Philippines, class always mattered more. Marcos did not rise within any single institution; rather he recognized that state institutions, perhaps more than land, could be powerful resources, particularly those without landed positions. Behind this recognition, he stitched together a coalition of new entrepreneurs, newly professional politicians and technocrats, all with the vision and skills to snatch up investment opportunities and wind-fall profits, and to forge the state into an active weapon against landed privilege. At the helm of this social coalition, Marcos was unbound by the constraints on any specific office. He grew formidable through skills useful in transforming any office into a vehicle for this new political style. As president, he centralized and empowered the state apparatus, both to face down rivals, and to attract entrepreneurs and technocrats fed up with policy paralysis. But unlike landed families building on their provincial power, Marcos *required* access to central institutions, and refused to vacate the palace: he declared martial law as his second term waned and his landed rivals seemed poised to bar him from further office.

The new regimes

Extreme violence against apparently helpless opponents cannot entirely be explained by the dictators' efforts to unseat incumbents or defend against challengers. The new regimes of Ne Win, Suharto and Marcos broke sharply with old political and social styles, and the violence with which each inaugurated his dictatorship (beyond helping to defeat rivals) established many of the new political rules on which dictatorship would thrive. Hence, these rising authorities often roused themselves to levels of repression out of all proportion to the apparent threats they faced. The relatively small and politically isolated contingent of student BCP sympathizers at the Rangoon University, for instance, hardly threatened the Revolutionary Council; nor, for all his talk of communist threat, was Marcos seriously jeopardized by the CPP in 1972. Each dictator's attack, however, aspired to rewrite existing political rules, and to issue warnings to future challengers, and this aspiration explains much about the character of their attacks.

The *Tatmadaw* set out to build a new political system, oriented toward a central military command of politics and modeled on its own anti-insurgent apparatus. It recruited activist groups behind its program of socialist transformation, but soon regarded these supposed allies less as political partners (or even vehicles for popular participation) but as sub-ordinate units to transmit central orders and programs down the line. The student-union murders proscribed open urban dissent that was both anathema to this hierarchical ordering of authority, and a key resource in the old parliamentary system that so confounded the military. It helped, of course, that the students under attack sympathized with a BCP at war with the army. Yet the bombing did not cut into BCP strengths as much as it shut down a political arena that the army despised. Thenceforth, the RC kept Burmese society atomized and weak, and pushed dissent to the criminal and insurgent margins. Not coincidentally, the *Tatmadaw* alone could respond to a criminalized opposition with no open political purchase on society, insuring both a fight on terms that the military favored, and that only the military would be equipped for the job. Hence in Ne Win's Burma, dissidents could become secretive, insurgent or compliant, any of which posed considerably fewer problems to the regime than would legal political opponents.

In Indonesia, Guided Democracy had long weakened the Jakarta politicians who were most like Ne Win's main rivals in Burma, and ABRI's field of real competitors dwindled to only the PKI. Unlike the *Tatmadaw*, however, ABRI was not primarily an insurgency-fighting army, and had not built the streamlined, battle-hardened units that made the Burmese military so coherent and confident against insurgents. Rather, ABRI had diverse and expanding economic, social and political interests, which diversified further as it took on new tasks during Guided Democracy. After the October 1965 coup, ABRI maintained Guided Democracy's centralized and corporatist character, for it suited the military just fine. Given the match between ABRI and PKI capabilities, however, either might prosper under such a regime – and ABRI had twice watched a scattered communist party regroup after an apparently shattering defeat. The PKI murders did not, therefore, address communist behavior (as the Burmese student union murders had prevented protest); they eliminated the PKI itself.

Indonesia's New Order, founded upon those murders, was therefore a different kind of dictatorship than Socialist Burma. In contrast to the RC's aloof hierarchical authority, the New Order's extensive corporatism drew all parties (even, to some extent, dissidents) into itself, and dominated society with its smothering pervasiveness. With the PKI destroyed, only state leaders could pull together and direct these associations, and while only official associations could function, ABRI would rest on firm foundations. The New Order unremittingly blocked the organization of non-state political groups, and incorporated existing groups into official associations. Parties and labor unions were consolidated into large, inefficient and heavily surveilled organizations. Prohibitions against new or unsanctioned organization, rather than restrictions on dissent *per se*, represented the very core of the New Order's repressive policies.

Philippine martial law did not establish a new military regime, but consolidated an incumbent, and so required less violence than either the Burmese or Indonesian coups. Marcos's empowered and loyal security forces ended representative democracy with a series of well coordinated raids, logistically impossible under earlier, decentralized patterns of military deployment. Marcos also enjoyed new US support, keyed to a Cold-War allegiance that portrayed martial law as a necessary measure against leftist subversion. Armed with new resources, the president did not need to destroy adversaries, but rather to scatter them enough to secure an environment of emergency in which martial law could operate unfettered. With no recourse to due process, political rivals (even from established, landed clans like the Aquinos and the Lopezes) had little leverage against martial law. But if they were initially impotent against the New Society, they nonetheless constituted an elite, fuming, opposition from the dictatorship's inception. As Marcos's constitutional authoritarianism emerged, these opponents would adapt, and eventually prosper.

Comparison between the Philippines, Burma and Indonesia suggests that the character of state attacks depended less on leader's capacities or animosities, and more on his vulnerabilities to rivals in the specific context of the dictatorship's emergence. Ne Win's violence eliminated open protest that underlay the political power of parliamentary factions. Perhaps, like Suharto, he also wished to exterminate the communist party, but needed instead to focus on gaining control over lowland Burma to eliminate the vestiges of parliamentary power. The 1962 student union murders drove dissent underground and into rural arenas the military could more comfortably engage. In contrast, Suharto's fear of the PKI *organization* lay behind the 1965 to 1966 massacre. ABRI did not need to secure strategic territory, as had Ne Win, and instead hunted down the PKI in its provincial bases. Suharto attempted neither to push back nor reform the PKI, and one cannot imagine him conducting peace talks with communists, as did Ne Win in 1964. The PKI's very existence threatened the idea of a New Order. Ne Win's socialist regime, in contrast, could accommodate an insurgent BCP far more easily than open protest. Marcos had less to fear from any rival social force than either Ne Win or Suharto; he mainly faced legal obstacles protected by parliamentarians. His moves against both the left and the parliamentary opposition produced space to redraft Philippine law to continue the centralization of personal patrimonial power. Indeed, Marcos probably felt most vulnerable to international criticism of his regime, and he therefore set about constructing a political order that he hoped to be able to defend, at least on paper. The bounded, punctuated liberalism that he deemed necessary for this defense, however, allowed his domestic opponents to regroup.

Hence these attacks bridge old and emerging political orders. Either by directly striking at its strongest rivals – as ABRI struck at the PKI – or by undermining the base of a rival's power – as did the Burmese RC's prohibition of protest – new authorities used specific patterns of violence and repression to shake themselves free of the old system. In so doing, they also established rules for future political dissent, and claim makers in Socialist Burma, New Order Indonesia, or New Society Philippines could look to state crackdowns to learn what to expect from authorities. From 1962, Burmese protesters more or less understood that demonstrations courted bloodshed that (even) insurgency and underground work could avoid. Open mobilization against Ne Win consequently required extra-ordinarily encouraging conditions, for no activist could reasonably expect to encounter understanding or receptive authorities. New Order Indonesia proscribed political organization, but allowed demonstrations and pro-test. The state's hold on power rested on its organizational monopolies, but *because* these measures defanged the opposition, the New Order could permit peaceful demonstrations that Ne Win would not. In the Philippines, both elite parliamentary opponents and radical organized and underground groups survived into martial law. Marcos's attention to the ruling apparatus gave each the chance to adjust to the new terrain. Marcos certainly assumed that a more centralized state could withstand (and perhaps even win over) the opposition. But these new rules, includ-ing the bankrupt constitution, also provided resources for an opposition that proved flexible and resilient – not least because both its parliamentary and underground modes survived 1972.

Conclusion

This chapter has attempted to explain contrasting patterns of authoritar-ian crackdown in terms of the power balance between each of the three rising dictators and their political opponents. State leaders in each setting had reason to fear at least some challengers, for dissent and protest under the turbulent conditions of post-colonial politics threatened to unleash catastrophic consequences: the loss of power, a country torn from their control, death and retribution. The three patterns of attack are consistent with the new regimes' senses of vulnerability to political challengers, in the context of evolving political relations. They represent crucial moments in longer, more strategic interactions between vulnerable regimes and social challengers. The next section extends this narrative into the three new dictatorships. If regimes act strategically, challengers do no less. Following regime attacks, dissidents eventually reassemble, sometimes discarding its shattered pieces, sometimes fitting them together to form new vessels for resistance. They mobilize resources and shape strategy in a society often fundamentally altered by repression – and these alterations constrain movement activity. Activists plan strategy and recruit support with at least some sense of danger and threat, culled from the memory of authoritarian crackdown. It is impossible for New Order Indonesians to contemplate an underground organization without considering the PKI's demise. Burmese activists cannot plan a demonstration without recalling the murdered students of 1962, or of 1975 or of 1988. From these fears, and from movement accommodations with state proscriptions, a political calculus emerges, born of different repressive patterns, and of claim makers' efforts, nevertheless, to be heard.

4   Protest in socialist Burma

Before it established the exclusive and repressive military regime that would dominate Burmese politics for decades, Burma's eight-person Revolutionary Council (RC) embarked on a path briefly notable for its show of consulting potential supporters (even mobilized, activist organizations) and soft-pedaling radical changes in the Burmese economy. Where it would soon arrest and murder demonstration participants, it initially attempted to recruit activist support to the new regime, and this seems strange in hindsight. Yet authorities' early policies also presaged the drive for political control that most characterizes the socialist period. The RC set aside the 1947 constitution, established state control over universities and the printing industry, and banned such innocuous practices as beauty contests and song and dance competitions.[1] Soon, moreover, what might at first have been new avenues for representation (under military supervision) began more obviously to operate as mechanisms to extend and consolidate military control.

At the outset, government efforts to organize support, coupled with its attacks on BCP sympathizers, appeared to discriminate between those allied with the RC, and those who opposed military rule. Student associations established by the new regime's Burma Socialist Program Party (BSPP), as well as National United Front (NUF) groups and newly constructed Village Organizing Councils (VOC), expressed initial enthusiasm for the RC. For many experienced, leftist activists, the opportunity to build mass associations and participate in Burma's socialist transition was utterly exciting, and early BSPP initiatives, like land to the tiller and rent reduction programs, as well as concepts outlined in the *Burmese Way to Socialism*, stoked that excitement. Officials depended on activist enthusiasm and support to pull together a network of grassroots associations ostensibly to participate in that transformation. Soon, however, state repression ceased to differentiate between regime allies and opponents,

---

[1] Taylor 1987.

84

and instead attacked *politics itself.* Demonstrations supporting the RC's stated goals of negotiated settlements with insurgents drew indiscriminate, escalating repression that foreshadowed more general measures to prevent any public political activity (apart from BSPP-staged events).

Village-level mass associations, organized by the RC in the eighteen months following the coup, illustrate how authorities curtailed their own meager efforts at fostering representation. To build these associations, the RC relied on security councils (built in the late 1950s to disarm private armies and regulate mass organizations).[2] Security councils established township peasant councils (later renamed township organizing committees) in which experienced organizers, often from NUF groups, played leading roles.[3] The councils, in turn, set up village-level mass associations, so that in theory a fully developed chain of participatory organizations connected local communities and national government. Council general assemblies allowed villagers to meet party officials, who were in turn connected to government actors further up the line, and these interactions seemed to constitute a foundation for participatory mass politics.[4] When the RC had consolidated its power on narrowing foundations of the BSPP, these opportunities disappeared. Authorities de-registered all parties apart from the BSPP in 1964, depriving village activists of contacts and allies between themselves and the national government. In 1966, village general assemblies lost their right to express grievances, and thereafter merely transmitted RC directives. Peasant leaders absorbed into the party often lost their connection to the villages. Hence when rice shortages arose in 1966, the village-organizing councils were no longer in position to smoothly transmit farmer demands to officials.[5]

The general story of Ne Win's regime follows lines laid out in this example. Until 1974, the BSPP remained a very small, very exclusive organization, open mainly to military elites who harshly proscribed

---

[2] Callahan 1996: 484.

[3] The transition from independence to BSPP affiliation was not always smooth. In the BWPP, for example, an acrimonious debate divided the U Ba Nyein faction, which wanted to join these new groups as individuals, and Thakin Chit Maung's faction, which wanted to maintain the BWPP structure. U Ba Nyein's position won out, but the debate was rendered moot when the government outlawed all non-BSPP organizations in 1964. (Interview B–5.)

[4] Taylor 1987: 292–294.

[5] Interview B–6. This informant belonged to the PVO before joining a labor union originally affiliated with the AFPFL, and later with the BWPP. After March, 1962, he was assigned to the Township Organizing Council in his area to set up village and township organizing committees.

politics of any kind outside their ruling circle. With political parties out-side the BSPP banned, associational life squashed (to the point of state prohibitions on football matches), and political demonstrations sharply proscribed, political activity of any kind was driven into clandestine, secret acts. Outside the major cities, the *Tatmadaw* fought sustained, brutal battles with ethnic and leftist insurgents, but these fights were increasingly isolated from the central urban areas, and so would neither support, nor draw support from, protest in the cities. Economic activity, dampened by policies isolating Burma from the rest of the world, was strongest among a stratum of so-called black-marketeers: both illegal and necessary to the regime, and so publicly criticized, periodically perse-cuted, covertly protected and consistently extorted.[6]

Within this stifling political climate, what forms did political conten-tion take, and what state responses did it encounter? In order to answer, our account begins by tracing student activity in the wake of the 1962 murders, and moves from there to a more general chronology of Burmese dissent under Ne Win.

After the July 7 university explosion, surviving BCP students spent months hiding on University campus, while the army waited for them to make a break for Rangoon's safer confines.[7] In the main, confronta-tions between students and soldiers appeared rather low key: students built a crude, symbolic structure where the old Union building had stood, and soldiers pulled it down; in the main, however, the military refrained from extensive raids on campus holdouts.[8] It was in some ways a puzzling stand off. Certainly, the troops did not want to provoke broader demon-strations by too-blatant attacks on students, but they were surprisingly passive and appeared content to contain campus activism while they established the foundation of the new regime. In particular, there were few of the sweeping arrests and interrogations that marked the rise of Suharto's New Order or even Marcos's martial law.

When schools and universities reopened in late 1962, campus politics had changed utterly. The RC replaced student groups with new BSPP associations that randomly divided students into teams for athletic and social events. Each had a name alluding to Burmese mythology, and an identifying color, but no whiff of politics or ideology to mark one from another (a sharp departure for a milieu in which even the control of university reading-rooms had been a matter for partisan dispute).[9]

[6] Steinberg 1982: 79; Kyaw Yin Hlaing 2001.
[7] Steinberg 1982.
[8] Interview B–4.
[9] Silverstein and Wohl 1964: 53.

A university administrator accountable to an army Security and Administration Committee (SAC) chaired each association, with a BSPP student leader as vice-chair.[10] In this climate, BCP sympathizers were completely isolated. Their former allies in the SUF largely supported the new government, and with their close former association with the BCP students, made particularly dangerous informants. In 1963, during peace negotiations with the government, BCP party leaders under safe conduct passes contacted student BCP members and sympathizers holed up on campuses. When the government peace parley broke down, many of these activists accompanied the guerillas into the hills. (The recruitment brought little advantage to anyone: campus activism did not prepare students for jungle warfare, and they dragged at insurgent forces.) Politics for those who remained on campus was more difficult than ever, but BCP remnants and sympathizers made cautious moves to build underground cells.

The term *underground* (UG) has a particular meaning in this context, which, given its importance to the discussion that follows, merits some explanation.[11] Commonly, the term *underground cell* denotes one unit in a larger network of covert groups that support illegal or insurgent activity either by working through legal front organizations or in clandestine, secret groups. In either case, individual cells acquire importance in a larger movement structure – they are cells in a biological sense. In Burma after 1962, heavy state repression and surveillance, as well as proscriptions against even the most innocuous associational life, eliminated any possible covering activity, and prevented cells from forming larger networks. According to one analyst, there was one spy on campus for every ten students, and so activist cells had to be self-sustaining and utterly discrete.[12] Arrested activists faced open-ended detention, draconian jail conditions, torture and execution. In this climate, UG cells were less units of political activity than small, defensive activist clusters, unable to cohere into a proper movement, but which nevertheless kept dissident skills and memories alive.[13] Some contained veterans of past demonstrations, who had earned whispered reputations for skill and experience, and

---

[10] Interview B–11.
[11] Smith provides a similar definition and discussion of underground activists in Smith 1999: 367.
[12] Selth 1986.
[13] Informant B–12 recalls: "Basically, the role of the underground was to try to keep a feeling of anti-government sentiment alive through the years. We trained urban activists and cadres in these cells, and also from time to time would publish and distribute anti-government articles and leaflets. This really was about all that we could do in the urban underground." From notes transcribed immediately following interview.

attracted students looking for guidance in times of mobilization and protest.

The few accounts of cell activity that exist describe small, cautious collectives of between three and five who gradually sharpened their critical consciousness by reading and discussing novels, political tracts, and eventually the government itself.[14] Some published heavily disguised political satire in popular literary magazines that for some reason remained open.[15] As one writer from that period recalls

We set up a newspaper that published on campus after the coup, and remained open right up until 1967, when (after anti-Chinese riots) the government shut down a lot of these papers. We tried to slip some political criticism into short stories and poems. We experimented with all kinds of literary mediums, always trying to pass our anti-government message past the censors.[16]

Another activist describes how he functioned in the national media:

I was put in the media field and worked there for many years, anonymously. I didn't show my (political) identity at any time since my student days. Nobody knows about me, even the leftist workers themselves didn't know about me. The communist party regarded this field as very important, very strategic. They told me to stay behind and not to expose myself.[17]

This pattern echoes BCP methods during the parliamentary period,[18] except that underground activists *after* 1962 mainly sympathized with, rather than belonged to, the BCP or some other illegal group. Nor did they commonly coordinate with one another. One leader in the 1988 democracy movement started a cell in 1984, and then pursued rumors of kindred dissident circles for years, to no avail.[19] More rarely, a full-time BCP activist (often trained in China) returned to conduct secret work, but most of these seem to have been relatively uninterested in actual organizing or resistance activity. One BCP member, reflecting on those

---

[14] Aye Saung 1989.
[15] Divisions between educated Burmese and the newly empowered (often under-educated) *Tatmadaw* became increasingly explicit toward the end of the Parliamentary regime, and into the Socialist period. Several informants speculated that at least some of the provocation for the military attack in July 1962 stemmed from student taunts at less-educated soldiers, and the soldiers' class resentment. In any event, most writers I interviewed believed that literary satire slipped easily past uneducated military censors who did not understand literary devices like allusion and irony. Interviews B–11, B–12 and B–1.
[16] Interview B–12; see also Article 19 1991: 22–23.
[17] Taped interview B–9.
[18] One activist recalls: "We formed small groups, gave out literature to discuss, and so identified those we might recruit. After a time, when we thought we knew who we were working with, we began talking politics and eventually built a cell." Interview B–1.
[19] Interview B–13; also see Aye Saung 1989.

years, argues that the party's gravest mistake was ignoring the urban political arena.[20]

As BCP sympathizers were forced underground, legal groups formally supporting the RC also encountered new constraints. In 1963, with insurgent organizations from across Burma traveling to Rangoon to join a peace parley with the government, legal organizations like the BWPP and the NUF formed a loose movement called the People's Peace Committee. The Committee staged a Peace March along the hundred-mile road from Minhla to Rangoon. Supporters lined the parade route and the march ended in a 200,000 strong demonstration in Rangoon.[21] The military exercised some restraint during this march, although it did arrest activists linked to the BCP or to U Nu's Union Party. The relative political openness surrounding the peace parley lulled NUF and BWPP supporters, and even BCP sympathizers, into a rash complacency, and military intelligence agents quietly identified many who participated in those demonstrations.

By November 1963, plans for a second peace rally in Mandalay triggered a crackdown and ended the parley. This time, however, authorities moved against NUF and BWPP members formally *allied with* the new regime. Beginning on November 14, security forces arrested over 900 activists in Mandalay, with similar sweeps in upcountry towns. By the year's end over 2,000 activists from groups that *supported* the RC were in jail, where many would remain for over a decade without being charged.[22] On March 28, 1964, all parties and political organizations save the BSPP were banned – a move that merely formalized relationships established in the 1963 arrests. From that point forward, mass protest was exceptionally rare and dangerous in Burma. In 1965, some 2,000 monks did protest the introduction of a state agency to control the Buddhist clergy, but authorities arrested more than 100, imposed monastic controls and so prevented monks from protesting in any numbers until 1988. Apart from that confrontation, protest in socialist Burma required an extraordinary exogenous spur, provoking widespread spontaneous mobilization.

The peace parley's end provoked renewed fighting in the countryside, and thenceforth, grievances that arose in connection to events like demonetization in 1964 strengthened insurgency more often than protest.[23]

---

[20] Interview B–9.

[21] Smith 1999: 210.

[22] Smith (1999) estimates that 4, 500 people were arrested in these sweeps from late 1962 to 1963. His account of political support for the 1963 Peace March is based on interviews with participants in those events, 210–214.

[23] The 1964 monetary policy produced a "new generation of ethnic insurgent movements (that) rose up overnight." Smith 1999: 219.

Indeed, Ne Win and the BSPP leadership seemed in some ways more committed to eliminating protest than insurgent groups. Authorities, at any rate, reached periodic accommodations with insurgent forces that would never have been conceived as a strategy against urban protest. The military, for example, followed the broad outlines of safe-conduct agreements with the rebels that allowed most to return to their bases after 1963, peculiar in a place where authorities seemed to care so little for established rules of engagement.[24] When insurgent activity increased in 1964, furthermore, Ne Win offered many new groups the opportunity to reform as semi-autonomous defense militia (Ka Kwe Ye).[25] No similar accommodation was ever attempted with urban protest groups.

Cultural Revolution and rice protests

If patterns of state repression atomized and isolated urban politics, developments in the late 1960s guaranteed that no compensating ties with insurgent organizations could develop either. The events began when protest mobilized during a rice shortage, itself partly due to declining production incentives under socialism.[26] When the dwindling rice supply drove up prices, riots broke out across Burma. Students joined in, but workers initiated most actions. Rangoon protests centered on river jetties, where rice was loaded and stored.[27] Elsewhere, impoverished farmers and workers raided rice storage facilities, and concentrated less on demanding political reform than on acquiring food. This contention is precisely what one would expect in settings where civil associations and movement organizations do not exist to plan and coordinate resistance activity: riots spread because the crisis struck scattered regions simultaneously, encouraging direct action against local resource depots, rather than more indirect actions against national authorities. Security forces responded brutally, arresting and shooting demonstrators and rioters in the cities, and using even stronger force further afield. In the bloodiest incident, the 20th battalion killed 270 people in Arakan.[28]

Shortly thereafter, Chinese students influenced by the Cultural Revolution began wearing Mao badges to schools and invoking other symbols of Chinese communism. The BSPP had not by then abolished the Chinese schools, which divided into those supporting Mao's

[24] Taylor 1987: 367.
[25] Lintner 1994.
[26] Silverstein 1977.
[27] Interview B–3.
[28] Smith 1999: 225.

revolution and those that backed the Republic. Hence despite depoliticizing pressure on other campuses, Chinese students often had access to more politically coherent networks than other students. When the Chinese Embassy began distributing Mao's publications in 1967, students in Chinese schools could brandish the famous "red book" just like Red Guards across the border. In early June, one group of students attacked several teachers, triggering an immediate and strongly xenophobic popular reaction.[29] Through June and July of 1967, many of those who had been mobilized during the rice shortage attacked Chinese teachers, schools, businesses, and on June 26, the Chinese Embassy. These attacks refocused mass anger away from the state in ways that seem more than mere coincidence.[30] Two months of rioting destroyed Chinese establishments across Burma, and probably killed hundreds of Chinese.

In response to the violence, China stepped up aid to the BCP, and granted it broad access to territory bordering Burma. These new resources encouraged the BCP to adopt a more exclusively insurgent line against the state. But the anti-Chinese violence (seemingly directed against the Chinese revolution) also shook some BCP members' faith in the urban arena (a faith already weakened by difficulties that 1963 student recruits encountered integrating with battle-hardened insurgents).[31] These considerations set off a violent Cultural Revolution-inspired purge inside the BCP in late 1967, killing most student recruits, but also some of the party's most dynamic organizers and leaders.[32] Although Chinese arms and logistical support helped the BCP gain vast territory over the next five years, Burmese communism never recovered its authority in urban politics, and its organizational separation from the cities, emphasized by the move to distant basing areas, was virtually complete.[33]

These developments closed the last possibility for any substantial link between underground cells, or people involved in periodic urban protest, and the rural insurgencies. The party was not eager to recruit

---

[29] *The Guardian,* June 23.

[30] Smith (1999: 227) interviewed an RC official who revealed how military officers spread news of anti-Chinese riots upcountry to areas where the rice protests had been most severe, in order to provoke further anti-Chinese actions and derail any further rice-related protests; see also Aye Saung 1989: 42.

[31] The exodus of BCP student sympathizers into the insurgent struggle is described in Lintner (1990), where the student exodus is described as boosting the BCP insurgency. Most informants I spoke with emphasized that trouble emerged almost from the outset between BCP cadres and their student recruits. Interviews B–12, B–14 and B–5.

[32] Lintner 1989 66–67; Aye Saung 1989: 42; Maung Maung 1999: 74–75.

[33] Lintner 1994: 203.

students – and after 1967, students were equally wary of the party.[34] With neither legal organizations nor receptive insurgent groups to absorb UG activists, most found some place in mainstream Burma:

Upon graduation, some went to the jungle – but only a minority. Most stayed in the cities and took up positions as journalists, lawyers, or like myself, government servants. I worked in government for a long time, and even joined the BSPP – there was no alternative for government employees – you either joined the party or risked being posted to some backwater.[35]

More important, it was less possible to imagine linking an underground cell to any organizational structure or systematic anti-government initiative. Underground activists had few options except to preserve dissident perspectives and wait for a change in political conditions; from 1968 until 1974, with the exception of a small and easily scattered protest march demanding democracy at the 1969 Peninsular Games in Rangoon, no protest of substance occurred in Burma. U Nu (released from prison in 1966) adopted an openly dissident stand in 1969; still, even this inveterate politician organized an ostensibly *insurgent*, rather than *political* challenge to the BSPP government.[36]

Protest in the 1970s

The next protests, from 1974 until 1976, began as strikes among oil field and railroad workers and then spread to Rangoon textile, ink and paper factories. Unrest mobilized spontaneously as food grew scarce and prices rose. Workers launched insurrectionary strikes that (as in 1967) spread because of the broad and general hardship that the economic crisis produced across working populations. Early strikes alternated periods of intense disruption with relative outward calm, but as work stoppages paralyzed communication and transportation industries, the rest of Burmese society quickly discovered that something was afoot. More important, over the course of this activity, demonstrators learned how to organize protest, and developed

---

[34] According to one informant, after 1967 to 1968, when the communist party murdered student recruits who were accused of harboring counter-revolutionary orientations, students who fled the cities to evade capture were more likely to take up with one or another ethnic insurgent forces than the BCP. The communists continued to focus their recruitment efforts among the minority populations living in frontier areas. Interview B–4. Lintner's account of the BCP's mass base at the time of its collapse also tends to corroborate this recruitment pattern. Lintner 1990.

[35] Interview, B–12.

[36] Taylor 1987: 369.

networks that were more open and political than any in the twelve years since the coup.[37]

In considering these strikes, it makes sense first to note a political exercise that passed *without* protest. In February 1974, authorities finally submitted their draft constitution to a national referendum. While rumors of cheating filtered in from various quarters, threats and intimidation, rather than ballot rigging after the fact, managed to produce enough votes to win approval for the constitution. Voting booths were constructed to allow officials to note who voted to approve the constitution, and who did not. This way of coercing a favorable vote individualized the encounter between potential dissidents and state authority, focusing repression on myriad but isolated acts of voting rather than on any more potentially collective complaint that votes were miscounted, misplaced or misrepresented. As elsewhere under Ne Win, the logic of repression aimed at preventing dissent rather than at overpowering it. (As we will see, Indonesian and Philippine authorities managed elections quite differently.)

Industrial strikes began on May 13, 1974 among oil workers in Chauk, then spread into Rangoon. A conservatism marked these actions: workers remained inside their factories, halted production, and demanded better working conditions and wages, but carefully avoided explicitly anti-government actions they thought might provoke authorities. When University of Rangoon students, excited by the protests, went to the nearby Thamaing spinning mill to invite strikers to a street march, the workers declined, with polite gratitude.[38] The caution seemed well placed: on June 6, the military closed in on the mill and fired on striking workers, killing between twenty-eight and a hundred.[39] After several such attacks, the *Tatmadaw* arrested students on University campuses who had supported the workers.

After more than a decade of dormancy, the student activism stirred by these demonstrations had few models or leaders to follow. The oldest 1974 activists were still children during the last protests, and most knew nothing of activist strategy or tactics. No student leaders existed apart from those in unpopular and compromised BSPP groups (*Lan Zin Lu Nge*)[40]

---

[37] Htun Aung Kyaw 1997.
[38] Htun Aung Kyaw 1997.
[39] Smith 1999: 269.
[40] One leader in the 1974–1975 Rangoon student protests, reports that an original movement leader, Soe Tint, was replaced on the U Thant funeral committee after one hour when companions discovered he belonged to a Lan Zin organization. Htun Aung Kyaw 1997: 26.

for state repression and informants drove all others to jail, exile, the grave or underground.

In such dangerous circumstances, how could students trust that a companion did not work for the regime? Who would spread word of demonstrations? How would leaders emerge? Who would teach new recruits? The rallies themselves provided initial answers – for UG activists remained cautiously aloof. Curiosity, compassion, and a certain adventurousness drew students to the strikes, where they learned about workers' goals and grievances. Soon, students picked up and amplified these demands at speeches delivered on university campuses and in the streets. At first, a small student circle initiated the activity.[41] Those who demonstrated the most initiative or courage assumed leading positions, for with no other yardstick available, one's conduct at public rallies proved one's anti-regime commitment, and action (not association) produced initial movement solidarity. These connections, and leaders' reputations, survived the violence that quelled the 1974 strikes, and UG cells began to take notice of the volatile situation.

From the 1974 strikes, campus activists (a meaningful designation once more) vigilantly searched for the next opportunity to mobilize. Six months later, the occasion presented itself when respected statesman and former UN Secretary-General U Thant died overseas, and was returned home for burial without honors in an isolated Rangoon cemetery, in conformity to regime orders. Outraged by the apparent snub of U Thant, thousands of students and monks at the funeral seized his body, and marched it through downtown Rangoon. Eventually, they buried U Thant in a makeshift tomb near where the student union once stood on the RU campus. This burial site framed the episode as an indictment of the BSPP's very foundations, and students soon broadened their demands to include democracy, and an end to government repression. On December 11, three days after the burial, military tanks crashed through the university gate, and soldiers dug up the Secretary-General's body for burial at a more suitable site than originally intended. In the commotion, soldiers shot students who jumped atop the coffin to resist the move, and protests and riots flared across Rangoon. Official reports

---

[41] Htun Aung Kyaw describes his own activity: "We wrote letters to distribute – only a few of us friends – addressed to Dear people, monks, students. My friend is a teacher, and so had a hand copier, the kind that rolls out copies by hand on an ink pad. So we borrowed this, wrote the letter on wax paper and rolled out 2,000 sheets to distribute on the university compound. When students got hold of this copy, they read it and got agitated, and started to discuss these issues." The next day, 2,000 students from the University of Rangoon marched to Insein road to support the workers. (Recorded interview B–15.)

claim that soldiers killed 16 people, injured hundreds more, and arrested 4,500.[42] Others estimate far greater casualties.[43]

Unlike the earlier strikes in May, the U Thant protests produced organizations apart from sanctioned campus groups: a central committee and soon a separate unit to design and then manage U Thant's tomb, which many activists hoped would serve as an operations base for future campaigns. As before, however, movement leaders established their authority through particularly courageous speech or action, for these organizations did not pre-date the struggle, and could not screen out government spies. They did, however, enable far more organized and coordinated activity. Students went through Rangoon collecting donations as they had during the 1963 peace parley: trucks passed along established routes in the morning, announced collections, and returned later to gather donations – often tens of thousands of Kyat, and more food than activists could eat.[44] Some activists had parents inside the BSPP, who leaked news of government plans against the movement.[45] Workers who had been reluctant to leave their factories in May and June marched with students, as did many monks.

If movement leaders only emerged through public acts of eloquence or bravery, most participants also assumed that military agents were everywhere, and looked suspiciously upon individuals whose views undercut more general opinion. This mistrust hampered activists' ability to make careful political distinctions or devise subtle strategies. Consider the decision to bury U Thant at the student union site. As some students marched his body through downtown Rangoon, others convened a committee to decide where and how the statesman's tomb should be built. When the Government announced concessions (a new funeral, with honors, at the more prestigious Cantonment area), U Thant's family and the tomb committee were inclined to accept. At that moment, however, a law student picked up a megaphone, and urged students to bury U Thant at the university as planned. A cheer went up, and the procession

---

[42] Silverstein 1977: 143.
[43] Smith 1997: 269–270; Shwe Lu Maung (1989) quotes a student participant in those demonstrations who estimates that over fifty were killed on the campus skirmish alone, and hundreds more in Rangoon.
[44] Selth 1989.
[45] Htun Aung Kyaw reports that, "We got all kinds of information about government preparations against the movement, leaked to us from inside the regime. On December 10, for example, we received news that the government was sending spies to infiltrate student groups, and they would be wearing a clip on their collars, to help identify one another. This information came to us from the BSPP central committee headquarters. We informed the movement security detail, and they captured twenty people wearing such clips." Recorded interview B–15.

continued as before. No member of the tomb committee, despite their misgivings, intervened.[46] Given the crowd's enthusiasm, and the slim solidarity binding students together, none dared: "We were on the spot – if we disagreed, we would be beaten or captured as spies, so we keep quiet."[47] The dilemma directly follows from patterns of regime repression, which assured that activists would have no public reputation *qua* activists. Debates within the movement were hence confined to virtually apolitical matters (i.e. which *dormitory* should lead) rather than issues of strategy or tactics. One activist leader recalls, "We really didn't know what to do..."[48]

In other ways, however, the U Thant demonstrations evidenced far stronger organizational involvement than the earlier strikes. In Burmese phrasing, the protests were supported and controlled by "rightists," a designation that must be understood in relationship to the prevailing left-of-center discourse. Activists like Tin Maung Oo were associated with (only moderately) conservative forces like U Nu's Parliamentary Democracy Party (PDP), and may have received resources donated by people once active in the outlawed Democratic Students' Organization (DSO) or the Union Party.[49] Unlike BCP sympathizers, who could offer training on activist strategy, "rightists" more often provided resources – like the trucks that collected donations – but had little experience in movement building. Inclined more toward conspiracy than organization, "rightists'" hold on movement structures proved vulnerable: those surrounding Tin Maung Oo controlled the central committee for the U Thant demonstrations, but on December 6, "leftist" members joined that committee and dominated it completely by December 11.[50]

---

[46] The committee itself was already preparing a longer term plan to accept the government's offer but also to participate in the U Thant's memorial at the Cantonment area. The funeral committee would establish an office at the Shwedagon Pagoda to coordinate and plan construction of the memorial building – in the hopes of providing a longer term base for counter-regime activity.

[47] Recorded interview B–15.

[48] Quoted in Shwe Lu Maung 1989.

[49] The term rightist, when used by Burmese activists, has particular connotations that reflect the dominant leftist terms of reference of Burmese politics. In the main, groups that reject socialist or communist principles and leaders, including those who advocate free market capitalism, or simple multi-party democracy, have been called rightist.

[50] While he does not identify specific political orientations Shwe Lu Maung's informant does say that the original group of students who had seized U Thant's body (presumably identified with "rightist" groups) feared that spies were everywhere on December 10, and went off to meet in secret. When they returned, another group that the informant suspected worked as government provocateurs, had already buried the body, an act that unseated the original leaders. Shwe Lu Maung 1989: 52–54. Htun Aung Kyaw mentions the same shift as a leftward shift. (Recorded interview B–15 and Htun Aung Kyaw 1997.)

The U Thant protests produced a more experienced and recognizable core of activist leaders, as well as students who considered themselves activists, and regarded the government with nearly open animosity. By June 1975, activism had so taken root at the university that the government sent officials to campuses to explain deteriorating economic conditions to students, hoping to enlist their support, or at least to fend off further protests. The first meeting, between BSPP central committee member Dr. Hlan Han and Rangoon students, proceeded without incident. That night, however, activist groups met to prepare for the next day's meeting at the Rangoon Institute of Technology (RIT).[51] At that meeting, student activists executed a plan that required more coordination than would have been possible a year earlier: as the official spoke, activists positioned throughout the audience rose to ask pointed questions about the regime's legitimacy. The speaker soon fled and subsequent meetings were rescheduled or canceled.

Students, led by Tin Maung Oo, recently returned from consulting with U Nu's PDP on the Thai border, planned demonstrations to follow up on the RIT event. They described government plans to shift or cancel further consultative meetings with students as insulting, and by then anti-regime students were keenly attuned to such insults. After the meeting, Tin Maung Oo approached a wall dividing workers' quarters from student dorms constructed by the authorities after the May 1974 demonstrations. With some twenty companions, he took up a log, and tried to batter down the barrier. Students watched from their dormitory balconies for several moments, during which time the activists below operated with neither secrecy nor mass support – a dangerous condition in Ne Win's Burma. Soon, however, the observers descended, and in the last mainly spontaneous act of this cycle, tore down the wall.

The next day's protests were more organized, for leftist UG activists who had directed the last portion of the U Thant demonstrations began to play a leading role once more. A general strike committee met that first night, with Tin Maung Oo in charge, and others from the newly organized "rightist" Anti-Fascist Students League in prominent positions – but with the left poised to grab control from the right. On the strike's first day, BCP sympathizers seized control of a march to Insein Jail to demand

---

[51] Htun Aung Kyaw had formed the Anti-Fascist Student League, which met on the eve of the RIT consultation to plan their response to Dr. Hla Han's presentation. But Htun also acknowledged that secret groups of BCP sympathizers were also meeting during that same period, and so the speaker confronted an audience that, at least in its initial opposition to his remarks, was more organized than had been the case for earlier protests. Recorded interview B–15 and Htun Aung Kyaw 1997.

prisoners' release. By the next day, one of their ranks, Myint Soe, replaced Tin Maung Oo as strike committee chair, and elevated other leftists to the committee. New tactics soon followed: the general strike committee began concentrating on constructing activist organizations and set up headquarters at the RU Arts and Sciences Convocation Hall. They unfurled the fighting-peacock banners under which anti-British nationalists had marched, and had leaflets (urging coordination between urban protests and the BCP insurgency) to pass out at daily demonstrations. The BCP itself, concentrating on its insurgent war with the government, took little evident notice of these protests, however. On June 11, troops moved in and arrested over 200 student activists, ending the general strike.

Leftists exercised even more control over the protests in the cycle's final March 1976 demonstrations. These protests responded to government plans to commemorate the anti-colonial movement's most respected writer, Thakin Kodaw Hmine. Two prominent leftist writers on the event's planning committee resigned when Ne Win named himself a member as well, providing students one more opportunity to emphasize issues of democracy they strongly associated with Thakin Kodaw Hmine. Writers and artists led this last short round of protest, for many such had sympathy for the BCP and ties to UG cells. Study circles produced anti-government pamphlets, but only grew aware of one another as the literature began to circulate. Several discussed the relationship between Kodaw Hmine's writings and the BSPP regime, and many gained renewed circulation. When demonstrations broke out, they were already planned and announced by UG activists, largely through printed circulars. Ideologically distinct demonstrations carried rightist and leftist banners, led by activists clustered around Tin Maung Oo and Tin Aye Kyu, respectively.[52]

On March 23, over 2,000 students marched off the campus to the poet's tomb, commemorated his birthday, and then returned to occupy the RU Convocation Hall, as in June. A great many pamphlets and flyers circulated prior to the demonstration, evidence of advanced, secret preparation. When students returned to the University campus, however, leaders slipped away to preserve their cell core for future struggle.[53] Without leaders at the demonstration (when clearly some group had called the assembly) the Kodaw Hmine protests grew confused.

---

[52] Tin Maung Oo, however, was picked up the night before the March 23 Thakin Kodaw Hmine demonstration, and so the movement lost the main thrust of its non-BCP leadership.

[53] Recorded interview B–15 and Htun Aung Kyaw 1997.

Participants milled around for some time, then most merely left. Military agents swiftly closed sites of campus protest, and picked up key student leaders and organizers, virtually ignoring rank and file participants. Tin Maung Oo was arrested on the eve of the March 23 protests, and executed three months later. Others in his circle had been arrested after the June 1975 protests. Members of Tin Maung Oo's family, who seem only to have been superficially connected to the protests, went to prison for between five to nine years.[54] Writers and activists associated with the BCP (and Tin Aye Kyu's circle of BCP sympathizers) also fell to government operations. From March 1976 until 1987, Ne Win faced no protests.

The left's rise during these protests flags something important. Rightist students had resources and links to U Nu's PDP, access to printing materials and money, which allowed them to print flyers announcing demonstrations, but they had no tradition of mass organizing beyond their small and secret circles. Even before the 1962 coup, organizations like the DSO worked mainly by providing logistical support to activists of the left. When the BCP seized control of the general strike committee, rightist students almost willingly stepped aside. Rather than organizing a movement the communists might dominate, rightists then attempted to attract international attention (as indeed, U Nu was attempting to do) through a program that included bombings and hijackings.

Protest and state repression under Ne Win

Burmese contention, though rare, followed rather clear patterns. The military was never comfortable with, nor particularly successful at, open politics, and resorted to repression to prevent or quash protest that did emerge. The 1962 explosion, mass arrests in the early 1960s, attacks on striking workers, and sweeps through student dorms all illustrate authorities' pursuit of this same basic objective. While state antipathy toward communists may underlie some attacks, 1963 demonstrations (also repressed) supported peace negotiations that Ne Win himself initiated, organized by forces pledged to support the regime. Repression decisively influenced dissidents' political calculations and strategies – driving many underground or toward frontier insurgencies. Nevertheless, links between the countryside and the urban sites of struggle never developed, and underground cells became so isolated that they could hope only to

---

[54] Information on who was arrested and what prison terms they received is available in Htun Aung Kyaw 1997.

preserve dissident perspectives and skills, rather than to sustain dissent itself. Most sympathizers graduated from college into mainstream occupations, and many even joined the BSPP. Cowed by this sustained repression, activists could protest only under cover of more spontaneous mass unrest. In 1967, and again in the 1970s, unorganized political contention began with broad economic crisis, arising first where working people gathered in normal workday interactions that helped them see individual hardship as collective grievance, but then developed in ways that suggest the organized activity of more experienced activists.

Initially spontaneous demonstrations making direct and often economic claims prompted more organized and planned demonstrations making indirect and more political demands.[55] 1967 rice riots paved the way for small political demonstrations at the 1968 Peninsular Games. In the 1970s, student support for strikes encouraged ties among them, giving subsequent campaigns more organization. Protests during U Thant's funeral, the June government consultation, and the Thakin Kodaw Hmine ceremony made progressively broader, more political claims. U Thant's funeral was arguably a bridge in this regard, for it gathered a disgruntled mass at the potentially routine burial ritual, and group dynamics at the site produced sharp protest, but also a committee structure to guide future resistance. Students may not have protested when authorities cancelled meetings with them, and could not have coordinated their questions at meetings which did take place, without prior planning and explicit leadership. By the Thakin Kodaw Hmine protests, leaflets were published in advance to stir up protest. This progression illustrates the deepening involvement of those loosely organized activists that I have described as underground cells.

As collective forms demonstrate more organization and planning, the events that trigger protest become more politically symbolic, rather than merely material. Given state repression, perhaps only massive socio-economic could initiate protest, for neither activist networks nor dissident practice existed in sufficiently robust form to mobilize dissent from the outset. Spontaneous activity, however, woke activists to the possibility that Burmese society had begun to quicken, and they watched for opportunities to frame events like U Thant's funeral in terms of broader dissatisfactions. Not surprisingly, in the political void carved out by state repression, planned protests strongly evoked earlier Burmese struggles, and quickly appropriated their sites and symbols: the University

---

[55] For a discussion of the relevant differences between indirect and direct forms of struggle in social movements, see Boudreau 1996.

convocation hall, the fighting-peacock flag and the demand for a student union remained the most vivid political themes in the struggle against Ne Win – testimony to both the power of the nationalist legacy, and the absence of anything after 1962 to displace it.

This evolution is crucial. UG activists sank below the surface of Ne Win's Burma, with little prospect of activity as either open dissidents or (after 1967) insurgents. Most kept Marxist perspectives alive, but probably devoted even more effort to avoiding state surveillance and repression. Activists required spontaneous unrest to provide them cover, to suggest broader possibilities and produce encounters between activist cells and unorganized demonstrators. This sequence also explains why the 1974 constitutional referendum sparked virtually no mobilization, but almost certainly would have following U Thant's funeral.

The interplay of experienced activists without public reputations and mass unrest structured important elements of Burmese contention. First, protest leaders had great difficulty directing mobilized activity. With no public organizations or leaders, the momentum of mass opinion became inexorable. Moreover, if leaders established themselves by brave words or deeds, spies were thought to reveal themselves by actions or speech that undercut mass opinion. Contention was therefore difficult to focus politically, vulnerable to state subterfuge, and prone to violent escalation. The 1967 rice riots deteriorated into anti-Chinese rioting (probably encouraged by the military). Second, the underground culture of secrecy made movement participants suspicious of potential supporters. At the U Thant funeral, activists confiscated and smashed foreign correspondents' cameras, thereby pre-empting potentially sympathetic international press coverage. Finally, because so much mobilization depended on the limited, everyday contact that the regime allowed, authorities could quash protest merely by closing universities. Ne Win used the tactic months after the coup, and repeatedly thereafter.

State repression also followed patterns suggested in 1962 that raised the costs of protest. Authorities responded to protest with indiscriminate shooting and sweeping arrest, but never allowed demonstrations for more than a few days – except the anti-Chinese riots. Prison terms grew longer and executions more frequent. In fact, it appears that in several respects – particularly in its periodic willingness to enter into peace negotiations and cease fire arrangements – Ne Win was more inclined to conciliate *insurgents* than *student protesters*. The government crushed 1974 labor strikes by interrupting ongoing counter-insurgency efforts, and bringing troops into the cities.

The expectation of state repression led UG activists, even during protest, to work with extreme caution, to the point of abandoning protest at the Thakin Kodaw Hmine events. In the long and oppressive calms between protests, cells slipped into virtual suspended animation. Hence, across Ne Win's reign, protest repeatedly mobilized apparently from scratch, but soon, under the leadership of a tentative underground, began to move in more political – but backward-looking – directions.

5   New Order repression and the Indonesian opposition

Despite the Indonesian New Order regime's inaugural mass murders, it has since been relatively lenient toward demonstrations *of a certain kind* particularly in comparison to socialist Burma. Student protests, localized land and labor disputes, NGO-led environmental demonstrations, provoke periodic (not inevitable) arrest, injury or murder. Participants in such action (at least into the 1980s and even acknowledging prominent state violence against labor activists in the 1990s) seldom experience the kinds of prison torment one associates with dictatorship, and commonly spent relatively short spans behind bars. Other forms of dissent and resistance, however, predictably called forth sharp state violence. Outer island separatist movements in East Timor, West Papua, and Aceh drew sustained, brutal repression, as did any movement that sought to develop strong organizational structures and capacities. Hence, for almost two decades, the New Order presented two contrasting faces, depending on the mode of resistance it confronted: one committed to bloody and unremitting repression, the other more willing to tolerate dissent that it probably still disliked, and also subjected to intense surveillance.[1]

The New Order wove a repressive strategy from two legacies of its bloody rise. First, the anti-PKI struggle physically eliminated the only force that, in terms of organizational capacity, could rival ABRI for pre-eminence.[2] Suharto then expanded corporatist structures that deepened his organizational monopoly and restricted the legal possibility of organizing dissent outside state agencies.[3] Second, intimations of anti-communist violence colored even the most oblique state threats, and many proscribed acts (but increasingly the act of *organization*) were cast as communist.[4]

---

[1] Tanter 1992.
[2] McVey 1996.
[3] King 1982; McIntyre 1990.
[4] Schulte-Nordholdt 1987: 41.

Restrictions on organizing emerged incrementally, for Suharto at first needed, and even helped organize, social support against President Sukarno. ABRI agents worked closely with students and rural Islamic institutions to build anti-communist groups. From late 1966, however, state actors seemed less interested in popular action. Soldiers took control of the anti-PKI campaign, and violence shifted from a public war against known PKI groups to more secret attacks on "conspiracies" and "underground cells."[5] This period produced the first antagonistic notes in authorities' relations to supporting movement organizations. By the middle 1970s, the New Order had established its mature strategy, using direct repression sparingly, but broadly proscribing organization. The 1965–1966 massacres, of course, underwrote these proscriptions, at times explicitly, but also through elliptical references to communist influence via "irresponsible people" or "formless organizations"[6] and its consequences.

The containment strategy worked well. Prohibitions and threats against dissident organization atomized and moderated dissent. With no organizational vehicles to sustain dissent, most activists preserved their ability to rejoin the social and economic mainstream as lawyers, journalists, writers and politicians, and movements became extremely respectful of state restrictions.[7] Indonesian dissent, in consequence, became elliptical and stylized, expressed (rather frequently, under the repressive circumstances) by small-scale demonstrations, local associations and independent intellectuals. In time, students found common cause with peasants, workers and slum dwellers, but continued to favor episodic and isolated acts of resistance. In this chapter, we trace links between state repression and this specific style of New Order contention.

Precisely because Indonesian state repression scattered and atomized dissent, descriptions of individual movement histories are of limited value, and a catalogue of all protest activity impossibly cumbersome. (Burma and the Philippines, for reasons directly related to key aspects of their states' repressive modes, produce far more coherent narratives: the former because protest is so rare, and the latter because it is so centralized and coordinated.) The main dynamics of Indonesian contention are most clear in shifts between state policies to control dissent and the adjustments these shifts produce in contention. Throughout the New

---

[5] Van Langenberg 1990: 50–61; Jenkins 1984: 4.
[6] "Orang yang tidak bertangungjawab" and "Organasisi tenpa bentuk," respectively. Both phrases were prominent codes for communism in New Order pronouncements. Van Langenberg 1992: 127–128.
[7] Liddle 1985: 74–77.

Order, authorities' efforts to control dissent motivated a succession of policies proscribing a succession of specific *organizational forms*. In 1974, 1978, and 1983 to 1984, following periods of disruptive and escalating mobilization, new state policies prohibited organizational modes that gave recent contention its particular power. Activists typically worked around (rather than challenged) new state proscriptions, engineering consequent shifts in contentious forms.

Accordingly, shifts in state policy and movement response provide the milestones in the narrative that follows. Legislation in 1974 made it illegal for students to protest off campus, and so they retreated to university institutions, and used them to put together strong mobilizations in 1977 and 1978. In 1978, after these protests, authorities passed legislation that prohibited the use of university facilities for political purposes, and activists eventually moved to set up small off-campus agencies and study groups. When *these* groups gained power and mass support in the early 1980s, authorities enacted legislation that prohibited political groups from legally organizing a mass base – and movements either eschewed mass organizing or retreated from political positions. We will concentrate on these shifts, but first discuss the period from 1966 until 1974, when for particular reasons, Indonesian students did have the organizational capacity to mount more or less coordinated national struggle.

Student protest and state sponsorship in post-coup Indonesia

While the New Order's first dilemmas resembled those confronting post-coup Burma, key differences also existed. Both militaries faced parliamentary and communist rivals, recruited disgruntled popular forces, but then shouldered mass allies aside. Yet the *Tatmadaw*'s organizational dominance *before its coup* made Burmese officers less inclined to cultivate social support; moreover, since the BCP had been at war with Burma's parliamentary regime, there was little danger that U Nu and the communists would unite against Ne Win. In Indonesia, the PKI had substantial and growing power within Guided Democracy, with nearly 20 million reported members.[8] Before Suharto's victory was evident, many officers feared communist counter-mobilization,[9] and for several years after

---

[8] McVey (1996) reports that in 1965, the PKI had 3 million party members, and some 20 members in affiliated mass organizations.
[9] Robinson 1995: 134–135.

1965, the New Order remained largely on the drawing board, its very design contested among officers.[10] Suharto's leadership continued to be tenuous, and Sukarno commanded enough support to prevent swift and summary moves against him. Sukarno even showed initial signs of mobilizing society against ABRI, as in 1952 and 1957. Under those conditions, ABRI turned to student activists, already protesting against Guided Democracy and fighting rival student groups of the left.

The coup provided anti-communist organizations with new allies and support, and they fell into step with the army's broadening anti-communist campaign.[11] At first, demonstrations closely paralleled the government's anti-PKI campaign. When officials concentrated on blaming the PKI for the coup (in October) students staged rallies leveling the same charge.[12] When authorities began arresting PKI members in government, students denounced specific officials, and military units (particularly the RPKAD[*Resimen Para Komando Angkatan Darat*, Indonesian Special Forces] and KOSTRAD) protected anti-communist demonstrations from pro-PKI groups.[13] But the early movement also lacked discipline and focus, as when October 10 anti-communist rallies in Jakarta and Sumatra degenerated into anti-Chinese riots that eventually assaulted the Chinese Embassy.[14] To address concerns raised by such intractable demonstrations, Major General Sjarif Thayeb (Minister of Higher Education and Education Sciences) met with student organizations[15] on October 25 and established the Indonesian Students Action Union (KAMI, *Kesatuan Aksi Mahasiswa Indonesia*). As one activist

---

[10] According to Jenkins (1984), the military was divided between radicals, who favored the abolition of representative institutions in favor of a junta, and moderates who expected to dominate a tractable corporatist system that nevertheless left opportunities for popular representation.

[11] ABRI closed several PKI newspapers on October 3, and on October 12 shuttered universities with strong communist movements. By October 16, authorities banned the PKI and several affiliates. Thereafter, ABRI chipped away at the PKI's hold on government institutions, and it began purging government officials and members of the military alleged to belong to the party. See van der Kroef's too credulous account (1970) of government moves against communist conspiracies. One of van der Kroef's key erroneous assertions in this piece is that the PKI launched a significant and vicious counter-strike. Many refute this view (e.g. McVey 1996: 116).

[12] See articles cited from the military newspaper, *Angkatan Bersenjata* by Robinson 1995: 124.

[13] Budiman 1978: 617; Sundhaussen 1982.

[14] Newspaper note on this.

[15] Saidi (1989) reports that among the student organizations present at that meeting were the Association of Islamic Students (HMI, *Himpunan Mahhasiswa Islam*) Movement of Islamic Students of Indonesia (PMII, *Pergerakan Mahasiswa Islam Indonesia*) and the Association of Catholic Students of the Republic of Indonesia (PMKRI, *Perhimuunan Mahasiswa Katholic Republik Indonesia*).

wrote, KAMI "rendered students more coordinated and easy to lead."[16] ABRI's role here is striking, for never again would it permit, let alone assist, efforts to build organizational power outside the state.[17]

KAMI demonstrations were larger, more coordinated, and more synchronized with ABRI. Its chapters launched simultaneous actions with standard demands across Indonesia, often in close coordination with military action. When, for instance, KAMI published one of its seminal documents (its *Tritura* or Three People's Demands) on January 10, 1966, RPKAD commander Sarwo Edhi attended the event.[18] The strikes that followed culminated an organizationally *internal* process, and Edhi's attendance signaled ABRI support for student activity, placing the movement in a strange, almost semi-official position. Thenceforth, KAMI protests often foreshadowed ABRI operations against the PKI or Sukarno. At KAMI seminars, students and invited guests (often soldiers) picked at the ideological fabric of Sukarno's rule, and fashioned alternatives around ideas of development and modernity. Regular KAMI meetings with Generals Dharsono, Kamal Idris, and Sarwo Edhi, allowed students to imagine themselves in an emerging governing coalition, meeting on the New Order's ground floor.[19]

When Sukarno relinquished his executive powers on March 12, student protests shifted. Earlier demonstrations against economic hardship, the PKI and Sukarno helped Suharto to power by making economic demands to attract mass support (for example, against high transportation costs and demonetization in January 1966) or by directly demanding that Sukarno resign. Thereafter, however, students also began advocating a clear restoration of democratic rule and launched an anti-corruption campaign that lasted until late 1967. In these new demands, students approached positions that would eventually divide them from the New Order.[20] Still, they retained the national organizations that ABRI helped them to build, including national councils, inter-campus coordinating bodies, radio stations and newspapers. These capacities cut sharply against the grain of the New Order's emerging corporatist strategy, by which authorities would soon combine political parties into the internally

---

[16] "... agar para aktivis mahasisiwa itu manjadi lehbi terkoordinir dan mudah depimpin." Saidi 1989: 76.

[17] Suryadinata 1989: 19.

[18] Sundhaussen 1982; Saidi 1989: 78.

[19] Aspinall 1995: 28–29; Suryadinata 1989: 32.

[20] The first outright clash between students and the regime they helped to set in place occurred during Bandung mobilizations, called by students when elections were postponed from June 1968 to some future date. These led to growing protests from students against the military's expanding power. Liddle 1973: 290.

heterogeneous Muslim *Partai Persatuan Pembangunan* (PPP, United Development Party) and nationalist Partai Demokrasi Indonesia (PDI, Indonesian Democratic Party), or press associations into official state-sponsored unions, farmers' organizations and the like.[21] Even when some student leaders accepted government posts, however, the activist machinery continued to function. Organizers experimented with mobilization forms to strengthen the movement: they staged demonstrations on symbolic events like the coup anniversary, adopted an anti-corruption campaign that played on growing mass discontent, and acted for the first time like entrepreneurs. The students had grown more capable than was entirely convenient for the state.

Because the student movement mobilized the precise mode of dissent that authorities wanted most to curtail, official responses provide an opportunity to examine New Order repression in some detail. By mid-1966, ABRI could be relatively certain of defeating the communists and Sukarno, and its second congress in Bandung strengthened the *dwifungsi* doctrine and also resolved differences between New Order radicals and moderates.[22] From this more secure position ABRI required less in the way of mobilized mass support, and was in any case moving to build the corporatist apparatus on which it would depend.[23] Moreover, the anti-communist campaign was then turning toward operations to unearth alleged underground communist networks: specialized work for anti-communist professionals, rather than a matter for public politics.[24] Government and military purges accomplished part of the task, but state agents also reported secret PKI cells plotting an insurgent struggle.[25] In this climate, officers began to undercut student protests; the last demonstrations clearly worked out between soldiers and students occurred on September 19 and 20, 1966, backing increased military efforts to arrest PKI members. After that, ABRI began to distance itself from student groups (i.e. *before* students began making demands that Suharto found uncomfortable). In early 1967, soldiers dispersed marchers demanding Sukarno's removal from office. On January 27, Suharto banned demonstrations. Students largely ignored this injunction from late January to early March, and celebrated the transfer of presidential power to Suharto on March 4. On March 6, the government again banned street demonstrations – though one last protest followed this announcement.[26]

---

[21] Liddle 1973; Schulte-Nordholdt 1987: 43–44.
[22] Suryadinata 1989: 39; Jenkins 1983; MacDougall 1976; Gunn 1979: 763–764.
[23] Anderson 1978.
[24] Van Langenberg 1992: 51.
[25] Van der Kroef 1970.
[26] Newspaper sources.

The first significant effort to undermine student power in a character-istically New Order style of repression came in late 1966, when students developed a new description of their political activity as representing a "moral force."[27] Officials soon accepted and used the formulation themselves, for it implied corollary restrictions that authorities found useful: a moral force was *not a political force*, and did not rely on massed pressure.[28] Rather, students were to use suasion, make their point, and then stand down. The concept was thus an encoded prohibition against using the political and organizational resources that ABRI helped stu-dents cultivate in 1965. Soon, students felt this prohibition more clearly. In April 9, 1968 soldiers attacked a gathering of students assembled to plan a demonstration, killing one high-school student and injuring three others. Around the same time, ABRI officials began to speculate more frequently that students were linked to a communist conspiracy. It was a significant charge. With the PKI's open machinery destroyed, author-ities had turned to rooting out secret communist cells.[29] In this climate, stories of communist conspiracy continued to rework popular concep-tions of what communism was: no longer an open parliamentary party, but an underground, secret organization, operating in defiance of the New Order's monopoly on legitimate political organization. To ignore prohibitions on *organization* thus opened one to charges of communist entanglement.[30]

The idea of the necessary morality of legitimate student activism also created new opportunities to discredit students. In mid-1967, military and police began warning of juvenile delinquents ("hell drivers" or "cross-boys"). Tales of rich kids smoking marijuana, racing expensive cars, and having sex with multiple partners appeared in the press.[31] One story described how police accosted young men in Beatle haircuts and forced them to have public haircuts. These accounts provided a context

[27] One of the earliest expressions of the moral force idea can be found in a series of articles written by Arief Budiman in 1967 (these articles are cited in Aspinall 2004).

[28] Arief Budiman describes the post-1966 student movement's use of the "moral force" position in terms of Javanese cultural idioms. In these terms, the idea of a moral force conjured the image of the *resi* (i.e. hermits and sages) who were traditional sources of moral and personally disinterested political criticism in Javanese literary and theatrical forms. Budiman 1978: 616–619.

[29] Van der Kroef 1970.

[30] McVey (1996) reminds us that the association between communism and organization was not merely a post-coup, New Order formulation. Akhmadi also expresses this association clearly (Akhmadi 1979: 165–166).

[31] A *New York Times'* article entitled "Wild Teenagers Bedevil Jakarta" describes these alleged acts, and claims that "Every day, the (local) papers are filled with reports on adolescent antics." *New York Times*, August 8, 1967.

of moral depravity within which authorities could situate student protest: later accusations of student involvement in communist conspiracies merely broaden this accusation from degeneration (hell drivers) to treason (communists). Nevertheless, although authorities intimidated and discredited student organizations, they left the associations, inter-campus councils and the student press, largely intact.

Officials' initial tolerance toward organized student protest represents a departure from larger New Order patterns, and was probably a consequence of the *Angkatan 66*'s earlier anti-communist support; the repressive strategy is far clearer, however, in relation to separatist challenges that also defied New Order proscriptions on organization. Starting in 1968, separatist organizations in West Papua (Irian Jaya) moved into a protracted insurgency that foreshadowed later struggles in East Timor, Aceh and (to a lesser extent) Ambon.[32] As others have argued, these regions had contentious, and often shorter histories within the Republic, and separatist movements in each attracted substantial popular support. The scope and the character of separatism posed obvious dangers in the heterogeneous Republic[33] – but also virtually assured that activists would assert these demands from within more formal, long-term insurgent organizations. Hence, an entirely different set of state–movement interactions emerged between Jakarta and separatists, precisely because it was virtually impossible (perhaps from the beginning, but certainly after a few months of state repression) to conciliate these movements into the New Order. In West Papua, ABRI massively repressed separatists, segregating the region from Indonesia and barring journalists as well. Isolated in this way, separatist movements calibrated their activity to their organizational capacities, troop strength, local support, and international attention (i.e. capacities they could use against authorities) rather than to their chances of winning over Indonesian allies. It is therefore difficult, and probably not particularly useful to assess whether separatism or movement organization most decisively shaped the New Order's response to these movements. As we will see, however, the pattern of the strongest state repression targeting the most organized movements, so clear in relation to separatist movements, is evident elsewhere as well.

---

[32] The resistance was stirred to life when Indonesia announced vague and shady plans to substitute consultations with 1,000 village representatives for a UN-mandated popular referendum on the territory's independence. Osborne 1985 (especially chapter 1).

[33] Indeed shortly after the West Papuan insurgency began, Ambonese separatists staged several terrorist attacks in Indonesia and in the Netherlands.

Protest in the 1970s

Two important facts shaped student protest against the New Order in the 1970s. First, with the communists eliminated and Suharto in power, students began to think more directly about Indonesia's future rather than about outflanking those they regarded as responsible for its past. In this shift, many moved toward a critique of modernization-based development models, and began also to identify and criticize local, sometimes corrupt collaborators in dependent economic relations. Protest hence began more often to target New Order authorities.[34] Second, for reasons that in retrospect seem a bit puzzling, the military refrained from prohibiting student organizations forged during the anti-PKI campaign, even as it was banning or "consolidating" other parties, unions and political associations. The regime intimidated, punished, conciliated, or discredited student political assertion, but did not eliminate them.

Students (and students alone) could therefore still plan and coordinate national protest based on their own organizational resources rather than exogenous sparks. Study groups turned the publication (in student newspapers!) of critical papers about state policy into occasions for mass action. University student councils (*Dewan Mahasiswa*, DM) coordinated campaigns between universities. Veteran of the 1966 movement assessed the New Order's progress against blueprints they helped draft years before. KAMI and related groups remained active,[35] but virtually every demonstration also produced new organizations around specific campaigns. Between 1968 and 1974, in fact, campaigns were more *organized* than *mobilizing*, and many featured small groups or symbolic actions accompanied by carefully drafted position papers.[36] Cadres ensured that movements responded to price increases, election campaigns or movement anniversaries, and sophisticated critiques of government programs touched off explosive anti-corruption protests in 1970, "Taman Mini" protests in 1971, and the Malari riots in 1974: loosely linked events that involved a fairly stable set of activists operating in movement organizations.

The Taman Mini Indah protests in 1971 to 1972 and Malari riots in late 1973 to early 1974 were but the high points of an extended student campaign. Starting around January 16, 1970, high-school students (organized in *Kesatuan Aksi Pelajar Pelajar Indonesia*, KAPPI, Indonesian Students' Action Front) protested fuel price hikes in demonstrations that

[34] Aspinall 1995; Budiman 1978; Akhmadi 1979: 168.
[35] Saidi 1989.
[36] Budiman 1978: 623.

soon spread to Jogjakarta; protests ended on the 26th, when the government banned further demonstrations.[37] Authorities pre-empted planned August protests by the student "Anti-Corruption Committee" (*Komite Anti-Korupsi*, KAK) by arresting activists for hanging anti-corruption posters near the Attorney General's office. In a typical but telling accusation, General Sumitro accused the students of communist connections and compared the situation to that leading up to the 1965 coup. The following March, protests mobilized in the run-up to scheduled elections, and sharply increased in May.[38] A *Golongan Putih* (White Group) formed in mid-May to advocate an election boycott, and the Opposition Young Generation Group projected a similar stance for the Islamic social organization *Nahdlatul Ulama*.[39] That September, students protested authorities' cancellation of an Indonesia Foundation discussion, and commemorated the anniversary of the anti-corruption movement. General Sumitro once more berated activists, and accused them of harboring communist sympathies.

The first crescendo in this activity was 1971 to 1972 students' protests against the Taman Mini Indah project, an expensive, frivolous theme park in which Suharto's wife Tien held a substantial interest. By January 15 demonstrations occurred in virtually every university center across Indonesia.[40] The demonstrations represented the sharpest anti-government criticism to that point, and were all the more volatile because they leveled charges at Suharto's family. Authorities responded with a mixture of violence against demonstrators, and a more concerted effort to undermine activist credibility. On December 24, hired hoodlums attacked twenty demonstrators, injuring three, on January 6, a visibly angry Suharto threatened to use deadly force, and the next day security forces attacked a student sit-in outside the project's headquarters, arresting several participants. ABRI linked the protests to the Golput electoral boycott, and both to the PKI.[41] On January 14, Minister of Interior, Amir Machmud claimed that PKI "terror campaigns" depended on criminal support. Other officials implied that activists were merely paid criminal stooges. Arief Budiman, a leader in these protests, took special pains at the time to refute government descriptions of the activists:

---

[37] Press announcement.
[38] *Pedoman*, May 24, 1971.
[39] From the outset, officials attempted to delegitimize these groups. They described activists involved in these actions as rapists and kidnappers carrying Mao's "red book". *Diwarna*, May 16, 1971.
[40] *Tempo*, January 15, 1971.
[41] *Angkatan Bersenjata*, January 6, 1971.

"[M]embers of the Austerity Movement are students of the University of Indonesia schools of (among others) letters, law and economics. GAPUR (*Gerakan Pemyimpkan Uang Rakyat*, Movement to Save the People's Money) consisted of KAPPI figures ... mostly 1966 activists, known to the military and neither rapists nor muggers."[42] Starting on January 18, state agents arrested prominent movement leaders, shutting down the protests.[43] Government reports once more decried long hair, drugs and promiscuity among the youth, linking moral decay to activism and criminality. Soldiers again administered forced public haircuts in what it depicted as a struggle to root out subversion on interlaced cultural, moral and political fronts. Since both government and student forces elected to define acceptable dissent in the language of the "moral force," this campaign in fact struck home, setting many actual (or alleged) student acts outside the realm of legitimate activity.

Still, the sanctions did not disrupt student organizations, particularly the student press and inter-campus organizations, which were instrumental in framing and mobilizing dissent. The DM's analysis of the economic roots of 1973 anti-Chinese rioting in Bandung, for instance, established positions that informed protest in 1974.[44] A series of small, but regular and organized student protests occurred in 1973's last quarter, against a ban on long hair, a visit by the Dutch Education Minister, and (in greater numbers) a marriage bill that offended Muslims. Organizations also allowed close contact between activist leaders and some sections of ABRI. At the time, two military factions, described by Crouch as professional and investment generals, struggled for power, with the latter more involved in economic affairs and more implicated in corruption.[45] A prominent member of the professional camp, General Sumitro (Kopkamtib) spent 1973's last months solidifying ties with student organizations, issuing statements supporting greater political freedom, and encouraging student demonstrations criticizing the finance Generals.[46] Aspinall argues that

---

[42] *Indonesia Raya*, January 18, 1972. The last remarks, that demonstration participants are neither rapists nor muggers comes in response to government charges, circulated in mid-January, that communists had hired gangs of criminals to fill out demonstrations ranks – with the lingering implication as well that activists and criminals were pretty much the same. See also Arief Budiman's Letter to the Editor, *Kompas*, December 30, 1971.

[43] Among those picked up were Arief Budiman, human rights activist Hadji Princen, *Sinar Harapan* editor Aristides Katoppo, and KAPPI head, Jusuf AR. Katoppo and some of his reporters were released after sixteen hours, others, like Budiman and Jusuf AR, were held longer.

[44] Ng 1976: 5–8; Akhmadi 1979; Aspinall 1995.

[45] Crouch 1978.

[46] Van Dijk 1989: 12.

students believed that Sumitro would seize power if university organizations could sustain protests.[47]

The protests that capped this activity were initially organized demonstrations against Japanese Prime Minister Tanaka's visit and the economic policies that visit represented, but soon spun off in violent
rioting, particularly when unorganized members of poor urban communities joined in.[48] The action was in some ways inherently vulnerable to
unruly non-student participation. As a self-consciously "moral force,"
students protested in expressly symbolic ways, as when three activists
calling themselves the *Komite Kabanggaan Nasional* (KKN, Committee
for National Development) draped the Japanese Astra building with
an Indonesian flag in late 1973.[49] Convinced that they functioned best
"morally," students used organizations to provide themselves with
credentials and to coordinate among leaders, rather than to draw in or
direct mass support, and the movement remained detached from
society.[50] Most students envisioned the economic policy debate as properly conducted among modern sectors of Indonesia, and were thus eager
to exclude mass society (and consequently unprepared to direct mass
participation). Deteriorating economic conditions and a rice shortage,
however, had driven working Indonesians to the brink of defiant activity.
Already scattered incidents of largely unorganized protest or conflict
across Indonesia seemed on the rise, and centralized, public student
protest proved an irresistible draw for many. Some evidence also suggests
that Ali Murtopo, a prominent finance general, countered Sumitro's
efforts to mobilize student support by recruiting slum dwellers to join
and radicalize the protests.[51]

For whatever reason, relatively peaceful student protests on January 14
gave way to greater violence the next day. Workers and slum dwellers
streamed into Jakarta, burning and damaging Japanese cars. By day's
end, mobs had looted and burned a major shopping center, smashed
the Toyota showroom in the Astra building, and vandalized the Japanese
Embassy. On January 16, 10,000 students gathered near the Japanese-
owned Presidential Hotel, but riot troops turned them back with warning
shots. Later, Sumitro disavowed the violence, depriving student leaders
(themselves badly shaken) of expected support. Students quickly endorsed
Sumitro's call. DM president Hariman Serigar recalls feeling great

[47] Aspinall 1995: 30.
[48] Budiman 1978: 618.
[49] *Kompas*, December 17, 1973.
[50] Ng 1976: 30; Aspinall 1995: 6–7.
[51] Ng Chin-Kaong 1976: 17–20; Hansen 1975: 150–152; Bourchier 1992: 193.

alarm as the demonstrations swelled beyond the DM's control, and relief when they ended.[52] Official estimates place the riot damage at 11 deaths, 137 injuries, and 1,000 destroyed cars and motorcycles.[53]

The government response, given this violence, was relatively lenient, and concentrated first on quelling the unrest and then on restricting student organizations. On January 18 troops occupied the University of Indonesia and set a curfew that remained in effect for only a week. Of over 800 students, journalists and teachers arrested, only 42 eventually faced trial, and they reported relatively privileged prison conditions.[54] More significant action came later, from the new Education Minister Sjarief Thayeb (who had helped organize KAMI in 1965). Aware of how organizations enhanced student power, Thayeb drafted law SK 028 (restricting off-campus student protest) and unsuccessfully attempted to elevate the KNPI (*Kesatuan Nasional Pemuda Indonesia*, the Indonesian National Youth Committee) to the status of sole legal student organization.[55] Despite a visibly less supportive government,[56] many students were inclined to accept SK 028 restrictions and view the Malari violence as reason to avoid broader political involvement. The violence also triggered a backlash inside religious organizations like the HMI (*Himpunan Mahasiswa Islam*, the Organisation of Islamic Students), behind the position that student leaders had become too political and secular.[57] Others merely reassessed the tactics surrounding Malari, re-embracing the "moral force" proposition to concentrate on discussions, cultural presentations, poetry readings and folk concerts.[58]

---

[52] Taped interview, March 6, 1998.

[53] These estimates were reported to the People's Representative Council's January 21 meeting (*Dewan Perwakilan Rakyat*, DPR). *Kompas*, January 22, 1974.

[54] Hariman Serigar, for instance, scoffed at the idea of overseas exile as an alternative to Indonesian prison: "Why do that? Things were so comfortable for me in prison – I was even able to go home when I needed a good meal." Taped interview, March 6, 1998. See also Southwood and Flanagan 1983: 184–185.

[55] First announced in a speech in Malang, July 17, 1974. In a general way, the editors of the journal *Indonesia* make this point in footnote 26 of their translation of "The *Exceptie* of Heri Akhmadi." (Akhmadi 1979). For a more particular example of an organization leader's successful work to fend off the centralizing efforts of the KNPI, see Saidi 1989: 115–122; Thomas and Soedijarto 1980: 51–55.

[56] HMI leader Ridwan Saidi, for instance, describes a meeting between student leaders and Misister of Religions, Mukti Ali. The Minister regarded the students with cool detachment, took a long pull on his cigarette and asked each what level they had attained in school. The students answered . . . and the Minister ended the meeting abruptly to demonstrate how little they mattered in his official calculations.

[57] Saidi 1989: 117–122.

[58] Hariyadhie described this evolution of student collective forms. Hariyadhie: 1997: 2–4.

Yet campus organizations did survive and could still coordinate and organize resistance (unlike in Burma, where such groups were eliminated). Hence when 1977 DPR elections drew near, and a government official named Sawito Kartowibowo published a series of papers alleging government corruption, students began once more to protest.[59] The actions occurred on individual campuses, in conformity with SK 028 restrictions, but soon also challenged those restrictions: Surabaya students joined ambulant food vendor riots, Bogor students protested land tenure patterns, and the *Mahasiswa Ujungpandang Bertanya* (Ujungpandang Students Ask) petitioned at Sumatra's local assembly.[60] Elections pushed activists to coordinate these demonstrations, and they met in East Java to discuss how their press might strengthen the national movement.[61] In February, students across Indonesia met university rectors to complain about SK 028 and began to demonstrate against issues of mass concern, like expensive bus fares.[62] Later that year, students from three universities organized a mock legislative session called the Provisional Parliament. Akhmadi recounts that, "By this move, we began the consolidation of student movements/activities by setting up coordination networks in each city ... (after our arrest) our ideas were then taken up by the student Councils/Student senates in Jakarta, Bogor and Bandung."[63] Larger student meetings in October produced stronger cooperation and a document called the "Students' Vows."

These efforts demonstrate a growing willingness among activists to struggle for organizational power (perhaps natural after three years of SK 028 restrictions) in place of earlier activists' inclinations to form small, excluding alliances with potential allies in the state. At large inter-university meetings, students agreed to "take advantage of every opportunity" to press their demands. They organized demonstrations on two November holidays and to meet a delegation of seven government ministers traveling to campuses and dialogue with students. In both cases, student organizations planned demonstrations and publicized them in the student press. Some even argued for joining forces with mass society, unimaginable earlier, and particularly hard to fathom so soon after the Malari chaos. By 1977, however, activists believed that

[59] McDonald 1980; Bourchier 1984.
[60] Hariyadhie 1997: 14–17.
[61] One participant in high-school protests at the time recalls how his campus, which eventually was the site of violent clashes between students and security forces, first grew political because they could obtain college magazines that inspired resistance. (Interview, Coki, February 13, 1998).
[62] Akhmadi 1979: 17–18.
[63] Akhmadi 1979: 18–19.

Malari escalated because the actions were unorganized, and the move-ment could correct that flaw, and even be more militant, if organized. Demonstrations mobilized despite military warnings, and began to leave campus despite SK 028. In some cases, students marched even when soldiers ringed their demonstration, and tanks patrolled their perimeter. The *White Book of the Student Struggle*, published by the Bandung Institute of Technology's Student Council on January 14, 1978, tried to explain student protests to a broader audience – a new and significant concern for the erstwhile "moral force."[64]

The paper was an anti-Suharto declaration of unprecedented strength, and days later student councils in Jakarta, Jogjakarta and Surabaya published similar documents. Kopkamtib troops moved into the larger campuses to arrest student leaders. On February 25, soldiers seized Gadjah Madah University with far greater force than anything in Bandung or Jakarta, killing six students and injuring many more. On smaller campuses, students built barricades – but these often only attracted determined commando raids. Into March, soldiers violently broke up demonstrations and arrested around 800 across Indonesia; as with the Malari riots, however, far fewer (150) spent more than a few days in jail. Authorities closed all student councils and eight newspapers regarded as having sympathized with the demonstrators (seven that pledged not to cover opposition news eventually reopened).[65] In late March, close Suharto ally Ali Murtopo became Minister of Information, officials seen as too close to students (for example, Generals Nasution and Kamal Idris) were repri-manded, and Association of Southeast Asian Nations (ASEAN) head General Dharsono was forced to resign. These measures took the wind out of the activists' sails: some demonstrations occurred during the *Majelis Permusyawaratan Rakyat* (MPR, the People's Consultative Assembly) General Assembly on March 3 and March 11, but a token show of military force scattered the crowd.

The strongest measures against further protest came in a package of policies called the *Normalasisi Kahidupan Kampus/Baden Koordinisisi Kamahahsiswaan* (NKK/BKK or the Normalization of Campus Life/The Body to Coordinate Students), drawn up by the new Minister of Education and Culture Dr. Daud Jusuf. The NKK/BKK imposed more stringent course requirements, placed student life under a campus bureaucracy with ABRI oversight, barred student organizations from political activities,

---

[64] Bandung Institute of Technology Student Council 1978.
[65] This pledge and its consequences for the media record concerning protest and dissent is one reason why Indonesian newspapers are unreliable sources of information about contention during the New Order.

and abolished institutions central to the 1978 demonstrations (especially the student councils and press). Unit *Kagiatian Mahasiswa* (Student Representative Bodies) were limited to sporting and social events, and could only exist on the individual faculty levels.[66]

Surprisingly, implementing NKK/BKK provisions required little direct repression, apart from threats to expel violators or restrict their employment potentials. Troops quickly disbursed each action that rose to protest the measures, but exercised enough restraint to avoid spin-off anti-violence campaigns.[67] Beside such one or two day challenges, fifty youths were arrested in early 1979 as members of an underground militant organization. In the main, however, activists complied with the new proscriptions and established study groups to review their pasts.[68] This relative meekness is puzzling, particularly given recent student concern about organizational power.[69] Some conjecture that most students grew disinterested in campus politics, and study groups eventually did argue that activists should seek closer ties with Indonesian society off-campus, and to that end, established small Non-Governmental Organizations (called LSMs for *Lembaga Swadaya Masyarakat*). The NKK/BKK legislation did emerge in conjunction with state moves to reprimand or purge government officials who supported student initiatives, and so students had little choice but to comply. Still, the absence of student struggle against the measures, particularly efforts secretly to defy the measures by building something akin to underground formations, is striking.

Consider, however, the larger context of Indonesian politics. Students had isolated *themselves* from mass society since 1965, and participated in processes establishing distinctions between campus and mass politics. Deeply involved in the New Order's emergence, they defined moral and modern politics mainly by its exclusion of unruly mass exercises, particularly of the left. Students did not suffer the campaigns to prohibit,

---

[66] Aspinall 1993: 8–9. For a more detailed justification of the measures' logic, see the paper written by Dr. Jusuf and sent to students, entitled "Normilasi Kahidupan Kampus" and included in Hariyadhie 1997: 171–179; see also Ministry of Education and Culture 1980.

[67] 500 University of Indonesia students protested the expulsion of 11 NKK/BKK violators on November 10, 1979. Ten days later, 100 students in Bandung protested the legislation. Other protests occurred over the next few years, but they were usually quite small and always fairly short expressions of dissent. *Kompas*, November 11, 1979; *Kompas*, November 21, 1979.

[68] *Tempo* magazine's April 22, 1989 feature on study groups served to inform many of one another's activities, and paved the way for visits and eventual coordination among them. See also Denny 1990.

[69] Hariman Serigar even recalls that he and other former activists urged students to stick to the campuses and struggle to re-establish the student movement there.

constrain or consolidate their organizations that reshaped other associations in the early New Order period, but there was not much they could
do *alone* to sustain activism. One could not, that is, graduate from campus
politics to a movement structure operating in the broader society, for
repression had eliminated such networks. Hence, by the time graver
consequences were attached to student defiance (particularly when
authorities began to present *organized* resistance as *communist* resistance)
campus dissent was largely isolated. Moreover, student activists (even
those from more disruptive, anti-state actions in the 1970s) often went on
to mainstream careers, precisely because of the credentials they established via campus politics.[70] By the late 1970s, the stakes riding on such
transitions were growing quite high. The Indonesian economy had
entered a period of steady growth, and prospects for educated
Indonesians with unblemished records were quite bright.[71] But such
careers depended on academic degrees, awarded only to those who
remained within the broad confines of state proscriptions. Students,
who constitute both an identifiable social group and individuals becoming something new, were in fact particularly vulnerable to NKK/BKK
prohibitions, for since activists only could anticipate futures sanctioned
by the New Order, apparently weak NKK/BKK threats of expulsion
represented central (not incidental) barriers to activism.

Contrast this situation with that of movements *not* dissuaded by heavy
state sanctions, which defied all manner of state proscriptions, including
those on organization. Separatist movements in West Papua, in East
Timor (after the 1974 Indonesian invasion) and in Aceh (1980s) developed
underground and insurgent organizations;[72] Maluku separatists in the
late 1960s favored dramatic acts of terror both in Indonesia and the
Netherlands. Each movement demonstrated resolve in the face of focused
state repression.[73] For instance, over 100,000 of East Timor's 600,000
residents died in the occupation's first years, and the New Order
responded to the West Papuan movement with armed military invasion.
These movements generated committed resistance with deeper, more
fully articulated anti-state organizations and alliances, partly because of
their physical and psychic distance from Jakarta, and perhaps also
because they did not occur where the PKI had been strongest, or bloody
anti-PKI massacres most intimidating. Hence, separatists never developed
the bounded symbiosis with authorities that led many Javanese students

[70] Lev 1996: 146–147: Adrinof 1988.
[71] Robison 1988: 64–67.
[72] Osborne 1985; Hill 1978; Kell 1995: 61–68; Tanter 1992: 239–244.
[73] Wessel 2001.

to define their actions as essentially *moral* rather than political. Separatists seldom sought *Indonesian* support, set out to preserve their own futures in an Indonesian mainstream, or to influence those who did. One East Timor activist reflected that, "We assume that there is no audience for us inside Indonesia. So when we demonstrate, we are either attempting to build our organization in East Timor, or to capture international attention."[74] Each movement developed an underground organization capable of surviving state pressure, concealing members, and training new recruits in an essentially insurgent strategy that required an organized network – and defied state proscriptions in ways that students never would.

After NKK/BKK

Before NKK/BKK, inter-campus networks and the suppression of non-student activism allow us to describe contention as possessing substantial central coherence. After 1978, student activists scattered and developed isolated formations that undertook limited episodes of protest, often (following recommendations of the post-1978 campus study groups) in cooperation with other Indonesian social formations. The result of these efforts would vary over the years (in response to shifting state prohibitions) but always reflected dissidents' inability to organize or broadly coordinate their activity, except under extraordinary circumstances.[75] Initially, students founded small LSMs to work with impoverished, marginalized Indonesians in what might broadly be called development programs, and avoided confrontation with state agents.[76] By the early 1980s, LSMs and other groups began taking more political, strongly anti-New Order positions, and less-organized riots, frequently against local targets, also increased.[77] Authorities often treated these outbursts as criminal or moral offenses that required suppression in the event itself, but no more comprehensive response. Local military detachments

---

[74] Recorded interview with East Timor activist, Jogakarta, March 4, 1998. See also recorded interview with Marcelino Magno, March 3, 1998; Naipospos 2000: 87; Chauvel 2001.

[75] Gayatri 1999: 104–105.

[76] Bunnell 1996: 181.

[77] Some evidence indicates that students in loose groups incited some of the unrest. On March 2, 1981, forty students were tried for roles in November 1980 riots. Hong Kong Radio reported that students led riots that same year in Maluku and Central Sumatra. Sometimes, loosely arranged, one or two day student demonstrations off-campus produced riots, as in Bandung on January 14, 1981, or Lhoksemawe, East Aceh on November 2 that year. See Uhlin 1995: 99–150; Eldridge 1989.

imposed curfews or increased patrols, and sometimes officers called the local Islamic clerics to scold people, but unrest remained fragmented, and offered a low-order threat to authorities.

Just as authorities seemed to have forced open contention into manageable forms, however, they began also to report underground, anti-government conspiracies. Often, media stories described the groups as mainly student led, but Michael Vatikiotis reports that radical groups may have been former Darul Islam activists assembled by Ali Murtopo to discredit Islamic parties in approaching elections.[78] Indeed, initial information about these activists described their secret work to disrupt the 1982 general elections. Later, a spate of militant attacks and government counter-raids indicated that the struggle was escalating. Intelligence agents arrested key leaders of a group called the Kommando Jihad on January 16 and 26, and killed another, Faisal Gozali, on January 18. The Mujahidin Command detonated a bomb on September 1, 1980 at a Jakarta hospital where Murtopo was to have been treated; ABRI operations smashed the group by October 21. In early 1981 the Indonesian Islamic Revolutionary Board (IIRB) began attacking police outposts, culminating in a Bandung raid that killed three policemen – but yielded many IIRB prisoners. On March 28, hijackers seized a Garuda Airlines plane to demand that arrested IIRB and Kommando Jihad members be released; three days later, commandos raided the plane, taking many prisoners. In such cases, arrested operatives received jail sentences ranging from seven to twenty years, starkly more than that meted out to student activists around the same time, and the secret organizations more generally received harsh and decisive treatment from authorities.[79]

Apart from the Islamic groups, another underground clash began in 1983: the so-called *petrus* (*Penembakan Misterius*, or Mysterious Shootings).[80] Dead bodies, often described as "tattooed," began appearing on the streets of large cities. By 1987 some 5,000 people had been killed in this manner, mainly via execution-style bullet wounds to the head, after earlier torture. Behind unconvincing government explanations that a gang war produced the casualties, Indonesians understood that both the killers

---

[78] Vatikiotis 1993: 129. The author acknowledges a debt to Sydney Jones Asia Watch for that information. See also Jenkins 1984: 56–57.

[79] In 1979, Heri Akhmadi received a two-year sentence for his role in the 1978 protests; in 1980 former UI student council president Dodi Suriadireja received ten months for insulting the president; in October of 1981, the University of Indonesia Rector received custody of student leaders arrested for inviting banned author Pramoedia Anna Toer to speak on campus. King 186: 344–347.

[80] Bourchier 1992b; see also Amnesty International 1983.

and victims belonged to covert networks,[81] partly discernible to ordinary Indonesians, but revealed most clearly in the grisly corpses discovered each morning. Killers and victims hence posed ominous contrasts to the rest of society – and the boundary between the covert and the open was thus marked by blood warnings.

While varied, each of these events represents a state attack on anti-regime *organization*. Actions against both the Muslim underground and criminals demonstrate the state's violent resolve to root out conspiracies and undergrounds, and probably also made the point that while criminals and terrorists lurked out of ordinary sight, they could not evade an omniscient state. As if to emphasize their commitment and power, authorities also periodically executed detained PKI members. The executions followed no discernible judicial timetable, but like *petrus* killings, were thrust suddenly into public consciousness – another underground, unearthed and vanquished, time and again. Student demonstrations probed NKK/BKK provisions, and found them firm. Subsequently, study groups avoided state pressure by remaining informal and fragmented, and by confining themselves to study and debate.[82]

Evolving repressive patterns also shaped LSM activity from that point forward.[83] LSMs initially delivered services and assistance to individual beneficiaries. LBH (Lembaga Bantuan Hukum, or Legal Aid Society), for example, provided legal assistance to individual clients, often on prosaic matters like divorce. New college graduates who had been active study group participants brought fresh, more explicitly political insights to the LSM movement. Under this new influence, LBH, like other LSMs at the time, shifted in 1983 from service provision to wider advocacy campaigns and more frequent recourse to demonstrations, and regularly began to situate disputes within integrated reform positions.[84] Crucially, as LSM activity adopted more radical tones and tactics, most still shunned formal organizational elaboration.[85] Networks that pulled together local communities for protest disappeared once LSMs took up other issues in other communities, and never set out to be long term or programmatically complex. The LSMs themselves remained small enough to escape strong state concern, or, when groups like LBH expanded, they did so in ways

[81] While most believed that the criminals or *galis* belonged to street gangs, there was also evidence, and substantial opinion, behind the notion that they were also members of networks set up by Ali Murtopo, organised as part of a plan to undercut his political rival, Benny Murdani. Bourchier 1992b: 189–193; Schulte-Nordhold 1987: 45.

[82] Aspinall 1993: 14.

[83] Eldridge 1995.

[84] Lev 1987.

[85] Bunnell 1996.

that conformed to state prohibitions. The LBH, for instance, renamed itself a foundation (*yayasan*), understood explicitly as *not an organization*. This semantic slight of hand demonstrates a more general LSM trend to avoid seeming to organize mass communities. Experience suggested that authorities would pre-empt and repress such efforts, but might tolerate looser advocacy.[86]

Within the structures of post-NKK/BKK restrictions, opposition movements began once more to gather steam. LSM expansion brought urban Javanese activists to rural and "outer island" cases, where authorities acted with less legal restraint and power issues were more fundamental.[87] In these local struggles, LSM activists and members of local populations often ran afoul of security forces striving to maintain order or protect their interests. Soldiers more commonly intimidated or threatened local advocacy efforts, but seldom resorted to the harsher measures, like murder and torture, of which they were institutionally capable. Initially scattered and small-scale LSM efforts began to grow larger and more politically potent as organizers gained experience and began also to criticize their own fleeting engagements with mass society. At the same time, the two largest Islamic networks, NU and *Muhammadiyah*, organizationally intact because they had designated themselves as religious and social groups, began more strongly political patterns of activity.

The state response to mounting unrest, when it came, was not a coordinated sweep to arrest or harm activists, but another round of legislation narrowing the permissible scope of counter-hegemonic organization. Mass Organization Legislation (*Ormas*) in 1984 restrained political organization outside the government's GOLKAR (*Golongan Karya*, Functional Groups) from recruiting and organizing constituencies. The legislation reiterated the intent of "floating mass" policies that prevented opposition parties from organizing stable mass support, but aimed specifically at non-party associations like Islamic organization, unions and LSMs.[88] The measures forced groups either to abandon mass constituencies (as most LSM would do) or to redefine themselves as social organizations (a path that NU and *Muhammadiyah* chose). On May 21, 1985 new legislation required all associations to adopt the *Pancasila* as their sole ideological basis, a rule that particularly affected Islamic groups.[89] The

---

[86] Eldridge 1995; Aspinall 1995.
[87] In 1983, for example, LBH opened an office in Irian Jaya, and almost immediately took in clients involved in the region's autonomy struggle. For patterns of LSM expansion more generally see Eldridge 1995.
[88] King 1982: 111.
[89] MacIntyre 1990: 39; Hari 1990; van Djik 1985.

NU and the *Muhammadiyah* rested on basic organizational building blocks that were also central to the Muslim religion: local clerics and teachers, Mosques and *Pesantren*. *Ormas* could not eliminate these organizations without attacking Islam itself. Hence, these "social" associations were allowed to maintain their organizations, but adopted orientations defined by the state.

The legislation generated even less protest than had the NKK/BKK, for by 1984, the New Order had substantially weakened its opposition. With no movement organizations to underwrite protracted struggle or counterbalance state sanctions by offering alternative activist futures, dissidents who defied *Ormas* would expect to act alone, risking both their present security and future prosperity. Other measures made this isolation more complete. Newspaper closures in 1978 intimidated the media from devoting substantial attention to opposition activity, and journalists began to practice self-censorship and a particularly circuitous mode of expression.[90] After September 1, 1980, foreign media sources were also barred from reporting on Indonesian politics within the Republic.[91] Mandatory state indoctrination (so-called p4 classes) and a pervasive effort to de-politicize the Indonesian language also contributed to the effort.[92] Authorities sometimes further strengthened corporatist institutions, as when the *Federasi Buruh Seluruh Indonesia* (FBSI, All-Indonesia Workers' Federation) gave way in 1980 to the more restrictive *Seriket Pekerja Seluruh Indonesia* (SPSI, The All Indonesia Workers' Union).[93] Together, these policies represent the New Order's mature repressive strategy, aimed at preventing dissidents from developing sustained, coordinated or national political expressions.

As activists internalized and worked around these restrictions, protest became more generally tentative, rhetorical and episodic.[94] Because secular protest worked within the state's paralyzing organizational restrictions, it seldom aroused the strong state violence. A contrasting glance at Islamic protest, which in the early 1980s did provoke substantial state repression, emphasizes this point. Islamic protest depended on local institutions like Mosques and *Pesantren* which left pious Muslims less "afloat" than most Indonesians, and so capable of sometimes-powerful unrest. Some of the most committed and energetic protest – against the state lottery (1991) or new marriage laws (1973) – had Islamic

---

[90] See Dhakidae 1991; Kitley 2001: 257; Heryanto 1996.
[91] Measures announced August 12, 1980 (*Kompas*, August 12, 1980).
[92] Heryanto 1988; Foulcher 1992: 304–305.
[93] Hadiz 1994: 194.
[94] Heryanto (1999) provides a fine statement of this position.

organizational foundations. Not surprisingly, resistant as they were to repression through organizational proscription, these protests also incited some of the most flagrant state repression. Soldiers killed between twenty-two and sixty-three at Islamic protests in Tanjung Priok, and around thirty more in later Muslim demonstrations in Sumatra.[95] One ABRI operation even removed the Ayatollah Khomeini's picture from West Java homes.[96]

By the mid-1980s, Indonesian contention took many forms, from student protests to secessionist insurgency, and including land, labor and water disputes, as well as those involving issues of Islamic faith. Nevertheless, the hallmark of the New Order's political success at domestic pacification was the *segregation* of different social forces and contentious forms from one another via proscriptions on their organization.[97] It was also difficult for ambitious university graduates to work for long in such small and limited LSMs. With scant room for either political success or individual advance, many LSM workers evolved into a particularly New Order-*style* activist: public intellectuals who criticized the regime in lectures, but strove to remain within what was legal and tolerated, and so eschewed movement building or any real calls to action.[98] Many of these public intellectuals emerge within some study groups that began to specialize in cultivating media exposure, and which developed a strategy of "information action" as an explicit alternative to "mass action." These individual activist careers combined to produce an extremely cautious movement culture. Barred from organizing sustained resistance, many came to regard dissident lectures and discussions as full-blown struggle. Reform professionals and public intellectuals stood in for movement cadres, and devoted considerable energy to dissident discussions. Significantly, these restrictions hobbled the New Order's opposition precisely as the Indonesian economy continued to grow and to offer opportunities to those outside the developmentalist state's originally narrow circle: expanding individual opportunities for economic gain overshadowed collective opportunities lost in the realm of forceful opposition.[99] The strategy was also self-sustaining: as activists accommodated

---

[95] The precise number killed at Tanjung Priok has never been established precisely. See the Petition of 50 1984 and Anonymous 1985.

[96] Liddle asserts that, as the Abangan Catholic Benny Murdani expanded his role in ABRI, "Many *santri* in society, particularly modernists, nonetheless believed that Murdani's army was an anti-Islamic force, willing and even eager to repress them." Liddle 1996a: 629.

[97] Aspinall 1993: 19.

[98] See Denny 1989; Aspinall 1993: 14.

[99] Robison 1988: 70; Adrinof 1988; Liddle 1992: 452–453.

state proscriptions, they sacrificed resources, like powerful movement
organizations or a strong opposition culture that would have allowed
sharper defiance. For authorities, this was precisely the point: by prohibiting movement organization and regulating access to the Indonesian
mainstream, they kept contention fragmented and manageable, even
when levels of protest rose.[100]

Protest and *keterbukaan*

On May 5, 1980, amidst growing dissatisfaction over the army's expansion into politics, spreading corruption and the regime's anti-Muslim
bias, fifty prominent Indonesians (many retired generals, but also two
former prime ministers) issued a statement of concern; the signatories
became known as the "Petition of 50", and from that point forward
served as a prominent oppositionist beachhead.[101] The group met frequently, and often issued statements criticizing the government.[102] When
the New Order encountered more broadly-based opposition almost a
decade later, the "Petition of 50"(still actively criticizing the regime)
provided examples of how dissidents might carve out space in the New
Order.[103] By then, ABRI was becoming a less reliable bulwark for
Suharto's controlling ambitions. *Within* the New Order, conflict emerged
between Suharto's patrimonial and nepotistic impulses, on the one hand,
and the interests of those undercut by those impulses, including formal
institutions like ABRI.[104] To thwart potential challenges and to weaken
prospective rivals, Suharto rotated senior officers out of power via territorial command positions, or into direct retirement.[105] He fostered service branch rivalry and constraint by placing adversaries together in
important service institutions, betting that they would keep one another
in check.[106] At the same time, outside the regime, opposition politics was
acquiring some important new foundations. Years of economic growth

---

[100] Liddle 1996b; Heryanto 1999.
[101] Jenkins 1984: 157–173.
[102] Sadikan 1985.
[103] See, for instance, the influential article in the *Far Eastern Economic Review* in which
Retired General Sumitro called for broader democracy. Sumitro 1989.
[104] Aspinall 1995: 28–29. Other locuses of tension included military dissatisfaction with
the rising influence of Islam. These tensions would continue and contribute to disputes
over the GOLKAR leadership in the early 1990s. Suryadinata 1997: 273–274; see also
Vatikiotis 1993.
[105] Most prominently, ABRI Commander and close Suharto ally Benny Moerdani was
dismissed in 1987 for voicing concerns about succession to the presidency and
corruption. Liddle 1996a: 629.
[106] Jenkins 1984.

and prosperity produced a growing stratum of professionals and entrepreneurs who did not automatically agree with regime policies, and often
supported public intellectual dissent.[107] As LSMs multiplied, many
moved away from narrow developmentalist positions, and began to
embrace more political advocacy.[108] In 1988, several forces broke with
the established pattern of simply accepting Suharto's nomination for the
Vice-Presidential position. The Muslim PPP party nominated an alternative candidate and strongly campaigned on his behalf. When Suharto's
nominee, General Sudharmono, eventually secured the nomination, an
ABRI officer took the stage to express military dissatisfaction.[109]

Pressure within the regime by the latter 1980s (especially because
parties to intra-state debates often sought social support, as had
Sumitro in 1973) opened the way for stronger social criticism and mobilization, producing a liberalizing thaw known as *keterbukaan* (openness).
But, *keterbukaan* increased opposition activity without initially changing
dissent's basic parameters, for habits of deference and restraint continued
to inhibit activist expressions. Protest remained issue-specific and local,
and often withered at the first sign of state disapproval. But in specific and
limited ways, dissent began also to acquire broader organizational
resources that would slowly change contention. In 1987, for instance,
Education Minister Wartasan sent a former activist (Surito) to recruit
university student support (although it has never been clear for whom).
Through those meetings, students pressured Wartasan to revive the
Ikatan Pers Mashasiswa Indonesia (IPMI or Indonesian Student Press
Union) and allow student newspapers gradually to publish once more.
Student government, confined to ineffective and isolated faculty units
since 1978, was reorganized into the new SMPT (a less autonomous
version of the old DM; *Senat Mahasiswa Perguruan Tinggi*, University
Student Senate) in 1990.[110] Small campus protests, although violations
of the NKK/BKK, began to slip by unmolested, and students also began
discussing activism in broader, multi-campus assemblies.[111]

New student activism advanced two kinds of demands. New impositions
like fuel and utility price hikes, currency devaluations, new traffic laws,
marriage laws and a state-run lottery produced uncharacteristically
strong and sustained protest, and often policy concessions from

---

[107] Robison 1988: 58–60; Lev 1996.
[108] Eldridge 1995; Uhlin 1997.
[109] Sudharmono had been a lawyer not an ABRI field commander, and this undermined
support for him among other officers. Liddle 1996a; Budiman 1992.
[110] Aspinall 1995.
[111] Hein 1990: 223–224.

government. Protests against power rate hikes (1988) new traffic laws (1992) a state-sponsored lottery (1993) and the construction of a tourist resort in Bali (1994) all extended over a period of weeks or months, while 1987 helmet laws in Kalimantan triggered extraordinarily violent exchanges between activists and authorities.[112] Second, students took up larger issues of democracy and freedom echoing groups like the Petition of 50. Participants in such protests were more often hurt or detained than those making limited and national claims, and the actions generally attracted a hundred students or less, and rarely lasted beyond an hour or two. Yet precisely because protests were small and episodic, some activists did risk making dangerous criticisms against some core regime policies.[113] Demonstrations decried state violence (particularly at protests) and also challenged activist arrest or sentencing[114] – especially when prominent figures, like labor leader Muchtar Pakpahan or Arief Budiman were detained (both in 1990). As in the early 1970s, symbolic occasions like anniversaries or holidays also triggered student mobilization: alternative independence celebrations occurred on August 17, 1994,[115] and protests marked the December 8, 1992 anniversary of the East Timor invasion.[116]

In contrast, ongoing LSM-led advocacy campaigns mainly focused on reversing specific actions against specific communities. These protests, largely over issues of land tenure and water usage, occurred across Indonesia, apace with expanding, community-displacing development projects (often owned by military-backed concerns). Activists threaded a careful line in these disputes, between helping local residents and observing laws against building mass organizations.[117] Meetings of more than five people, for example, were not allowed without prior permit, and when two LBH lawyers met four clients in Badega, all six landed in jail.[118] LSM organizers refrained from building mass bases, but slid past *Ormas* laws by providing education seminars on organizing strategies to farmers, who then constructed political groups themselves. Struggle organizations that did emerge remained utterly local and

---

[112] In those protests, soldiers killed fourteen students and arrested forty. *Kompas*, November 16, 1987.

[113] Widjojo and Nurhasim 1998.

[114] Following violence at the 1987 helmet law protests, for example, students across Indonesia staged November protests, and the legal aid group LBH held a three-day symposium to decry state violence. *Kompas*, December 10, 1987.

[115] *Kompas*, August 18, 1994.

[116] *Kompas*, December 9, 1992.

[117] Eldridge 1995.

[118] Rianto 1996.

embedded in the fabric of community relations. LSMs and students did set up politically ambiguous and *ad hoc* solidarity committees that could be dissolved and reconstituted at little cost. Farmers soon learned to seek out LSM and legal foundation assistance: the Badega dispute alluded to above began when farmers traveled to Bandung to enlist LBH lawyers' help; the next month, in March, 1987, LBH mobilized (but did not organize!) 500 Bandung students to march supporting the farmers. In stand offs between residents and bulldozers, soldiers often resorted to violence against mass participants, but tended not to hit student or LSM members.[119] While the incidence of such protest increased, they remained atomized and isolated from one another: neither a unified movement nor entirely separate events.[120]

Most important, student activism began to augment LSM work, and those who joined LSMs in the 1990s frequently were not seeking a *substitute* for the campus dissent (as in the late 1970s) but its post-graduate *continuation*. But no formal organizational connection between campus groups and LSMs existed, and differences still marked their politics. Students more boldly confronted state authorities, and were critical of LSM caution and moderation.[121] Student activists joined land and labor protests from a clearly prominent, sometimes national campus base. In traveling between the sites of struggle and of study, they came to insist on a more political approach to advocacy, and often produced uncomfortably apparent activist constituencies. Demonstrations protesting the dam construction at Kedung Ombo in 1989, for instance, began in LSM efforts to help residents affected by the proposed flooding to seek redress.[122] Student involvement politicized the protests and activists pushed LSMs more extensively to coordinate their activity. Soon, a broad front of LSMs and student activists converted the case into a national cause, and demonstrations in large cities augmented those at the dam site.[123] In similar ways, students continued to avoid formal organization and protest forms remained atomized and episodic, even as they pushed a more coherent opposition movement into existence.[124]

---

[119] See, for example, the twenty-nine cases of land tenure dispute discussed in Rianto 1996.

[120] Bunnell 1996; Eldridge 1995; Lucas 1997.

[121] Among a group of hunger-striking student activists I interviewed at Gadjah Mada University, for instance, most anticipated graduating into work in some LSM – although most also expressed resentment at LSM conservatism. Interview with Author, February 28, 1998. See also Budiman 1990; Lucas 1992: 91.

[122] See account in Rianto 1996; also, Budiman 1992.

[123] Lucas 1992: 86–87.

[124] Gayatri 1999.

Labor strikes increased from 1988 to the middle 1990s. Government restrictions had virtually prevented labor stoppages since 1973, but *keterbukaan* and LSM support emboldened workers to adopt land-case models (i.e. localized stoppages that often subsequently ventured "long marches" from factories to petition government agencies).[125] As with land and water cases, LSM workers and lawyers intervened to help workers on an individual, case by case basis. Soon, however, a distinct group of labor organizers, supported by international allies and norms, began to build an unofficial national labor union – among the first national acts directly to defy state organizational proscriptions. While initially illegal, the *Sejahtera Buru Seriket Indonesia* (SBSI, Prosperous Workers' Union of Indonesia) was first tolerated, and then grudgingly accepted by authorities.[126] SBSI began by using safer symbolic tactics, like one-hour national strikes in February 1994, in place of longer protests. Explosive, multi-factory Medan strikes in May 1994 raised the stakes. Rioting and clashes between soldiers and strikers killed one person, wounded fifty and led to the arrest of over a hundred more.[127] Government agents arrested SBSI leaders over the next months, and tried them for inciting to riot. But the government also increased the minimum wage, and regularly urged factory managers to raise salaries. Thenceforth, military teams investigated (and often supported) worker charges against sub-minimum wages. The message was vintage New Order: strikes were barely tolerated, but those who organized opposition activity (instead of keeping it looser and less coordinated) would be punished. After the Medan strikes, labor protests retreated from the large organization model, and once more concentrated on factory level strikes in which LSM organizers played key roles.

Keterbukaan perhaps provided the broadest latitude for public intellectuals who in greater and greater number spoke out on what was essentially a professional oppositionists' lecture circuit. In part, the rise in intellectuals' demand for democracy reflects the expansion of the Indonesian middle class after sustained economic growth.[128] Journalists, writers, lawyers, religious leaders and former activists began more frankly to advocate democratization, to criticize Suharto's autocracy, and to decry corruption, human rights violations, and electoral constraint. NU leaders organized what we might consider the prototype for these groups: the

---

[125] The most comprehensive discussion of this upsurge appears in Kammen 1997. Budiman 1992; Evers 1995.
[126] Bourchier 1994; Liddle 1996b.
[127] Asian Labor Update 1994b (nos. 15 and 16).
[128] Mallarangen and Liddle 1995; Robison 1993.

Democracy Forum. No single force dominated Democracy Forum, nor did it attempt to build any substantial machinery. Rather, its members staged periodic events that the media prominently covered, and articulated (in a sense general enough to remain barely safe) demands for reform and democracy. This activity, however, remained largely within the New Order's understood political parameters and "favor[ed] genteel seminars for intellectuals, civil servants and businessmen."[129] Speeches were cautious and rhetorical, and speakers often withdrew or modified remarks following government criticism. Groups like Democracy Forum almost never urged political action. Discussions centered on what a democratic society should look like, or how it would benefit Indonesia.[130] Sometimes speakers revealed particular acts of state corruption, and when elections drew near, they dwelt on the unfolding political process, or sometimes unveiled (usually limited) opposition candidacies. Lacking support from other elites or institutions, LSM members and activists paid fairly close attention to the faltering leadership that these forums provided.

Eventually, activist organizations apart from those on campus also began to emerge. In 1989, security forces arrested several students, ostensibly for selling banned books by Pramoediya Anna Toer. While in Jakarta's Cipinang jail, they met East Timorese separatists, learned about separatists' more complex and covert organizational machinery, and began to think more seriously about cultivating international support.[131] Separatists responded to the association by augmenting their outer island insurgencies with demonstrations in Java's major cities. Years of insurgent struggle, however, had convinced separatists that they had no significant Indonesian support, and so such demonstrations usually occurred when an international audience was also present.[132]

In other ways, activists acquired stronger organizational resources, despite existing prohibitions. As we will discuss in more detail later, some developed the covert, multi-sectoral and national network eventually known as the *Partai Rakyat Demokrasi* (People's Democratic Party or PRD). More openly, dissidents began more seriously to operate within

---

[129] *The Economist*, 1991.
[130] Uhlin 1997.
[131] Naipospos, interview with author February 1998; Naipospos 2000.
[132] Examples of this strategy abound. On October 12, 1989, East Timorese activists mobilized during the Pope's visit to their province; on January 18, 1990, East Timorese students protested during a US envoy's visit to their province; on April 15, 1994, protests in East Timor met a delegation of foreign journalists; in November 1994, protests in both Jakarta and East Timor met US President Clinton's state visit, and activists stormed the US Embassy.

organizations the regime formally permitted, like the PPP and the PDI.[133] The move to take electoral parties as more serious opposition vehicles followed PPP examples set in a surprisingly strong 1988 election campaign. An infusion of campus and LSM activists in 1992 revitalized the PDI and pushed it toward a more energetic 1993 campaign. No one then seriously anticipated a PDI victory, but the party's organizational potential nevertheless attracted activists in droves, forming a radical wing that pushed the party to redefine itself. PDI activists focused their attention on supporting the reticent, but politically evocative Megawati Sukarnoputri, the image of whom conjured her father's leadership and provided a symbolic umbrella for ideas about democracy, socialism, and struggle. At the party's December 1993 congress, activists backed Megawati for party president. Despite government pressure against Megawati, her candidacy prevailed, setting up a 1996 confrontation between her supporters and the New Order. It would be the first public act in the regime's end game.

Conclusions

The history of contention outlined in this chapter emphasizes how New Order repression influenced the institutions and strategies available to aggrieved populations. From its inception, the New Order sought to maximize the organizational advantage it gained by slaughtering PKI members by tightly limiting all other opposition organizations. Attacks on the PKI established a pervasive threat to enforce with prohibitions, but also established a New Order convention of equating communism with attempts to organize dissent: communists (and only communists) meet secretly, print underground pamphlets, infiltrate unions, and build networks. Hence, long after the PKI had been eliminated, charges of communism could be used to tamp down opposition activity the state preferred not to allow.

Read in this light, styles of protest, and the Indonesian opposition's general circumspection directly descend from state repression. The New Order's elimination and consolidation of most political organization early on amplified student protest in the 1970s – but students also adapted their actions, under the *moral force* banner, to a climate in which political organization was suspect, and mass participation unwelcome. Later state moves against students forced those who might have become activists

---

[133] Although, for limits on that permission, consult Body for the Protection of the People's Political Rights Facing the 1992 General Election 1994.

under other conditions into a less contentious developmentalism that the state itself pioneered. Organizationally, inter-campus organizations gave way to scattered LSMs. Fragmentation and political inhibition diffused student protests, and made LSMs compliant when further organizational restrictions emerged in the early 1980s. This compliant activism contrasts sharply with patterns we will examine in the Philippine case, where front organizations struggled against state impositions precisely because of the more strongly organized opposition networks that supported that struggle. In Indonesia, LSMs stood in for movement organizations eliminated by New Order repression. Over time, the restrictions grew self-enforcing. With no organizational basis for activist careers and an economic boom rendering the social mainstream more attractive, proscriptions on dissent became embedded in a depoliticized New Order culture. As we have seen, even as *keterbukaan* revived some institutions central to earlier movements, public intellectuals, LSMs and activists remained initially quite cautious.

The chronicle of Indonesian contention, finally, is cumbersome, for its scattered and atomized events confound efforts to write a central narrative. Yet this pattern precisely reflects state repressive activities. The culture of political caution, the circumspect professional dissident circle, the occupational segregation of protest all follows from state repressive patterns. New Order protest emerged in thousands of local, small-scale and short-term events, some spontaneous, some partly organized. Those who have described patterns in these events as provocations hatched by conspiracy or the interest of some hidden hand may in some cases be correct. Yet the more general context of Indonesian contention, its fragmentation and its caution, surely allows such conspiracy greater latitude, and is a testament to more fundamental state efforts to eliminate dissident organization.

6   The Philippine new society and state repression

Earlier, I argued that Marcos's distracted authoritarian crackdown demonstrated more interest in state building than in defeating adversaries.[1] In fact, Marcos detained many *political* rivals (i.e. excluding activists) for only a few months after martial law's onset. In late 1972, as the draft martial law constitution approached its referendum, he even released some prominent dissidents and encouraged them to debate the new document.[2] They mounted so strong a campaign that Marcos canceled the vote, and rammed the constitution through an impromptu local assembly (*barangay*) approval process.[3] Yet why allow the campaign at all? Neither Suharto nor Ne Win would seriously have tried conciliating such adversaries, nor have been surprised (as Marcos apparently was) at staunch resistance. Marcos, however, rose through a world of bounded political struggle, where electoral losers quickly accommodated themselves to victors – and he perhaps too readily expected support from those he jailed. He also expected *all* elites to support his regime, particularly if the alternative seemed communist revolution.[4] Indeed, martial law's anti-communism *might* have attracted elite oppositionists like the Lopez or Aquino families – but in 1972 Philippine communism was still fairly ephemeral, without deep national roots, so intra-elite conflicts seemed far more pressing than any between the ruling class and insurgents. Accordingly, many elites were less inclined to accept martial law than Marcos expected, and authorities never devoted themselves to eradicating the communists they pretended so to fear.[5]

---

[1] A Staff Report Prepared for the US Senate Committee on Foreign Relations corroborates this: "Since declaring Martial Law, President Marcos has put less emphasis on the threat from insurgent groups (which he claimed led to the action) and on measures to control that threat and more emphasis on the reforms necessary to build what he calls the 'New Society'..." Staff Report Prepared for the US Senate Committee on Foreign Relations 1972: 32.
[2] Van der Kroef 1973b–74: 55; Rosenberg 1974-1975: 477–478.
[3] Stauffer 1977: 401–403.
[4] Marcos 1978.
[5] Tiglao 1988: 30–31.

Of the three dictators, therefore, Marcos alone consolidated power without eliminating either open dissent or more radical opposition organizations. Instead, he focused on discouraging alliances between the political center and the left. Given what seemed a basic tension between moderate and radical opponents, Marcos proceeded as if limited reform would divide the opposition. While he vigorously pushed war against communist and Islamic insurgents, he was more flexible with the rules of political participation. In time, dissident labor unions, peasant associations, and opposition parties re-emerged, many operating as legal fronts for banned movements.[6] Members of these groups faced harassment, arrest, torture and murder – but the violence was less assured or public, and Marcos typically treated individual attacks as mysteries or mistakes.[7] (Suharto and Ne Win, in contrast, more often *claimed* their murders.) Periodic elections, typically called in response to internal or international pressure, almost certainly involved massive and widely recognized cheating, but the campaigns themselves produced rallies, speeches and party building beyond what either of the other regimes permitted. How did this repressive strategy influence contention?

Martial law, protest and resistance

Contention under Marcos demonstrated many organizational forms and strategic orientations: moderate protest, radical insurgency, and myriad interactions between them applied variegated pressure on the state – even when different movements did not explicitly cooperate.[8] Basic philosophical differences marked the boundaries between the anti-dictatorship movement's different sections. The National Democratic (ND) left, linked to the communist party, treated participatory opportunities as inherently illusory, useful mainly to expose the limits of reformist possibilities and to recruit for the armed struggle.[9] Liberal and Social Democratic (SD) dissidents often accepted participatory opportunities more at face value, as chances to make concrete advances.[10] Hence, moderates often mobilized when the regime undertook what would prove insubstantial or temporary liberalizing measures – while the

---

[6] *Southeast Asia Chronicle* 1978.
[7] Clarke 1998.
[8] This heterogeneity had roots in the pre-martial law movement: in 1970, for instance, the CPP instructed members to engage the Constitutional Convention campaign, but to boycott the actual vote; more moderate groups backed delegates they thought might win and draft a progressive constitution. Pimentel 1989; Franco 2000; Rivera 1985.
[9] Jones 1989.
[10] De Dios 1988: 71.

insurgent left more reliably expanded during authoritarian crackdowns that usually ended such liberalization. These differences partly undermined opposition unity, but also meant that authorities could not attack one opposition flank without energizing another: liberalizing reforms designed to diminish communist power enabled moderate protest, while repression aimed at controlling rambunctious legal protest often radicalized liberals and increased support for the left.

Martial law virtually ended protest until 1975.[11] The campaign against the constitutional plebiscite produced some demonstrations in 1973, but only until Marcos canceled the plebiscite. Student protests, once tumultuous affairs, became small campus events as surveillance tightened. Labor strikes, relatively frequent before martial law, ceased altogether when Presidential Decree (PD) 823 banned labor actions in any vital industry.[12] Press restrictions ended in May 1973, but because the president issued all media licenses (renewed every six months) reporters remained mainly compliant.[13] The strongest initial anti-dictatorship moves occurred in the courts, which still functioned in order to bolster Marcos's claims for martial law's legitimacy. Five opposition Senators (from the closed legislature) were able to file a motion against the 1972 Constitution's ratification, arguing against martial law itself (hard to conceive of a similar case making it to Burmese or Indonesian courts).[14] Benigno Aquino's extended trial, interrupted by his hunger strikes and jurisdictional disputes challenging the regime's legitimacy, provided a pulpit for lawyers to attack martial law, and kept Aquino in the spotlight. Under cover of organizations that Marcos permitted in order to maintain his legal veneer (like the Civil Liberties Union) men like Senator Jose Diokno issued dissident reports that both exiles and international human rights' organizations picked up.

This elite legal (and legalistic) opposition had no formal ties to the underground left, but provided it propaganda opportunities, and important mainstream support. In fact, more explicit moderate-left cooperation was reported to have occurred between Aquino and the CPP before martial law, and Aquino seems also to have courted NPA support for his electoral activity.[15] Under martial law, however, even general support for liberal principles could provide resources to the left. Diokno organized the Free Legal Assistance Group (FLAG) in 1974 to help the group Task

---

[11] Rivera 1985.
[12] Dejillas 1984: 29–30.
[13] Wurfel 1988: 122.
[14] Muego 1983: 96–102; Tolentino 1990; Tiglao 1988: 29.
[15] Burton 1989.

Force Detainees (discussed below) defend men and women accused of subversion and rebellion; but frequently turned these trials into indictments of martial law.[16] FLAG began from narrow concerns about due process, but its members soon developed deeper sympathies with the left.[17] Other civil organizations survived martial law by holding fast to slender legal footholds that remained.

The regime also failed to control the influential Catholic Church, which had both a strong Philippine hierarchy and formidable transnational links. Even before martial law, progressive Papal Encyclicals inspired some Catholics to organize community associations, but 1972 brought most of this activity up short.[18] Thereafter, some clergy opposed martial law (and one group formed the underground Christians for National Liberation or CNL) but the hierarchy was silent.[19] Raids on fourteen churches in martial law's first months annoyed Catholic officials, but only full-scale raids on two seminaries in mid-1974, and Church outrage at the regime's account of cordial inspections, moved the Archbishop to such guardedly anti-dictatorship actions as a protest/prayer rally that drew over 5,000 participants. Established Church organizations began to take firmer action.[20] The Association of Major Religious Superiors of the Philippines (AMRSP) at its 1974 meeting, founded the Task Force Detainees, (TFD) to keep track of political prisoners and advocate their fair and humane treatment. TFD became a model of how legal institutions could provide support to broader, and even underground, struggle.[21] It established branches across the Philippines, and attracted underground activists who used the Church's sheltering support, and the broad issue of human rights, as an entering wedge against the state. Similar service organizations began also to act in ways not obviously linked to the underground struggle – but which still criticized the regime, and recruited support for more pointed struggle.

Because civil, legal and religious institutions provided cover for banned political organizations, underground activity was a more integral element of on-going Philippine dissent than in Burma or Indonesia. Even moderate social democrats developed a *formally* radical underground: some descended from the progressive Christian Social Movement as a secret network that eventually emerged in 1977 as the Philippine Democratic

---

[16] Thompson 1995: 73.
[17] Clarke 1998: 168–171.
[18] Youngblood 1990: 83–83.
[19] Bolasco 1984; Youngblood 1981; de La Torre 1986.
[20] Wurfel 1988: 220; Pasquale 1988; Hardy 1984.
[21] Clarke 1998: 167–169.

Socialist Party (PDSP), and others more directly from Church or campus groups.[22] But the CPP built the main underground. In 1974, it announced plans for its National Democratic Front (NDF), containing civil associations that could get by under martial law. Activists formed or infiltrated such groups, and then steered them toward movement positions, and also recruited for the armed struggle. Before martial law was formally lifted in 1981, the NDF was a more entirely clandestine network, with the strongest presence among campus organizations that survived because Marcos would not move against the universities.[23] The *Kabataan Makabayan* (KM or Nationalist Youth) in 1973 had around 112,000 members in 300 chapters. Other activists worked in student government, the campus press, or even in what might have been apolitical academic groups. After 1981, front organizations acquired more leeway off campuses, and became more politically explicit. But from the first, the simultaneous existence of underground and civil institutions allowed activists to link legal and underground struggle.

In the early 1970s, the CPP's New People's Army (NPA) had bases only in Isabella province. The NPA initially cultivated scant village support, and adopted Yenan-style fixed bases that over-estimated rebels' military power. Sharp counter-insurgency drives, using as many as 7,000 government troops in northern provinces, reduced NPA troop strength from around 500 armed guerillas and perhaps 2,000 civilian supporters in 1972 to approximately 500 combined fighters and supporters by 1974. Also in 1974, the AFP over-ran expansion areas in Bicol, Zambales, Tarlac, and captured four important education and training facilities in 1974.[24] Under pressure, the CPP turned more careful attention to political tasks, and implemented more cautious and systematic expansion plans. The care was well placed, for the early 1970s also marked the regime's populist high water mark, buoyed by a relatively ambitious agrarian reform program that undercut some of Marcos's bitterest rivals.[25] Predictably, the program bogged down after a few years, but for a time it also hampered CPP recruitment.

---

[22] De Dios 1988: 71–74; Abinales 1985.
[23] Unlike Ne Win or Suharto, there was substantial sociological affinity between Marcos and his campus rivals, and this prevented a wholesale anti-campus campaign. Both Marcos's rivals and his allies' supporters educated their children on these campuses. Moreover, Marcos never doubted his regime's fundamental modernity, and hence his ability eventually to conciliate university graduates and use the universities to bolster his regime. On martial law campus politics, see Abinales 1985.
[24] Tiglao 1988: 64; Jones 1989.
[25] Kerkvliet 1974: 287; Southeast Asia Advisory Group to the Asia Society 1975: 25; Wurfel 1977: 8.

Marcos also faced a strong Muslim insurgency from 1971, mainly on the southern island of Mindanao. Unlike the CCP/NPA, the Mindanao Independence Movement (forerunner of the Moro National Liberation Front – MNLF) received regular overseas and strong village support. Although the Muslim insurgency was formidable, however, it progressed through provincial battles that distracted, but did not disrupt state-building projects so important to the early martial law program.[26] Moreover, differences between Islamic separatists and Catholic Marcos opponents reduced the chance of alliances between them at first, although in the 1980s, some agreement was reached. Still, campaigns against Southern rebels sapped AFP energies that might otherwise have focused on Northern communists, unarguably helping the NPA to survive.[27] The Mindanao wars were also important counter-insurgent training grounds, and AFP soldiers who fought the NPA in the late 1970s and 1980s were battle hardened and formidable.[28]

By 1975, then, the anti-Marcos resistance had recovered somewhat from early martial law setbacks.[29] Legal regime opponents adjusted to new conditions, some via high profile court cases, others forming civil associations with no open anti-regime activity.[30] Street demonstrations remained rare, but universities and the Catholic Church established offices that provided cover for activist work.[31] Marcos's desire to legitimize the New Society (as he now called the dictatorship) led him to constrain the courts and the media, but allow both to function, providing activists with additional resources and opportunities.[32] In secret, the underground also expanded, both within these institutions, and as a proper insurgent army. In explicit counterpoint to both radical left and rightist dictatorship, the Catholic Church strongly supported Social Democratic movement organizations, which also combined moderate legal and underground struggle.[33] Across this political range (but far more directly on the communist left) insurgencies supported the legal struggles, which benefited from opportunities that such struggles created. Hence while legal activists themselves made little headway against the dictatorship, the combination of their activity and armed insurgency formed a larger, more tenacious and disruptive movement complex.

[26] George 1988; Tiglao 1988: 67–68.
[27] Overholt 1986: 1147–1148.
[28] McCoy 1999.
[29] Kessler 1989: 52–54; Muego 1982.
[30] Rivera 1985.
[31] Celoza 1997: 42; Allen 1976.
[32] The Lawyers Committee for International Human Rights 1983: 115–132.
[33] Fagan 2000: 459.

Protest did not fail or succeed merely on its ability to influence government or change policy; it expanded support for the longer-term revolution – which itself encouraged and validated legal activists' struggles and sacrifices.

International pressure, regularization and protest

In late 1975, renewed protest and demonstrations produced a loose alliance between illegal underground activists and opposition politicians. The communist underground had spent three years rebuilding networks among the urban poor and workers. By 1975, they established several clandestine labor associations under the *Bukluran ng mga Mangagawang Pilipino* (BMP or Association of Filipino Workers) with similar activity among Manila's urban poor, peasants and university students. Such groups undertook open struggle and mass demonstrations, but concentrated on providing an operational and recruitment base for the armed struggle.[34] Nevertheless, new state restrictions, (PD 823 in November 1975 banned all labor strikes) and new support from prominent individuals like Cardinal Sin (who in November urged Marcos to reconsider that decree) convinced cadres to experiment with mass action. 4,000 students, workers and slum dwellers demonstrated against the decree in late November, and 6,000 repeated the action when US President Ford visited in April 1976.[35] Marcos responded by easing labor restrictions on December 16 – but these events had invigorated mass organizations. In late December, BMP members at the La Tondeña distillery launched the first illegal strike under martial law, attracting substantial support.[36]

Parliamentary forces undertook a parallel effort in late 1975, led by former Philippine President Diodado Macapagal and timed to coincide with the International Monetary Fund's (IMF) 1976 Manila summit. He called for an Interim National Assembly (INA) as mandated in the 1972 Constitution. Encouraged by on-going labor protests and needing a machinery, Macapagal met with the CPP's Manila Rizal section (a party branch quite open to tactical experiments) and planned several large demonstrations in January to demand the INA. Marcos responded by ordering arrests that netted 300 La Tondeña strikers and students; over 1,000 more fell in the weeks that followed.[37] Still, the campaign accomplished three things. It demonstrated the possibility of political struggle

---

[34] See *Southeast Asia Chronicle*: 1978: 7.
[35] Wurfel 1977: 15–16.
[36] Pimentel 1989: 137–140.
[37] Franco 2000: 204–207.

against the regime and underscored basic regime abuses. Over the next year, members of the Catholic Church, parliamentarians and civic organizations began also to protest. Second, it revived contacts between moderate parliamentarians and the communist party – or at least its Manila Rizal branch. Finally, Macapagal's gambit pushed Marcos to announce elections for an *Interim Batasaan Pambansa* (IBP, Interim National Legislature) providing further opportunities for collaboration between moderates and radicals.

An upsurge in student-led protest backed by new insurgent activity in 1976–1977 followed the 1975 labor actions,[38] and signaled the first real strains in martial law. The communist insurgency had clearly begun to recover by 1977. Not only had the NPA expanded into new Visayan base areas, it was also exploring alliances with Muslim insurgents in Mindanao.[39] Security forces had clear ideas that Church and university organizations supported the left, and were probably front organizations – but Marcos was constrained in his countermeasures. The parliamentary opposition, resurgent and excited in advance of the 1978 elections, and the Catholic clergy (now routinely criticizing regime repression and human rights violations) consistently protested state attacks on civic, (even front) organizations. Counter-insurgency techniques like the strategic hamletting program, began in 1977 raised objections from both domestic and international human rights' advocates.[40] Newly elected US President Jimmy Carter, moreover, made US support for Marcos less exclusively dependent on his anti-communism and more connected to his human rights' record; the State Department's January 1, 1977 report was the first in a regular series of US criticisms against the regime.[41]

Unable to eliminate political organizations or dissent, authorities continued almost randomly to harass and intimidate front organizations,

---

[38] For example, in the campaign surrounding the October 17, 1976 plebiscite, large anti-martial law demonstrations occurred repeatedly. Over 2,500 people – mainly students, workers and members of the urban poor – demonstrated against martial law on October 3. On October 10, the largest and most violent demonstrations to that point under martial law occurred, mounted by the same coalition that organized the October 3 demonstrations. Large protests occurred also on May 1, 1977, and five separate demonstrations, resulting in arrests and injuries, occurred from September 19–25. These examples demonstrate that the Philippine left had acquired the organizational muscle to mobilize demonstrations and strikes virtually on command. Boudreau 2001; Franco 2000.

[39] Molloy 1985.

[40] The outcry against the strategic hamlet program only grew over the next several years. Integrated Bar of the Philippines: 1983; Lawyers' Committee for International Human Rights 1983: 72–87; *Far Eastern Economic Review*, 1982.

[41] Daroy 1988: 76–78.

but regime elites always preserved their ability to disassociate themselves from any attack. Marcos periodically closed newspapers, ordered campus raids, harassed church or labor organizations, and had critical parliamentarians arrested. Often, he released detainees after a short while, claiming that lower-level security agents arrested them in error. These moves obscured the boundary between tolerable and illegal dissent, fostered an immobilizing confusion among opponents, and allowed the regime to depict repression as incidental, rather than central to the exercise of state power. At the same time, Marcos undertook measures like 1978 elections, designed to divide opposition moderates from radicals by conciliating the former and leaving the left more isolated and vulnerable. The plan, however, had an important flaw: Marcos would only contemplate the most insubstantial reform and genuine participatory opportunities touched off such protest that he seldom allowed them much play. Hence, crackdowns against moderates who engaged reform-driven political opportunities ended each liberalizing thaw. Martial law elections, for instance, were violent and dangerous for campaign workers, and unfailingly fraudulent. Rather than satisfying moderate dissidents, they were often radicalizing experiences, and also provided them with political experience and organizational vehicles.

The 1978 IPB elections demonstrated the Marcos plan's promise by touching off debates inside the opposition. In the end, Benigno Aquino campaigned from his prison cell, under his newly organized LABAN Party (*Lakas ng Bayan*, Strength of the Nation), supported by other prominent oppositionists.[42] Jesuit-backed Social Democrats like the PDSP became a key element of LABAN's machinery.[43] Senators Lorenzo Tañada and Jose Diokno, each drifting toward movement organizations, led a boycott campaign, arguing that Marcos would cheat anyway. The CPP also advocated a boycott, but instructed cadres and mass organizations to use the election period's political thaw to recruit support and conduct anti-regime propaganda. The party's Manila Rizal branch, (MR), and particularly its United Front Commission, however, saw a chance to solidify links with moderate oppositionists, and seriously engaged the election, in defiance of CPP policy.[44] MR pursued an alliance with Aquino that recalled pre-martial law arrangements. However, the MR/LABAN alliance did not hold. Aquino had limited faith in the left, and party discipline prevented MR from evading the boycott policy for long. Eventually, the party reined in its maverick cadres, disciplined

---

[42] Bonner 1988: 232–233.
[43] De Dios 1988: 71.
[44] Weekley 1996: 38–42; Malay 1988.

those most responsible for the alliance, and nullified important promises MR made to LABAN.[45] For Marcos, of course, this all ran according to plan.

But the April 7 election also demonstrated the Marcos strategy's central flaw. In prison and allowed but one televised speech, Aquino's Manila-only campaign still was strong enough to cast suspicion on Marcos's claims of sweeping victory. Reports of campaign violence and ballot theft augmented this suspicion,[46] and led to unruly but organized protests, backed by social democrats with some unorganized and ND support as well. The first protest came on election night, when frustrated voters banged pots, honked horns, and exploded firecrackers; organizers planned a ten-minute noise barrage, but it lasted for three hours.[47] Demonstrations continued over the following days, particularly between April 9 and 11. The regime swiftly repressed these protests, arresting 561 demonstrators on April 9, and raiding a seminary office at the Ateneo de Manila University (a center of Jesuit support for SD movements). Although 540 of the April 9 detainees were freed in a matter of days, the experience radicalized many.[48] Despite martial law restrictions, reimposed on April 10, protest never entirely returned to pre-election levels. Broader student protests – both short, small "lightning" rallies and longer marches and demonstrations – occurred regularly thereafter. Workers more directly challenged restrictive labor laws in the courts, and in Negros, sugar workers undertook demonstrations and strikes.

What of the crucial moderates that Marcos had set out to co-opt? Many were mobilized by the campaign and radicalized by the fraud.[49] When Marcos stole the 1978 elections, he convinced many that civil resistance and opposition was futile. Aquino's LABAN party remained an important symbolic rallying point, but efforts to build opposition organizations, like former Defense Minister Salvatore Laurel's National Unity for Democracy and Freedom,[50] also suggest that moderates had begun to think in movement terms. One segment of the parliamentary opposition, led by Lorenzo Tañada, advocated explicit alliance with the communist left, and only Aquino's staunch opposition thwarted that plan.[51] From late 1978, several armed and clandestine organizations with SD bases formed. In July, 1979,

[45] Malay 1988.
[46] LABAN submitted a formal complaint to the Commission on Elections, published in *The Philippine Times,* May 11–17, 1978; see also Machado 1979: 133.
[47] Lande 1978.
[48] Machado 1978 133–134; Abueva 1988: 59.
[49] De Dios 1988: 72–74.
[50] Organized in September, 1976; Machado 1979.
[51] Thompson 1995: 82.

soldiers arrested 100 armed men, erstwhile moderates, undergoing military training in North Cotabato.[52] Members of the opposition reportedly also discussed plans for a *coup d'état* with Defense Minster Juan Ponce Enrile, who had then just lost an intra-military power struggle to Fabian Ver. But the clearest story of moderate radicalization describes two linked urban terrorist movements – the Light a Fire Movement (LAFM) of 1979, and the April 6th Liberation Movement (A6LM) in 1980.

A small group close to Aquino began discussing insurrectionary strategies in 1977.[53] The parliamentary opposition had then formed an "inner circle," that was considering extra-electoral activity – initially via alliances with CPP cadres. Somewhat on the fringe of that group (more central during the 1978 election) SD activists argued for combining movement politics, electoral campaigns, and – in proportion to their limited capacities – armed struggle. When Marcos repressed post-election protests, these activists were positioned to put the new, more radical strategy into effect. Leading figures included Aquino (eventually freed from prison in 1980 to seek medical treatment in the US), Social Democrat Charles Avila, and members of the powerful Lopez clan; supporters included industrialists, priests, lawyers, community organizers and academics. In 1978, after inner-circle talks, a representative traveled to the US to solicit money and support from the Filipino exiles.[54] The LAFM expanded along elite social connections, but remained small and conspiratorial.[55] Rather than mass demonstrations, it favored acts of arson and sabotage, torching several Manila buildings in 1979. The conspiracy collapsed when customs agents caught Ben Lim smuggling explosives into the country; before dying in state custody, Lim revealed the names of many LAFM members.[56] The A6LM pulled

---

[52] This Mabuhay Philippines Movement was not, however, the social democrats' first experiment in armed struggle. Since the middle 1970s, the PDSP (Philippine Social Democratic Party) had been training an exceptionally small army in Sabah – having established ties with Muslim insurrectionary forces at the very outset of martial law. This small force, however, never really engaged the Marcos state, and perhaps served more as a destination for social democrats who felt then needed to go underground. Boudreau 2001; Psnakis 1981.

[53] This account largely follows the excellent history in Thompson 1995. See also Neher 1980: 263–265; Toye 1980.

[54] Many of Marcos's elite opponents fled martial law and established overseas solidarity networks. Among those that LAFM enlisted were Raul Manglapus, Heherson Alvarez, and Steve Psinakis, a Greek American married to a Lopez. Psnakis 1981. See also Aquino 1980.

[55] For instance, Eduardo Olaguer came to it through his Jesuit brother's SD activity; Teodoro Yabut knew Olaguer from country-club connections, and also brokered financial support from the Puyat family. Psnakis 1981.

[56] See Psnakis 1981 for an account of the Lim heart attack.

together LAFM remnants, but rested more heavily on the US-based contingent, and the more organized SD group, KASAPI (*Kapulungan ng mga Sandigan ng Pilipinas*, Organization of Defenders of the Philippines). Like the LAFM, the A6LM struck several Manila targets, from August 22 to an October 19 meeting of the American Society of Travel Agents. But the A6LM effort was also more public than the 1979 arson binge, selecting more dramatic targets and issuing advance warnings.

Thompson argues that the travel agent attack moved Marcos to speed up the lifting of martial law, a move he was considering in any case.[57] The measure potentially divided the moderate opposition from radical allies or tactics, and so was a typical Marcos maneuver. Still, the repeal of martial law did not fundamentally change things. Formal arrests dropped, and many of the political prisoners held as subversives were released. Yet as open repression dropped, secret, extra-judicial killings increased. What Filipinos called "salvage" victims – nabbed in secret by authorities, tortured, killed, and left at some public place, sharply increased.[58] In the countryside, counterinsurgency intensified, with over 500,000 village residents forced into strategic hamlets.[59] The number of strikes initially increased sharply, but then new restrictions came into force that virtually banned strikes entirely.[60] Marcos also retained power to legislate by presidential decree.

He also ignored key elements of his 1980 pledge to social democratic activists, and ordered many A6LM members arrested in the following months. SD leaders linked to the A6LM fled to safety, sending ripples of dissent through movement organizations left behind and under the gun.[61] Some organizers renounced their leaders, re-evaluated the SD program, and drifted toward independent politics, often developing new shades of social democracy. A new round of organizing followed, closely tied to communities and often committed to active non-violence.[62] Other activists began to search for safer organizational expressions, often in small advocacy, education, research or organizing institutions (what would soon be called NGOs). In consequence, the SD movement became organizationally quite differentiated by 1983.[63]

---

[57] Thompson 1995.
[58] McCoy 1999: 204–207; Clarke 1998: 173; Youngblood 1981.
[59] Leary, *et al.* 1984: 35–39.
[60] Dejillas 1994: 30.
[61] *Far Eastern Economic Review*, April 14, 1978: 14; Boudreau 2001: 38.
[62] Among these were the Pandayan group, based in Ateneo de Manila, and organizations like Tambuli and Tambunting. Rivera 1985: 5–7.
[63] Soriano 1987; Kimura 1997: 51–53; Thompson 1995: 109.

Further left, the ND movement was itself evolving. Although CCP leaders resolved their 1978 conflict with Manila-Rizal cadres by asserting the insurgent line, opportunities for semi-legal political action in alliance with moderate activists remained.[64] Even before martial law formally ended in January 1981, the parliamentary opposition had softened the regime enough to make semi-legal politics more promising, and to draw CPP attention. US pressure on Marcos to "normalize" politics and respect human rights, and the surprising activities of what some NDs called "bourgeois bombers," suggested growing possibilities for protest. By 1980, moreover, ND activists had lived through several cycles of authoritarian thaw and crackdown, witnessing how that process radicalized moderates. As party activists expanded in frontier areas such as Mindanao, they gravitated toward more dynamic united front strategies, while at the center, a substantial group of older cadres also supported a more political (as distinct from military) revolutionary strategy.[65] For all these reasons, the party created new mass organizations, designed to use protests to bridge the divide between themselves and political moderates.[66] When more political unions began to form after labor lawyers overturned the ban on multi-industry unions in 1980, ND cadres founded the *Kilusang Mayo Uno* (KMU, May First Movement).[67] The CPP took longer building farmers' associations, for cadres feared introducing a reformist note within their presumed main revolutionary base, but the *Kilusang Magbubukid ng Pilipinas* (KMP, Movement of Philippine Peasants) emerged in 1983.[68] The party began establishing women's organizations along initially sectoral lines, such as WOMB (Women Against Marcos Boycott) for Professional Women and SAMAKANA (*Samahan ng mga Malayang Kababaihan na Nagkakaisa*, The Movement of Free and Unified Women, Philippines) for the urban poor, culminating in the umbrella organizations Gabriella, in March 1984.[69] Nevertheless, party strategy still emphasized armed struggle, and held neither hope nor affection for a reforming process. Rather, by supporting front organizations, CPP leaders hoped to radicalize and recruit among political moderates when the state resorted to violence.

Hence the ND dynamic differed substantially from that among the less organized moderates. Via centralized organizational control, cadres

---

[64] Porter 1989; Weekley 1996; Jones 1989: 146–147.
[65] Kessler 1989: 69–71; Jones 1989: 145–154.
[66] Franco 2000: 232.
[67] Dejillas: 1994.
[68] Jones 1989: 301.
[69] Raquiza 1997: 175.

steered members to serve insurgent (rather than legal, political) ends. NDs had the potential to deliver *command demonstrations*, so-called because participants mobilized on party directives, even when external conditions hadn't stirred more general contention to life.[70] Graffiti and poster campaigns, often in the very teeth of harsh regime repression, called out from the underground, reminding society of the secret opposition crouched just beyond reach, preparing to strike. Following this logic, NDF groups mobilized in response to both state attack and expanding opportunities, but less enthusiastically for the latter. Cadres sought to harvest the anger and frustration that state repression provoked among regime opponents, and engaged participatory opportunities to position themselves for that harvest. They expected more effectively to recruit as repression rose, and were inclined to *accelerate* demonstrations, in so-called "outrage rallies," when government seemed least forthcoming or most aggressive. Projecting an underground and largely invisible left also made cadres eager to mobilize on symbolic occasions like anniversaries or working-class holidays. The KMU's own figures, for example, state that its biggest demonstrations between 1980 and 1986, occurred annually on May 1, in large, orchestrated, and diverse protests.[71] This development marked a new stage in the anti-dictatorship movement, in which semi-legal or underground associations played stronger roles in open political arenas.

In the end, however, it was neither the expansion of the underground nor legal movement institutions, on either moderate or radical movement flanks, that most decisively shaped political contention under Marcos. Rather, *interactions between* differentiated movement groups stymied regime repression. This is particularly clear, as we will see below, when members of the establishment began to break ranks with the regime. For now, consider an early example. On August 28, 1980, 72 leading opposition figures signed the "National Covenant for Freedom," a wholesale critique of martial law.[72] Despite the document's brave criticisms, parliamentary opponents had no organizational apparatus, and its signatories had no plans to organize one. They did, however, show interest in working with mass organizations to build a broader anti-dictatorship movement, and this interest motivated the CPP to accelerate its efforts to form semi-legal organizations. New bonds between underground, semi-legal and parliamentary dissidents allowed them to unite behind a widely successful electoral boycott campaign that

[70] Porter 1989: 15.
[71] Scipes 1996.
[72] Overholt 1986.

prevented the election from dividing moderates and radicals.[73] The campaign also provided a model for broader anti-dictatorship mobilization following the 1981 economic crisis and the 1983 Aquino assassination.

Conclusions: insurgency, party, movement organization, NGO

The anti-dictatorship movement eventually blossomed in the early 1980s, when important anomalies in Philippine fiscal policy came to light. Following revelations that the Philippine Central Bank overstated currency reserves by $600 million, the IMF withheld import credits, closing down the Philippine economy.[74] Large segments of Philippine business, already disgusted by rampant graft and corruption, adopted aggressive anti-regime positions that blossomed into mass protest when soldiers assassinated Benigno Aquino in 1983.[75] While those protests depended on a large measure of spontaneous mass participation and elite resources, movement organizations set the Philippines on a path that differed from that in either Burma or Indonesia. By way of concluding this discussion, let us review the movement structures that grew under martial law, and underscore the broader logic of state society interactions as they stood on the eve of Marcos's decline.

Despite periodic spontaneous mobilization through the 1980s, the anti-Marcos opposition emerged atop a largely *organized* base that eventually included NGOs, broad ideological organizations, specific sectoral groups (i.e. peasant, labor, student and women's associations) church organizations, electoral and underground parties, and insurgent armies.[76] Movement organizations differed functionally, in their social constituencies, and in their ideological orientations, but most ideological currents possessed the full complement of parties, mass groups, NGOs and armies. In the public and legalistic discourse governing interactions between state and movement, distinctions between legal and illegal *actions* mattered more than distinction between radical and moderate programs, for a revolutionary rhetoric pervaded activist culture. The formal repeal of martial law in 1981 allowed for legal dissent, and above-ground movement groups functioned as if they possessed clear political rights, and were separate from the underground.[77] Moreover,

---

[73] Youngblood 1981: 229.
[74] Manning 1984–1985: 398.
[75] Lindsey 1984: 1185–1186.
[76] Weekley 1996; Porter 1989.
[77] Rivera 1985: 17.

state officials acted publicly as if strong correspondences existed between modes of struggle and movement ideology (i.e. political moderates were expected to prefer civil struggle).

By the early 1980s, however, movement centers were *not* separated: organizational webs linked underground and open groups together, and movements with moderate and radical political visions no longer stuck exclusively to *tactics* that were correspondingly moderate or radical.[78] In fact, ideologically diverse coalitions around common programs of action proliferated in the early 1980s.[79] Working within integrated movement structures stretching across legal and illegal realms, moderates responded to state attacks on radicals, and radicals benefited from state reprisals against moderates. Authoritarian crackdowns spurred recruitment into underground armies, and drove measured institutions like the Catholic Church to more critical stands.[80] Because the boundary between legal and illegal dissent blurred in both activist tactics and state views, clandestine state violence often struck down formally (or marginally) legal dissidents, even as thin participatory reforms attempted to conciliate moderates and isolate radicals; both efforts aimed at preserving divisions (that public discourse and policy could not maintain) between legal and illegal anti-dictatorship forces.

Yet the Marcos strategy was wearing thin. Moderates, particularly after the 1981 financial crisis, responded to reforms by mobilizing in large numbers, but were no longer as averse to sharper confrontation. The resulting activity reliably precipitated new rounds of regime repression and subsequent radicalization. Years of alternating reform, mobilization and state crackdown multiplied the legal organizations poised to resist Marcos. In the countryside, extreme agrarian poverty and periodic political crackdowns on legal institutions combined to enable steady CPP/NPA expansion, particularly when state agents began more regularly to use violence against citizens after 1981. As moderate and radical opposition wings grew, the state had more trouble separating them.

In consequence, social movement institutions accumulated, as they could not in Indonesia and Burma. Activists built organizations of all kinds, and then worked within them for years: many movement leaders in 1985 cut their political teeth in the early 1970s, and had lost little steam since. Not only did movement networks and organizations permit such enduring activity, but their explicit state power objectives promised almost unimaginable rewards for sustained activism: the same cataclysmic

[78] Franco 2000: 200–222; Boudreau 2001: 22–30.
[79] Overholt 1986: 1151–1153.
[80] Youngblood 1990.

change toward which Burmese activists struggled, but with far better odds. The opposition evolved via splits and schisms, as disgruntled cadres formed new movement vehicles and institutions, and in consequence of new cycles of liberalization and repression. But the state power mission had such historical standing, such support from accumulating opposition organizations, that established movement groups dominated most contention and absorbed more spontaneous or parochial resistance into the anti-dictatorship movement. Protest always occurred against the deeper shadows of this historically durable and evocative mission.[81] Movement leaders examined changes in the Marcos state, tested the winds of social support, and asked, "What kind of activity best suits this situation?" But *some* activity was always imagined as fitting the bill.

Organizational networks also allowed movement leaders to design extremely flexible and tenacious strategies (blending legal and insurgent struggles) that made any state move, short of a retreat from power, likely to produce *some* movement gains. Often, movements choreographed campaigns that included a build-up phase of education and propaganda activity, and then a series of mass actions and demonstrations. When the campaign met resistance, more spontaneous actions might follow and sustain the push. The 1978 IBP campaign followed set plans and used organizational resources; similar campaigns developed around opposition to the US military bases, or a nuclear power plant, slated for construction in Bataan province. In such cases, broader more spontaneous expressions of outrage and protest followed regime repression leveled against initially more planned protest actions. Elsewhere, movement cadres discovered aggrieved populations and attempted to attract them to more comprehensive struggle, as when the NDF recruited Cordillera people (displaced by the Chico River Dam) into the NDF. Yet even without unorganized support, movement organizations could still plan and execute protests and strikes – and the insurgency continued to expand.

For years, Marcos kept this growing movement at bay. The opposition was still arrayed to pose fairly stark choices between a capitalist dictatorship and communist insurgency. Ironically, because the regime did not wipe out NPA insurgents at the outset, when the movement began to recover in the mid-1970s, the state strategy grew more credible than it had first been, buying Marcos some important time, and stirring concerns about communist revolution among regime critics that had earlier refused to kindle. Soon, however, men like Aquino faced a ticklish dilemma: they both deeply mistrusted the left and utterly hated the regime, and so were

[81] Boudreau 2001.

compelled to undertake independent radical programs, like the urban terrorist campaigns of the late 1970s, that attached moderate political programs to radical forms of struggle. Because they stood apart from the broader complex of left organizations, however, these movements were, for Marcos, quite manageable.

Two things changed in the 1980s, foretelling the regime's end. First, the gap between political moderates and radicals narrowed because periodic interactions between them, mounting moderate frustration, and the growth of NDF front organizations with stronger legal dynamics suddenly made broad coalitions more viable. As the center-left political alliance grew more possible, Marcos's strategy faltered. Liberal thaws provided occasions for stronger anti-regime protest, rather than mere opportunities for authorities to co-opt the center. Stronger opposition efforts in compromised elections made regime cheating more apparent.[82] Second, and more important, the 1981 financial crisis increased dissatisfaction among moderates and the business community, and allowed an angry political center to become a force in its own right. From 1981 on, the dilemma that held that center in check – the Faustian choice between a repressive and corrupt state and the CPP – loosened. As the center roused itself, it became a true alternative to rightist authorities *and* the communist party. The massive outrage and protest following Benigno Aquino's assassination in 1983 was therefore the clearest public sign of a process underway for some time. We will, of course, have more to say about these events in chapter 8. For the moment, I wish to emphasize that this mobilization occurred in the context of accumulating movement institutions, the political geography of which, particularly in relation to state repression, was changing considerably.

---

[82] Carbonell-Catilo, *et al.* 1985.

7 Repression and protest in comparative perspective

That contention broadly differs across the cases should by now be reasonably clear. This chapter endeavors to set forth the dimension and logic of those differences in more explicit terms. First, however, consider for a moment the significance of that variation for the study of protest. I hope in part to be demonstrating that one cannot characterize contention in these cases merely by how they differ from baseline cases in the industrial world, better represented in social movements theory: since the set does not hold together as *similar* examples of "third-world" or even "Southeast Asian" contention, it confounds efforts to concentrate merely on the variables that distinguish first- and third-world cases (i.e. levels of development, democracy or state capacity). Instead, the cases demonstrate the central importance of how interactions between states and societies create an institutional, political and cultural terrain that shapes subsequent contention.

To broadly restate these differences: In Burma, years of quiet were punctuated by massive protest that invariably began with widespread economic dislocation, moved to more coordinated struggle and ended with radicalized protests and state violence. During each upsurge, demonstrations grew more organized as the ferment produced new leaders, and underground activists emerged from hiding to play stronger roles. Apart from these demonstrations, ethnic and communist insurgencies consistently engaged state forces, but seldom coordinated with urban protest movements. In Indonesia, protest occurred more frequently, and with less necessarily dire consequences. Changes in demonstrator identity and activity reflect changing state proscriptions designed to keep protest unorganized, for dissidents generally obeyed state rules and tailored activity around state prohibitions. Hence, student-based national demonstrations dominated protests from 1965 to 1978, but NGO-assisted land and water protests increased thereafter (reflecting the influence of the NKK/BKK legislation) followed by increases in labor and finally democracy protests. In the Philippines, national movements amassed broad bases by constructing functionally diverse and startlingly dense movement organizations. Movement leaders orchestrated campaigns that combined electoral work, marches and strikes, and included or threatened armed struggle. As the anti-dictatorship movement grew, contention acquired a more coordinated, organized, and sustained dynamic than in either Burma or Indonesia.

These different patterns of contention suggest the influence of past interactions between states and societies. Previous struggles eliminate some social institutions and call others forth, dispose of some movement leaders but maybe not all, illustrate how potential movement adversaries or allies will respond to a collective strategy, and (in consequence of all of these) shape counter-hegemonic cultures. Patterns of state repression left marks particular to each society, reflecting how different authorities, equipped with different capacities and facing different challenges, attempted to maintain control. We will examine several of these legacies in turn.

Repression and the arrangement of contention

State attacks restructured opposition vehicles in each case. Robust and rowdy popular associations existed before and during each dictator's rise, but soon came under fire. State repression followed definite strategies, rather than the haphazard whims of men merely drunk with power or poisoned by cruelty. The Burmese military, with the strongest counter-insurgent capacities of the three (and unsuited for open election-based politics), violently ended open dissent and protest, driving political groups underground. (It is also true that Burma faced the strongest insurgent challenge of the three, which serves to emphasize a key element of the argument: authorities do not merely respond to their most potent adversary. Rather, they respond to adversaries that seem most to *outmatch* state capacities. Armed with a potent counter-insurgent force, Burmese authorities preferred to drive contention into insurgent postures.) Indonesia's New Order, in contrast, eliminated many non-state organizations, replaced others with new corporatist bodies, and consolidated remaining groups into large, heterogeneous and divided formations. Behind a new organizational dominance, authorities could tolerate (within limits) protest that did not organize. Marcos, more concerned with state-building than with any particular challenge, scattered both underground organizations and open political rivals – but eliminated neither. In consequence, he began his dictatorship facing powerful elite opponents and underground insurgency; both groups would soon help political organizations to emerge and take root. Marcos tried to isolate the left by implementing weak participatory reforms to conciliate moderates, by using sporadic, unpredictable violence to frighten semi-legal activists into inactivity, and by concerted military campaigns against insurgents.

Beyond reshaping movement structures, early repression also influenced subsequent development by obstructing or encouraging particular lines of growth or change. Early state repression appears most clearly to have shaped three elements of contentious politics: the potential relationships between protest movements and insurgencies; the potential connection between elite and mass strata of the opposition; and, finally, the availability and autonomy of non-movement institutions (i.e. religious institutions, community organizations) that could provide cover or support for anti-state activists. We will examine each dimension in turn.

Protest and insurgency

Connections between open political and insurgent struggle vary across the three cases – sometimes reflecting pre-dictatorship patterns, but always also in ways that state repression at least enforced and sometimes established. The matter is essential, because connections between protest movements and insurgencies change mobilization's entire calculus: insurgency adds a new dimension to protest, changing how participants and authorities calculate victory and defeat, expense and opportunity. Connected to insurgency, protest movements can both press for proximate demands and undertake actions to support the armed resistance. Power struggles between state and social forces are not, in such cases, limited to individual cycles of protest, for cadres may design campaigns primarily to recruit insurgent soldiers, raise movement resources, or soften society up for revolution. In Burma and Indonesia, the state disrupted or prevented links between political and insurgent struggles. In his initial nonchalance about adversarial social forces, Marcos did not eliminate or isolate either legal protest or insurgent organizations, and so political and insurgent modes of opposition interacted to form a more resilient, cumulative and flexible opposition than that which emerged in Burma or Indonesia.

The Burmese *Tatmadaw* closed legal avenues of dissent by jailing members of parliament, blowing up the student-union building, and even arresting activists still allied to the BSPP in 1963. Its moves against legal political figures were more decisive than those following the Indonesian coup, and more committed than Marcos's. By late 1963, only insurgencies openly opposed the Revolutionary Council (RC). Stranded urban dissidents and BCP sympathizers formed small underground circles, but never connected them to larger opposition networks. Regime pressure and surveillance prevented activists from building a legal movement, and after BCP purges and anti-Chinese riots in 1967 and 1968, the communist party lost interest in urban recruits for their jungle war. Hence, the activists who formed underground cells had little connection to communist or ethnic insurgencies, and no network of civic associations to provide them cover. Hounded by the regime and isolated from insurgencies, cells remained exceptionally cautious. Members adopted largely defensive and anticipatory postures and under normal circumstances, most reached some provisional *modus vivendi* with the regime – but also studied and waited.

In Indonesia, student movement participation in the New Order's rise left several important legacies. Student activists mobilized *against* the PKI (the sole social force potentially able to conduct anti-state insurgency[1]) and in alliance with New Order anti-communist forces; the combination eroded student affinity for or interest in insurgent modes of struggle. While ABRI initially helped students build strong movement associations, it dismantled most other popular organizations, or replaced them with domesticated corporatist associations. Student protest in the next years stood apart from other social forces – and students valorized this separation in the idea of their privileged and moral access to policy makers. This pose partially sheltered student activism when New Order pronouncements began equating *organization* with insurgent and communist plots – which, given the memory of anti-communist slaughter, represented a formidable proscription against new organizations. Hence even when students began more to criticize Suharto, they had neither the resources nor the will to contemplate insurgent or underground activity.

Student isolation helps explain the subsequent evolution of Indonesian movements. Restrictions on student protest in 1974 and 1978 met little defiance, despite fairly weak sanctions, principally expulsion from school. But threats of expulsion worked because an expelled student had little future in Indonesia's mainstream, and no movement network could provide alternatives *to* that mainstream (a movement career or a fundamentally changed Indonesia). Activists preserving mainstream futures for themselves conformed to state prohibitions, and this rendered protest extraordinarily compliant.[2] Individual demonstrations acquired meaning largely in the immediate, usually limited concessions they could win, not

---

[1] McVey points out, however, this capacity was certainly over-stated. The PKI had never been attracted to insurgency, preferring instead moderate parliamentary politics. Indonesian communists hence made no credible counter-strike against the anti-communist campaign. McVey 1996.
[2] Heryanto 1999.

as movement-building events. Student study groups and mass advocacy in the 1980s stimulated new ideas about cross-class alliances, but still *complied* with state proscriptions. In deference to 1984 Mass Organizations laws, LSM activity remained localized and fragmented. Stronger and more coordinated movement activity only re-emerged under *keterbukaan* – but remained weak relative to Philippine parallels.

Philippine authorities did not prevent links between legal and underground or insurgent organizations. As in Burma, martial law clamped down on urban centers and drove many legal activists underground by closing representative institutions and the press, arresting opponents, imposing curfews, banning assemblies, and generally curtailing civil liberties. Soon, however, space for legal dissent began to open, parliamentarians emerged from jail, and institutions like the Church established advocacy centers to promote civil liberties and human rights. From the first, however, legal activists had an insurgency to join or emulate when state pressure grew too strong, and underground networks had formidable legal associations that provided them with support and cover. CPP cadres, unaffiliated activists and young senators, moreover, had some history of cooperation before martial law, and renewed those ties when their leaders met in martial law prisons. Soon, organizational and tactical connections linked some legal opposition groups and the illegal, underground resistance. These connections prevented authorities from eliminating the civil space that claim makers required, encouraged quite conservative opposition groups to adopt more radical forms, and provided broad institutional support for anti-dictatorship struggle.

The Philippine anti-dictatorship movement hence steadily accumulated in ways not possible in Indonesia or Burma. The underground provided a destination and sanctuary for political fugitives, and the idea of revolution, regime change and a clean start fortified activists' willingness to break with the main currents of Philippine society. As the insurgency grew, Marcos resorted more regularly to what he hoped would be demobilizing reforms – but in the context of his dictatorship, these measures triggered anti-regime mobilization and subsequent repression, not demobilization. Cycles of reform, mobilization, repression, and radicalization produced stables of well-known and experienced movement leaders, in whom the skills and prestige earned over decades of struggle accumulated. Movement organizations also accumulated: while an Indonesian land or labor protest left ephemeral, experiential residue among participants and Burmese struggles left hidden, largely underground legacies, Philippine efforts almost always sought to establish more open organizational vehicles that would last.

Mass society, elite support and mobilization

State repression also influenced relationships between cosmopolitan political forces and mass society in each case, greatly influencing contention. Before each dictatorship, national political forces were developing styles of mass politics that depended on, but also enabled, robust dissent. Burmese peasant and labor groups were organized and attached to political parties; PKI mass organizations shouldered an agrarian reform campaign, and Philippine labor and transport strikes combined with student protests and some congressional endorsement in the "First Quarter Storm". In each place, mass poverty provided a strong material basis for mobilization, while political activists (seizing opportunities like a Burmese election, Sukarno's favor or rifts among the Philippine elite) channeled mass unrest into protest, elections and even insurgency. State repression in each case initially disrupted connections between elite and mass activists, but policed the division with varying degrees of resolve and success.

In Burma, the state assault on civil society marginalized both mass and elite populations and initially divided one from the other. By directly linking Township Peasant Councils (TPCs) and similar mass associations to the BSPP, authorities severed connections between mass organizations and activists – even activists *supporting the new regime*. Subsequent regulations reduced the TPCs' prerogatives and powers, even as arrests and threats during the 1963 Peace Parley intimidated activists into paralyzing caution. Soon, activist leaders and their organizations were either eliminated or driven into hiding. Yet by cutting down both mass and elite political dissent, authorities inadvertently thrust all classes into a shared marginality, inadvertently encouraging broader empathy between different movement constituencies. Hence, university students in the mid-1970s readily identified with striking workers, as no Indonesian student ever could.[3] This empathic potential produced rapid contagion and mobilization across Burmese society during crises.

Indonesian student access to New Order leaders, student opposition to Sukarno's mass politics, and the idea that student power was moral and intellectual (not political) made *Angkatan 66* activists initially uninterested in mass organizations, even had ABRI allowed such initiatives. Under Guided Democracy, the PKI dominated organized mass politics, and student activists and ABRI were equally wary of mass alliances. Of course, Islamic organizations also played lead roles in the anti-PKI campaign, but authorities swiftly denied organized Islam any share of power.

---

[3] Budiman 1978.

When the killing abated in 1966, the regime began chipping away at remaining political organizations, unions and parties, and by 1971, students alone retained strong movement organizations. By then, however, barriers to student-mass alliances were even stronger, and new legislation dissolved mass membership in political parties and reinforced this decoupling. Under attack as communists, pressured to join corporatist associations and ignored by students, Indonesian mass society produced only local, unorganized and short-term contention.

Things changed after the 1978 NKK/BKK legislation drove students off campus. Forced to re-evaluate their seclusion, activists founded NGOs (LSMs) to help them reconnect to village and factory life. The effort advanced in small, mainly uncoordinated formations. Still, regular LSM contact with mass society marked a critical departure from developments in Burma. From the early 1980s onward, Indonesian working people did not need to wait for grievances to generalize to the point of mass rebellion. Rather, LSMs helped local communities grapple with local grievances. LSMs in the early 1980s emphasized self-help and moderation, and their involvement rendered grassroots' protest less explosive than either Burmese equivalents or Indonesian precedents. Even in later, more political phases, LSMs operated under de-politicizing constraints that limited dissident expressions. Hence the most explosive mass actions were unorganized, violent but local riots in which cosmopolitan activists played no role, and the more organized separatist insurgencies that recruited mass support with no moderating thought to preserving participants' futures in mainstream Indonesia.

Martial law drove elite Philippine dissidents to stronger connections with mass society, and most demonstrations had working-class constituencies organized by movement cadres. Activists who left Manila in 1972 began building bases among rural populations. Had these activists been Burmese, they would have been among those who fled to the countryside in 1964, but could not mesh with BCP insurgents. In fact, neither Filipino nor Burmese students proved immediately adept at jungle warfare, but unlike Burmese students, Filipinos were starting mainly from scratch: their insurgent setbacks led them to recalibrate revolutionary practice, but they (rather than experienced insurgents) stood at the party's core. In Burma, more experienced BCP fighters purged students in the late 1960s, and then turned away from the cities (where elite and mass dissidents were both marginalized from power and isolated from rural guerillas). Outside the Philippine insurgency, clear differences persisted between elite and mass capacities – for elites *remained elites*, with resources to contribute to the struggle, and distinct perspectives on that struggle. Had Filipino activists in 1974 been *Indonesians*, they would have joined *anti*-communist protests, and then adopted the moral force positions that distanced them from mass society. Eventually, of course, Indonesian LSMs adopted a mass advocacy line that initially *replaced* national political struggle, and state proscriptions on movement building kept elite-mass alliances weak and fragmented. In the Philippines alone, therefore, committed activists guided virtually all mass protest toward one of several national anti-dictatorship networks, virtually from the dictatorship's inception.

Supporting social institutions

Apart from reconfiguring movement collectives and organizations, repression also profoundly changed the social institutions available to support anti-state activity. All three dictators set out to control and subordinate elite political party members, but adopted different strategies to do so. The Burmese *Tatmadaw* swiftly imprisoned civilian politicians and expropriated their holdings, and so effectively eliminated local dissidents that when U Nu left prison and began organizing his resistance, he settled on Burma's frontier, and relied more on foreign assistance than domestic support.[4] Parliamentary dissent posed even weaker challenges to the Indonesian New Order, for Guided Democracy had already marginalized most parties and their leaders in the late 1950s. After 1965, most politicians reluctantly accepted their consolidation into the PDI and PPP parties and so were mainly unavailable to support anti-regime movements.[5] Marcos alone had powerful political adversaries with strong and independent resource bases. Even after the regime closed political institutions, Marcos's elite opponents would still materially support opposition movements.

Burmese and Indonesian authorities were also more willing than Marcos to repress elite educational institutions. Suharto and Ne Win set themselves against political rivals who differed utterly from the dictators both with military backgrounds. U Nu, BCP students, Sukarno, Indonesian party members, and Indonesian student leaders in the 1970s, all came from privileged social strata unfamiliar to either general. Not surprisingly, both men had no compunction about moving against university campuses. Marcos, on the other hand, himself graduated from the University of the Philippines and sent his children to study there. He also needed to move carefully against national universities

[4] U Nu 1975.
[5] Although disgruntled PSI remnants did support the Malari protests.

that still-powerful elites cherished and would defend. Shuttering these campuses would surely broaden and radicalize the opposition and ran against the grain of Marcos's own sociological disposition. Hence, despite the comparatively strong hold that activism had on students, Marcos never shut down the campuses. Despite significant state surveillance and repression, universities hence provided movements with recruitment bases and arenas of struggle.[6] Ne Win deprived activists of university resources so central to pre-1962 protests, and Suharto did the same after 1978.

Religious institutions also provided stronger support for Philippine opposition movements than either the Burmese Sangha or Indonesian Islamic institutions. Some authors have argued that the Philippine Catholic Church was inherently quite resilient against regime repression, but Ne Win and Suharto also more actively restrained potential religious opponents than did Marcos.[7] In 1965 Ne Win established a state agency to replace the independent Sangha and drove the monastic resistance underground, from which it periodically re-emerged in connection with broader protests, like the U Thant funeral demonstrations in 1974. In Indonesia, ABRI's deep mistrust of political Islam led the regime to keep its organizations in check: despite Muslim assistance in the anti-PKI campaigns, Suharto never restored Islam's position in national politics, and party consolidations undercut Islamic parties no less than others. Underground Islamic groups were crushed with great violence in the middle 1970s, and the sole basis legislation in 1984 primarily strove to reduce Islam's political appeal.

Viewed in this light, the comparative strength of Philippine Catholicism seems significantly a consequence of less dogged state repression. Marcos concentrated on state building, rather than on his adversaries, and the Church had not in any case been as strongly political as it would later be. Although Jesuit priests sponsored moderate labor and peasant associations like the Federation of Free Workers(FFW) and the Federation of Free Farmers(FFF), they were among the easiest groups for Marcos to co-opt. Church diversity also allowed Marcos to direct policies at its different branches, arresting strongly dissident clergy while conciliating the hierarchy (with its early "critical collaboration" posture). Hence the Philippine Church survived the construction of martial law relatively intact, and was able thereafter to increase its criticism of Marcos. By 1976, martial law's early open moment had passed, and authorities

---

[6] Abinales 1985.
[7] Youngblood 1990.

could no longer freely rework social relationships or directly inhibit the Church (as Ne Win and Suharto had their respective religious opponents). Perhaps Marcos's most effective threats then were relatively private warnings about potential tax increases on Church property.[8]

While other social institutions influenced mobilization patterns, they did so in ways that conformed to patterns suggested in the above examples. Burmese authorities generally eliminated public associational life at all strata between the RC and the neighborhoods. Universities, monastic associations, even production groups fell before this state campaign, leaving virtually no social institution to support any dissent. Opposition moved underground: writers penned cryptic, heavily disguised stories they hoped to pass by censors, hushed tea-shop conversations replaced open discussion, and people were otherwise frightened into silence – but that silence also served as a strong box that protected dissident perspectives for the future. In Indonesia, as organizations and associations fell under stronger state regulation, those looking to prosper under the New Order shied away from dissent. Potential sources of opposition – parties, Muslim associations and the Universities – grew compliant. Dissent more often mobilized outside these institutions, in *ad hoc*, temporary or small-scale networks. But the marginal and ephemeral character of these collectives limited their power. Only in the Philippines did independent social institutions survive the dictatorship's first repressive wave to play strategic roles in subsequent struggles, sustaining and directing activism and mediating alliances between open political and armed underground struggle. Moreover, independent civic organizations also encouraged Marcos to continue attempts to reconcile moderates to his regime by introducing weak participatory reforms.

Movement strategy and patterns of contention

The memory of state repression also shaped movement strategies and mobilization patterns by suggesting the costs and consequences of collective action. State action, particularly the violent convulsions at the dictatorships' rises, eliminated some modes of contention, and rendered others so precarious that activists could only contemplate them under extraordinary conditions. These legacies helped activists determine what forms of resistance the state would tolerate, and how far activists would risk offending state tolerance under given conditions. These calculations influenced particular acts of protest, but in time also produced distinct patterns of contention.

[8] Wurfel 1988.

Burmese protest occurred in bursts of activity, separated by long periods of almost total calm. While we have but three real examples of these cycles, they follow rather clear patterns, particularly once arrests and harassment in 1964 eliminated all parties but the BSPP. From that point, sustained dissent survived in weak, isolated underground cells, but seldom risked exposure via precipitous mobilizations. Instead, cells functioned mainly as study groups, periodically producing opposition fliers or graffiti. Rare public demonstrations usually started in informal school or factory networks, and responded to strong generalized grievances like rice shortages or currency devaluation. Initial, spontaneous mobilization emboldened the cautious underground. In 1967, protest began with rice riots, led to pro- and anti-Chinese demonstrations and finally to small but explicitly anti-regime protests. In the 1970s, workers' strikes against low wages and harsh working conditions ignited student interest and sympathy. After mobilizing outside factories, students protested the regime's funeral plans for U Thant, and opposed government officials who visited the campuses. In both instances, unorganized episodes of unrest broke a sustained public calm, and led to more organized and political demonstrations.

Burmese state repression eliminated movement leaderships and traditions of collective struggle to shape protest across each contentious cycle. Early mobilized activist circles began almost from scratch, following leaders who did not pre-date protests: brave men and women became movement leaders within specific cycles via particular acts of defiance or eloquence.[9] Movement collectives formed around institutions like university dorms or particular tea shops. Cell members understood the dangers of protest, and strove above all to preserve their precarious organizations: the underground, consequently, only weighed in once protest acquired a certain momentum, but its activity changed protest. In the 1970s cycle, for example, underground cadres planned and controlled protests surrounding the Thakin Kodaw Hmine anniversary. From that point, both activist slogans and the strike committee membership changed. As the cycle progressed, demonstrations became more pugnacious, for activists did not expect amicable settlement with the regime, but rather to replace authorities or be crushed by them.[10]

During the period when students alone were allowed to organize under Indonesia's New Order, the campuses utterly dominated contention.

---

[9] The activity, referred to as "signaling" by collective action theorists, was particularly important in Burma because few organizations or associations existed to provide that information. McAdam, Tarrow and Tilly 2000.

[10] Htun Aung Kyaw 1997.

Demonstrations *then* (particularly those related to complicated economic positions) required substantial groundwork to mobilize movement consensus, usually accomplished by formal student organizations. But protest also coincided with important changes in the New Order: it accompanied the first post-coup elections in 1971 and Sumitro's seemingly serious challenge to Suharto's leadership in 1974.[11] In both, students partly mobilized because they identified themselves as New Order insiders, and even their more direct anti-Suharto criticisms through 1974 mainly weighed in on a power struggle among the regime's factions. Hence, at the height of their organizational power, students seldom suggested alternatives to the New Order, but rather advocated positions to be taken *within the existing arrangement.*

Indonesian students hence avoided mass mobilizations, seeking instead private and exclusive influence within the state. Still, as they turned more critical of the regime, one might expect student activists to have cultivated mass support (as did pre-war Philippine bureaucrats who fell out with Philippine Commonwealth President Quezon). The Indonesian students' forbearance on this point certainly reflects the dangerous New Order association between mass politics and communism. But students also had developed their own perspectives around ideas of a moral, rather than political force, rendering mass support less necessary or attractive. This orientation harkened back – sometimes nostalgically – to the largely cooperative *original* relationship between the *Angkatan 66* and the state.[12] When students turned more critical of the regime in the 1970s, state restrictions on political organization foreclosed sharper, broader or more sustained resistance, and left students a little marooned, socially and politically. In fact, restrictions on opposition organization made resisting the New Order juggernaut from the outside nearly inconceivable: despite an apparent desire to force Suharto's resignations, students in 1974 only pursued that goal in cooperation with regime insiders, and hurriedly *demobilized* when working-class crowds joined them. Students seemed only fully to grasp the importance of organizations and mass support after the 1979 NKK/BKK legislation began to take effect.[13]

By then, of course, it was too late. Student acceptance of the NKK/BKK, and their shift to an off-campus NGO (LSM) strategy, was an

---

[11] Aspinall 1995.
[12] Note for instance, the language used by students in 1974: "No matter what, we are only a group of youths who in 1966 had a meaningless share, which is nothing compared to the share in establishing this New Order Government... We are only made of soft flesh and hopeful eyes looking toward the future." Budiman 1978: 619.
[13] See Akhmadi 1979.

instructive surrender that both reflected the balance of power during 1978, and weakened activist power thereafter. LSMs directed activism toward short-lived, issue-based engagements, seldom toward nationally coordinated campaigns and never into broad, permanent or clandestine opposition organizations. Urban demonstrations against price hikes, new traffic laws or a state lottery never built durable organizations, or expanded into heterogeneous or extensive protest. Authorities met some protest demands, but more often needed only threats and curfews to end unorganized protests. Unable to apply real pressure on government officials, activists still expressed themselves in terms of moral positions and political ideas, and concentrated on influencing the courts and reform-minded officials, rather than on building a strong movement apparatus.[14] Even when LSM activists adopted stronger anti-regime postures, they obeyed government proscriptions on organization.

The dynamics of protest in Indonesia and Burma differed significantly, particularly in terms of mobilization and demobilization processes. Explosive but unorganized mass protests against economic hardship in Burma triggered more organized activity by the cautious underground. The very breadth of the events necessary to trigger organized Burmese protest assured that big demonstrations concentrated in the country's largest cities. State moves against mobilized demonstrators – arrests or murder – eventually crushed protests, but demonstrators often grew violent as well, building to centralized, cataclysmic confrontations. In Indonesia, student activists and later LSM organizers frequently *initiated* protest, either on their own (in the late 1960s and early 1970s) or in connection with mass communities. Events that triggered protest ranged from new state impositions – laws, projects or policies – to disputes among New Order factions that produced new allies for activists (as in 1974 and 1988). Protest was scattered and localized – as likely in a Javanese village as in Jakarta. Government threats and military patrols usually ended clusters of protest, often with little violence or detention (except when mass activity escalated into riots). Decisive state action, in the form of policies against organizational forms that activists had used to good advantage, usually *followed*, rather than *ended* protest.

Authorities in the two countries, moreover, imposed different kinds of sanctions on adversaries. The limits and circumspection built into Indonesian protest allowed officials to tolerate demonstrations with little fear of broader contagion. Urban Javanese demonstrators adhering to state restrictions seldom encountered harsh repression – and the prospect

[14] Lev 1996.

of reconciliation moderated interactions between the state and such activists. Rural or outer island protesters encountered more regular and intense repression, and built more durable and clandestine organizations to cover their activity and protect their members. In Burma, protest cycles ended in gunfire, bloodshed and lengthy imprisonments designed to wipe out dissent altogether. Rarely, authorities negotiated with dissidents (as during the U Thant burial agreement) but police, soldiers and military intelligence more commonly hunted activists down, even following such negotiations, and few activists were themselves disposed to negotiate. In sharp contrast to Indonesia, Burmese authorities reacted with greater urgency to urban and cosmopolitan protests than to armed frontier insurgency. More than once, Ne Win relieved pressure on his military by deputizing insurgent armies within their territories. For much of the socialist period, anti-insurgent campaigns unfolded in seasonal thrusts, rather than constant assaults, although they were savage affairs once underway. In contrast, ABRI has been more relentless and cruel against its insurgent and separatist movements than against central anti-regime protest, and routinely resorted to broad and brutal attacks in East Timor, West Papua and Aceh.

Despite these contrasts in strategy, however, protest movements did not accumulate over time in either Indonesia or Burma. The Burmese state eliminated activist remnants at the end of each cycle, and demonstrators in the mid-1970s and in 1988, report initially knowing nothing about movement politics or tactics (although such knowledge often re-emerged when underground activists joined the fray). In Indonesia, state measures restricting opposition organizations, fragmented protest and limited activists' careers. No LSMs, student activists, labor or farmer associations ever developed a strong and broadly based anti-regime network to support extended oppositionist careers. In an important sense, the initial student framework for regime change – that it required sponsorship from inside the state – survived throughout the New Order. When the regime seemed willing to allow more political liberties in the late 1980s, activists had already internalized the rules of Indonesian protest. *Keterbukaan* produced freer dissident writing and more protest, but little movement building, coalition politics or cross-class associations.

In the Philippines, legal dissidents and underground insurgents existed throughout the Marcos dictatorship, reinforcing one another even without explicit cooperation or coordination, though such cooperation also occurred. Open civil associations established moderate political centers that provided cover for the underground, and also resisted too sweeping attacks on civil liberties. Repression of underground activists often provoked broad protest, for many victims also worked in formally legal organizations, and Marcos was unable convincingly to discredit such groups as mere fronts. Hence expanding state repression in the 1980s took the form of surreptitious murders (dubbed "salvagings") and other acts of clandestine brutality to which authorities never admitted (unlike winking denials about the *petrus* killings in Indonesia). The Philippine underground reinforced even moderate regime resistance and offered organized and guided radicalization as an alternative to demobilization. This heterogeneous movement complex grew despite (or perhaps because of) the Marcos strategy of implementing disingenuous reforms to prevent broad center-left alliances. Theoretically, reforms and elections could divide those who sought broader participation in the polity from those more committed to armed revolution. The IPB campaign of 1978, however, illustrates that elements of the left allied with Aquino's LABAN party were more flexible than Marcos anticipated, and moderates who build opposition organizations in time also proved resistant to facile co-optation. Moreover, and crucially, Marcos would not actually *implement* reforms. Initial liberalization always encouraged broad anti-regime activity that triggered new repression. Hence the central dynamic of Philippine contention was the mobilization of moderate regime opponents under conditions of temporary liberalization, regime crackdowns and then dissident radicalization – causing a parallel expansion of the more radical left. Particularly after recent liberalization, renewed authoritarian controls bitterly disappointed parliamentary and moderate regime opponents, and drove them toward radical action and alliances.

Compare this dynamic with Indonesian events, where sham elections also regularly occurred. State attacks on independent political organizations in the early 1970s shaped the numb pageant of Pancasila electoral democracy, where apron-string opposition parties raced one another to endorse the president and his policies. Certainly most Indonesians disliked *their* electoral system no less than Filipinos disliked *theirs*. Why did equally unfair Indonesian elections seldom provoke sustained protests as in the Philippines? The answer may lie in how the political opposition was structured and related to authorities. With no strong elite opposition when he took power, Suharto never needed really to pacify or coopt elite or parliamentary opponents, and so could simply proscribe opposition activity that he disliked. In fact, the regime felt the strongest pressure to maintain its initial electoral timetable from students *within* the New Order coalition, rather than from displaced parliamentarians. The New Order regime did not occupy a pole in a divided society as did the Marcos dictatorship, but monopolized political and economic life by its sheer mass. The disgruntled could protest election results, but did so with no strong support from an organized opposition, confronting a state that controlled most avenues to power and prosperity. Hence, the period leading to elections and the *Majelis Permusyawaratan Rakyat* (MPR, National Assembly Meeting) produced demonstrations geared toward influencing policy, or cultivating support within sections of the state's several factions. But protests ended soon after the election itself, because activists had no leverage against authorities.[15]

In contrast, Filipino activism rose during the elections, but radicalized *after* poll results underscored the regime's betrayal. Election malfeasance increased cooperation between moderate and radical dissidents, and more generally broadened the opposition. Further, Marcos's political crackdowns ripened conditions for national democratic protest. ND groups, unlike more moderate associations, did not anticipate winning reforms from mass protest, but sought to shepherd moderates toward revolutionary struggle by demonstrating the limits of legal protest. State repression provided the precise conditions to accomplish this goal. Moreover, because the NDs had stronger organizational control of their base, they could command demonstrations, and so for them, political opportunity was less a question of individual participants' willingness to protest than of a leadership's decision to deploy resources. After the 1981 repeal of martial law, smaller cycles of openness and closure provided conditions under which opposition organizations grew larger and more powerful; under *keterbukaan*, protest and dissent became more prominent and frequent – but powerful opposition organizations never emerged, and movement power remained diffuse.

Economic dynamics, factors we have touched on at different points in the case narratives, interacted with the political considerations to reinforce emerging patterns of contention. For different reasons, neither Burmese nor Indonesian society ever produced a strong economic elite in opposition. In Burma, generally desperate economic conditions meant that no social group ever accumulated substantial economic power outside the BSPP's inner circle, with the possible exception of vastly dependent and so politically tractable black-market merchants. Hence although protest frequently mobilized among different social strata, relatively privileged Burmese dissidents had few distinct resources, save education and experience, to contribute to the movement. Everyone, excepting insurgents, was more or less politically supine; everyone required some powerful external stimulus to provoke waves of spontaneous rebellion. In Indonesia, from the middle 1970s onward, rapid economic growth

---

[15] An important exception, however, does exist: in the provincial assembly elections, local protests over cheating constitute one of the main arenas of mobilization in Indonesia since the late 1980s.

(so profound as to allow broad social advance even after rapacious state corruption) compelled dissidents to balance their desire for political reform against opportunities to make a comfortable living in the social and economic mainstream. The pull of mainstream careers and a flush economy took a toll on activist ranks, both by encouraging moderation among protesters, and convincing many to end activist careers and start working for pay. Generations of protesters hence dissipated into New Order society, and this provided conditions under which the New Order strategy of scattering and dis-organizing dissent would work.

Philippine conditions were, in many ways, exactly the reverse. In his rise, Marcos expropriated many established, landed elites, and then shouldered aside others by establishing crony-run monopolies. As we have seen, this produced an angry, wealthy stratum of anti-dictatorship activists from early on. As economic conditions deteriorated seven or eight years into the dictatorship (precisely, that is, at the stage when things began radically to improve in Indonesia!) fewer and fewer Filipinos could hope for mainstream, upwardly striving careers. This is not to say that decisions to join or stay with a movement had economically individualistic foundations, but rather that movements did not have to compete with as apparent and accessible a gravy train as existed in Indonesia. The economic crises of the early 1980s, of course, did much to push more upper-class Filipino business people and organizations toward strongly oppositionist stances. But particularly in contrast to strong and steady economic growth in Indonesia, Philippine economic decline probably helped solidify resistance and diminish the chances that activists would break from the movement. In this light, the longevity of the Indonesian dictatorship, and the state's efforts to scatter Indonesian dissent and resistance received substantial enforcement from an economically conducive context, while patterns of state repression that still allowed Philippine protest organizations to expand were reinforced by a steady economic decline.

In short, conditions that allowed Philippine anti-dictatorship institutions steadily to accumulate distinguish Philippine protest from that in Burma or Indonesia. As movement organizations expanded Marcos needed *even more* regularly (if disingenuously) to respond to dissident concerns (unlike either Suharto or Ne Win). His strategy *depended* on capturing support from moderate forces against the left, and so he needed to distance himself from human rights' violations, establish investigative commissions, and periodically liberalize the rules of engagement (similar developments marked only the *end* of Suharto's rule, when things had begun to collapse). In the Philippine atmosphere, protest was merely *part* of a longer-term movement strategy, and often secondary to concerns about organization building and insurgent struggle. Burmese protest radicalized when activists lost hope of political advance (or often, survival) while Indonesian protest petered out when participants lost faith in their ability to influence authorities or continue demonstrating unmolested. In the Philippines, closing opportunities and state intransigence drew more people into movement structures, and helped convert spontaneous political activity into organizational gains for the movement. Hence movement leaders often planned their largest demonstrations in the very teeth of rising state repression.

As movement networks thickened from the mid-1970s, Philippine protest increasingly occurred when organizations decided to march, strike or do something else. Different forces seized upon different events as politically opportune, and whether one mobilized during liberalization or repression, for instance, depended on one's line of march. Often, protest fell on holidays and anniversaries – Labor Day, Bonifacio Day, or some martial law anniversary – for on those occasions, organizations felt compelled to demonstrate their strength, and reiterate their positions. Dynamics that emerged *periodically* in Burma or Indonesia (as when activists attempted to drum up support in a specific campaign) were more routinized for the standing armies of Philippine dissent. Propaganda committees worked steadily and organization committees continually sought likely expansion areas. Lacking strong or public organizations, Burmese and Indonesian protests required external events to rouse people into action. Organizational processes in the Philippines also influenced *unorganized* individuals and new recruits, and encouraged all claim makers to mobilize in ways authorities would have liked to prevent. Movement organizations provided strong models for protest and focused anger against the regime. Even when authorities proscribed movement activity, the stronger opposition structure allowed Filipinos (more than Indonesians or Burmese) to defy those proscriptions: one could have a career as a Marcos-regime opponent, conceiving of the anti-dictatorship struggle remaking Philippine society and sweeping the old regime aside. This possibility helped radicalize the expression of all dissent, even from comparative moderates.

Visions of transition, oppositional cultures and implications for the struggle

Within the established relations between these states and their societies, broadly different oppositional cultures developed. Burmese pursued protest and demonstrations at great personal risk, as a kind of cataclysmic undertaking that would either topple the regime or bring state violence down on demonstrators. More circumspect Indonesian protest attempted to compel political change by exerting moral pressure, and by establishing relations with authorities inclined to echo or sponsor movement demands. Philippine movement organizations steadily amassed constituencies and liberated territory behind a vision of steady revolutionary growth dislodging Marcos and remaking the government. These orientations, of course, are partly aggregations of the smaller institutional and political legacies we traced earlier in this chapter; yet they also suggest that important themes in oppositional cultures do not inhere in one setting or another, but reflect regime structure, and histories of patterned, often violent contention.

Burmese movements, particularly after peace parley arrests cleared the political stage, were closely chained to volatile mass anger. Activists had neither intact organizations nor continuous traditions to help sift earnest participants from informers, and movement decisions often emerged in the public flow of events, where daring, often reckless, acts demonstrated commitment and trustworthiness. These conditions, however, diminished chances that reasoned debate would finely tune or temper movement strategies, for those who disagreed with the dominant opinion on the streets risked drawing suspicion as spies,[16] and demonstrators even attacked foreign journalists (who could have helped their cause) in the 1970s. Particularly after 1962 and 1975, activists surely understood that security forces would try to kill or imprison them, and could not contemplate staged or protracted struggles. Instead, they tended to bet on intense but limited clashes. With no strong social institutions to protect or support protest, activists collected individual donations of food and money from the fragmented society – and in these public collections (rather than the secret efforts that often backed Filipino and Indonesian activists) the movement seemed to embrace, and be embraced by, the entire population. Finally, movements often had no political program, nor any clear demands, at least initially. Students who traveled to investigate workers' strikes in 1975 did so out of curiosity and a kind of nascent rebelliousness, but weighed workers' demands against only a raw sense of justice. As we will see later, Ne Win *himself* first broached the concept

---

[16] I attribute the suspicion surrounding political debate in Burma to the absence of movement organizations, which provide a structure for continuous interaction, and so stronger trust, among activists. One can compare this more or less typical condition inside the Burmese movement to the atypical suspicions that surrounded political debate during the *Kahos* purges in the Philippine left (1987–1988). In *Kahos*, cadres became convinced that military spies had infiltrated their organization, and the party could not longer certify any cadre as legitimate. In that context, debate and disagreement (as in Burma) came to be viewed as evidence of betrayal. Abinales 1996.

of multi-party elections in the 1988 democracy movement; it did not come from the activists' program of struggle.

But because protesters expected state violence, because authorities so successfully marginalized and disrupted dissident networks, and because activists had virtually no political or strategic models, these brief and rare moments of protest bore vast, cataclysmic burdens of aspiration and hope. Participants seldom seemed to expect that their activity would produce regular or more accepted opposition vehicles – although student leaders at the U Thant protests *had* hoped to acquire a mausoleum office from which to manage future demonstrations. Rather, demonstrations constituted all-or-nothing gambles, wagered against an ante of state violence. Activists attempted to hold violence at bay by sustaining mass mobilizations – and sometimes the regime did hold off while protests were large. But the entire gambit balanced atop the shaky calculus that massive unrest alone could bring down the regime, that before mass support dwindled, the movement would sweep away the regime. Protesters did not appeal to state reformers, and had no reason to expect government concessions. Instead, they escalated the struggle, calling forth (or perforce, accepting) more violent contention that they often could not control.

As the underground grew more active across any cycle, speeches and demonstrations changed as well. Activists adopted more explicitly political terms – often drawing comparisons between Burma and other countries that would never have occurred to original demonstrators. Underground activism also brought forth some of the important symbols of the anti-colonial struggle – the fighting-peacock flag, student unions, meetings at the Shwedagon Pagoda – for it was mainly the underground that nurtured these traditions. The vast gulf between the insular Burmese state and society lent resonance to images that first emerged in opposition to foreign colonial rule.

Because Indonesian protest was fragmented, decentralized and heterogeneous, it is harder to summarize the ideas of struggle it embraced. Separatist insurgencies combined armed struggle and protest (particularly when they had access to international audiences) to press for autonomy or independence. Periodically, in localized, violent outbursts, mass communities took direct action – seizing and redistributing a Chinese merchant's stock, or ransacking a factory whose owner paid low wages. LSM-led local protests often sought to resolve specific land tenure disputes or labor struggles, leaning heavily on a discourse of legal rights. Anti-regime protests in urban centers either targeted specific policies in sometimes forceful protests, or larger issues of democracy, corruption and human rights violations in more restrained, limited actions. Some of the boldest *rhetorical* attacks against the regime were also the most *tactically* tame:

speeches, lectures and articles by members of the urban, semi-professional pro-democracy lecture circuit.

Often, excepting separatist insurgencies on their home ground, contention demonstrated a peculiar combination of radical, and sometimes violent activity on the ground that in the larger scheme of things was nevertheless manageable for authorities. Even riots, though furious, were unorganized, largely reactive and usually local; military authorities seldom had trouble restoring order in such cases, and some evidence suggests that military men sometimes incited riots to advance one agenda or another. Because LSMs could not build mass organizations, their protests remained episodic. Labor strikes initially occurred at the factory level or (if more extensive) were entirely symbolic. After violent and more organized strikes in 1993 called forth substantial repression, worker support for off-factory actions once more waned. National student groups and pro-democracy professionals kept their activity unorganized, and usually complied with curfews and military warnings. Over-bold pro-democracy speeches often called forth oblique but effective warnings in the press: typically something like an affirmation of the right to free speech, coupled with expressions of regret about those who used that right irresponsibly, and sometimes, speculation about communist involvement. Authorities arrested and tried activists in explicitly public ways, usually inhibiting protest for months thereafter. The New Order's entire propaganda and language policy supported these trends to depoliticize society.[17]

How, then, was Indonesian protest supposed to work? Limited issues generated some of the most sustained and focused protest during the latter New Order, and perhaps these very limits emboldened participants. Broader, more cautious pro-democracy protests were directed toward fissures in the New Order and responded to signs that members of the state itself wanted change. *Keterbukaan* initially reflected disagreements within the state. ABRI's 1988 rejection of Suharto's vice presidential candidate shocked Indonesian society; Benny Murdani's dismissal and the regime's turn toward Islam (and away from the military) emphasized rifts that further encouraged protest. By the late 1980s, New Order repression had shaped protest so that it was seldom associated with organizations, but with social *groups*, like youths and peasants. Ideas were still discussed as if they were more important than political power, and this allowed orators or editorialists to imagine their rhetorical support for democracy as full-blown struggle. Despite the devalued currency of language in the New Order, then, speech acquired an unfounded reputation for import.

---

[17] Heryanto 1999; Crouch 1992.

In most respects, Filipino dissidents' self-confident assertions starkly contrast with Indonesian caution. Filipino activists disagreed about how Marcos would be driven from power: some planned insurrections, others, protracted insurgency, and still others, effective electoral campaigns.[18] But this lively debate indicates something more than mere disagreement. It suggests that for activists, strategy and tactics mattered, for most seemed confident that they (not larger social processes, or internal state convulsions) would eventually overcome the dictator. This idea, validated by steady movement expansion, lent broader meaning to individual protest actions. Each march, each sit-in or class boycott had significance as a building block toward that eventual transition. Activists planned the seizure of state power as if it lay inevitably on their path.

In this context, even acts of defiance that could not produce short-term gains could make long-term sense. "Outrage rallies," conducted on the very heels of state repression, ran greater than normal risks, but also promised to recruit moderates to radical struggle. More stylized protest at political anniversaries and holidays, graffiti and lightning rallies signaled the movement's presence. Students routinely left elite universities without degrees, for what qualification trumped a prominent role in a regime transformation? This particular way of imagining a connection between eventual revolutionary transformations and finite acts of resistance helped cultivate a more overt culture of resistance and revolution in the Philippines than elsewhere. Cadres submitted their romantic lives to party authority. Activists described beach outings as "consolidation exercises." Small protests, student arguments with teachers, even, one former activist recalls, complaints about filthy university toilets could all fit into a larger, revolutionary agenda. The movements produced protest songs, activist cafes and bars, and a fashion that would have cut against the grain of activists' restraint in Indonesia[19] and been suicidal in Burma.

Opposition culture pervaded the Philippines. People knew University of the Philippines' students as activists, understood that an active underground existed close at hand. They read revolution from graffitti-stained

---

[18] Rivera 1985.

[19] On the subject of student activist fashion in Indonesia, a group of protesting Gadja Mada university students once told me that some of the activist fashions common in the Philippines, particularly clothing and jewelry association with ethnic minority groups, would not work in Indonesia because activists wanted to emphasize their message about a united Indonesian society, rather than associate themselves with any individual group living within Indonesia. More evident at that interview were women activists in Jailbabs, one of which, in the privacy of the interview room, had unbuttoned the garment to reveal a Che Guevara T-shirt. Guevara's image is particularly popular in Indonesia because of his resemblance to East Timorese activist Xananna Gusamao.

walls, and sensed something building in shanties bordering strike areas, and out past Manila in particular villages and along specific mountain ranges. The revolution weighed on mainstream Philippine society, and pushed ideas of struggle and opposition further into the realm of public debate.

At the same time, activist leaders' increasingly explicit quest for center-left unity steered protest away from some of the most explosive elements of contention in the other two cases. Riots, looting and mass property destruction virtually never occurred in the Philippines – except, ironically, in urban bombings fueled by the outraged sensibilities *of moderate elites themselves*. Organized political movements recruiting from mainstream society took pains not to frighten off moderates. Long-term struggle based on increasingly broad alliances made Filipinos (unlike Burmese counterparts) disinterested in pushing each confrontation to murderous conclusions. Strong movement organizations also made Philippine demonstrations less likely than those in Indonesia to spin off unintended violence, looting or vandalism. And finally, the sociological similarity between many movement leaders and their government adversaries (more like the Thai situation than anything in Burma or Indonesia) also moderated the conflict.[20] Hence, an apparent paradox, resolved: the movement posing the strongest revolutionary threat to its regime exercised the most restraint in its public demonstrations.

Conclusion

Authoritarian regimes in these three countries began as hard-pressed organizations using repression strategically to defeat specific challenges. To understand how environmental changes influenced contention – let alone what changes constituted mobilizing opportunities – one must evaluate protest, repression and social support for either in terms of established interactions between states and societies: the logics they obey, and the legacies they leave. Activists and authorities *both* attempt to press their advantage within a specific context, in light of particular relationships to one another. I have argued that initial patterns of state attacks evolved into institutionalized programs of containment with relatively clear practices and logics that create distinct patterns of contention, producing some collective options and cutting others off. Movement actions prompt different state reactions across the three settings, because the meaning of political activity (its threat or subversiveness) resides in

---

[20] Anderson 1990.

unique histories of conflict between states and societies. Even as repression rewrote political rules in the three dictatorships' genesis, it remained intelligible in terms of ongoing histories.

Nor, of course, do differences between the cases merely reflect different *degrees* of democracy, or repression, or opportunity or support. Were Indonesian or Burmese authorities, for instance, more repressive? Does the question even make much sense? Both killed dissidents, both resorted to arbitrary arrest and imprisonment. It was probably safer in Burma to be an insurgent than a protester, while in Indonesia precisely the opposite was true. In both cases, and in the Philippines as well, dictatorships took whatever measures they felt necessary to consolidate and preserve power, and these measures varied from place to place. Quantitative assessments of these factors, I have tried to show, do not provide the information necessary to interpret the dynamics of repression in any of these settings. To understand when protest mobilizes, what forms it takes, how powerful it may be requires an appreciation of the larger strategic contest between authorities and challengers: Who enjoys democratic rights and who does not? What kinds of people (or collective forms) do states repress, and why? What risks do activists run, using specific strategies against particular states? We require qualitative information about patterns of strategic interactions between dissidents and state authorities, histories of strike and counterstrike, to answer these questions.

The disadvantage to the approach, of course, is its unwieldiness. The complex and structured comparisons that inform this analysis (far less detailed, of course, than a country-specialist might desire) yield cautionary notes and models for further work, rather than immediate generalizations beyond these cases. At present, however, one pay-off does seem clear: in the final section, building on these comparisons, we examine the democracy movements that ended each dictator's rule. If my arguments hold water, comparisons between these democracy struggles will make sense against the history of regime and movement interaction, in patterns that began in state violence, proceeded as more institutionalized repressive policies, and eventually shaped movement participants' most basic strategic and tactical calculations.

8 People power and insurgency in the Philippine transition

Many descriptions of the 1986 Philippine anti-Marcos rebellion emphasize the largely mistaken notion that an unorganized force (more moral than political, in the Indonesian sense) swept the dictator from office. This impression, however, neglects how organized political struggle against the regime maneuvered to set up this transition.[1] In *that* process, each side strove to polarize Philippine society in ways that would leave its opponent isolated and vulnerable to direct violence: authorities looked to isolate the NDF by co-opting moderates away from potentially broad revolutionary alliances, while the left sought to recruit among the political center by demonstrating the limits of state-sponsored reform and the wisdom of the revolutionary alternative. Still, the regime did not end in violent revolution, nor did authorities launch a military counterstrike against anti-dictatorship protests. Non-violent protests supporting military defectors and fortified by domestic and international pressures did Marcos in, and he left office without a bloodbath. Here, then, we find a puzzle: with the regime and its most organized and apparently powerful opponents *both* angling for social polarization and one another's violent dispatch, what explains the *peaceful* transition in which neither prospered?

The answer lies in how cycles of reform and repression under Marcos nurtured open and semi-legal anti-dictatorship organizations. Marcos continued to try dividing moderate and elite dissidents from those who adopted armed underground struggle, though the boundary between these camps constantly shifted, often as moderates radicalized following regime repression. By 1981, the relaxation of martial law and growth of NDF front organizations encouraged open resistance to the regime, and diminished Marcos's ability to attack his opponents without stirring up broad protest. A great deal of subsequent repression (which expanded steadily into the 1980s) aimed at legal and semi-legal activists.[2] Economic

[1] Boudreau 2001.
[2] Overholt 1986: 1151–1152; Lawyers Committee for International Human Rights 1983; Kessler 1989.

deterioration in the early 1980s provided the opposition with new allies and divided regime elites. The 1979 oil shock and a forty-percent decline in the country's terms of trade created widespread hardship,[3] emphasizing unhappiness about flamboyant regime expenditures like the Cultural Center of the Philippines, the ill-advised Bataan nuclear power plant, and an $8 million bust of Marcos in Northern Luzon.[4] Business groups complained about state corruption, particularly the conversion of crony liabilities into public debt,[5] while local economists chronicled extensive, and often politically motivated state intervention in the economy.[6] The Catholic Church broadened its criticisms of the regime, notably in the Catholic Bishops' Conference of the Philippines's (CBCP) 1983 pastoral letter, and the organization of Basic Christian Communities in poor barrios swelled.[7] In the light of these developments, the dilemma between revolution and authoritarianism (a dilemma that once froze moderate political initiative) began to ease. As centrist political forces roused themselves to action, they sometimes joined radical groups, but increasingly also formed politically moderate, though tactically radical, protest organizations.

Marcos's obviously deteriorating health created further opportunities by raising the issue of presidential succession. Since the late 1960s Marcos had personally controlled the state apparatus, and his inner circle remained stable but constipated: so unmoved by either purges or promotions that many who helped implement martial law remained in power.[8] (In contrast, Suharto rose within a military that threw up powerful rivals to his authority, and secured his position by periodically purging those who had grown too strong. Shifts in the Indonesian regime sometimes, therefore, produced allies for protesters.) The comparative stability of Philippine state personnel, in contrast, initially created fewer top-level renegades to support or encourage the opposition – and even those who did defect (as we will see) typically joined the movement as individuals, rather than allying with the movement as factions.[9] Yet when Marcos fell ill in August 1982, a minor, premature succession crisis rippled through his regime, eventually producing an Executive Committee tasked with leading the

---

[3] Manning 1984–1985: 396.
[4] Rafael 1990; Diokno 1982.
[5] De Dios 1984: 17; Mayo 1984.
[6] University of the Philippines, School of Economics 1984.
[7] Youngblood 1990; Consolacion 1983.
[8] Miranda 1990.
[9] Two illustrative examples are Primitivo Mijares, who did Marcos substantial damage by publishing the scathing *The Conjugal Dictatorship* in 1976, and Victor Corpuz, whose defection from the AFP to the NPA captured widespread attention. See Jones 1989.

country should anything befall the president. That committee became an arena for second-line competition in which Fabian Ver and Imelda Marcos eased out men like Juan Ponce Enrile and Fidel Ramos, opening new rifts in the regime.[10] Entering the critical years of the middle 1980s, therefore, an increasingly viable political center had begun more assertively to rise against a newly divided regime. And then Benigno Aquino was killed, and that changed everything.

The Aquino assassination

Benigno Aquino almost certainly returned to the Philippines in 1983 because of the politically auspicious combination of a weakened president and a disturbed economic elite. He had pursued a broad range of opposition activities throughout the dictatorship: had campaigned against the regime from prison in 1978, backed the LAFM and the A6LM in the late 1970s, founded the LABAN party and also influenced Salvador Laurel's UNIDO.[11] For many, he perfectly combined a flamboyant oppositional style with essentially moderate political perspectives, and represented the greatest hope for political change.

His assassination at the Manila Airport on August 21, 1983, moments into his return from exile, triggered broad and intensive protests.[12] Many of the 2 million who joined Aquino's funeral march were neophyte activists, but the sanctioned, familiar ritual of mourning eased them into the protests that followed. The breadth and power of these protests encouraged fairly extensive cooperation among the different opposition currents. Social democrats joined the ND-organized Justice for Aquino, Justice for All (JAJA) and later the National Movement for Freedom Justice and Democracy (NMFJP).[13] NDs attended prayer rallies and marches that social democrats set up. Despite his recent rift with NDF organizers, Senator Jose Diokno accepted a leading position in the NMFJP – at least partly because ND groups demonstrated greater interest in and respect for the integrity of centrist partners to the alliances. Cardinal Sin condemned the murder in his strongest anti-regime statements ever, calling Aquino a martyr. The United States and the Vatican, among other foreign powers, expressed concern over the murder. Military

---

[10] Overholt 1986: 1153; Muego 1983; Kessler 1984.

[11] Franco 2000.

[12] Thompson quotes government estimates that 165 "rallies, marches and other demonstrations" occurred in the month following the assassination, with more than 100 between October 1983 and February 1985. Thompson 1995: 116.

[13] On JAJA, see Diokno 1988: 133–135; and Lane 1988: 4; Kessler 1989.

officers (not associated with Fabian Ver) expressed condolences to Aquino's widow, and Defense Minister Enrile even visited mourners.[14]

The assassination provoked further economic worry, and international creditors began more carefully to scrutinize the Philippine economy. In the light of this new attention, the IMF discovered that the Central Bank has been overstating its currency reserves by between forty-two and fifty-eight percent.[15] Sensing disaster, investors shipped dollars abroad at a calamitous rate of 5 million a day before settling, in 1984, at a still-crippling 2 million per day average. The IMF suspended import credits and nearly 1,000 firms went bankrupt in the next year.[16] In response, Philippine businesses began sponsoring weekly protests, known as confetti demonstrations (after the shredded yellow telephone directories that cascaded from the skyscrapers).[17] While no activist organization initially coordinated these events, corporate resources sustained regular demonstrations, partly by closing offices and reconstituting workforces as movement bases. Not coincidentally, the canyons of office buildings in the Makati business district provided relatively safe, pleasant and familiar places from which employees could watch or join the activity.[18]

Spontaneous anti-regime protests persisted for months after the Aquino assassination, but established groups also expanded, working mainly through broad coalitions and sectoral organizations. In time, the demonstrations began to dwindle, and to attract fewer unorganized participants – but they did not end. Rather, organized forces that had previously *directed* spontaneous mass activity shouldered larger and larger demonstration burdens (for example, food and transportation costs) rather than merely planning events and hoping that people would show up. Protest forms shifted from mixed mass marches directly following Aquino's death, to demonstrations of more discrete participant categories – a phalanx of workers one day, youths on another, farmers on a third.[19] Protest thus grew more tractable for organization leaders, but also more expensive. Still, movement organizations were particularly successful in recruiting middle-class and elite activists following Aquino's assassination, and this new constituency underwrote repeated and sustained mobilizations around issues of democracy and regime brutality.[20]

---

[14] Fact-Finding Commission 1990: 120–122.
[15] De Dios 1988: 109–111.
[16] Hutchcroft 1998: 170–184; de Dios 1988: 120–122.
[17] Macaranza 1988: 39; Diokno 1988: 136–137; Tiglao 1988; Lindsey 1984: 1201–1204.
[18] Coronel 1993.
[19] Franco 2000; Thompson 1995.
[20] Diokno 1988.

As the crisis peaked, Marcos allowed repression to fall more heavily on legal and semi-legal dissidents.[21] Security forces fired upon Manila demonstrators on September 21, 1983. By the end of a constitutional referendum in January 1984, clashes between anti-referendum activists and security forces had killed eleven activists and injured thirteen others.[22] By mid-1984, authorities regularly repressed protest – mainly with teargas and truncheons, but sometimes also with bullets. Moreover, authorities seemed no longer clearly to distinguish between moderate or radical regime opponents, and even attacked one demonstration that included Catholic nuns and priests. The next day, newspapers related that, "Riot Police fired into the air and clubbed nuns and priests with rifle butts and truncheons." It would be hard to conceive of a more inflammatory story line. Still, repression was random *enough* that demonstrators did not always expect repression, and people were not frightened away from marches. Protest thus became a regular event, but increasingly mainstream participation made *periodic* state violence more shocking. As stronger resistance mobilized, cooperation within anti-dictatorship coalitions waxed and waned.[23]

Under earlier polarized conditions, moderates were torn between supporting the state and the radical left, and they often had to piggyback on more organized NDF efforts. By the mid-1980s, however, business associations, human rights offices, political parties and the Church hierarchy, as well as a mobilized public, provided stronger and more assertive bases for politically moderate anti-regime struggle.[24] Hence, the assassination both strengthened relations between left and centrist activists (by mobilizing the latter and orienting the former more strongly toward protest politics) and granted moderates the political strength to walk out on radical alliances without caving in to authorities. For instance, anti-dictatorship actors from Cardinal Sin to the NDF formed KOMPIL (*Kongresso ng Mamamayan Pilipino*, Congress of the Filipino People) to boycott 1984 elections, sparking the largest demonstrations since Aquino's funeral.[25] But KOMPIL's boycott consensus collapsed when several coalition centrists, including UNIDO,[26] PDP-LABAN, the Kalaw wing of the Liberal party, Cardinal Sin and Corazon Aquino decided to participate in the

---

[21] Clarke 1998: 172.
[22] *Reuters North European Service*, January 28, 1984.
[23] Crouch 1985: 7; Diokno, 1988.
[24] Consolacion 1983.
[25] Over a half million people welcomed a smaller delegation marching from Central Luzon to Manila. Soriano 1984.
[26] United Nationalist Democratic Organization.

elections.[27] Boycotting groups established an anti-election coalition CORD (Coalition of Organizations for the Restoration of Democracy) that included such anti-dictatorship luminaries as Diokno, Tañada, Aquino, former president Macapagal, and the Liberal Party's entire Salonga wing.[28] Through March and April, CORD held several powerful boycott demonstrations, highlighted by provincial marches leading to a large Manila rally. But opposition candidates also drew strong popular support. Corazon Aquino emerged as an effective campaigner and Cardinal Sin explicitly endorsed opposition candidates, to great effect. To guard against election-day cheating, the opposition revived NAMFREL (National Movement for Free Elections) organized with US support in the 1950s, but dormant for decades.[29] Despite violence, widespread government cheating, and limited media access, anti-Marcos candidates won 60 of 183 contested legislative seats, and 15 of the 21 in Manila.[30] Elections still divided Marcos opponents precisely as the President would have wished, but the divisions no longer forced moderates toward the New Society. *Both* opposition's center and the left were approaching political viability, and the dictator was hence as likely as anyone to be isolated by political polarization.

The electoral campaign, like the Aquino funeral the year before, provided a sanctioned framework for collective action that dissidents built on afterwards. Some of the largest and most violent events in May and June protested cheating – particularly in provincial cities like Cebu.[31] As the campaign faded, however, demonstrations once more depended on organizational resources more than on spontaneous mobilization, creating tactical flexibility at increased movement expense. NDF groups, for instance, led 700,000 people (nationally) in demonstrations on the anniversary of Aquino's murder. After the government released its account of the assassination on October 25, Agapito Aquino (Benigno's brother) led protests by NDF organizations, while Corazon Aquino led a less organized, more diverse protest. Overall, 10,000 people demonstrated on that day. Prompted by the confetti rallies that began around this time, NDF groups held several surprise demonstrations in Makati (also supported by contributions from business people). Labor unions coordinated their strikes across sectors, and when fuel and commodity prices rose in 1984, transportation workers struck from October 22–23. But workers

---

[27] Thompson 1995: 124.
[28] Franco 2000; Diokno 1988.
[29] Byington 1988.
[30] Franco 2000; Thompson 1995: 125–131; Kessler 1984.
[31] Franco 2000.

responding to organizational directives also struck concerning issues that did not directly touch on livelihood issues. In 1985, for instance, as corruption linked to the Bataan nuclear power plant came to light, the NDF's Bataan labor network paralyzed that province's export processing zone with a strike that freed workers to demonstrate at the plant site.[32]

With organizations shouldering greater mobilization expenses, activists had more reason to establish broad movement coalitions, but these remained fragile. In 1985, CORD and Nationalist Alliance leaders began to meet with Liberals, Social Democrats and independent Socialists to form a "Convener's group" to plan what was to be an anti-dictatorship front of unprecedented breadth: BAYAN (*Bagong Alyansa Makabayan*, New Nationalist Alliance).[33] But the NDF was more isolated in its 1984 boycott campaign than at any time since 1978, and the rising urban mass movement made protest seem ever more crucial. Hence, despite agreements distributing coalition leadership positions among participating organizations, NDF delegates to the BAYAN conference elected members from their own organizations to virtually all positions.[34] The move stirred resentment among liberals, socialists and social democrats, many of whom abandoned the project and formed an alternative anti-dictatorship coalition called BANDILLA(*Bansang Nagkaisa sa Diwa at Layunin*, The Nation,Unified in Spirit and Purpose).[35] These moves deepened and ossified divisions between radical and moderate activists, and all positions on the opposition spectrum subsequently had an anti-dictatorship coalition to coordinate their mass organizations.[36]

BAYAN and BANDILLA committed their now formidable organizations to sustained protest, and almost any occasion sparked fresh demonstrations. When agricultural input prices rose in January 1985, farmers' organizations marched on Manila. Squatter organizations regularly protested community demolitions and labor unions struck against price increase. In 1985, movement organizations demonstrated on August 21 (Aquino's assassination), September 21 (the declaration of martial law) International Women's Day, Human Rights' Day, May 1. July 4 demonstrations denounced the US at its embassy, and during Holy Week, clergy members staged protests that equated the plight of the Filipino poor with Christ's passion. On February 19, Cardinal Sin denounced the government's policy of "deliberate brutality and senseless violence" at protests.

[32] Macaranza 1988.
[33] Weekley 1996.
[34] Rocamora 1994; Abinales 1988.
[35] Villegas 1985: 130–131; Boudreau 2001.
[36] KSP 1984.

Aquino's widow Corazon more forcefully condemned state violence, and moderate, middle-class dissent blossomed. On April 17, after military men killed an Italian priest in North Cotobato, 300 priests and nuns demonstrated outside Camp Crame in Metro Manila. Other human rights' violations (when the military killed twenty in Escalante, or a reporter in Davao on September 23, or when the police fired into a crowd of demonstrators on October 21) triggered some of the largest anti-regime protests, and deepened elite support for the anti-dictatorship movement.

As pressure mounted, the regime's international support also waned. US officials wished to avoid the mistakes of Iran and Nicaragua, where they over-committed to faltering regimes that were soon eliminated by revolution.[37] Since a moderate and capitalist anti-dictatorship movement had emerged in Manila, US policy makers had clearer policy alternatives in the Philippines than in either Nicaragua or Iran.[38] US support for Benigno Aquino had been ambiguous before his death, but the late Senator also had friends on Capital Hill, and a substantial PDP-LABAN lobby formed in Washington after his death. As the US position began to waver, Marcos finally made his move. Drawing on his standard plan for dividing the opposition, he scheduled presidential elections for early 1986. Significantly, Marcos revealed this plan on American television, perhaps more to appease Washington than his own population.

Several early developments suggested that the 1986 election could not be stolen as deftly as those in the past. The US pressed the regime for free and fair elections (although President Reagan and the Pentagon remained more committed to Marcos) and gave some support to NAMFREL and (more quietly) to opposition candidates. The US Embassy also kept in touch with a group of officers (largely Philippine Military Academy graduates) who had set up the Reform Armed Forces Movement (RAM) ostensibly to promote democracy, but mainly to protect Philippine Military Academy graduates from the growing influence of General Ver and political appointees inside the AFP. RAM's activity further restricted Marcos's room to maneuver.[39]

The Epifanio delos Santos Avenue protests

The confrontation between Marcos and his opponents built through the 1985–1986 campaign, and ended in massive Manila street protests

---

[37] Bonner 1988; Thompson 1995.
[38] Staff Report Prepared for the use of the Senate Select Committee in Intelligence 1985.
[39] McCoy 1999: 230–234; Villegas 1985: 124–126.

between February 23 and 27. As in 1984, the movement's different flanks disagreed on how to engage elections and who would lead the struggle's final act. After the failed BAYAN conference, the two opposition wings were almost as wary of one another as of Marcos, and those tensions informed the debate about whether to boycott the 1986 elections.[40] Once more, elections divided the opposition, but moderate political forces were even stronger in 1986 than in 1984 – and the regime was weaker. Following CPP directives, the NDF called its members to boycott the elections, while Liberals, Social Democrats, Democratic Socialists and even some dissident NDs supported the PDP-LABAN ticket of Corazon Aquino and Salvadore Laurel.[41] Provincial protest had expanded between 1981 and 1985, and paved the way for Aquino's rowdy and mass mobilizing presidential campaign. But Aquino also enjoyed strong support from NAMFREL, the Catholic Church, the Philippine Business community, and (more obliquely) the RAM.

The protests that ended the Marcos regime began almost immediately after the polls closed, when PDP-LABAN activists began planning a civil disobedience and consumer boycott campaign.[42] Poll counters (many married to young RAM officers) exposed regime cheating, and locked themselves inside the Commission on Elections headquarters. The NDF announced plans for a national strike, and newspapers openly reported electoral fraud. As domestic and international opinion turned against the regime, members of the military, particularly inside RAM, moved against the government. Defense Minister Juan Ponce Enrile and Philippine Constabulary Commander Fidel Ramos planned to replace Marcos with a military Junta, but General Ver's agents discovered the plot. Exposed, vulnerable, and besieged inside Camp Aguinaldo, Enrile and Ramos crossed the EDSA(Epifanio delos Santos Avenue) highway to the more logistically crucial Philippine Constabulary Headquarters in Camp Crame, and appealed to Archbishop Jaime Cardinal Sin for help.[43]

Sin used the Catholic Church's *Radio Veritas* to call citizens to support the besieged generals. Political organizations involved in the Aquino campaign viewed the rebellion as backing their own protests, and soon tens of thousands streamed to the highway dividing the camps.[44] But the uprising was not primarily an organized event. Religious communities came in parish groups or convents. Students came in classroom clusters,

---

[40] Rivera 1985.
[41] Weekley 1996.
[42] Macaranza 1988: 48.
[43] The best scholarly treatment of the coup conspiracy is McCoy 1999.
[44] Magno 1986.

joined by neighborhood cohorts and families. The rally built upon networks mobilized during the election, and reinforced by earlier dissent from journalists, ballot counters, teachers, and the clergy. In the rebellion's first days, Marcos (or possibly Ver) ordered attacks against protesters – but soldiers refused. In any case, field officers who would have been most useful against the demonstration were *least* likely to support Ver or to turn against Ramos.[45] Demonstrations greeted soldiers with religious images, prayer, and explicitly peaceful overtures; as military men began to side with the anti-Marcos assembly, intoxicating mass celebrations broke out. When a helicopter gunship fired at Malacañang, Marcos gave in and fled the Philippines aboard a US military helicopter on February 27.[46]

The coup plotters never intended to support an Aquino presidency. But with nearly a million people in the streets demanding that Aquino be sworn in, and celebrating Enrile and Ramos for making that possible, the would-be generalissimos swallowed the pill, announced their support for Aquino's presidency, and accepted positions in the new government. Many who joined the new regime had been officials under Marcos, and switched sides at the last minute, but others among the anti-dictatorship activists, particularly economic and political elites marginalized by the New Society, had substantial political plans and skills. Hence the centrist, yellow movement, more than any other force, set the initial terms of the transition.

Thinking about the Philippine transition

Interpretations of Marcos's demise often stress the *discontinuity* between the normal politics of New Society repression (Marcos as shrewdly calculating, society as largely contained and controlled) and the dynamically explosive end game.[47] In important ways, however, the 1986 rebellion depended on developments *continuously* in play since the regime's inception. Marcos's plan for snap elections in 1985 resembled those he had followed all along, and were designed to exorcize moderates' political ambitions while dividing them from radicals. The strategy failed, however, because the complex of movement organizations that initiates the EDSA protests had steadily grown during the dictatorship. Organization had been important to the underground left since the early 1970s, but after 1981 all opposition tendencies deepened and expanded their organizations, rendering even centrist regime opponents more capable of

---

[45] McCoy 1999; Nemenzo 1987.
[46] Arillo 1986: 82–83.
[47] See Johnson 1987; Komisar 1987; Burton 1989.

creating their own opportunities and directing mass energies against specific targets. The combination of open resistance (backed by formidable elite opponents) and an armed insurgency derailed authorities' anti-opposition strategy. Liberal reforms encouraged protest and opposition participation in open political arenas; stronger state repression and aborted reform pushed moderates to sharper dissent and provided the NDF with new recruits. The financial crisis broadened support for the movement, making centrists more autonomous from the revolutionary left and more able to resist regime overtures.

As the opposition expanded, moderates began pursuing activity (protest, demonstration, movement building and even terrorism) once associated only with radicals, and the NDF built mass legal organizations. Suddenly movement organizations along the liberal and social democratic flank could decide, as insurgents did, how and when to strike, and regularly protested. As the struggle accelerated, the entire trope of resistance radicalized to favor revolution, avoid co-optation, and invest in organization.[48] In this climate, authorities could no longer sort the radical left from the political center by moving against specific forms of struggle. As both moderate and radical organizations grew and occupied overlapping tactical territory, Marcos lost his ability to play either side against the other, even when the opposition could not unite on a single anti-dictatorship program.

Because organizational decisions strongly shaped Philippine protest, movement ideas and strategies mediated activists' responses to external political events, creating diverse but more constant mobilization across the ideological spectrum.[49] Liberals and Social Democrats believed the transition would occur through some combination of protest and electoral struggle, and were most active around elections, surrounding the Aquino assassination, and in efforts to utilize and expand participatory rights. National Democrats thrived on events that polarized society between the state and its radical opposition, such as when participatory opportunities ebbed or repression increased, and used protest to generate support for the armed struggle. Less organized forces often reserved their protest for moments of moral outrage, when regime violence or duplicity were particularly salient. Hence, whatever authorities did, some section of the opposition was likely to mobilize.

Protest organizations also mediated the relationship between opposition elites and mass strata, with important consequences for contention.

[48] Boudreau 1996.
[49] Rivera 1985.

Movements typically incorporated mass demands for land reform, higher wages, and even regional autonomy into multi-faceted anti-dictatorship programs, and independent working-class protests seldom lasted for long without attracting organizers from established and multi-class movement networks. Indeed, aggrieved communities often assumed that contacting more experienced national activists was part of the mobilization process.[50] Connections between movement summits and bases also steered mass members in directions that did not threaten movement elites' economic and class privileges. In the National Democratic Movement, the ostensibly temporary synthesis of mass and elite interests was explicitly called the National Democratic "phase," in which local capitalists displaced imperialists; only in subsequent socialist phases would domestic capital and proletarian interests directly clash.[51] Outside the ND movement, the synthesis of mass and elite interests was less formally theorized, and more a tacit promise that anti-dictatorship struggles would trigger a post-dictatorship golden age of just social and economic relations. Everywhere, however, the organization-mediated harmony between mass and elite interests-in-struggle, meant that *all* movement activists viewed *any* political or economic crisis as undermining the state and so benefiting the movement. In pressing a foundering Marcos regime, economic elites and business people seemed never to fear mass anger, or to think of moderating their anti-regime statements to prevent anarchy in the streets. Mass anger was reliably mass *base* anger, linked to organizational leadership and discipline. Protest virtually never deteriorated into looting and rioting, or turned against secondary targets of opportunity such as Chinese traders. Indeed, many anti-dictatorship elites were themselves Mestizo Chinese, justifiably confident in their ability to rally populations against Marcos. Hence, the mobilization of movement energies against Marcos was utterly unconflicted and committed, for even elite activists never seemed to anticipate that their actions would have *socially* revolutionary consequences.

The prominence of social and economic elites in this anti-dictatorship complex had several other striking effects. Besides wielding substantial movement organizations, elite activists had other resources: friends in Washington or links to foreign investors. Many were prominent politicians before martial law, or had won positions in Marcos-era assemblies. Others were lawyers, professors, writers or priests, whose activism carried

---

[50] See, for instance, how BISIG (*Bukluran sa Ikauunlad ng Soyalistang Isip at Gawa*, The Federation for the Advancement of Socialist Theory and Praxis) typically recruited new community groups in Boudreau 2001: 38–42.

[51] Guerrerro 1979.

a striking sense of entitlement and self-assurance. From the outset, they imagined themselves, rather than Marxists or reformers within the state, as Marcos's successor.[52] When defectors from the state approached the movement, activists did not defer to the new arrivals, or strongly hope for internal state reform. Defectors were assumed to be joining the movement, and submitting themselves to movement authority. Hence the February-coup plotters, once discovered and vulnerable, had few options other than to come out for Aquino.

Movement elites' moderation and stature also made it easier for former state officials to support demonstrations. State defectors and movement leaders often were sociologically similar – graduates of the same universities, members of the same fraternities, often linked to the same families.[53] While the struggle pushed many activists toward revolutionary rhetoric and socially transforming programs, these positions partly resembled promises that Philippine politicians had made since the first mass-mobilizing elections, and could be regarded as safely empty rhetoric. People fleeing Marcos's sinking ship could trust that the transition would still leave them on rather comfortable ground. If there was any doubt of this, the relationship between the movement's leadership and its left flank helped clarify things. As the movement grew more internally divided in the 1980s, the basic animosities between Marxists and liberal reformers reasserted themselves, and probably assured Marcos defectors that the transition would have limited social consequences.

These considerations lend the climactic Philippine anti-dictatorship protests their distinctiveness. The emergence of an elite and moderate movement leadership commanding strong mass support meant that protest was a safe and effective weapon against the state – and organization leaders intensified their resistance at every opportunity. Movement elites' social standing, and organizational control also helps to explain why disenchanted state officials joined up, rather than attempting to broker or initiate internal reform. Movement elites and state reformers were available to one another outside the regime, in what was *for both* the relatively congenial vessel of a liberal and peaceful anti-dictatorship movement. This movement could advance itself as the new regime, and approached the transition through demonstrations rather than violent confrontation. Without moderate protest that engaged participatory opportunities (i.e. elections) and movement organizations that were powerful and credible to disaffected state actors, the regime's decay

---

[52] Anderson 1988.
[53] Wurfel 1988; Thompson 1995: 153.

might well have polarized society between authorities and the armed left, and officials almost certainly would have closed ranks against the movement. As things transpired, interactions between the repressive state and its society created an organized but liberal anti-dictatorship option that state defectors could support, and this made all the difference.

9   Protest and the underground in Burma

Several months after the September 1988 coup installed the military State Law and Order Restoration Committee (SLORC) in Burma, Intelligence Chief Khin Nyunt held a series of press conferences, largely in English for expatriate journalists and diplomats to set forth the regime's account of the 1988 democracy protests. The conferences seemed laughable and received substantial ridicule from anti-regime activists and foreign observers. One conference exposed a *rightist* conspiracy in which secret cells and subversive foreigners worked against the regime. The next unmasked a *leftist* underground conspiracy to overthrow the state. At each event, SLORC presented a lengthy narrative of the 1988 protests, augmented with biographical dossiers on key conspirators, in what seemed obvious and clumsy propaganda.[1] That the press conferences occurred at all is notable, for Ne Win never cared much what the outside world (save immediate neighbors) thought. But few beyond the new government's thrall seemed even to consider the possibility that the state reports had any basis.

Neither, however, do alternative descriptions explain the events. Such accounts often attribute movement power to its leaders (like Nobel Laureate Aung San Suu Kyi and Generals Aung Gyi and Tin Oo), to widespread economic crisis and currency demonetization, to regime brutality, to foreign radio broadcasts and even to the auspiciousness of the August 8, 1988 (8–8–88) demonstration date. As a group, these positions share an important feature: they all argue that protest blossomed *spontaneously* from the righteous anger of a society pushed to the brink. There are, of course, political reasons why a spontaneous cry for democracy is an appealing frame for the protests, and why Burmese might choose to package the movement as unorganized. Burmese citizens were deservedly angry at their country's economic collapse and the government's reliable brutality and determined autocracy. But accounts of largely spontaneous activism fail to explain the movement's extraordinary

---

[1] Khin Nyunt 1988a; Khin Nyunt 1988b.

190

level of coordination, and the remarkably similar, sophisticated tactics that its branches adopted in very short order. Across Burma, strike committees formed, adopted the same symbols, published strike newspapers, made similar speeches, and coordinated activity. That a society with no protest experience for over a decade could achieve such organization *spontaneously* makes little sense.

The extended interplay between state repression and social response perhaps provides a context to help assess these competing interpretations. Anti-regime protests under Ne Win often began with an economic crisis sparking synchronized anti-state mobilizations, and so providing cover for subsequent, more organized activists working in the particular, Burmese version of underground cells.[2] Cell members or veterans directed protest along more politically pointed and powerful channels. In this light, might we take a less dismissive approach to SLORC reports? Interviews that I conducted with 1988 movement veterans suggest that underground activists in fact played important roles in the 1988 protests, particularly after June. Moreover, these informants tended to confirm many press conference details. As one put it, "The problem with the SLORC intelligence is not its minor details, but the larger argument that underground cells acted under central party supervision. Those ties were disrupted in the 1960s, and the party neglected the urban arena ever since. But you must take claims of UG involvement seriously."[3] This chapter does not depend on the SLORC press conferences, but on interviews conducted inside Burma during 1998, and with exiled activist leaders both before and after that research visit. Still, the interviews suggest that as protest spread and progressed, organized or semi-organized underground collectives increasingly shaped it.

Burmese democracy protests passed through several distinct phases in 1988. Violent state action during what began as an apolitical March disturbance, under conditions of simmering resentment against authorities immediately provoked strong university student protests, followed by predictably violent repression. In days, unrest moved from the campuses to the neighborhoods, and to several nearby cities. But the movements' leadership remained unorganized and inexperienced, and demonstrations spread largely through word of mouth. Authorities closed the campuses in late March, and sent students home for an enforced vacation. When schools reopened in June, students resumed anti-government protests – but the movement had changed, marking a new phase in the

[2] Smith 1997: 367–368.
[3] Interview B–13 (transcribed from notes immediately following the interview). Smith (1999: 367–373) makes this same point, relying in part on interviews with BCP cadres.

conflict. An entirely new leadership controlled the protests, emphasizing meetings, organization, and more explicitly *political* demands. Movement practice acquired more uniformity, and strike committees emerged as its main instrument, even in far-flung places. Activity accelerated over the weeks that followed, particularly when Ne Win and then his successor, Sein Lwin, resigned. But as strike committees multiplied and state authorities withdrew in August, something else happened. More organized and experienced activists began losing control of the movement, and the resulting confusion set the stage for a state counterstrike and the re-imposition of authoritarian rule. This chapter explores these phases of the democracy movement, and their relationship to established patterns of state repression and social response.

Early protest, spontaneous mobilization and state repression

By 1987, Burmese authorities faced acute and mounting financial pressure that they had avoided for decades of socialist isolation. Burma then had a staggering 3.5 billion dollar debt and currency reserves of only between 20 and 30 million dollars; debt service ratios stood at over fifty percent of the national budget.[4] Sustained counterinsurgency required continued involvement in the international market, and insured that the government would try to meet these obligations, however difficult they were. To ease the burden, the government secured Least Developed Country (LDC) status from the United Nations Economic and Social Council, and also required farmers to sell their harvests below market prices, to create greater revenues through resale on the international market. That latter policy deepened rural resentment and led to several violent rural protests.[5] At that point, Retired Brigadier General Aung Gyi wrote an open letter, reminding Ne Win of 1967 rice riots, and suggesting broad economic reforms.[6] At a BSPP conference on August 10, Ne Win responded by speculating that the Burmese Way to Socialism was conceptually flawed. The government deregulated trade in important agricultural products, including rice and beans on September 1.[7] Soon after these apparent concessions to Burmese producers, however, authorities demonetized 25, 35 and 75 Kyat notes, and redirected foreign reserves into debt repayment. The policy devastated sections of society more

[4] Lintner 1989: 94–95.
[5] Yitri 1989.
[6] Aung Gyi 1988a.
[7] Aung Gyi 1988b.

involved in the cash economy or with cash savings – including university students preparing to pay their tuition.[8]

Almost immediately, students at the Rangoon Institute of Technology (RIT) ran riot through town, smashing glass and traffic lights along the Insein road.[9] In response, Rangoon universities closed and sent students home. Larger Mandalay protests involved more monks and workers, and participants burned several government buildings, ransacked state cooperatives and smashed cars from a local fire brigade.[10] While the highly regulated media reported little of these events, students sent home carried news of the protests. When schools reopened in late October, underground campus groups in Rangoon and Mandalay published dissident pamphlets. In November, university students in Arakan and Pyinmana demonstrated several times and some bombs exploded in Rangoon. On December 11, Voice of America (VOA) and BBC broadcasts reported the UNDP's earlier decision to grant Burma LDC status, which underscored the depth of government mismanagement.[11] Soon, police in Mandalay received threatening letters from underground groups, and small, elusive protests flickered around the RIT campus and its surrounding neighborhoods.[12]

These protests, though significant, mainly set the stage for what followed. In March 1988, students in a Rangoon tea shop argued with out-of-school youths about the music playing on the sound system. A brawl followed, in which security forces arrested, then released a youth charged with injuring a student. The next day, students protested at the local police department, and authorities shot and killed one of their number. The next day, more students marched and rallied at the RIT, but protests soon spread to other Rangoon campuses.[13] One Rangoon University (RU) student recalls rounding up ten classmates on March 14 and setting off to investigate events at RIT. At the rally, he encountered other RU students (with whom, however, he had never discussed politics) and gained an initial sense of their group as *activists*. They marched back to RU, took up positions where students normally congregated, and denounced government brutality at RIT. Thus, the movement came to RU.[14]

---

[8] Mya Maung 1992: 93–135.
[9] Nyi Nyi Lwin 1992.
[10] Interview B–6. The informant was a Mandalay lawyer whose original movement activity involved assisting those arrested in these anti-demonetization protests.
[11] BBC's Summary of World Broadcasts (henceforth SWB) December 12, 1987.
[12] Lintner 1989: 95–97.
[13] Smith 1999: 1–14.
[14] Interview B–2.

For early participants, it mattered immensely that RIT lay just down the road from RU, for they could walk between campuses and spread news of the events. Because campus political organizations did not exist and early leaders were inexperienced, collective action identified potential comrades and fostered solidarity and courage. At RU, those who spoke that first day acquired status and celebrity, at least through the end of March. Yet their inexperience was also on display. Activist speeches expressed discontent in very personal terms, describing how demonetization wiped out family savings, or their humiliation about living in the newest LDC. Yet the discussion produced few *political* proposals or action points.[15]

On March 15, riot police (*Lon Htein*) moved into RIT to arrest students. The next day, students from RU set off for RIT campus to lend support, but met *Lon Htein* crouched in ambush near a small white bridge at Inya lake. The information we have about what transpired next comes primarily from a letter that Brigadier General Aung Gyi wrote to Ne Win, which others cite at length.[16] The soldiers opened fire on the advancing students, shooting even those swimming away or scrambling ashore. Police piled wounded students several deep in a sweltering paddy wagon, where they remained for an inexplicable four hours during what should have been a brief ride to Insein Prison. Eventually, the government admitted that forty-one students died on that journey, but originally it owned up to just two casualties.[17] Perhaps 200 more died at the white bridge, after which troops occupied the RU campus. With no political vehicles at their disposal, and scant protest experience to draw on, students resurrected the model that Ne Win destroyed in his rise and organized a new Rangoon Student Union the next day. (In contrast, Filipino activists *constantly* reinvented their organizations, and showed little interest in reviving past efforts.) That same day, occupying troops arrested around 1,000 more RU students.

As troops descended on the campuses, activists fled to the city, and people from working-class neighborhoods joined in. In immediate consequence, demonstrations grew larger but also more dispersed, for new

[15] The RU student who first visited RIT demonstrations explains: "At the start of all this, we were very young and inexperienced. When I stood to make a speech, it was mainly about how I felt, about the frustrations I had at the government and my difficulties as a student." Interview B-2. See also interview with activist Nyi Nyi Lwin, who describes how older students had to explain about earlier demonstrations in 1962 and 1975. Nyi Nyi Lwin 1992: 16.

[16] Aung Gyi 1988b; Lintner 1989. Smith cites other sources who also confirm these stories of brutal and determined violence. Smith 1999: 2.

[17] *Burma Watcher* 1989: 175.

participants ceased to relate only to the university campuses, and Rangoon landmarks like the Shwedagon and Sule Pagodas also became sites of struggle.[18] Protest grew more rambunctious and less manageable for the loose student leadership. On March 18, demonstrators torched government facilities (state stores, offices, and automobiles) near Sule Pagoda and the *Lon Htein* began shooting demonstrators. Headstrong high-school students and workers returned fire with rocks, firebombs and other projectiles, drawing infuriated police and army units into one-sided battles that killed scores more activists in several Rangoon neighborhoods. That evening, the government closed schools and universities and announced plans to ship students back to their home villages and cities. Despite a few small protests, the March uprising essentially ended on that Bloody Friday.

It is difficult to pin down precise casualty figures for these events. In several of his open letters to Ne Win, Retired Brigadier General Aung Gyi claimed that 283 died in the March protests. He reiterated this figure in his later narrative of the Inya lake slaughter and of torture in Insein gaol.[19] An AP wire report cited diplomatic estimates that over 3,000 protesters were arrested, particularly noting that hundreds of Muslim students of Indo-Burmese origin, not involved in the protests, were also detained.[20] Bertil Lintner put the death toll near 300, and offers graphic evidence that the slaughter was systematic.[21]

Hiatus, movement spread and organization

When schools closed at the end of March, authorities shipped students home to prevent angry and idle youths from loitering around the tea shops, looking for trouble. Yet the remove from Rangoon did little to assuage student anger, and those who traveled home (as in 1987) carried stories of repression and resistance. Provincial populations would have had a vague idea that something had transpired in the city, but media sources predictably described the unrest as hooliganism, and denied that serious casualties occurred. Indeed, the only clear initial evidence of the violence was the homeward flow itself. But students bore stories of Inya Lake and Bloody Friday across Burma, and so authorities' desire for

---

[18] See Sein Win, 1988.
[19] Aung Gyi 1988a (June 9). Aung Gyi's August 6, 1988c contains more detail about military atrocities in March, and a particularly vivid perspective on how methodically Burmese troops beat protesters to death.
[20] AP Wire Report, June 23, 1988.
[21] Lintner 1989.

peace in the capital helped overcome the fragmented communication and transportation networks that often limited social unrest. Student return-ees also brought experience and a perspective on struggle to rural communities that may not directly have experienced demonstrations in decades. They re-introduced the Rangoon University Student Union, with its familiar independence-era fighting peacock, and explained how marches and demonstrations worked, rekindling a long dormant activist spark.[22]

The full influence of these student returnees would not be apparent for several months. When protests eventually spread to the countryside in late July and August, students from larger cities established strike com-mittees and organized demonstrations that closely paralleled urban activ-ity. The absence of opposition institutions, however, made it hard to trust any new arrival in town, particularly those claiming to represent move-ment collectives, or urging local residents to action; such emissaries could as well be spies ferreting out movement sympathizers and democracy activists. Returned students, however, could quiz new arrivals about mutual friends or shared experiences, and were also among the first to contact activist leaders in larger cities concerning movement develop-ments or plans:

At first, nobody believed (that a new arrival was really a student). You have to ask a lot of questions. In our state, we had some students who studied in Mandalay and in Rangoon (who had been sent home). So if somebody said he was from Mandalay, students from Mandalay in our town would ask them a lot of ques-tions: Who do you know? Where do you study?[23]

Hence, returning students represented a foundation for movement building that allowed Rangoon and Mandalay protests to nationalize.

But students also spent the interval between March and June learning from current and former underground activists. It bears repeating that Burmese cells were seldom linked to a party structure or to movement organizations, for neither existed in the lowlands cities, and frontier insurgencies were too involved in battlefield struggles to take much account of urban politics.[24] State repression had eliminated protest since 1976, and even underground groups had done little since then beyond publishing rare pamphlets and preserving dissident knowledge.[25] Not surprisingly, then, the Burmese underground had diverse origins and

---

[22] Interview B–18. See also published interview with student leader Kyaw Kyaw Htut 1992.
[23] Taped interview B–16 with Maung Win, in Washington, 1997.
[24] Smith 1999: 367–373.
[25] Aye Saung 1989.

orientations. Some cells contained independent social critics who read and discussed Marxist literature, while others had more precise sympathy for the BCP (i.e. detainees released after years in prison, or cadres returned from frontier camps or Chinese study tours). Still others were not Marxists at all, but liberals associated with the 1974–1976 U Thant events.[26] These activists helped to preserve knowledge and experience scattered by state repression. After the school closings, interactions between activists and underground cells changed protest utterly.

Particularly in Mandalay, movement leaders recognized underground activists they had known as NUF members in the late 1950s. A strike committee leader living near Mandalay recalls that, "A couple of local underground people were at the center of the movement. I knew these people years ago as BCP activists, and they hung around the village ever since."[27] A senior advisor to the Rangoon movement described the underground as a loose circle of experienced activists, most effective as teachers:

In 1988, students approached (underground activists) including myself, for leadership and support. Remember that Burma is a country with no recent tradition of open struggle. When the demonstrations began, students had very little idea what to do, and didn't even know where to acquire this knowledge.[28]

Students sought activists with experience, even as underground cells sought out students with energy. Htun Aung Kyaw, a veteran of the non-communist demonstrations in 1975 and 1976, taught protest strategy and tactics: how to distribute leaflets on the sly, or how to hold small and lower-risk lightning rallies:

(Students) came to me in June, when things were rolling along. I told them how we started the movement – how to use the media, how to organize people using issues of economic hardship, political freedom. The slogans, I told them, had to be short, precise and to the point so people will understand. I told them to form small and closely linked groups, with four or five people to a cell, and then each cell member should organize one additional cell. I told them also how to use a cipher.[29]

Renewed protest

On May 30, schools and universities reopened. Students who returned to classes were newly angry, for the government had just released the account of Bloody Friday that acknowledged a mere three casualties.

---

[26] Recorded interview with Htun Aung Kyaw August 1997.
[27] Interview B–4 (Transcript made from notes immediately following an interview.)
[28] Interview B–12. Earlier in the discussion, the informant had taken great pains to explain that the underground networks were no longer attached to the BCP.
[29] Interview with Htun Aung Kyaw August, 1997 (taped).

Crowds gathered on most Rangoon campuses and leaflets appeared almost immediately (an early sign of clandestine preparations). Activists arrested in March began to return to universities, describing torture and hardship, but also with new connections to those they met in jail. Against this backdrop, Aung Gyi issued another open letter to Ne Win, this one containing shocking details of the March repression (including eyewitness reports of the Inya Lake slaughter, and an accusation of state premeditation, and an estimate that 283 had died).[30] The campuses were ripe for unrest, but most March leaders remained in jail.

Other signs indicated that students were also more organized and politicized than before. Demonstrations resumed at RU on June 15, when activists with covered faces burst into a crowd near the campus center, and delivered a well-informed speech. Years later, *March* leaders recalled wondering who these new activists were, and where they came from. Where earlier speakers mainly expressed personal anger and frustration, May and June speeches featured data on Burma's economic decline and about other anti-dictatorship struggles. New activists decried human rights' violations and used speeches to announce plans for political demonstrations.[31] (The initial leadership had of necessity been fairly open, making decisions at anarchic public meetings, usually following some persuasive speaker's suggestion; in June, nobody seemed to know who planned things.) Similarly, the idea of a strike committee as the movement's basic unit arose at this time, but nobody from the March leadership knew from whence it came. Small lightning rallies flashed across the capital's streets, and leaflets regularly appeared – but at whose initiative? By June 16, all Rangoon universities had protests, and students busied themselves organizing committees and linking campuses together. Masked speakers continued to emerge suddenly from crowds. Some, like Maung Maung Kyaw, were recognizable March leaders;[32] others were unknown even to prominent March activists.[33]

On June 20 and 21, larger but more scattered demonstrations occurred in Rangoon, in part prompted by the Education Ministry's decision to close Rangoon University.[34] These actions posed new difficulties for security forces. Individual neighborhoods became centers of activity,

---

[30] Aung Gyi 1988a. In part, the letter ran: "The lady students suffered the worst beatings at Inya Bund. Some were dragged by their hair and beaten; some jumped into the lake, and upon clambering back, were beaten."

[31] Interview B–2, from notes transcribed immediately following the interview.

[32] Lintner 1989: 104.

[33] Informant B–13 was an RU student and B–2 was a medical student. Both recall initial confusion at the new June leaders.

[34] Smith 1999: 4.

and repression that previously concentrated on university buildings now had to contain entire sections of the city. Confrontations now played out in full public view and rallied support to the movement. When riot police attacked marchers on the 20th, protesters answered with jinglees (sharpened, poisoned bicycle spokes, fired through a slingshot). Almost 100 people died in the exchange, over 20 of them on the government side.[35] On June 21, students marching near Myenigone Market met *Lon Htein* forces and scattered into the neighborhoods, while residents held soldiers off. Elsewhere, smaller bands of demonstrators roamed the streets, dodging the *Lon Htein*, firing jinglees, and shouting demands. Students briefly regrouped at the Shwedagon Pagoda, but were dispersed. Battles between Rangoon residents and security forces lasted through the night, ending late on June 21. Security forces captured hundreds more students and imposed a sixty-day curfew. By then, authorities could no longer end protest by closing the campuses. They had to shut down Rangoon itself.

As support for the movement broadened, student (and underground) abilities to control things generally diminished.[36] June 21 most pitched battles, for instance, occurred while student leaders discussed strategy and organization at Rangoon's Institute of Medicine, and they barely prevented a crowd outside the meeting from killing a government agent captured in their midst.[37] Other towns began anti-regime activity, largely prodded by Rangoon students sent home in March (only thirty percent of whom returned in May).[38]

As in March, police and military agents brought hundreds of activists to Insein Prison, temporarily ending protests. Again, however, the end of movement activity initiated a period of organizing both inside the prisons and without. In the prisons, differences between March and June detainees jelled into factional divides, and both groups developed more cohesiveness than they might have on the outside.[39] Released after July 7, they rejoined the movement as powerful activist collectives. Outside prison, underground organizers redoubled efforts to forge stronger connections with cities and villages outside Rangoon. From late June to the end of

---

[35] *Bangkok Post*, June 29, 1988.
[36] Interview B–7 (transcribed from notes directly following the interview).
[37] Lintner 1989: 108–110.
[38] Moksha Yitri (a pseudonym for a Burmese activist) writes that, "Some student activists had also gone to Pegu, a town 50 miles to the northeast, and the ensuing protests there caused the deaths of a number of police personnel in addition to demonstrators shot and killed." Yitri 1989: 546.
[39] Interview B–2, transcribed from notes immediately following the interview.

July, delegations from Rangoon collectives spread across the countryside to recruit support.[40]

On July 7, Ne Win called a special BSPP congress, a meeting that would produce a potent combination of outrage and hope, making demonstrations between late July and mid-August the most volatile since before 1962. At the congress, Ne Win announced the release of detained students, and admitted that forty-two had died in police custody that March day. He forcefully restated his earlier reservation about the *Burmese Way to Socialism*, admitted personal responsibility for March and June shootings, and in a stunning conclusion, resigned from the party and government. He also suggested that a national referendum on multi-party democracy might resolve the political crisis.[41] But the dictator also left grim legacies of his rule: Ne Win named *Lon Htein* commander Sein Lwin, the man most responsible for the June slaughter, as his successor, and then warned protesters to cease demonstrations, reminding them that, "When the army shoots, it shoots to hit."[42] These events galvanized the movement in three ways. First, Ne Win's resignation made it clear that fundamental change was at least possible at the government's highest levels, inspiring hopes that the army might support calls for democracy.[43] Second, Sein Lwin's appointment redoubled social anger, and protest flared once more. Third, ironically and perhaps accidentally, Ne Win's referendum suggestion was the first public statement of multi-party democracy as a movement goal, and from that point forward, activists had a clear programmatic rallying point.[44] The hope for multi-party democracy also welded movement constituencies onto a single national

---

[40] Htun Aung Gyi's Freedom Fighters of Burma, for example, decided in mid-June to move to central and Northern Burma to build broader popular sympathy for the Rangoon movement: "Some of my friends went to Prome and some of my friends went to Mandalay and we tried to organize people, and tell them what is going on. Many groups did the same – lawyers' committees and workers' committees." Interview B–15 (taped).

[41] *Burma Watcher* 1989.

[42] Mya Maung 1990: 617.

[43] Informant B–9, who was a close advisor to Aung San Suu Kyi, recalls that this was one of her particular hopes: "Every day, she asked me, 'What's the news from Mandalay? What is the military doing? Have the military changed sides in Mandalay yet?' You see, they were expecting that the military would split, and that it would happen in Mandalay." Taped interview B–9.

[44] Informant B–12 recalls: The question of multi-party democracy was never one of the movement's agendas until Ne Win mentioned it in his speech. From the time he said that there would be discussions of multi-party democracy, this became part of the movement's agenda. We took up this theme, and soon it was in all of the strike papers and leaflets, and it passed from here to other towns as well." Interview B–12. Transcribed from notes.

framework more effectively than earlier student demands that expelled activists be reinstated and soldiers be punished for campus violence.

The 8–8–88 protests

As the movement developed stronger organizational capacities, underground cells became more active. One March leader recalls initial confusion, as underground influence grew more apparent:

> After that second wave of arrests, we began to hear rumors of some big action on August 8th, and I remember a big, secret meeting among all the different student groups sometime in the middle of July. At that meeting, we decided that the time wasn't ripe for a big mobilization, that we were not prepared organizationally...Afterwards, we all went into the countryside to build movement networks for a big mobilization drive in the future. When 8 August came, we were all so surprised when the mobilization went ahead, despite our agreement. There was only one person from the March leadership group left in Rangoon, so we all rushed back, but didn't get to the cities until days later. The groups most involved in that 8–8–88 demonstration were the ones I have associated with the communists – from the June leadership group.[45]

As underground influence increased, movement leaders began to make sharper decisions. Consider its interactions with BBC reporter Christopher Gunness. In July, Gunness interviewed Burmese activists who described how soldiers had raped women during the March protest, then announced that large national demonstrations would occur on the astrologically auspicious August 8. Activists on the air thus circulated a shocking story to Burma's furthest reaches, and then tied that story to a call for action – very sophisticated stuff. Yet at least one analyst has uncovered evidence that movement activists *invented* stories of rape to mobilize opinion against the regime.[46] Even Bertil Lintner, in an account consistently sympathetic with the democracy movement, includes a curious half-caveat when he describes those interviews: "One of the alleged victims was said to be the daughter of an army major. Whether that particular case was true or not was actually irrelevant. The rumor had

---

[45] Interview, B–2. Transcribed from notes.

[46] Kyaw Yin Hlaing (1996) interviewed many of the activists who went on the air with Gunness, and they admitted to fabricating some of the stories. Informant B–12 agrees: "I knew a lot about what was being planned and who was doing the planning, and I have talked a lot to the different movement participants since then, and nobody can say for sure who it was that decided on this date and made the announcement, and that's why I have assumed that it was the small group of people that were directly involved in the radio broadcast, and that that broadcast, more than anything else, was responsible for that demonstration and focusing the movement around those dates."

spread and people believed it."[47] For our purposes, the importance of these fabrications rests with the capacity of secret activist groups in late July to take movement-shaping decisions under cover of the broader contention. They used the media to advance movement goals in ways that sharply contrast with the suspicious aggression that led 1970s activists to smash reporters' cameras.[48]

Posters and pamphlets also appeared in Rangoon announcing the demonstrations, many bearing the fighting-peacock insignia of the underground All-Burma Students' Union. In Rangoon, the first strike committees (initially community defense committees) formed at this time on the advice of underground activists seeking to broaden the movement's base. By July, underground forces openly organized neighborhood committees. A Rangoon cell member describes the process: "When the students came onto the streets, leftist organizations tried to enter the field, and eventually began to lead the students and their movement in the strike committees. The movement thus became well organized and strike committees easily spread from one city to another."[49] Some strike committees were able to draw on influence that underground cells had cultivated among workers and monks in the 1980s.[50] As neighborhood defense committees became more prominent, they emerged in working-class neighborhoods, often following underground plans.[51] Between August 2 and 10, protest occurred in virtually every Burmese town of any size, using a relatively stable and consistent range of tactics and symbols: they synchronized marches, protected rally speakers, published movement newspapers and unfurled fighting-peacock banners.

In Rangoon, the first signs of movement resurgence occurred at the Shwedagon Pagoda on July 28, the Buddhist full moon of Waso. Student activists suddenly emerged from the crowd to denounce the government and urge support for new democracy demonstrations.[52] Protests blossomed over the next few days, with community defense groups and strike committees barricading and defending neighborhoods, coordinating information and mobilizing isolated townships for central demonstrations.

---

[47] Lintner 1989: 99.
[48] Soe Lwin 1992.
[49] Taped interview B-9.
[50] Taped interview B-9.
[51] Lintner dates these local movement committees in July, but describes them as spontaneously emerging in "almost every ward and township in Rangoon." Lintner 1989: 126. Informant B-2 recalls that students assigned by central strike committees to establish organizations in working-class communities often had great trouble dissuading these groups from using violence or looting. Interview B-2.
[52] Lintner 1989.

In many neighborhoods, strike committees built makeshift stages where movement activists addressed crowds of supporters, and to which people brought donations to support the rallies.

While activists' recent protest experience perhaps explains how Rangoon demonstrations mobilized so effectively, activists' speed and skill *outside* Rangoon is another matter. Demonetization produced small 1987 demonstrations in Mandalay, and people there followed Rangoon events with great interest, but without themselves undertaking similar protest. In August, however, Rangoon activists contacted Mandalay lawyers and monks (two categories of people with strong internal networks and some underground collectives as well) to urge them into activity. When news of the August demonstrations reached central Burma, the first Mandalay response came from a somewhat rough Buddhist monastery whose members demonstrated with others in a group soon known as the Galoni.[53] Students from local and Rangoon universities participated in the demonstrations, but these protests *began* off campus, and students never clearly took the helm.[54] The first August 8 demonstration march circled the town, stopping periodically for people to speak. The day's only casualty occurred at the corner of 28th and 84th Streets, when a frightened traffic policeman fired into the crowd, killing one and then fled. Marchers continued to a space called the 45 Hta Field, and erected a platform where monks and students made speeches. Such marches recurred almost daily until September 19.

The Mandalay strike committee formed on August 18, uniting forty-nine separate organizations, pulled together over the preceding days. While monks and students led earlier protests, lawyers organized the actual committee, beginning when the Mandalay Bar Council received a fax from its Rangoon counterpart.[55] The fax inspired one lawyer to spend the afternoon recruiting support among his colleagues, including many who (like himself) had been associated with the BCP or the BWPP. The next day, lawyers organized what was called the Opinion Taking General Assembly at the city's Centenary Grounds, where organized and experienced activists (many in underground collectives) took control. The Mandalay strike committee hence had a clearer and more political orientation than the Galoni, and soon forced the Galoni (in the words of one committee member) to stop making speeches full of

---

[53] Interview B–6, transcribed from notes.
[54] Many village strike committees followed the same pattern (taped interview B–16).
[55] Informant B–6 received that fax. As he had already made several speeches and was relatively certain that authorities could identify him, he decided to take a leading role in convincing Mandalay lawyers to join the protests. Interview B–6.

nonsense.[56] Afterward, debates concentrated on issues of multi-party democracy and human rights. The many lawyers and monks in the cohesive Mandalay leadership contrasted to the higher percentages of workers and slum residents in Rangoon's more decentralized and organizationally inchoate movement – and helps explain why Mandalay protests produced less violence and fewer casualties than those in Rangoon. Even before the Mandalay Strike Committee formed, however, organizers recruited support from nearby towns. For instance, organizers arrived at one medium-sized town about twenty kilometers from Mandalay on August 8, but made rambling, nonsensical speeches, rife with parochial attacks and personal complaints, and similar to those that Committee members ascribe to the Galoni monks. After the Opinion Taking General Assembly in Mandalay, new organizers arrived at that city, stressing, "concepts of multi-party democracy and democracy struggle . . . From then on, all speeches made in (the town) emphasized multi-party democracy, and the earlier emphasis on rumors and personality . . . began to fade."[57]

In smaller villages and cities across Burma, students and underground members returned from the cities to direct resident activities. One who left Mandalay for a town in central Burma recalls wanting only to stay home and study after March. Around August 10, however, village mates who had joined the Rangoon protests cajoled him into action – citing his responsibility as a student. Farmers were then so angry at taxation and marketing policies that the movement immediately won broad support – and perhaps 2,000 participated in August demonstrations, from a village of around 5,000 residents. Unlike Rangoon protests, these demonstrations began by building organizations,

> for this was the idea of students who had these committees in their city campuses, and also of local monks. We established committees for organization, for propaganda, and other tasks, but the strike committee's real work was to organize mobilizations and demonstrations.[58]

Soon, local students themselves sent organizers to surrounding villages, sometimes to establish strike committees, sometimes to spread news of demonstrations. By August 26, the village committees formed a township-level strike committee; when the local government threatened

---

[56] Interview B–6; informant B–4 makes the same point. Interview B–4, transcribed from notes.

[57] Interview B–7 transcribed from notes.

[58] Interview B–7 transcribed from notes.

reprisals, residents contacted the Galoni, who coerced administrators into giving way.[59]

An account from a Kayah state village presents an essentially similar story. Protests began when students returning from Mandalay and Rangoon shared their experiences, and began to lay plans. Activists soon formed a local strike committee, in part because some belonged to the underground All-Burma Students Union. Having formed the Kayah State Strike Committee, however, activists were at a loss as to what to do, when one member suggested contacting strike committees from larger towns:

We contacted some of the student-union organizations in Rangoon, especially those in the *ma ta ka* (All-Burma Student Union). There is a township between Mandalay and our home state, and we contacted their strike committee. Soon, some students came down to talk. We planned how we would engage the national strike, marching through the towns where we had established some strike committees. After, they sometimes sent down slogans and papers to distribute to people.[60]

Rangoon demonstrations began on July 30 and built steadily until August 8. On that day, hundreds of thousands converged on the downtown from diverse Rangoon neighborhoods each group marching under identifying banners – called forth by interviews broadcast over the BBC and the VOA. Marchers appealed to soldiers for support and encircled security forces to protect them from protesters' hostility – explicit and organized attempts to prevent earlier violence. By that first evening, however, soldiers opened fire on demonstrators, scattering them into smaller crowds that authorities pursued through the streets.[61] Protesters often remained close to their neighborhoods and defended themselves with rocks, firebombs and jinglees. On August 10, soldiers fired into the Rangoon General Hospital, killing nurses and doctors ministering to the wounded.[62] Protesters also grew more violent, at one point burning a police station and tearing apart four officers who fled the flames. On August 12, after days of violence in which as many as 2,000 died, Sein Lwin resigned.[63]

The resignation produced confusion across Burma, but also jubilation. Rangoon security forces exercised comparative caution, particularly in working-class neighborhoods that demonstrators almost entirely controlled.

---

[59] Interview B–6 transcribed from notes.
[60] Taped interview B–16.
[61] Yitri 1989.
[62] *Burma Watcher* 1989: 177.
[63] United States State Department 1988.

Activists were not initially eager to resume protests after the latest violence, but took heart when more established forces criticized the regime.
On August 16, the Burma Medical Association denounced the recent
hospital attack, provoking a solidarity demonstration at the hospital's
gate. That same day, the US Embassy happened to lower its flags to
half-mast (for reasons unrelated to the protests); demonstrators read
this as a gesture of support, and gathered outside.[64] When these demonstrations provoked no violence from soldiers, the movement surged ahead
once more, both in Rangoon and upcountry. Security forces exercised
uncharacteristic restraint in the days of protest that followed, which also
allowed movement groups to deepen their organizations. The Mandalay
Strike Committee first met in this period, and across Burma, committees
began to publish the first newspapers reporting their activities.[65]

On August 19, Dr. Maung Maung – a more moderate Ne Win insider
than Sein Lwin – became president. Still, activists were poised to reject
anything short of multi-party democracy, and gamely took on this new
target. Movement groups were now more coordinated, and announced a
national strike for August 22 that paralyzed Burma and solidified strike
committees nationally. Committees developed regular communication,
published more and more newspapers, and sent stories by fax to one
another. But the most surprising consequence of Dr. Maung Maung's
rise occurred on August 24, when he lifted martial law, and the military
stood down (in many places, disappearing altogether). The largely underground movement burst into the open, and dominated political life for
the next several weeks, not knowing whether they had finally won or
merely entered a new stage in the struggle.[66]

In light of the rapid change following this announcement, it is worth-
while to consider things as they stood at martial law's end. The democracy movement had a coordinated network of strike centers, controlled by
people with some political experience and (recently secret) links to collectives elsewhere. Demonstrators by then embraced more focused
demands for multi-party democracy, and had also suffered such stark
repression that most viewed the regime as an utter enemy. The strongest
remaining constraint on mobilization or organization ended when

---

[64] Lintner 1989.
[65] Informant b–12: "At the same time, the general strike committee took in representatives
of newly established strike committees in the quarters, so almost from the very
beginning the central committee had a great deal of contact and information . . . By this
contact, as well as the mediums of the newspapers and wallpapers, it was really amazing
how quickly and efficiently news spread throughout the movement." Interview b–12
transcribed from notes.
[66] Smith 1999, Lintner 1989; Yitri 1989.

soldiers withdrew on August 24, but demonstrators had been more willing to challenge soldiers even before that – particularly where movement organizations may not have been strongest. After August 24, organized activists (in networks still somewhat lacking public standing or reputation) would have less difficulty mobilizing mass support – but more trouble directing mass efforts in politically productive directions. The movement underwent a new, uninhibited round of committee formation, governed by more celebratory and anarchic dynamics.

The national strike

The apogee of the Burmese democracy movement stretched from August 24 to the military's violent return on September 18. As the fear of state violence receded, people began taking pleasure in giving voice to long suppressed protests, and one might easily have mistaken demonstrations for festival processions, but for their banners and slogans. One man watched a Rangoon intersection from 7AM to 5 PM on August 26 as 372 separate strike unions marched by:

Everyone wanted to be part of the movement, and so all different social groups eventually created a strike committee or a union. There was a gay union, a housewives union, a kindergarten union, and a grave-diggers' union. Can you imagine a kindergarten union demanding its rights? ... [D]emonstration was a sort of fashion, but also a way to get food: the really rich people never joined the rallies, but would donate money and, above all, food.[67]

Apart from marching, some collectives worried about the movement machinery, particularly its lack of a credible or prominent national leadership; others took over local governments – both matters that would compete with mobilization for movement attention and energy.

The festival of democracy, however, also obscured problems eating away at the movement. Because pre-demonstration underground networks were neither public nor connected to insurgent groups, they had no strong public followings and no disciplined mass machinery. The movement's consequent radical democracy therefore meant that experienced activists were quite effective building strike committees, linking them together and getting the strike started, but had more difficulty maintaining discipline, particularly as the movement expanded. When martial law ended, the strike ballooned out of control. Strike activity was in particular exceptionally vulnerable to external provocation.

---

[67] From interview with informant B–3.

In Rangoon undisciplined community defense committees may have first formed when students took refuge in working-class slums during the June dispersals, inspiring the people who hid them to organize. Such committees were probably mainly governed by local power dynamics, with more the character of gangs than activist cells. In August, one university teacher (paralyzed with fear) listened from his room as the local committee captured, interrogated and eventually beheaded a couple caught with what seemed a bomb (later discovered to be equipment pilfered from their workplace).[68] Outside his window, that committee routinely extorted money from passersby, nominally for movement defense. Across Rangoon, crowds accosted soldiers, policemen, or "suspicious" looking strangers – but *every* stranger seemed suspicious in those days. Organizers sometimes attempted to temper this violence but lacking a strong or public structure, had little authority in the neighborhoods. Moreover, the movement was subject to rumor and intrigue at all levels, and hardly less prone to violence at its summit than at its base. When 9,000 inmates escaped Rangoon prisons, many deemed it a state plot, particularly when word spread that convicts were poisoning food and water supplies, and shooting at crowds. A kind of panic set in, rooted in the impossibility of screening movement participants or verifying rumors.[69]

Beyond Rangoon, isolated strike committees organized by inexperienced activists also ran into trouble. As in Rangoon, activists struggled to direct mass protest, but these struggles depended on local conditions. The Mandalay strike committee was largely non-violent (partly because more organized monks and lawyers controlled things) but not necessarily more effective.[70] When security forces and government officials abandoned their positions, activist committees that replaced them soon encountered problems of maintaining order, policing food supplies, preventing smuggling and resolving local disputes. But strike committee decisions to undertake local governance seem not to have been

---

[68] Interview B–3, transcribed from notes.

[69] *Burma Watcher* 1989: 178. Informant B–12 reflected on how difficult these rumors made movement control: "It was hard to keep people calm when the rumors flew round. There was a rumor that the government was putting out poisoned food and water during the demonstrations. This was dangerous because we had so many people donating water and food for those in the demonstrations, and it was an important resource sustaining the movement. Those rumors flew round after the government had done some beheadings, and so when people got enraged, of course they also undertook some beheadings – it had already become an established model. But we tried as much as possible to keep this in control."

[70] Sheo 1992: 19.

underground decisions, and experienced activists argued against diverting movement attention to government administration:

We students wanted to keep the strike committee focused on activities related to organizing demonstrations and protest, but notable people in the village insisted that we take over the village administration and run the local government: that we manage the police department, the village fund, and the local rice supply – all local government functions became our responsibility.[71]

In Mandalay, lawyers with underground experience advised against taking on government tasks, and urged activists to spend greater energy spreading the movement to nearby villages and publishing committee newspapers.[72] In one central Burma town, Mandalay activists convinced the local committee to avoid village administration. One resident recalls that

We set up a local court where people could bring grievances – on the suggestion of the Mandalay underground people – but nobody used it. When the village administration faltered, respected people in the quarter, rather than strike committee members, picked up its responsibilities.[73]

In places with weaker underground leadership, strike committees seem to have turned more attention to taking control of apparently powerful village administration offices. Activists first took over local offices in Moulmein, after an angry and unorganized countercharge against officials who authorized a murderous state attack,[74] and the isolated strike committee in Kayah state also came to its own decision to occupy government offices as well.[75]

To that point, personalities associated with the movement – Aung San Suu Kyi, Tin Oo, Aung Gyi and U Nu – operated mainly on their own; during the national strike, however, student activists attempted to forge them into an explicit leadership council. Activists arranged a meeting among them for August 26, but the invitees were lukewarm on the project: "It was something of a forced marriage, and they had no independent inclination to work with one another," one meeting organizer reports.[76] Nor, either before or after that meeting, was the group entirely in step with the mass action. On his release from prison on August 24, for instance, General Aung Gyi addressed an eager crowd of activists without

[71] Interview B–7.
[72] Interview B–6.
[73] Interview B–7.
[74] Forty-seven activists were murdered in that state assault. Lintner 1989: 154.
[75] Taped interview B–16.
[76] Interview B–8.

fully understanding how they had been affected by the mid-August violence, or comprehending the crowd's deep outrage at security forces. He advised activists not even to *think* hostile thoughts against the military. The crowd turned away in disgust and disappointment.[77] U Nu made his own error after August 26, when he declared himself the legitimate prime minister and named a shadow government. The move eradicated any remaining unity among the leadership group and confused the movement.[78] (*Philippine* movement leaders provide a useful contrast, for they mainly rise through movement organizations that provided rather strict guidance and constraint on individual initiative; very few leadership moves in the anti-Marcos struggle occurred without careful planning and coordination.)

By mid-September Rangoon protests grew more violent and lawless, and soldiers also goaded demonstrators into making ill-advised attacks leading to skirmishes that soldiers easily won. President Maung Maung made several shows at meeting movement demands, but many activists, particularly in student groups, ignored more moderate advice and mistrusted proposals for compromise or incremental reform.[79] Instead, they demanded the regime's immediate replacement with an interim, transition government.[80]

On September 18, the military retook the country, in ways utterly consistent with its established custom of using raw force against protesters. In Rangoon alone, soldiers killed thousands, but bloodshed was not confined to the capital. Everywhere, soldiers smashed strike committees, pursued students into the jungle, and violently enforced new and rigorous curfews. Early estimates of the September casualties ran as high as ten thousand, but subsequent figures incline more to three thousand – still remarkably high.

Thinking about the national strike

Consider the national strike within the flow of Burmese history. What explains the rapid spread of strike committees? Why did massive and sustained demonstrations fail to force a transition to democracy?

---

[77] Informant B-2 was in that crowd, and recalls feeling that something important ended that day. (Interview B-2.)

[78] *Burma Watcher* 1989.

[79] For President Maung Maung's own, certainly slanted account of these events, see Maung Maung 1999.

[80] Informant B-9 reports that by late August, "in the middle of the demonstrations, some military intelligence officers came to me, and they asked me, 'what do you want?' They said 'Let's form a coalition government.' But students refused." Taped interview B-9.

Answers to both questions lie in the institutional, political, and cultural residues that state repression left on Burmese contention. When state repression destroyed civil associations and eliminated the possibility of open dissident expressions, it forced regime opponents and critics underground. Because underground cells could not work through legal associations or in alliance with frontier insurgencies, they never formed a broad network. Still in 1988 the underground was experienced enough to suggest models of struggle but these mainly came from pre-1962 protest (like the student union) or corrected old mistakes (as when activists attacked the foreign media in the 1970s).[81] Underground activists were also connected enough to coordinate activity, but ultimately unable to discipline the movement's base. As one underground activist put it:

A lot of the movement's most important organizational structures arose in the course of struggle, guided, I am sure, by the efforts of the UG activists, but also in response to more fluid conditions. You know about the incident that occurred at the General Hospital? There were some old people that were being brought in for treatment and the military showed up and shot a group of nurses. This was something that enraged our people, and very shortly, that hospital became the sort of spiritual but also organizational center of the strike.[82]

Activists created strike committees, community defense groups, movement courts, security patrols and newspapers almost entirely from resources generated during mobilization. The underground cells' only resources existed in the realm of knowledge, experience and connection, and such resources could shape movement claims and tactics, but could not, ultimately direct movement politics.

Yet activists' inability to achieve clear and lasting reforms probably also reflects other legacies of repression. Long-term repression destroyed any moderately empowering perch for dissidents: no opposition parties, newspapers, or even consultative state offices existed to provide dissident intellectuals or elites with some stake in an incremental transformation or standing among regime elites to allow cooperation in that transition. Writers, lawyers, monks and intellectuals had scant option save to ally with mass social strata. That alliance had few internal programmatic differences or tensions, for pervasive repression and poverty, especially after 1987 demonetizations,[83] drove everyone toward similar circumstances (particularly compared to persistent class differences within

---

[81] Informant B-9 (recorded interview) and informant B-12 (interveiw transcribed from notes) both stressed the line of descent between earlier struggles and underground formations and the 1988 strike committees.

[82] Interview B-12, transcribed from notes immediately after the interview.

[83] Mya Maung 1990.

both Indonesian and Philippine democracy movements). While the pattern of state society relations influenced Burmese protest, it also narrowed options available to any government official contemplating a democratizing defection from the regime: the political distance between regime and movement (in consequence of regime repression) was apparently too great for many to undertake the journey. Morcover, the fate of Retired General Aung Gyi – isolated from his former colleagues, imprisoned for a period, in some ways leading a mass movement he ultimately failed to understand, was probably a cautionary tale. Authorities' retreat on August 24 may have hampered prospects for a democratic transition, for though it stimulated protest, it also widened gaps between potential state defectors and movement leaders.

Hence, despite energy and popular support, the movement reached an impasse by September, with the chance of progress hinging on three hopes. The first was that daily demonstrations would leave the regime little choice but to capitulate. Second, movement activists hoped that soldiers would defect to the movement – even during violent August 8 protests, demonstrators protected members of the *Tatmadaw*, and attempted to engage their sympathies.[84] Third, the movement appealed to international audiences for help and August rumors circulating among activists suggested that US or UN troops would soon arrive. Let us examine these three possibilities in turn, to see why none eventually produced the transition.

Had the BSPP been a different kind of party, with a larger middle stratum or deeper roots in society, popular pressure might have deprived it of resources central to its stability. BSPP members did respond to protests by turning in their party cards *en masse*,[85] but the move merely diminished insignificant outer circles, and never disturbed the BSPP's core. Local government officials permitted the movement to seize what seemed like important positions in local government, but the *Tatmadaw* ultimately benefited from these occupations, for they dissipated activist energies into protecting rice supplies and arresting criminals. The movement operated with a conception of power geared toward marginalizing and replacing the regime rather than establishing influence within it. Behind this vision, activists in late August and September regularly

---

[84] We have already seen how Suu Kyi anticipated a military split that would benefit the movement. Across Burma, however, activists also attempted to cultivate sympathy with soldiers, and a Kayah state activist recalls how students, weak with hunger after a two-day stand-off with soldiers, still passed their own food to the military: "We just want to show that we really don't hate soldiers...that we are not the enemy." Recorded interview B–16.

[85] Lintner 1989.

rejected intermediate proposals from the Maung Maung government, declining, for example, to participate in a government commission to solicit opinions for reforms, or to back any election administered by the existing government. By the end of August, the movement demonstrated virtually no inclination to compromise on the issue of these elections.

What, then, of military defection? By late August, some *Tatmadaw* members reportedly did join protests, but only to a limited extent.[86] The Burmese military remained far more cohesive than either its Philippine or Indonesian counterparts, with neither the external political interference that split the AFP nor the rivalries (central *v.* outer island commands, finance generals *v.* professionals, service branches against one another) that divided ABRI. Military elites who opposed Ne Win, such as Aung Gyi or Tin Oo, tended to represent individual, rather than factional positions in the *Tatmadaw*, and most such were regularly purged.[87] The few soldiers who joined democracy protests came mainly from lower ranks of the Air Force (more politically marginal than the army) and did not indicate struggles between higher echelon protagonists. Moreover, Sein Lwin brought combat troops from insurgent areas to deal with protesters, and they did so in ways modeled on their ongoing war.[88] Interesting counter-examples, however, also exist on this score: in a village outside Mandalay, local youths erected a security checkpoint, and were standing guard on September 19 when troops (long garrisoned in the area) acted on the national order to retake the country. When the soldiers arrived at the checkpoint, the officer in charge approached, and asked the students what they were doing. "Guarding the village," they reportedly replied. "Who the hell told you to guard the village?" the officer raged – but he sent them home, after spanking (!) each.[89]

Finally, the idea that international support would help demonstrators unseat the dictatorship reflected the large role that foreign media services like VOA and the BBC played in mobilizing movement activity, and on the extraordinary international attention the demonstrations attracted. Stephan Solarz, fresh from democratizing successes in the Philippines and Korea, brought his road show to Burma in September, both encouraging protest and attempting to pressure the regime toward reform. US President Bush sent the regime a diplomatic note reiterating the Solarz message.[90] Still, even had the US been more committed to doing

[86] Callahan 1999: 1.
[87] Interview B–9; See also Smith 1999.
[88] Callahan 2001.
[89] Interview B–7, transcribed from notes.
[90] United States State Department 1989.

something direct in Burma, the regime had fewer ties to or dependencies on the outside world than either the Philippine or Indonesian regimes, and many closer states soon resumed relations with the new government.[91] Moreover, Burma's proximity to China made Western states even less willing to contemplate serious intervention than they otherwise might be. Rather, from August through September the international community made supporting gestures sufficient to inspire in activists the hope of more concrete help, without delivering on those gestures.[92]

On the government's side, the regime's very isolation helped authorities close ranks as protests mounted. The *Tatmadaw* was not divided, nor were many of its counter-insurgent soldiers particularly tied to lowland Burma's society. The state didn't require strong social support, and was not materially hampered by its withdrawal, particularly when demonstrations grew more anarchic. The regime was not troubled by internal dissent on the question of the coup and repression – those siding with the movement left the party early on. Hence despite unprecedented social mobilization and the truly surprising degree of organization among its various centers, the protest movement never split the state or applied significant drag on the repressive apparatus. Nor could it counter regime gunfire with its own military counter-strikes (apart from street-quality weapons like rocks and jinglees): the BCP, the movement's most logical armed ally, only got around to forming a position on the democracy movement after the guns of September had fallen silent in Rangoon.[93]

[91] Yawnghwe 1995.
[92] Bray 1992.
[93] Lintner 1990.

10 Indonesia's democracy protests

1998 Indonesian democracy protests marked an important break with established patterns, in which state policies scattered and fragmented all opposition movements (apart from those operating in insurgent areas like East Timor and West Papua). Although sustained national protest took almost a decade more to mobilize, *keterbukaan* in the 1980s paved the way for this movement. On a number of important fronts, long-standing restrictions on political activity relaxed, and activist institutions like the student press or independent unions revived. By the early 1990s, the regime's ability to suppress political organization began to slip. Some of the more radical local struggles, such as the Kedung Ombo Dam campaign, produced (tentative) national coalitions among LSMs. Legal aid groups, particularly *Lembaga Bantuan Hukum* (LBH, Legal Aid Foundation) adopted a structural approach that systematically opposed regime policy and built a national network.[1] Incarcerated student leaders in the late 1980s met and learned from members of the comparatively well-organized East Timorese independence movements, and after, began thinking more seriously about organizational styles and secessionist movements.[2]

Keterbukaan encouraged activists more extensively to utilize electoral opportunites and institutions. In 1987, under Suryadi's new leadership, the *Partai Demokrasi Indonesia* (PDI, Indonesian Democratic Party) gradually sharpened its opposition, recruiting members of the Sukarno family to draw on the first president's charismatic legacy, and attracting in consequence young activists seeking new venues for dissent. Somewhat unrealistically, Suryadi strove both to play by the regime's rules and expand the PDI's power. New PDI recruits had other ideas, mounting an unusually strong anti-Suharto campaign in 1992 (behind Sukarno's son Guruh Sukarnoputra).[3] Despite internal support for this more

---

[1] Lev 1996.
[2] Naipospos 2000.
[3] *Tempo*, June 20, 1992.

215

confrontational stance, PDI leaders voted to re-elect Suharto at the March 1993 MPR meeting, antagonizing party radicals without dispelling authorities' anger at the recent electoral campaign. At the PDI congress in December, ABRI intervened to remove Suryadi and install an interim caretaker council.[4] Activists began shifting support to Megawati Sukarnoputri (another Sukarno offspring). Despite ABRI opposition, Megawati became the PDI leader in December 1993.

By then, Indonesia stood on the brink of something new. Authorities could still enforce proscriptions on dissident organization, and predictably also accused those who flirted with direct, organized resistance of harboring communist sympathies. Years of New Order repression so deeply planted state prohibitions and taboos in activist imaginations that these rules became virtually self-enforcing. Hence, political contention remained fragmented, local and episodic – particularly in comparison to coordinated Philippine campaigns.[5] But *keterbukaan* also undercut some proscriptions on formal organization, sparked activist interest in legal organizations like the PDI, and encouraged some brave souls to defy other proscriptions and begin organizing. Anti-organization laws like the NKK/BKK remained in effect, but students began testing their boundaries, experimenting with new and more powerful modes of struggle. We begin with the PDI story, for that is where the opposition first found a large, stable organizational vehicle.

The struggle for the PDI

The PDI under Megawati was something new to opposition politics. Not since the 1970s could dissidents work within an organization with the standing and security that official parties offered, for while the regime could meddle in party affairs, the parties themselves were central to the New Order's governing philosophy, and so relatively protected.[6] The PDI provided activists with organizational resources long denied them, although one shouldn't overstate the case. Mass organization restrictions remained in effect, and only the regime's official electoral vehicle, GOLKAR could maintain branch offices outside the major cities.[7] Still the PDI represented a marked improvement over the ephemeral collectives through which activists otherwise worked. Moreover, when authorities

---

[4] Zulkifli 1996: 89.
[5] Or, as one Indonesian analyst has noted, in comparison to conditions that obtained in 1966 Indonesia. Soewarsono 1999b: 13–14.
[6] Liddle 1996c.
[7] Liddle 1996c.

set out to unseat Megawati and re-install a suddenly more attractive Suryadi as PDI head, activists' general demands for democracy acquired a specific focus. By 1996, the issue of Megawati's leadership was a fulcrum on which an organized and resilient campaign turned.[8]

With regime support (including strong pressure on media to secure favorable coverage) Suryadi formed a breakaway PDI faction and scheduled its congress in Medan for June 1996. In advance of that congress, Megawati supporters began to demonstrate in Jakarta and other large cities.[9] The main party leadership also adopted more activist overtones, threatening to "bring tens of millions of people into the streets of every major city and town in the country."[10] Despite protests, which occasionally flared to violence, the Medan congress continued as scheduled, elected Suryadi as faction president, and then declared itself the true PDI. Meanwhile, Megawati supporters dug in at Jakarta's PDI headquarters, beginning a siege that would last over a month. Party headquarters provided activists with an operations base and helped sustain and focus protest. On June 20, 5,000 activists rallied outside the building, until police violently dispersed the assembly. The next day, 500 PDI demonstrators returned to the party headquarters at Diponogoro Street, but went home after receiving ABRI assurances that they might return and protest in the days that followed.[11] Fresh demonstrations greeted the Medan congress results on June 24, and demonstrations occurred every day thereafter. By June 28, 1,000 people marched to support the Megawati faction. 2,000 marched to parliament on June 29.[12]

The stand off began in earnest when Medan delegates returned to Jakarta to claim the PDI building. By then, activists guarded party headquarters, and soldiers patrolled its perimeter. Beside street demonstrations, activists erected a podium at the PDI building for what they called a *mimbar bebas*, or open forum, at which anyone could air grievances against the regime.[13] In ways that suggest the Burmese experience in mirror image, speakers and speeches in these fora evolved. Party activists prominent in the encampment's early days (lawyers and writers focused on the PDI's leadership dispute) gave way to workers, vendors, farmers

---

[8] Bertrand notes that even some powerful figures inside the regime, including members of ABRI associated with Benny Murdani, lent support to Megawati during this period. Bertrand 1996: 332.
[9] YLBHI 1997a: 9.
[10] *Jakarta Post*, June 13, 1996.
[11] *Jakarta Post*, June 22, 1996.
[12] *Jakarta Post*, June 30, 1996.
[13] Wardhana 1997.

and fisherfolk who described lives of hardship and injustice. The shift suggests a growing sphere of party influence, beyond the functionaries that the New Order permitted to members of a more prohibited mass base. More ideologically explicit activists aired ideas about long-term structural change, and used the forum to urge broader democracy protest. The podium became a place to announce marches that fanned out from the PDI headquarters to other points in Jakarta: 3,000 on July 14, 1,000 on July 15. On July 18, 1,500 demonstrators carried a one-kilometer length of white cloth, on which passers-by wrote supporting messages. In bolstering the movement by demonstrating popular support, activists had departed from the moral force tradition, and were playing at demonstrating mass power. On July 20, the military banned further demonstrations, but PDI forces vowed to defy that ban. On July 25, between 500 and 1,000 people took to the streets; the *mimbar bebas* inside the compound continued uninterrupted.[14]

Early in the morning of July 27, trucks containing people dressed as members of the Suryadi faction pulled onto Diponogoro Street. The new arrivals charged the building and began swinging rattan canes at its occupants. As fighting spilled into the streets, soldiers and police arrived on the scene, but initially took little action. When they did move, it was to arrest and restrain Megawati supporters, not to interrupt the attack. Megawati supporters then moved across Jakarta, burning buildings and smashing cars. Bystanders, particularly from Jakarta's poor and marginal classes, joined the fracas and soldiers began to use teargas and rattan canes against them. As evening fell, military head Faisal Tanjung issued a shoot to kill order against remaining protesters, and rioting ended around 8:30 PM. 5 people were killed, 23 were missing, and 124 were under arrest in the worst Jakarta riots since 1974.[15]

The struggle for the PDI illustrates two important developments that would be crucial to the 1998 democracy movement. First, actors within accepted New Order institutions began to use those institutions to demand more substantial political reform. Conflict within the state that triggered *keterbukaan* allowed familiar New Order parties like the PDI (and the PPP) to act more defiantly.[16] Megawati's leadership wove radical demands for democracy into conventional complaints about

---

[14] An account that takes careful note of the protest's evolution from a PDI member-action to one joined by Jakarta's working and marginalized classes can be found in YLBHI 1997a; and Santoso 1997.

[15] This account is based on Luwarso 1997; National Commission on Human Rights 1996; YLBHI 1997a.

[16] Vatikiotis 1993; Bertrand 1996.

procedural justice, in terms the regime had sanctioned. Megawati evoked her father, and so the *perjuangan* (struggle) tradition that he deftly commanded.[17] Hence, the first signs of a resilient democracy movement materialized behind someone whose antagonism to the New Order seemed (quite apart from her own actions) both moderate and irreconcilable. The combination attracted significant support. Nataduul Ulama head and Democracy Forum member Abdurrahman Wahid spoke in support of Megawati and the larger democracy agenda.[18] LSMs like KIPP and LBH issued statements of solidarity, and many at the PDI site belonged to these groups.[19]

Second, new, more organized and militant groups also gravitated toward the PDI encampment, none more influential than the PRD (*Partai Rakyat Demokrasi*, People's Democratic Party). The PRD leadership consisted of young activists dissatisfied with decentralized, LSM-based advocacy, who developed a model of explicitly organized, clandestine movement formations of exactly the kind the New Order sought most to prohibit. PRD cadres (some of whom had contact with Philippine movement organizations) paid explicit attention to the advantages of movement organization, and attempted to build a network in which their central political leadership directed mass organizations with distinct sectoral constituencies such as workers, farmers, urban poor and students (an organizational pattern that ABRI linked to communist influence).[20] The PDI conflict provided the PRD with a national focus and a new arena: throughout the July stand off, some PRD groups gathered at the PDI headquarters, while others staged coordinated solidarity actions across Indonesia.[21] According to PRD sources, the *Solidaritas Mahasiswa Indonesia untuk Demokrasi* (SMID, Student Solidarity for Indonesian Democracy) formed in 1992, but was announced only in August 1994. Other PRD organizations began as apparently small and scattered community actions (the sort generally permitted by the state) that subsequently formalized.[22] Among these, the *Pusat Perjuangan Buruh Indonesia* (PPBI, Indonesian Center for Labor Struggle) was

---

[17] Brooks 1995; Aspinall 1996. Megawati's political weaknesses were also one display from early on. For instance, she provided virtually no support for activists detained during the PDI protests, and seemed more to distance herself from them.

[18] This endorsement, poorly disguised as a legal opinion, came close to violating mass organization restrictions, for the NU was barred from political activity.

[19] *The Economist* July 26, 1996.

[20] Honna 2001: 74.

[21] Such as labor and student protests in Surabaya on July 9–12. *Jakarta Post*, July 10, 1996; *Kompas*, July 14, 1996.

[22] PPBI 1997.

particularly visible during the July 1996 confrontation. It staged a solidarity strike in Surabaya on July 8 to support Megawati's PDI faction, an action that also attracted support from students and other PRD constituencies.[23]

Again, we should not over-emphasize these new capacities, for years of repression left the state overwhelmingly powerful against social opponents. After the July protests, repression increased, despite objections from pro-democracy leaders like Wahid,[24] the "Petition of 50's" General Nasution[25] and international human rights' groups.[26] PDI leaders (Megawati, Alexander Litaay, Sophan Sophian, among them) and LSM members were interrogated and detained. But investigators paid particularly fierce attention to the PRD.[27] Even before July 27, government sources labeled the PRD neo-communist, and Suharto claimed that it demonstrated the PKI's "way of thinking and acting."[28] In early August, security forces arrested leaders of PRD mass organizations across Indonesia.[29] On August 11, more PRD leaders, including overall head, Budiman Sudjatmoko, fell in raids. Altogether, thirteen PRD members, as well as labor leader Dr. Pakpahan, were charged under the 1963 anti-subversion act. Most were tortured and denied council for weeks – practices not usually applied to cosmopolitan, elite and *Indonesian* activists.[30] Still, despite authorities' undiminished capacity and willingness to use repression, the 1996 protests suggested that anti-regime forces had begun to gain new kinds of organizational resources, and these gains also partly explain the intensity of anti-PRD measures.[31]

Run up to the election

Between August 1996 and May 1997, elections spurred increasing protest and violence that we can understand in terms of two interacting

---

[23] Interestingly, however, even as the PRD lent its organizational muscle to the PDI protests it remained a tractable ally for other members of the pro-Megawati coalition, and in the aftermath of the July 27 confrontation, it anchored its own denunciations on those of established pro-democracy forces in that coalition. See Sudjatmiko 1996b.

[24] *Jawa Post*, August 5, 1996.

[25] *Republika*, August 5,1996.

[26] YLBHI 1997a: 31–34.

[27] Honna 2001: 70–75.

[28] *Kompas*, August 18, 1996.

[29] Specifically, the chair of an artists' group in Solo, SMID chairpersons in Jakarta, Bandar Lampung and Bogor and the head of the SBSI, Dr. Muchtar Pakpahan (also accused of provoking violence in the 1994 Medan strike) Soewarsono 1999b: 138–139.

[30] For details of this torture, see Sudjatmiko 1996b.

[31] McRae 2001: 5.

cycles. First, the gradual process of *keterbukaan* diminished prohibitions on dissent, and provided some leeway for political organization, a long, escalating cycle of mobilization. Activists in LSMs, labor unions and political parties initially moved with great caution, and ABRI quelled most demonstrations with threats or expressions of displeasure.[32] Gradually, stronger activist organizations allowed more defiant and sustained demonstrations. Second, shorter cycles of mobilization and protest, associated with elections, had been part of the New Order's rhythm since the early 1970s: Indonesian electoral campaigns, though entirely rigged, provided opportunities for demonstrations. In the 1970s, regime elites jockeying for position often engineered such rallies, but as *keterbukaan* took hold, more truly oppositional activities (like PDI and PPP protests in 1992) showed that oppositionists had begun more seriously to seize opportunities to campaign against the regime. 1997 protests were hence partly an election-based mobilization pattern that authorities had withstood in the past, occurring, however, further along a *keterbukaan*-driven cycle. The combinations of these two cycles made the 1997–1998 protests potentially more powerful than many previous mobilizations from the outset (even before one factors in the influence of the monetary crisis).

Strong movement organizations allowed dissidents to plan more powerful actions for the election. Though ABRI banned street demonstrations in December 1996, activists in Megawati's faction (now called PDI-*perjuangan*, or struggle) planned defiant new protests. On December 29, 500 marched against Suryadi in Surabaya.[33] When the national election board excluded Megawati's name from the list of eligible candidates, she denounced the government and the PDI-*Perjuangan* held rallies and marches in Jakarta and in other Indonesian towns.[34] The government dampened Megawati's own militancy by suspending her parliamentary immunity on January 28, but as May neared, PDI members began to threaten an election boycott. By April 15, pro-Megawati demonstrations attracted nearly 2,000 in downtown Jakarta, and despite prohibitions, about 100 marched to the Central Jakarta State Court to file a lawsuit against Suryadi's leadership the next day.[35] The PPP launched a sustained string of demonstrations from late April through May in Jakarta, Surabaya and Jogjakarta, against rules requiring them to clear campaign material with state watchdogs. Riots flared almost before

---

[32] Bunnell 1996.
[33] *Jawa Post*, December 20, 1996.
[34] *Kompas*, January 22, 1997.
[35] *Jakarta Post*, April 16, 1997.

voting ended on Madura, and continued until June 2, when officials announced plans to re-poll 121 stations. On June 14, PPP members demonstrated in the East Javanese town of Jember, but party leaders approved the official election results soon after, ending protests.

Other organizations also figured prominently in the building contention. Labor strikes in 1996 more frequently involved national organizers from independent unions, or linked to the PRD.[36] In a June 9 Surabaya strike, for instance, activists from the STI (*Seriket Tani Nasional*, the National Peasants' Union), the SMID and PPBI all turned out. The resulting *multi-sectoral* mobilization attracted allies committed to a broad national reform – something alien to most groups except students and LSM workers.[37] As elections neared, protests made national policy demands (for exmaple, against a proposed nuclear energy program and opposing expanded alcohol sales).

Increased organization among activists allowed them to cultivate international support more easily, as secessionist movements had for some time, and this support served to sustain and focus protest in new ways. In early February, the US AFL-CIO launched a campaign for the release of Muchtar Pakpahan, jailed in the August crackdown and facing the death penalty.[38] In March, British human rights' activists protested plans to train Indonesian officers at Kings College, and disrupted British Aerospace's annual meeting to protest company sales to Indonesia.[39] In April, international labor groups attacked Nike Corporation for using child labor in its Indonesian factories, and over 10,000 workers in these Indonesian plants struck.[40] East Timor separatists, always cognizant of opportunities provided by forces external to Indonesia, held demonstrations when UN special envoy Jamsheed Marker visited Dili on March 23; soldiers killed two protesters and injured twenty-eight others, triggering months of protest from national and domestic human rights' groups, including the state's National Committee on Human Rights(NCHR). An alliance of East Timorese and Indonesian protesters staged another rally in Jakarta when Marker arrived on March 26.[41] Soon after, the US state of Massachusetts imposed a largely symbolic trade embargo on Indonesia. Indonesian unions, human rights' organizations and separatist

---

[36] PPBI 1997.
[37] YLBHI: 118–120.
[38] *AFP Newswire*, February 5, 1997.
[39] *The Guardian* (London) March 18, 1997. These protests led to several acts of civil disobedience over the next several weeks in Britain, aimed at disrupting arms sales to Indonesia.
[40] *Antara News Agency*, April 23, 1997.
[41] *Jakarta Post*, March 27.

groups sustained relatively large and durable demonstrations in conjunction with each exercise of international solidarity.

More mobilization, however, did not always redound to activists'
power – and indeed rising unrest provided elements in the regime with
opportunities to reiterate that mantra of Suharto's rule: that mass activity
was dangerous, chaotic and apt to spin out of control. Indeed, the new
organizations that grew up under *keterbukaan* were far from entirely in
control of things, and at times, movement leaders and public intellectuals
seemed as much to fear as to invoke mass political activity.[42] This
ambivalence was naturally ripe for exploitation, and authorities may
have nudged some incidents down the road to riot and violence to
cultivate fear regarding all mass activity.[43]

Several uncharacteristically large episodes of community violence
broke out in the period before the 1997 elections. In October 1996,
anti-Chinese violence flared in East Java's Situbondo after a court issued
what local Muslim groups regarded as a light sentence in a blasphemy
case.[44] Human Rights Watch reported "evidence that the violence was
deliberately instigated, and local security forces made no effort initially to
stop it." On December 26 in Tasikmalaya, Muslim groups initially protesting a teacher's torture at a police station turned on Chinese targets,
killing four and destroying shops, cars, factories and churches. The
NCHR suggested that "a third party" provoked the riot, but did not
name the group.[45] In late January, Wahid accused rightist Muslims,
particularly in the Humanika Foundation and CIDES (Center for
Information and Development Studies) of provoking riots.[46] Anti-
Chinese riots occurred in Rengasdengklok, West Java (after a Chinese
man allegedly insulted Islam); military sources again implied third-party
provocation.[47] Through March, violence flared in West Kalimantan

---

[42] Siegel 2001: 90–95. Quotations in the newspapers often revealed this same anxiety. For
example: "Pengamat politik Dewi Fortuna Anwar Khwatir dampak naiknya BBM dan
tariff listrik bias mengundang rakyat turun ke jalan." (Political commentator Dewi
Fortuna Anwar worries that the effect of increased fuel and electricity rates could cause
the masses to take to the streets.) *Inti Jaya*, May 3.

[43] Eklöf 1999: 50–74.

[44] *Wawasan*, October 13, 1996; see also Gerakan Pemuda Ansor 1996.

[45] *Kompas*, January 8, 1997. On January 13, police raided student residences in Jakarta
looking for documents that would implicate the students as members of the banned
Negera Islam Indonesia (NII, Indonesian Islamic State). The NCHR declined to confirm
that this group was the organization it suspected in the December riots. (*Kompas*,
January 14, 15, 1997.) See also YLBHI 1997a: 75–90.

[46] *Suara Karya*, January 30, 1997. *Jakarta Post*, January 30, 1997. According to Wahid, a
leader of a local NU chapter had been "fooled" by members of CIDES and Humanika
into believing that the riots would be in line with NU policy.

[47] *Kompas*, February 1, 1997.

between Dayaks, Madurese immigrants and Chinese.[48] Other clashes
followed confrontations between GOLKAR supporters and PPP parti-
sans, at least partly fueled by PPP election-rules protests. In Banjarmasin,
Kalimantan, motorcycle-riding GOLKAR campaigners disturbed Friday
prayers, leading to riots that killed over 120.[49] No wonder that democracy
advocates would be cautious about broadly mobilizing movement
strategies.

By 1997 the concept of *keterbukaan* had developed its own particular
dynamic in Indonesia. Frequent protests, a sporadically assertive media,
and prominent and vocal public intellectuals all combined to make the
liberalization seem at least a superficially pervasive phenomenon.
Enough former or current regime members echoed the call to make
the demand for reform seem reasonable and mainstream, rather than
radical. Even Suharto incorporated terms like *reformasi* into his public
statements. But the New Order was neither willing to institute substantial reform nor to allow others to make much headway. *Keterbukaan* still
operated within relatively restricted parameters, and authorities cracked
down without compunction on those who transgressed them. Hence in
1994, four newspapers were shuttered for discussing political dissent
too frankly, and as riots began to occur in 1996, media editors were
enjoined from devoting too much attention to the events.[50] Activists,
particularly workers and farmers living outside major cities, were often
harassed, intimidated or physically harmed by security forces.
Periodically, more focused violence was brought to bear against some
dissident force. After the July 27, 1996 conflict, over seventy-five people,
many belonging to the PRD were arrested, and authorities roundly
denounced the organization. Perhaps more important, most dissidents
never ventured directly to oppose the regime, to undertake sustained
acts of resistance, or to build organized (as distinct from fortuitous)
movement associations.[51]

[48] *Suara Pembaruan*, February 20, 1997.
[49] YLBHI 1997b.
[50] *Jakarta Post*, September 21, 1996.
[51] In what seemed to me an extreme case of this, several student activists (who identified
themselves, perhaps accurately, as among those who planned the PDI activities on July
1996) described what they did on the evening of July 27. "We all gathered together, and
listened to as many radio stations as we could find, hoping against hope that the
violence would trigger something more sustained, like Philippine people power. But it
didn't happen." It never occurred to them, they revealed after some questioning, that
such follow-up activity required organization and planning – that it was not likely to
happen spontaneously. Interview with three PDI activists, March 13, 1998.

The 1997 financial crisis and the MPR

Through this rising mobilization, government officials kept different groups of claim makers separate from one another, and continued to enforce enough anti-organization restrictions to prevent a national anti-dictatorship movement from ever taking shape. The 1997 currency crisis, however, synchronized and focused grievances across groups in ways that pushed unrest past what the regime could contain. Village riots proliferated from January 3 (starting in the East Java towns of Tamanan and East Jember) until February 13–16 (where they crested in the West Java towns of Ceribon and on Sumatra). Near the end of that period, riots also occurred on Sumatra (February 13) Sulawesi and Lombok (February 14).[52] While riots had grown more common since mid-1996, this outbreak was, in significant ways, different. Earlier riots had often been more or less contained episodes centered on single locations. Even exceptionally violent outbreaks seldom spread, and if authorities did not always move quickly to end them, they at least kept them contained. The 1998 events, though often sparked by particular local triggers, occurred in such rapid succession that many saw them as a single wave of chaos creeping across the countryside. Soon, the idea of *spread* – a domestic domino theory – began to dominate the nervous responses to the riots. Security forces blocked traffic flowing from Bandung to Jakarta to prevent riots from *entering the capital from the West*. Bus terminals, many suggested, were particularly dangerous, because the virus of contagion entered communities (from infected areas) at such places. Eye-witness accounts from successive conflagrations described men in black with short haircuts who appeared before each riot to set things in motion – although to this date, there is no reliable way to ascertain whether the riots were provoked by conspiracy or something else.[53]

Provoked or spontaneous, however, the riots were profoundly isolated *socially,* involving poor and restless sections of society, and never linked with (or recruited into) some of the more explicitly pro-democracy protests. The crisis hurt many businesses with smaller capital reserves and a dependence on international exchange, particularly when the Rupiah fell to 12,000 per dollar in February.[54] Many businesses failed, defaulted on

---

[52] Data on these strikes comes from a review of reports in the Indonesian periodicals *Jawa Post, Kompas,* and *Media Indonesia;* see also the table of strikes compiled in McRae 2001: 9.

[53] See for examples of this coverage, front page articles in *Kompas,* February 15, 1996, and *Jaharta Post,* on February 17 and 19, 1998.

[54] This dramatic decline immediately announced Suharto's nomination of B. J. Habibie for Vice President.

debts or drastically reduced production, and foreign investors across the country pulled up stakes and took off, particularly as the riots grew. Still, urban elites never pushed the crisis in order to unseat the president. Indeed, most of their clearest efforts and demands suggested measures to moderate economic hardship to stave off mass unrest. Many of the democracy-minded intellectuals, in fact, seemed to regard democratic reform and mass unrest as alternative trajectories, and enjoined government officials to enact reforms to *avert mass unrest.*[55] Hence, calls for reform did not exactly overlap with the riot wave, and while the democracy circles feared rioting in the streets, few ventured anti-regime demonstrations.[56]

Rather, elite responses to the crisis were initially rhetorical. Discussions linking the upcoming MPR and the economic crisis began on January 7, when *Muhammadiyah*'s Amien Rais, Megawati and Abdurrahman Wahid[57] found themselves together to bless the fasting month of Ramadan. Rais (and the press) made much of the meeting, and he later called for a national dialogue between government and leaders like himself and the other two.[58] These remarks dominated the media for several days, and government figures announced themselves ready for dialogue; in the same breath, however, most also undercut the idea, stipulating that talks should follow constitutional procedures, fretting that they might pre-empt the MPR, and ultimately dropping the whole thing. It was a classic and effective New Order response: an initial welcome, followed by increasingly explicit conditions and stipulations which, taken together, constituted a warning. By then, however, the media and lecture audiences had seized the next idea (in a pattern repeated several times over the next months): Rais or Megawati might nominate him- or herself for the presidency. Both government and opposition figures seemed to herald this prospect – though officials mused that such candidacies should not "disrupt national unity" – another killing stipulation. By mid-January, authorities launched a counter-offensive. Several military officers speculated (in coded threats) that Rais might mobilize *Muhammadiyah* for

---

[55] A leaflet produced by a group of critical intellectuals calling itself the "Thursday Night Club" ended, after demanding reform, with the unintentionally self-revealing line: "Baiklah, kita tunggu saja." ("Alright: We'll wait and see.") "Thursday Night Club" 1998.

[56] Rural riots tapered off during the second week of February, ending when authorities began to release emergency relief stores of basic commodities. Only after the riots ceased did pro-democracy demonstrations begin once more.

[57] Wahid would soon suffer a stroke that kept him hospitalized over much of the next few weeks; hence his absence from much of the account that follows.

[58] *Kompas,* January 7, 1998.

political goals (violating 1984 restrictions). On January 20, both Rais and *Muhammadiyah* were in full rhetorical retreat. One leader denied that Rais consulted the group about supporting Megawati, while Rais disclaimed any intention to turn *Muhammadiyah* to political ends. House Speaker Harmoko put the matter to rest that same day by announcing Suharto's willingness to stand for a *final* term.[59]

By mid-February, the opposition began focusing on Suharto's nominee for Vice-President – a tactic military officers pioneered at the 1988 MPR. At a February 11 democracy seminar, Emil Salim (Minister of Natural Resources and an official that many activists respected) allowed that he might accept a nomination for Vice-President, and this sparked a new round of excited speculation.[60] On February 21, Suharto's son-in-law, Lieutenant-General Probowo Subianto, described his friendship with both Salim and Amien Rais, stressing that no impediment existed to either making *constructive* criticisms against the government, within constitutional limits: another threat. By the time Suharto nominated B.J. Habibie, the prospect of an opposition candidate had fallen utterly apart. Moreover, unspecified government sources leaked reports that Amien Rais and supporters had convened a meeting at Gajah Madah University to plan demonstrations. Most accused of attending the meeting spent the next several days deflecting charges of subversion, and the alleged anti-regime plans never came off.[61]

It would be possible, of course, to trace the rise and demise of other rumors in the pro-democracy salons, moving from initial excitement, through government embrace, warning caveat and disintegration. No single rumor, however, was more important than the pattern that all inexorably followed. Crucially, public intellectuals would not violate anti-subversion laws in ways that really defied regime threats, and this deep reticence utterly affected dissent. Sometimes, dissidents made stronger motions toward political action.[62] *Suara Ibu Peduli* (Voice of Concerned Mothers) demonstrated outside the Hotel Indonesia (following a press conference in the hotel's coffee shop!) to denounce rising basic commodity costs. That the women planned to march despite recent regime proscriptions on street demonstrations marked it as a promising

[59] *Kompas*, January 20, 1998.
[60] *Kompas*, February 11–16, 1998; *Suara Pembaruan*, February 11–16, 1998.
[61] *Kompas*, February 26, 1998; *Suara Pembaruan*, February 26, 1998.
[62] At one Halal Bihalal ceremony, for instance, Amien Rais set out a sweeping critique of the regime, asserted that Indonesians who launched a "people power" revolution would be justified ... but only if things were not properly handled soon. It was, in the end, a typical deflection: apparently radical, ultimately tame, and in both respects characteristic of the democracy circuit. (From author's notes, February 23, 1998.)

departure for standard democracy discussions, and the entire event was planned with a fair amount of cloak and dagger (announced via secret fax and e-mail messages to supporters, the press and, without doubt, a few security types). Still, it remained an elite action, taken on behalf of impoverished Indonesians rather than in league with them. Without mass participants, the rally came off without any real violence – but the urban, elite marchers were a vulnerable and small assembly, and soldiers rounded them all up in less than two minutes.[63]

More organized activists (PRD members, students and LSM workers) were caught between elite dissidents and mass communities. Although a growing presence at the urban democracy forums, they also favored more concrete action than public intellectuals openly condoned. With mass unrest growing in early 1998, however, even organized activists seemed unsure how far to push mass protest – particularly as rumors spread that General Probowo was provoking riots to provide cover for authoritarian retrenchment. Hence organized labor and land protests dropped in 1998s first months, even as generalized unrest grew.[64] Moreover, while authorities frightened elite opponents with veiled threats, they had recently taken more direct measures to prevent organized challenges. On March 5, 1997 PPP leader Sri Bintang Pamunkas was arrested on subversion charges, linked particularly to his efforts to organize an unofficial opposition party, the *Partai Uni Demokrasi Indonesia* (PUDI, United Democratic Party of Indonesia).[65] In April 1997, authorities sentenced detained PRD members (arrested in the months following the July 27, 1996 unrest) to some of the harshest penalties meted out in years.[66] In early 1998, dozens of labor activists, particularly in the East Java industrial corridor, were arrested or disappeared.

---

[63] From notes taken after observing the rally.
[64] Rustam Ibrahim for LBH described the diminution in labor and land protests to me as a consequence of both the economic crisis (workers who had jobs didn't want to provoke lay-offs) and organizers' disinclination to jeopardize the precarious collectives that they had put together. Arrests and disappearances had increased during this period, and mass protests seemed more vulnerable to repression than usual. Interview with Rustam Ibrahim at LBH.
[65] *Jakarta Post*, March 6, 1997.
[66] Human Rights Watch 1997. In part, the report states that, "Budiman Soedjatmiko, head of the PRD, was sentenced to thirteen years in prison, and Garda Sembiring, head of the group's student affiliate, to twelve. Seven others were sentenced to prison terms ranging from eighteen months to eight years. In Surabaya, East Java, three other students associated with the same organization – Dita Indah Sari, Coen Husein Ponto, and Mohamed Soleh – were also sentenced to heavy terms. Dita's sentence of six years was reduced on appeal to five; the four-year terms of the two others were reduced to three and a half years."

More organized, but smaller and secretive demonstrations began once more as the general assembly approached – just as the rioting began to abate. Street protests started on February 9, when a group called the Red and White Front (*Barisan Merah-Puti*) marched in and around Bandung.[67] Riots had recently occurred in the area, and the demonstrators seemed interested in harnessing that unrest by demanding political transparency, an accounting for the Rupiah's fall, and reduced basic commodity prices. Like many late New Order demonstrations, this assembly, and those that followed over the next few days, were small and brief, but they were also more organized and secretive – and initiated nasty state reprisals. On February 12, eight Bandung student leaders were kidnapped in moves later attributed to special forces under Probowo's command, briefly ending Bandung demonstrations.[68] Beginning on February 11 in Jakarta, a group calling itself the *Tim Pembela Demokrasi* (Democracy Defense Team) held a series of demonstrations with between 200 and 400 participants (including many veterans of the 1996 PDI conflict). Most marches were unannounced – although about twenty minutes before each, organizers faxed demonstration plans to the press club to insure a media presence.[69] By February 20, these demonstrations ceased as reports of activist abductions once more came in.[70] (In July and August 1998, Kopassus troops began to admit what many dissidents suspected in March: that they abducted and tortured twenty-five activists between February and March – of whom only thirteen resurfaced alive.)

Through the end of February, despite rising pockets of unrest, authorities managed to maintain at least the most crucial element of their program against unrest and mass politics: they kept it fragmented.[71] Elite activists and dissidents remained easily intimidated, more organized and radical political activists had been hounded into watchful hiding, and mass protests and rioting had been socially isolated and partially mollified by the release of relief goods. Despite *keterbukaan*, monetary crisis and increased anti-regime mobilization, the New Order kept dissent internally divided enough to clip its wings.

[67] *Kompas*, February 10, 1998.
[68] Interview Mulya Lubis from KIPP(*Komite Independen Pemantau Pemilu*, Independent Election Monitoring Committee).
[69] Taped interview Naipospos February 1998.
[70] On February 21, for example, I went to the main office of the YLBH in Jakarta, in the company of a friend well known to the staff there. We were informed that the foundation's leaders were keeping a low profile because of all the disappearances, and that parked cars containing people who seemed to be surveiling the office had been seen in the area. (Field notes, February 22, 1998.)
[71] See Siegel 2001: 91–92.

At this point, however, the regime made a critical mistake, inadvertently granting student activists the resources to form a single movement. In a move that seems designed to further quarantine activist constituencies from one another, on February 20, Major General Djadja Suparman (denying that demonstrations were prohibited) stipulated that they should "occur in participants' respective places." He went on to promise that if activists moved into the streets, the military would take firm action.[72] Other authorities soon echoed the announcement. Students took this announcement to mean that long-prohibited campus protests would thenceforth be *tolerated,* particularly when other officials picked up on Suparman's distinction between the permissible and the prohibited. From that point, campus lawns, university buildings, student and alumni associations all became resources for movement activity.[73] Prior to that, and despite the partial revitalization of student institutions (the press and university councils) under *keterbukaan,* authorities had prevented widespread student movements, and used violence (as in Ujang Pandang in 1986) when protests grew too strong. From February 23, 1998, new and stable access to university resources allowed sustained, daily student protests across Indonesia. The protests soon grew less isolated as well: if Indonesian students were in general allowed to protest on campuses, then *any* university campus became a protest arena, and any campus action became part of an apprehensible and single-student movement. Any attack on a student assembly, similarly, came to be viewed as an assault on a national student body – and reliably triggered further demonstrations across the country. On February 25, a banner "New Order Struggle Campus" stretched across the entrance to the University of Indonesia.[74]

After February 23, campus demonstrations spread rapidly across Indonesia and adopted a dynamic array of tactics. Students held *mimbar bebas* (open fora) that evoked the PDI siege. They marched and rallied inside campuses, undertook hunger strikes, and organized *aksi kaprihatinan* (demonstrations of uneasiness) designed to avoid antagonizing authorities and to send principled messages (in the moral force tradition). Since most Indonesian elites had graduated from some university, many

---

[72] *Jawa Post,* February 20, 1998. The exact words were: "Asal aksi itu dilaksanakan di tempatnya masing-masing. Kalau sampai turun ke jalan, kami tindak tegas."

[73] Others have described the shift in the student movement at this moment as mainly one involving new actors in the protests – formal student organizations and members of the campus faculty and educational bureaucracy. That these groups undertook demonstrations on campus is presented as a natural consequence of the new forces involved – but I think the key to the entire shift lies in the new permission given to use campus facilities. See Soewarsono 1999a: 159–163.

[74] Nusantara *et al.* 2001: 35.

began to return to what seemed protected demonstrations, as alumni, for the campus was, to use Suparman's permitting phrase, "their place" as well.[75] Public intellectuals and university administrators defended the protests, and kept security forces off university grounds. In early March, Gajah Mada produced the largest demonstrations since the NKK/BKK, when over 10,000 students marched down the university's main avenue. A small hunger strike preceded that action – a strike that soldiers had harassed before General Suparman's announcement, but left alone thereafter. Interestingly, students at that hunger strike, interviewed days before the mobilization, expressed feeling isolated from larger political currents, and ignored by their classmates.[76]

The sudden reversal of long-standing prohibitions on campus politics is rather surprising. Since the early 1970s, New Order policies that fragmented and localized dissent, and particularly prevented aggrieved individuals from forming action-oriented associations that could sustain dissent. Even as *keterbukaan* had liberalized many of Indonesia's political rules, it maintained established efforts to keep dissident organizations fragmented. Moreover, by the late 1990s, most Indonesians, as we have seen, had internalized most of these rules, making their enforcement quite simple.

The economic crisis, however, made fragmenting policies more difficult to sustain and less likely to work, particularly as international actors entered the picture. In 1998, the IMF demanded political and fiscal reforms (a revised national budget, an end to consumer subsidies that successfully moderated village unrest earlier in the year, and measures against corruption and nepotism). It also criticized plans to fix an exchange rate, ending an alternative to which the regime had committed a great share of its dwindling prestige. With Suharto visibly weakened – and receiving almost daily, publicized calls from global leaders pleading for reform – a broader and broader range of Indonesian society was drawn into demonstrations. Faced with the deepening economic crisis, an approaching MPR, stronger internal regime conflict and intense international pressure, the regime needed to create some space for itself. The Suparman announcement *inadvertently* gave students new resources, but seems more designed to segregate students from other potential demonstrators. Security forces were almost certainly concerned to prevent mixed street demonstrations, particularly as the 1998 MPR meeting approached, and would have known that similar large and diverse rallies had recently toppled other dictators in Asia.

[75] Siegel 2001.
[76] Interview with author, February 27, 1998.

Beyond the MPR

The MPR meeting passed without producing any particularly large or explosive protest, but also without undercutting the momentum building on university campuses. From the beginning, these campus protests defied new regulations and strove to gain the streets. Many initially adopted tactics suited to fixed-site protest: the *mimbar bebas,* sit-ins and the hunger strikes. Soon, however, parades around campus grew routine, particularly as activists began regarding authoritarian control itself as the dominant issue.[77] From March 20, most campus demonstrations tried to *turon jalan* (to gain the streets, a term that invoked student calls in the early 1980s to *turon massa).*[78] The effort drew students into clashes with soldiers at campus exits. Students sometimes retreated after minor skirmishes, but often stood their ground and fought it out with under-matched security forces. Violent confrontations in one campus sparked protests in others, and the movement gathered force daily, particularly when missing activist reports began to circulate, or detainees returned from custody with stories of torture, interrogation, and the first eye-witness testimony linking Probowo's troops to kidnappings.[79] Student activists did not initially engage mass society,[80] and often when they broke through to the streets, their demonstration dissipated with no clear sense of purpose. At the same time, some students seem to have discussed reform with some soldiers at university gates; cultivating ties to Navy, Air Force and Marine officers led to later supporting relationships between those service branches and student demonstrators. By April 15, the first coordinated, multi-campus protests were taking place, on the initiative of a broad activist front called the Urban Forum (*Forum Kota,* or *Forkot).*[81]

In May, IMF pressure forced Suharto to lift consumer subsidies on gas and oil, and he lost his remaining ability to keep protest segmented. The move had been scheduled many months before, probably on the reliable assumption that protests would have abated after the MPR elections. But access to campus resources prolonged student demonstrations, which were in full swing when oil and electricity price hikes took effect. Immediate and massive violence across the archipelago directly followed these measures. Mobilized students joined these new protests, and

---

[77] Pattiradjawane 1999: 121–138.
[78] The efforts of students to leave campus in their demonstrations are reported as something new in a *Kompas* article on April 3, 1998.
[79] McRae 2001: 11.
[80] Siegel 2001: 91–93.
[81] Siegel 2001: 37–39.

suddenly defying military blockades at university gates was not a merely symbolic act, but an effort to join something larger, building on the streets. Unlike 1974 Malari protests, students and activists in 1998 had considerably more experience with mass communities, and were initially able to keep demonstrations focused on issues of democracy, corruption and economic mismanagement. By May's second week, sustained demonstrations across Indonesia even won guarded approval from some sections of ABRI – and particularly from Marine, Air Force and Navy service branches.

On May 12, soldiers fired at demonstrators from Trisakti university, killing four, and ongoing protests surged to a paroxysm of violence.[82] Almost immediately, rumors began linking the worst violence to mysterious provocateurs sporting military haircuts, even suggesting that such agents had executed the Trisakti students on purpose. Undercover Kopassus men, angling to provoke chaos to justify martial law under General Probowo, seem to have teased what might have been peaceful demonstrations into looting and vandalism. Mobs ransacked and burned some of Jakarta's most affluent shopping centers, and more focused attacks on Chinese people and businesses occurred in other neighborhoods – attacks once more strongly linked to troops that Probowo commanded. The greatest violence occurred from May 13 to May 14 while Suharto was in Cairo. On May 14, much of Jakarta was on fire, and would continue to burn for three days. Troops then spread across Jakarta to restore order, and students retreated to their various campuses, badly shaken. Around 2,250 people died in the rioting. 31 remained missing and over 150 Chinese women had been raped in what seemed a coordinated assault.[83] (By November 1998, government and independent human rights' bodies agreed that troops loyal to Probowo raped Chinese women in an organized and coordinated manner during these days, and also reported that many of these actions were planned at a May 14 meeting among twelve influential Probowo supporters.)[84] 40 large shopping centers, 4,083 shops and 1,026 private homes had been attacked, burned or looted.[85]

After May 15, students went to their campuses to regroup. On May 18, they again moved off campus, this time to the MPR building across town.

---

[82] Siegel 2001; see also Sembiring 1998; *Furom*, June 16, 1998; Pattiradjawane 1999.

[83] *Tim Relawan untuk Kemanusiaan* (Volunteer Team for Humanitarianism) July 28, 1998. These figures are generally supported by the government-sponsored *Tim Gabungan Pencari Fakta* (TGPF, Consolidated Fact-Finding Team). "Pemerintah Akui Ada Perkosaan Massal." Reported in *Media*, September 22, 1998; Sumardi 1998.

[84] *Jakarta Post*, November 4, 1998.

[85] National Committee on Human Rights' estimates, reported in *Kompas*, June 4, 1998.

Students wore identifying university jackets, distinguishing them from non-student elements they thought were most responsible for the riots. Military officers, especially form the Air Force, Navy and Marines, flanked the students to buffer them from hostile government forces, but also echoed some student demands in guardedly supportive statements. Several times students tried to march from Parliament to the national monument near the Presidential Palace, but troops blocked the road, containing protests at the MPR building, but not dispersing students.[86] Outside Jakarta, similar rallies occurred: half a million gathered on May 20 at the Sultan's palace at Jogjakarta; thousands marched to the provincial legislature in Benjarmasin; 20,000 demonstrated at Surakarta's city council – and so on across the archipelago.

The break came when Suharto returned from Cairo. Even in Egypt, he expressed some inclination to resign his office, although back in Jakarta he demanded the right to name a new transition cabinet. By then, however, Suharto's allies were fast deserting him, and conflict within the regime, particularly between Wiranto and Prabowo, was escalating dangerously. On the evening of May 20, General Wiranto pressed Suharto to resign. At around that same time, GOLKAR head and MPR speaker Harmoko also withdrew support for Suharto both publicly and privately. On May 21, Suharto resigned and turned power over to Vice-President Habibie. That night, a stand off occurred between troops loyal to Wiranto and those backing Prabowo, outside the new president's house. Wiranto's troops eventually escorted Probowo's to the barracks – beginning a series of demotions and transfers that eventually left a marginal Prabowo in undeclared, self-imposed exile.[87]

The new regime was structurally, and in its personnel, little changed from the New Order. Habibie replaced Suharto and named a cabinet that included several reformers, but the New Order's essential structure and staffing remained. The democracy movement had not the capacity to demand representation from its own ranks, let alone to displace old regime members immediately. Those who remained in power had few debts to the mass movement, and the transition initially emphasized continuity and order. Still, authorities had to rapidly adjust the rules of participation. Restrictions on non-state political organizations fell away, and by June, new political and activist organizations, such as Forkot GERAK (Anti-Anarchy Reform Movement) and KEPARAD (Committee for the Struggle Against Armed Forces Dual Function)

---

[86] McRae 2001: 14.
[87] *Straits Times*, November 5, 1998.

regularly demonstrated. Many formerly weak associations, able for the first time to expand, also joined the demonstrations.[88] Habibie was forced to authorize several inquiries into New Order brutality and corruption, and these produced evidence of ABRI's horrendous and sustained violence, particularly in Aceh and East Timor. On the strength of these revelations, Wiranto was eventually promoted to defense minister, a sly move from Suharto's play book that removed him from the ABRI command; then President Wahid subsequently replaced Wiranto in the Ministry, appointing the first civilian to that post since before the New Order. The suddenly free media eagerly covered this activity, and helped publicize more common activist campaigns. Activists resisted efforts to re-impose authoritarian controls (such as "Government Regulation Number 2" forcing all assemblies to register march routes and destinations with authorities).

Nevertheless, activists remained relatively weak and vulnerable to external provocation and intrigue. Mysterious "ninja" killings in Eastern Java in late 1998, reportedly yet another destabilizing plot from a military faction, terrorized the populations. New freedoms provided leeway for bloody communal violence, as in Maluku and Kalimantan. Weak movement organizations had trouble directing mass action, and political conflict often flared between activist collectives. When soldiers killed seven more student demonstrators on November 1, 1998, democracy activists mobilized once more, this time pushing through some important elements of their program to dismantle some of the structures of the New Order – pushing the democracy process further than many officials would have preferred.[89] Popular protest encouraged broader investigations into human rights, the separation of the police from ABRI, the reduction of military seats in the DPR, the further investigations into Suharto's ill-gotten wealth, and a review of the regime's policies in East Timor.

Still, the movement's general disarray meant that it was unable, as a political force, to exact a share of political power, and access to government positions only broadened in earnest after 1999 elections, in which activist constituencies played strong roles. Elections followed in stages as the New Order had mandated: a popular election chose a national assembly in 1999, and that assembly chose a president (Abdurrahman Wahid) in March 2000. But the elections also ushered in myriad new political parties, with supporting mass organizations pursuing far

---

[88] For a discussion of the variety of student organizations that emerged during this period, consult Saunders 1998.

[89] See, for instance, student protests against Government decree Number 2 on September 17, 1998. (*Kompas*, September 18, 1998.)

less-restricted campaigns. Still, the work of rebuilding a democratic Indonesia had only begun, and both entrenched forces like ABRI, and unruly communal relations have threatened Indonesia's new freedoms. Nor have either of the post-Habibie leaders been particularly successful in forging an apparatus that could both govern and represent. This, too, is surely a legacy of the New Order's particular style of repression.

Thinking about the Indonesian transition

The New Order decayed in ways that prevented both state agencies from reconsolidating power, as SLORC did in Burma, and social movements from acquiring strong, organized and coordinated perspectives on governance, as occurred in the Philippines. Three forces combined to bring down Suharto, but the process left no clear successor organizations to fill the void the New Order left. First, social protest undoubtedly provided some of the more important blows to the regime, particularly since Suharto had premised his entire regime on its ability to restore and maintain order. Yet Indonesian protest never was able to arrange itself into a government in waiting, and for this reason advanced as much by dint of demonstrating that the existing political arrangement could not prevent unrest as by posing any clear alternative. Second, divisions in the New Order destabilized the regime, but Suharto had done such a good job balancing his rivals against one another that no faction emerged in control of the state. While state officials were perhaps alone powerful enough to convince Suharto to resign, they have been, individually and as agencies, marked by weakness and vulnerability since. Wiranto dispatched Probowo, Wahid neutralized Wiranto and subsequent power struggles in ABRI have been far more defensive than aggressive. GOLKAR failed miserably in its initial post-Suharto campaigns, and other political parties, such as those that supported both Wahid and Megawati, have demonstrated their ability to mobilize supporters, but not to help stabilize a government. Third, the massive Asian currency crisis proved too much for the corrupt regime to manage, and as the economy collapsed, both domestic and international forces bore down on Suharto, demanding change. But in the absence of either a strong successor faction within the regime or an organized and capable alternative from society, structural conditions weakening the regime did little to promote an alternative.

Because the New Order countered most dissent with efforts to fragment opponents, accumulating regime weakness did not immediately signal an impending regime change. Proscriptions against organized dissent, like efforts to foster service branch and personal rivalries inside the military, meant that even when state agents fell on hard times, alternatives to the New Order did not immediately arise. The end of the New Order therefore came both as a complete surprise and as the natural consequences of decay begun a decade earlier. Although Filipino activists doubtless benefited from economic collapse, they still had the organizational power, in Marcos's final two years, to make their own political opportunities, and drive the regime into crisis. Indonesian oppositionists had no such capability, and relied rather more on the coincidence of economic crisis and political election to generate the anti-dictatorship movement's final thrust. Initially, moreover, they had to rely on the stronger positions of defecting regime officials, stirred less by assertions of mass power than by desires to avert unfettered mass violence.

These processes have had important legacies for Indonesian politics after 1998. Every successor institution – state or social – has been significantly fragmented by the New Order's political style, and this has created a substantial social void. Political leaders do not control mass energies so much as they have hoped to direct and claim them. Other legacies of New Order rule (ethnic conflict resulting from forced or state-sponsored internal migration policies; rural violence fostered by state-sponsored militia designed to keep East Timor, or Aceh, or West Papua in the fold; social dislocation resulting from the past impossibility of building social or political organizations to direct social demands and claims; and, continuing economic crisis) have also destabilized post-Suharto Indonesia. More damagingly, it is difficult to imagine resolving many of these problems without some level of organized political and social life capable of connecting mass society with national leaders. The absence of just such connections traces directly back to the old dispensation's desire to rule by scattering its opposition, fragmenting its society, and monopolizing political organization.

11   Democracy protest and state repression

How do patterns of contention shape transitions to democracy? Many describe protest as essentially an accelerant, pushing state reformers toward making broader concessions than they originally had in mind. Others reduce democracy struggle to almost an epiphenomenon: waters rushing along channels already carved by shifts in regime member interest, by class development and economic growth[1] or some other essentially evolutionary dynamic. Some look to explain regime transitions via alliances between reformers inside the state and moderates in society, as if these identities were significant independent of, and prior to, democracy struggle.[2] Others argue that analysts should write a clearer role for processes of struggle into explanations for these events,[3] often examining how mass-mobilization pressures regime and social elites into democratizing agreements.[4]

Most of these approaches, to my mind, share a central flaw: the process of economic development, changing elite interest or political struggle are judged in terms of how they bring social and political arrangement toward democracy, rather than in how they break down tyranny. Even demonstrating shifts in some elite interests toward democracy falls short of the task, because authoritarian regimes often persist despite the democratic proclivities of some of their members. The real phenomena we should address do not concern the emergence of forces demanding democracy, but the evolution of conditions that undo programs of repression and domination on which dictatorships depend. Any account of democratization processes needs to explain mechanisms that pry open the dictatorship. Consider, as an example of one such effort, Elizabeth Wood's work on El Salvador and South Africa. In her account, the rising costs that guerilla warfare in each country imposed on members of the oligarchy

---

[1] Cutwright 1963; Lipset 1959; DiPalma 1990.
[2] O'Donnell and Schmitter 1986; for a critique, see Collier and Mahoney 1997.
[3] Bormeo 1997.
[4] Bunce 1999; Ekiert 1996.

diminished political and economic elites' commitment to repression, dividing them from members of the security apparatus. In this reading, repression required the joint efforts of political, economic and security force elites, and with the business classes seeking a separate peace, the military was unable to retain its authoritarian posture.[5] More generally, we have seen that authorities' actions to consolidate power and defend against specific challengers create unique political circumstances in each of the cases. If we understand dictatorship in terms of particular mechanisms to bear down on particular challengers, then we should also understand democracy movements via their abilities to break these strategies down.

Three main themes emerge from the case narratives that will structure this final chapter. First, events that encouraged democracy movements acquire significance as political opportunities only in connection with ongoing modes of contention. Opportunities that attract our greatest concern do not merely encourage mobilization, but encourage *modes* of mobilization with particular power to undercut established state–society relations. Second, interactions between state repression and claim making (i.e. contention) influence who will be available for the democratizing coalition, and on what terms. Third, the political character of alliances among democratizing forces *in turn* influences movement power, coherence and capacity – factors that all matter immensely in the post-dictatorship settlement. We might retrospectively describe transitions as pacted, negotiated or something else, but the likelihood that a struggle will move in one or another such direction has much to do with established patterns of contention.

Mobilizing opportunities

In both the Philippines and Indonesia, long-term trends toward political openness (martial law's abolition and *keterbukaan*) increased protest levels, but developments most crucial to increasing anti-dictatorship pressure (as opposed to mere mobilization) allowed modes of struggle that regimes had previously inhibited. Marcos's recurring pattern of reform and crackdown originally demobilized most moderates, and radicalized others (sending them to ND networks.) After 1981, however, economic crisis and martial law's end combined to encourage more resilient movement organizations of the political center, alongside strong movement growth on the left. Under these conditions, state repression

[5] Wood 2000.

ceased to inhibit centrist protest, and in fact triggered large anti-regime mobilizations in which more reform-oriented forces played larger roles. The simultaneous operation of both moderate and radical networks, moreover, rendered state gestures toward reform or popular participation even less effective demobilizing strategies. Not only did reform (intended to diminish support for armed struggle) continue to mobilize moderate networks, but moderates were now more able to respond to repression with their own mobilization – though some still radicalized into ND groups. Hence, attacks on moderate leaders like Aquino produced the broadest possible protest, and both participatory opportunities *and* repression began to trigger assertive, sustained protest.

Despite *keterbukaan,* Indonesian authorities retained strong and successful prohibitions on opposition *organization.* Activists did begin to use official parties to evade some New Order regulations, but this did not reverse the general consequences of state prohibition. Anti-regime groups usually could not command demonstrations (as in the Philippines), and most powerful episodes of contention (like the 1996 PDI protests) required direct and powerful external provocation. Without the economic crisis, and the fear of rioting triggered by that crisis, protests surrounding the 1998 MPR would likely have been weaker, shorter and less threatening. Authorities allowed student demonstrations on campus in view of these developments, and that change gave protest a more sustained central thrust. Simultaneous rural violence, economic crisis and urban protest, now more coordinated by activist centers, hampered Suharto's ability to maintain order, and eroded his legitimacy. Massive May riots finally convinced ABRI and GOLKAR leaders to withdraw support from the president.

The difference between events that produced movement opportunities in these two cases reflects two separate factors. First, the centrality of movement organization in the Philippines, and its virtual absence in Indonesia, meant that anti-regime pressure worked off different triggers. The Philippine anti-dictatorship movement decisively benefited from opportunities that expanded organizational resources (over two years before the dictatorship fell) and movements then purposively deployed their forces, making their own opportunities as they went. Despite modest Indonesian organizational growth, political opportunities that spurred contention were more directly mobilizing, and less mediated by organizational structures or decisions. Indonesian activists could not coordinate protest until powerful unorganized mobilization produced new (i.e. campus-based) organizational resources. Second, particularly subversive mobilization forms were subversive *in relation* to specific modes of state domination. Philippine authorities depended so heavily on portraying dissidents as communist that they rapidly lost support when ordinary people (businessmen, housewives and clergy) moved to the opposition's fore. By easing the political polarization that Marcos required, moderate resistance became far more subversive than radical insurgency. In Indonesia, sustained multi-sectoral protest (as Marcos had endured for years) was particularly corrosive to a state founded on the idea of order. Broad and sustained unrest signaled Suharto's inability to deliver on the New Order's central domestic objective: a docile and fragmented society.

Unlike either Philippine or Indonesian protests, Burma's democracy movement did not benefit from any liberalizing trend; Ne Win's regime on the eve of the March 1988 Rangoon demonstrations remained committed to preventing anti-state mobilization in lowland Burma. Routine political processes did not contain participatory moments (like elections) that periodically spurred mobilization in the Philippines and Indonesia, and repression had driven activists to the insurgent countryside or into fragmented and isolated underground cells. By utterly proscribing dissent, the regime prevented anyone from demanding limited reforms. Moreover, the arduous and precarious construction of underground cells made their members unwilling to risk rash or early action, and so nothing encouraged activists to probe for some sign of an authoritarian thaw. Protest mobilized following steep economic declines triggering mass unrest, rather than hints of political change exciting activist hopes. With social networks and associations pruned back to the township and village levels, only markets efficiently diffused grievances and unrest (as in the 1987 demonetization). Furious local mobilization early on, such as March 1988 student protests, responded to specific state attacks on definite and proximate groups (i.e. students) but then established networks that could coordinate later, broader mobilization.

As underground activists became more involved, however, new sorts of events stimulated mobilization. As in Indonesia, the Burmese movement lacked an initial organizational apparatus, but activists in submerged networks soon began planning activities with a degree of control that Indonesians never achieved. By late July, activists were already planning nationwide demonstrations for August 8, indicating that mobilization no longer needed a particular exogenous provocation (apart from general anger at the regime) and movement leaders could create and define their own opportunities. The rapid, simultaneous emergence of strike committees, strike newspapers, and national protests all reflect a degree of central coordination more like Philippine contention than Indonesian – although the movement's descent into chaos also illustrates this coordinating authority's comparative weakness.

As in the Philippines and Indonesia, Burmese subversion acquired meaning in relation to the history of Burmese contention. Since 1962 the regime had been most determined to prevent open dissent in lowland cities, with important consequences for 1988. Beyond harsh, immediate repression, authorities responded to urban dissent by closing universities and sending students home – providing two advantages to the embryonic movement. First, university closures halted urban activity (school life as well as protest) so underground activists could begin contacting and training university students. Second, the arrival of cosmopolitan activists at rural villages spread news of the movement and established connections that underground activists would build on over the next several months. Nevertheless, the national coordination of Burmese protest did less than one might think to weaken the regime. Because authorities held power by holding the cities, they withstood the movement's assault by murdering students, and chasing survivors into the countryside. Authorities had good reason to prefer this kind of fight to protest in the streets, for they had stable, almost routine ways of dealing with insurgency, and surely could accommodate an influx of inexperienced fighters into enemy camps.

What, then, can we say about the events that triggered these democracy movements? First, initial movement opportunities led to riper, democratizing challengers by encouraging *modes* of resistance that authorities had tried to repress, resistance that pushed directly against the state's particular containment strategy. Hence events that mobilized and angered the political center fueled democracy protest in the Philippines, while the movement in Indonesia blossomed when events allowed sustained, and eventually more coordinated protest from diverse social groups. In Burma, economic crisis provoked such strong anti-regime protests that underground activists could plan a more sustained and extensive public attack than Burma had seen for decades (although by rising earlier in the cycle and avoiding some prominent mistakes, the Burmese underground also made the most of these opportunities).

Second, where activists could draw on stronger organizational resources, protest required less exogenous stimulus. 1986 electoral cheating in the Philippines was not entirely out of proportion to earlier fraud, but the mass mobilizing presidential campaign and the expansion of movement organizations positioned activists to seize upon those events to new effect. Indonesia had far fewer organizations, and protest consistently required external events like the MPR meeting, or the Trisakti student murders to trigger and coordinate activity. Indonesian protest, moreover, was strongest when it threatened to loose the pent up energies of mass society in a wave of chaos and destruction. In Burma, initial mobilization required the massive provocation of demonetization, but later protests were increasingly planned – until the state retreat opened the field of play to less organized collectives, and over-ran the movement leadership's organizational capacity.

Links between specific political opportunities and forms of struggle in each case therefore retrace established patterns of contention. These links not only explain why each democracy movement achieved broad scope, but also imply why particular styles of mobilization subverted particular regimes. Nevertheless, these associations tell only half of the story. The other half involves constraints on the state's ability to survive popular pressure. In this realm, too, established patterns of contention influenced state activity. As things began to deteriorate for each regime, the prospect of widespread defections from regime circles increased. Whether or not these defections occurred, however, depended on the availability of state and social reformers to one another – an availability also molded by years of contention.

Regime repression, modes of struggle and the movement's constituent alliance

Most theories of democratic transition emphasize the role that middle classes play in that process, either because this class produces the democratic agenda, or because it moderates political demands by limiting distributional claims in favor of procedural reform.[6] Such arguments undoubtedly carry a significant freight of truth, but not the entire load. The cases suggest more contingency: patterns of contention influenced how social reformers (middle-class or otherwise) and disgruntled regime members would be available to one another, if at all. Some patterns of repression drive all activists toward the political margins (where they likely develop coalitions around radical challenges to the regime); others distinguish between legal and illegal modes of dissent, between moderate and radical claims, or among claim makers from different social classes. Some repression criminalizes movement organizations or eliminates experienced activists; other repression allows activists to survive and lead subsequent protest. Repression directly influences how existentially, politically or ideologically available social reformers will be to potential regime defectors. This availability, in turn, shapes the likelihood of defections from the authoritarian coalition, and so the regime's resilience in the face of protest.

Years of Marcos-style repression produced an organized, moderate and increasingly hardy faction of the Philippine anti-dictatorship movement;

[6] Higley and Gunther 1992.

as the regime imploded and communists gained strength, this faction's availability helped rouse nervous or dissatisfied regime members to action, and certainly explains the movement's subsequent centrality to the transition. In Burma, by contrast, social elites were every bit as marginal as mass members of society. Pro-democracy elites could hence never present themselves as an incremental reform movement that provided state actors an alternative to *both* a fundamental transformation (in which all regime members would lose out) and deepening authoritarian rule. In Indonesia, as in the Philippines, a distinct elite and moderate pro-democracy force existed. Unlike Filipino moderates, however, this stratum was left unorganized and fearful of mass unrest by regime repression – with little option but to ask authorities to lead the reform process. Violence and chaos, rather than potential support from social moderates, therefore triggered actions against Suharto from within the state, and also ensured that regime members would dominate the early transformation. Hence the most successful and stable transitions occurred where committed opposition leaders, astride independent political bases, stood in useful proximity to wavering members of the authoritarian regime. Where such leaders did not exist, or were unavailable to regime members, the struggle moved toward open warfare (Burma) or a palace coup (Indonesia). Let us look more closely at these two developments, before returning to the more stable Philippine transition.

Ultimately, the Burmese struggle failed, despite sustained mobilization, because no connection was possible between movement leaders and regime members. The struggle, moreover, developed in directions that *shrank* possibilities for such connections. Decades of repression wiped out any open or accepted dissent and prevented a dissident discourse from gaining influence within the regime. Indeed, most regime members were shocked by concessions to reforming ideas that Ne Win seemed to make at the 1988 party congress, and evidence suggests that they lobbied for stronger authoritarian impositions, not reform.[7] Impoverished, weak and often fearful, excluded elites remained elite only in their intellectual capacities and experiences: *that* poor man used to be a powerful lawyer, *that* quiet woman was a respected student leader. Excluded elites were no more able (or willing) to cut a separate deal with the regime than anyone else, and this encouraged strong solidarity between the movement's summit and its base, governed by stable anti-regime orientations. Still, as things developed, ties between movement leaders and mass society, if extensive, were also quite weak. Recall how completely retired General

[7] Mya Maung 1990.

Aung Gyi misread mass sentiments in his August 24 speech, or how underground activists could not dissuade mass members from seizing local government offices. The divide between state and movement also explains why the *Tatmadaw* never lost its ability to use violence. Troops from bloody frontier counter-insurgency saw protesters as another "other," and were summoned by authorities for exactly that reason.

With no bridge between Burmese society and the state, political contention moved toward a peculiar combination of protest and insurrectionary strategies, premised on the disbelief that authorities would ever make real concessions to democracy advocates. With virtually the whole society backing the protests in August and conditions utterly polarized between the (absent) state and a movement at floodtide, sustained massive demonstrations applied little *additional* pressure. Indeed, this very polarization distanced authorities from movement appeals, and allowed many sections of the movement to shun conciliatory overtures from the Maung Maung government.[8] Starting on August 20, strike committees also embarked upon a more insurrectionary path, seizing local government offices and assuming their functions. Administering these offices often overshadowed the need to build stronger movement mechanisms or to attract support from wavering members of the ruling elite. Hence, the dramatic exercise of movement capacity never diminished the state's ability to respond or divided regime unity.

In Indonesia, groups available to challenge the state had adapted to repressive patterns restricting movement organization: free-floating public intellectuals, cautious activists working in (mainly) small NGOs, members of official opposition parties, and a small cadre of new and secret activists in the illegal PRD underground. Mass society had little direct place in this group, but counted in two indirect respects. First, though political activists could not organize mass bases, they drew poor communities into local campaigns, and advocated more general reforms *on behalf* of the poor and marginalized. Second, greatly threatened by the economic crisis, many poor communities rioted between late 1997 and 1998. Still, without significant organizational machineries, pro-democracy activists did not possess the authority or experience to direct mass unrest against authorities. As mobilization increased through 1998, therefore, it was not clear how activists would translate their own dissent or mass energies into political influence.

---

[8] Maung Maung (Dr.) 1999; this account is partially confirmed by interview with informant B–1.

Unable to control the violence that periodically emerged from mass society (often with military provocation), democracy activists never acquired the insurrectionary self-confidence sometimes evident in a more fragmented Burmese society (or, more predictably, in the Philippines). Even at its most assertive, therefore, Indonesian protests never angled to seize state power outright. Demonstrations appealed to forces within the regime, often ABRI, to take charge of a government in disarray. In the appeal, demonstrators occupied an ambiguous position, speaking both on behalf of impoverished Indonesians and as a class jeopardized by (and fearful of) unruly mass riots. Sustained, more or less coordinated protests (particularly escalating student clashes with security forces from February through March) triggered broader support from Indonesian society for a reform process. But the violence, especially in May, also lent urgency to authorities' efforts to contain student protests and helped convince (perhaps allowed?) military and party leaders to force Suharto's resignation.

Only in the Philippines did state repression allow elite dissidents to develop a machinery that both gave them control over mass constituencies and allowed a stable movement leadership to form. Anti-dictatorship leaders often grew within the movement, and could claim to represent mass society by virtue of concrete organizational ties rather than a privileged moral or intellectual vantage point (as Indonesian activists frequently claimed). Moderate movement leaders were credible and familiar to regime members concerned about the economic crisis, corruption, political polarization and presidential succession. The movement's strong elite base and established institutional support, moreover, helped assure potential regime defectors and undecided elites that the democratization process would keep the genie of social redistribution in the bottle. Because democracy protests were organized, the movement could present itself as an alternative to the regime (as Burmese activists did) rather than appealing, for instance, to a faction of the AFP. Marcos's repressive strategy – which needed to leave some room for political freedoms – thus enabled moderate leaders to develop ties to both mass society and the regime.

This organizational power, emerging as it did in a society that Marcos had contrived to polarize politically, made massive, peaceful and programmatically moderate demonstrations both possible and effective. A powerful moderate movement wing, in turn, placed the relationship between the movement and the regime on a different footing than that in either Burma or Indonesia. Movement leaders never seemed caught between a repressive state and a dangerously violent society (a common theme in Indonesian protest). Rather, they embraced mass struggle as their own, apparently collapsing the class distance between movement constituencies. Political contention cemented the movement's internal class alliances, allowing movement leaders to modulate mass activity and produce comparatively little violence or property damage. In the Burmese example (more like the Philippine than the Indonesian in terms of its elite/mass cooperation) Rangoon strike committees often sank to levels of violence beyond leaders' preference or control. Burmese underground groups were loosely connected with shallow social roots, and could not exercise much control over these formations – although stronger movement networks in Mandalay meant more control and less violence.

The Philippine movement coalition produced a curious mix of radical political tropes (many borrowed from the dynamic insurgency) and essentially moderate political objectives, held together by a usefully plastic and vague invocation of revolution.[9] Under the prevailing conditions, it was possible to contemplate a bloodless revolution against Marcos, for moderate leaders could select peaceful struggle, and the movement's organizations could control mass members. Most groups made appropriate gestures toward redistributive reforms, but could also contain mass struggle (and eventually compromised away most mass demands). But what accounts for the subversive power that peaceful demonstrations attained in the Philippines? Again, we must consider authoritarian rule's particular Philippine imprint. The burgeoning moderate movement challenged a core Marcos claim: that he alone prevented communist triumph. By demonstrating an explicitly non-violent and democratic alternative to either, the movement triggered defections from the state and diverted international alliances in ways that critically weakened Marcos.

Another set of contrasts between the Philippine case and the other two also depends on differences in movement organization. Both Burmese and Indonesian movements proved extraordinarily susceptible to external provocation. In Burma, rumors that military agents and released convicts were poisoning activists' food and water created panic toward the end of August – and movement participants killed more than one person who, to their eyes, looked like spies.[10] In Indonesia, movement members made similar attacks on bystanders who could not, for example, show student ID cards, and the massive May violence (to say nothing of the mysterious "ninja killings" in East Java after Suharto stepped down)

---

[9] For a fuller discussion of this, see my argument in Boudreau 2001.
[10] Smith 1999.

seem to have been instigated by state agents of some kind.[11] In both cases, external provocation triggered frightened and murderous activist reactions because movement organizations could not screen outsiders, identify threats and discipline participant activity. Mobilized activity, particularly under circumstances where a repressive state might do *anything*, was therefore governed by a fear that a comrade could be an enemy. Violence provoked by state infiltration naturally would give some potential movement members pause, and increase chances that some potential dissidents would seek old regime protection. In the Philippines, stronger movement organizations largely prevented this sort of provocation, and the transition probably retained strong elite support because it never entailed violent or unrestrained attacks on adversaries or secondary targets of opportunity. Efforts to infiltrate Philippine anti-state movements seem only to have worked when authorities devoted considerable time and resources to the project, as with the long-term military efforts to infiltrate the communist movement in the mid-1980s.[12] Instructively, some have linked the CPP's vulnerability at that time to an earlier period of heedless expansion, in which new recruits were insufficiently scrutinized.[13]

Movement outcomes

The failure of Burmese democratization, relative to Philippine and Indonesian processes, can probably be explained both by factors discussed here and by those emphasized by other democratization theorists. Burma had a small middle class, a cohesive state and a fragmented civil society, all of which diminished prospects of a transition. Yet those who would doubt that Burmese democracy had sufficient middle-class support to divide the regime would also have been surprised by Burma's strong pro-democracy mobilizations, and would have difficulty accounting for its defeat by the regime. This work helps explain why the regime could so thoroughly crush the movement: in contrast to developments in Indonesia and the Philippines, nothing in Burma altered authorities' established line of defenses against social challenges. Kyat demonetization, police violence and Ne Win's willingness to speculate on alternative governmental forms incited mobilization, but did not weaken authorities' hold on power, alter state–society relations, or diminish the military's ability to kill, intimidate and imprison dissidents. Some speculate that when soldiers retreated in mid-August, they set a trap to entice

[11] Siegel 2001.
[12] Abinales 1996; Garcia 2001.
[13] Jones 1989.

pro-democracy activists into the open.[14] Troops vanished from the street, participants recall, precisely as rumors began to describe military strike committees joining demonstrations. It is difficult to corroborate these conjectures, but whatever was *then* going on, the military eventually lashed out at protesters with undiminished violence.

Philippine and Indonesian events were quite different, for in each, new forms of mobilization undid established and successful repressive strategies. In the Philippines, the combination of a newly viable centrist opposition and an expanding armed left constrained the regime's ability to repress demonstrations without creating an overwhelming social reaction, and so prevented Marcos from achieving a political polarization between the communists and everyone else. Ultimately of course, the regime itself was so isolated that soldiers refused to follow orders to fire upon the EDSA demonstrations.[15] Organizational prohibitions fragmented Indonesian dissident expressions, but an increasingly divided state and powerfully collectivizing financial crisis overwhelmed authorities' efforts to keep dissident centers isolated from one another. Mobilization attained new power in both cases, not merely in terms of raw demonstration size, but also in relationship to strategies of repression and regime survival.

That said, the Philippines and Indonesian transitions also differed vastly from one another. With its formidable organizational apparatus, the Philippine movement could itself step into power, and was credible enough to attract support away from the old regime. After an unsettled period that included two serious coup attempts and several smaller adventures, the military and state bureaucracy more or less fell into step behind the new president. The movement itself supported the new regime long enough, and with sufficient enthusiasm, to allow the Aquino government to consolidate. While consolidation took the new government far from its movement origins, and the movement fragmented after 1986, activists' initial power, both relative to defecting regime members and to Philippine society, seems to have stabilized the transition, if not to have democratized its social outcomes.

Suharto's resignation did not end Indonesian protests. On the one hand, the new president, B. J. Habibie, was no more beloved than Suharto had been, nor viewed as entirely free of Suharto's influence. After the dictator left office, therefore, the new dispensation's democracy was by no means assured. But the atomized and fragmented movement could not push the post-Suharto settlement in any single, clear direction, and instead championed competing political demands, ranging from liberal reforms to a more Islamic ordering of Indonesian society. Not surprisingly, therefore, the transition's early stages remained largely in the hands of the regime (minus Suharto). In the months that followed, the liberalized rules of engagement allowed broader protest and new organizational formations, but the old regime's influence lingered. With neither strong associations nor experience at building them, mass contention often strayed toward communal violence or undisciplined direct action. Those who emerged from the New Order with an organizational network (including, of course, the military, but also business people and GOLKAR members) used the unsettled months to make political and economic hay. With no apparatus to link mass society to coordinated political activities, and in particular to activities with national and cosmopolitan referents, Indonesia was vulnerable, volatile and chaotic.

The contrast with the Philippine post-Marcos period is striking. Even when various Philippine movement organizations began seriously to question some of President Aquino's decisions, they also worried that a weakened administration would provide opportunities for a Marcos- or rightist-resurgence, and so most activists provided critical support on items like the new constitution. Movement leaders could even sell such campaigns to their increasingly disenchanted mass bases. National political calculations, that is, continued to govern mass political activity, because that activity was organizationally mediated.[16] If the results were neither perfectly democratic nor (even approximately) just, there was a participatory order to things that recalled pre-Marcos conditions. Deprived of political organizations, Indonesian movements were less able to represent social interests, or even frame coherent programs. In some instances, people who led the democracy movement sought allies from the old regime; after the 1999 popular election, but before the Presidential vote, democracy leaders Amein Rais and Abdurrahman Wahid both made overtures to GOLKAR's Habibie. More important, even political organizations that emerged during the regime transition have been weak and difficult to control.

Larger issues: democratic transitions and political protest

Why do we need a more contextually and historically rich social movements-based interpretation of democracy movements? Principally, I have argued

---

[16] Boudreau 2001.

that to understand how regimes change, we need to understand the precise formula according to which, for a time, they endure. I placed repression at the very heart of that formula, both because it represents the state's exact answer to concrete social challenges, and because it indelibly marks the social forces present at the dictatorship's end. Democracy movements rise when the state's established repressive strategy, for some reason, can no longer contain social challengers. In some cases, as in the Philippines, social and political developments make styles of repression (i.e. Marcos's efforts to polarize society between the left and the state) ineffective: while Marcos could still steal elections and attack protests in the middle 1980s, those efforts enraged, rather than cowed moderates. The Burmese democracy movement provides a strong counter-example to both the Philippine and Indonesian cases: despite massive and sustained protest, Burma's 1988 movement never eroded the state's capacity for repression, and the military eventually crushed protest, as it had for decades.

Democracy movements are less about building representative systems than they are about cutting down practices (and practitioners) that obstruct representation.[17] To identify signs that favor transitions to democracy, then, we must look for progress against those specific prohibitions that have sustained an undemocratic regime. Interactions between states and societies during the dictatorship provide a context for these inroads, establishing both their political significance in the struggle, and their analytical significance in our interpretations. At the most superficial level, that context consists of a power balance between the two sides – but this power is calibrated in terms of particular proscriptions and prohibitions that authorities seek to enforce, and society accepts, works around or defies. Regimes that have ignored distant insurgencies, therefore, may well survive their expansion; authorities that tolerate peaceful protest may weather a cycle of demonstration. In such cases, the *apparent* expansion of social power does not breach the state's main defenses, nor does it undermine state claims to hegemony. But members of repressive states also draw lines in the sand, marking off activities that are genuinely subversive to their power, and that marking defines actions corrosive to regime prestige. A movement that defies such proscriptions may both land a telling blow against authority, and signal wider audiences that the hegemonic hold has loosened. Given the dictatorship's ability to shape information and provide a covering bluster to

---

[17] Tilly 2000.

hide its failings, such confrontations are often necessary steps to making political opportunities salient.

This, perhaps more than anything, may account for the acceleration of events in the dictatorship's closing hours – for one of the most universal expressions to follow a democracy movement's triumph has been participants' sheer disbelief at their improbable success. This surprise is no accident. Apart from the determined application of repression against those who defy the state, dictatorships survive by isolating their opponents, each of which seem frail against leviathan's power. The Philippine political center, accordingly, was caught between a left with which they were uncomfortable, and an unjust state. Fragmented and localized Indonesian groups and the disconnected, cautious Burmese underground could never feel capable of exerting real power. Under such conditions, who would first rise above the crowd to denounce unjust authority? The military captain: employed, in power, but mistrustful of politicians' excess? The party leader, on whom it has begun to dawn that the dictator permits no upward mobility? The technocrat who has seen her best plans undermined, or the businessman forced to pay tribute and bribes? All must balance their growing discomfort against undeniable prerogatives and the suspicion that, should they take action, they would do so alone. New and subversive (rather than routinized) forms of collective action, however, signal shifts in the political wind. People who have grown accustomed to a dictatorship's boasts and threats will quickly recognize activity that defies authority, will interpret acts of contention, as we have attempted to do, within the established authoritarian context.

But if any of this is true, comparisons between democracy movements, stripped of their context, are likely at best to be incomplete, and at worst, misleading. In each case, similar developments preceded the democracy protest: economic crisis mobilized all three societies, and in each, illness, old age or both hampered a dictator of long standing. Regime fragmentation accompanied Philippine and Indonesian transitions, although in both, regime divisions preceded the transition by several years. In each case, one might even say, a dynamic woman outside the political mainstream played a leading role in the anti-dictatorship movement. Do any of these factors constitute clear, or clearly general causes of democracy struggle?

The answer, I think, is that they do so in only the most superficial sense. These developments influenced the balance between state and society and provoked broader contention, but did so only within the larger, older political relations between state and social power. The interplay between how authorities exercise power, and how society attempts to counter that exercise, provides the context for democracy struggle. Understanding the logic governing the thrust and parry between social and state forces helps us to interpret whether events have weakened the regime, strengthened society or left the balance between them unchanged. In striving to understand the strategic games central to contention, we begin to apprehend an episode of mobilization as progress toward democracy or a false start down an unpromising road.

This interpretation of democracy struggle, I hope, is both compelling in itself, and persuasive as an advertisement for a way of thinking about contention under conditions of great repression, or outside the liberal and industrial societies generally. The key to understanding contention in such settings rests in the logic of its interactions, rather than in identifying events that touch off collective action.[18] In these cases, very different goals and risks often animate activity. Activists may not merely pursue policy reform, and state actors do not merely defend preferred policy positions. Rather, they struggle over state power, over national autonomy, over political, social, cultural and individual survival. Because the stakes of struggle are comparatively high, modes of struggle vary across a tremendous range. In theory, everything from cyber-protest to warfare is in play, largely because collective repertoires are drawn both from local experience and international example. In practice, particular histories of state–society interaction, and the institutional, organizational, political and cultural residue they leave will push contention in one or another of these directions.

For researchers, alas, this means that deeper and more theoretically guided analysis of contention outside the industrial North will probably not produce a tight and generalizable list of factors likely to stir mobilization or regime transformation . . . but recent writing is already beginning to despair of such lists, even relative to Northern contention.[19] Rather, we might pay closer attention to political context and history, and strive to discover or interpret the strategies and perspectives that guide contentious interactions between states and societies. Where repression has significantly marked those interactions, it will naturally work its way to the fore of activist calculations, and become recognizable as particular, and context-specific contentious dynamics. As repressive regimes give way to more liberal and representative arrangements, contention's logic may also evolve. In all settings, however, modes of activity, political opportunity and democracy struggle acquire contingent, context-specific meanings. Early struggle and repression structures subsequent

---

[18] McAdam, Tarrow and Tilly 2000.
[19] McAdam, Tarrow and Tilly 2000.

contention and influences movement capacities, organizations, calculations and cultures. Influences like regime fragmentation or economic crisis may increase chances and levels of anti-regime mobilization, but in order to interpret the effect that such protests will have, we need to consider interactions with established patterns of contention. Where lists of events that qualify as "mobilization opportunities" have been more or less accurate, therefore, we might suggest that the context of struggle has been stable within individual settings, and similar among them – perhaps a fitting description of conditions in advanced industrial society over the past several decades. Even then, however, contemporary debates about what constitutes a political opportunity and why events that trigger mobilization in one country fail to do so elsewhere suggest the importance of context and history. If this matter is more obvious in places like Burma, Indonesia and the Philippines, then surely that is another example of how researchers may benefit from broad comparative study.

References

Abinales, Patricio, N. 1985. "The Left and the Philippine Student Movement: Random Historical Notes on Party Politics and Sectoral Struggles." *Kasarinlan* **1**(2): 41–45.

— 1988. "The Left and Other Forces: The Nature and Dynamics of Pre-1986 Coalition Politics." In *Marxism in the Philippines (Second Series)*, pp. 26–49. Third World Studies Center, University of the Philippines.

— 1996. "When a Revolution Devours its Children Before Victory: *Operasyon Kampanyang Ahos* and the Tragedy of Mindanao Communism." In Patricio N. Abinales, ed. *The Revolution Falters: The Left in Philippine Politics After 1986*, pp. 154–179. Ithaca: Cornell University, Southeast Asia Program Press.

— 2000. *Making Mindanao: Cotabato and Davao in the Formation of the Philippine Nation–State*. Quezon City: Ateneo de Manila University Press.

Abrahamsen, Rita. 1997. "The Victory of Popular Forces or Passive Revolution? A Neo-Gramscian Perspective on Democratization." *The Journal of Modern African Studies* **35**(1): 129–152.

Abueva, Jose. 1988. "Philippine Ideologies and National Development." In Raul P. De Guzman and Mila A. Reforma, eds. *Government and Politics of the Philippines*, pp. 18–73. New York and Oxford: Oxford University Press.

Adler, Glenn and Eddie Webster. 1995. "Challenging Transitions Theory: The Labor Movement, Radical Reform and Transition to Democracy in South Africa." *Politics and Society* **23**(1): 75–106.

Adrinof, A. C. 1988. "Kemana Perginya Aktivis Mahasiswa?" In J. A. Denny, Rahardjo Jonminofri, eds. *Kesaksian Kaum Musa*, pp. 47–63. Jakarta: Yayasan Studi Indonesia.

Akhmadi, Heri. 1979. "The *Exceptie* of Heri Akhmadi. Bandung Court of First Instance, February 5, 1979." *Indonesia* **27**(April).

Alatas, Farid Syed. 1997. *Democracy and Authoritarianism in Indonesia and Malaysia: The Rise of the Post-Colonial State*. New York: St. Martin's Press.

Allen, Alex. 1976. "The Christian Left? Just what is it?" *Philippine Daily Express* **9&10**.

Allen, Louis. 1984. *Burma: The Longest War, 1941–1945*. London: J. M. Dent & Sons.

Amenta, Edwin and Yvonne Zylan. 1995. "It Happened Here: Political Opportunity, the New Institutionalism, and the Townsend Movement." In Stanford M. Lyman, ed. *Social Movements: Critique, Concepts, Case Studies* pp. 199–233. New York University Press.

Amnesty International. 1977. *Report of an Amnesty International Mission to the Republic of the Philippines, 22 November–5 December 1975.* London: Amnesty International.

— 1983. "Indonesian Extrajudicial Killings of Suspected Criminals." London: Amnesty International.

Anderson, Benedict. 1966. "Japan: The Light of Asia." In Josef Silverstein, ed. *Southeast Asia in World War Two*, pp. 13–50. Southeast Asia Studies Monograph Series No. 7, New Haven: Yale University Press.

— 1974. *Java in Time of Revolution: Occupation and Resistance, 1944–1946.* Ithaca: Cornell University Press.

— 1978. "The Last Days of Indonesia's Suharto?" *Southeast Asia Chronicle* **63**: 2–17.

— 1983a. *Imagined Communities: Reflections on the Origin and Spread of Nationalism.* London: Verso.

— 1983b. "Old States, New Socieities: Indonesia's New Order in Comparative Historical Perspective. *The Journal of Asian Studies* **42**: 477–496.

— 1988. "Cacique Democracy in the Philippines." *New Left Review* **169** (May–June).

— 1989. "How the Generals Died." *Indonesia* **54**.

— 1990. "Murder and Progress in Modern Siam." *New Left Review* **181** (May–June).

— 1998. *The Spectre of Comparison: Nationalism, Southeast Asia and the World.* New York and London: Verso.

Anderson, Benedict and Ruth McVey. 1971. *A Preliminary Analysis of the October 1, 1965 Coup in Indonesia.* (With the assistance of Frederick P. Bunnell.) Ithaca: Modern Indonesia Project, Cornell University (Interim Report Series).

Anonymous. 1985. "Bloody Wednesday Night in Tanjung Priok." *Indonesia Reports Politics Supplement* (June 15).

Aquino, Benigno. 1980. Speech Delivered Before Asia Society, New York City (August 4, 1980). Mimeograph Copy.

Arillo, Cecilo, T. 1986. *Breakaway: The Inside Story of the 4-Day Revolution in the Philippines, February 22–25, 1986.* Manila: Cecilo Arillo.

Article 19. 1991. *State of Fear: Censorship in Burma (Myanmar).* An Article 19 Country Report. London: Article 19.

Asian Labour Update. 1994a. "Indonesia: Medan awakes." *Asian Labour Update* (**15**): 1–5.

Asian Labour Update. 1994b "Indonesia: Crackdown in Medan." *Asian Labour Update* (**16**): 20–21.

Aspinall, Edward. 1993. *Student Dissent in Indonesia in the 1980s.* Clayton, Monash: Center of Southeast Asian Studies Monograph, Monash University Press.

— 1995."Students and the Military: Regime Friction and Civilian Dissent in the Late Suharto Period." *Indonesia.* No. 59(Oct).

— 1996. "What Happened Before the Riots?" *Inside Indonesia* **48**: 4–8.

— "Student Activism in Indonesia: The Burden of Purity." Paper presented at the Association for Asian Studies Annual Meeting, March 6, 2004. San Diego, California.

Aung Gyi 1998a. *Personal Letter to General Ne Win, June 9th, 1988*. Unpublished, Wason Collection, Cornell University.
— 1998b. *Personal Letter to General Ne Win, June 29th, 1988*. Unpublished, Wason Collection, Cornell University.
— 1998c. *Personal Letter to General Ne Win, August 6th, 1988*. Unpublished, Wason Collection, Cornell University.
Aurora, Catilo and Prosperpina Tapales. 1988. "The Legislature." In Raul De Guzman and Mila Reforma eds. *Government and Politics in the Philippines*, pp. 132–163. Singapore: Oxford University Press.
Avineri, Shlomo, 1991. "Reflections on Eastern Europe." *Partisan Review* 3: 442–448.
Aye Saung. 1989. *Burman in the Back Row: An Autobiography*. Kowloon, Hong Kong. Asia 2000 Ltd.
Badgley, John. 1958. "Burma's Political Crisis." *Pacific Affairs* 31(4): 336–351.
Badie, B and P. Birnbaum. 1983. *The Sociology of the State*. Translation by A. Goldhammer. University of Chicago Press.
Baldwin, Robert. 1975. *Foreign Trade Regimes and Economic Development*. New York: Colombia University Press.
Bandung Institute of Technology Student Council. 1978. "White Book of the 1978 Students' Struggle." *Indonesia* 25. Ithaca: Modern Indonesia Project, Cornell University, Southeast Asia Program Press.
Becky, Shelley. 2001. "Protest and Globalization: Media Symbols and Audience in the Drama of Democratization." *Democratization* 8(4): 155–175.
Beissinger, Mark R. 2002. *Nationalist Mobilization and the Collapse of the Soviet State*. New York and Cambridge: Cambridge University Press.
Beltran, H. S. 1983. "The Ten Day Dress Rehersal: The Days After August 21 as Lessons for the Cynical, the Apathetic and the Politically Naïve." *Diliman Review* 31(6): 1–12.
Benda, Harry, J. 1965. "Decolonization in Indonesia: The Problem of Continuity and Change." *The American Historical Review* 70(4): 1058–1073.
Bertrand, Jacques. 1996. "False Starts Succession Crisis and Regime Transition: Flirting with Openness in Indonesia." *Pacific Affairs* 69(3): 319–340.
Body for the Protection of the People's Political Rights Facing the 1992 General Election (BPHPR). 1994. "'White Book' on the 1992 General Election in Indonesia." Translated by Dwight King. Cornell Modern Indonesia Project no. 73. Ithaca: Cornell University Southeast Asia Program Press.
Bolasco, Mario. 1984. "Marxism and Christianity in the Philippines: 1930–1983." In *Marxism in the Philippines: Marx Centennial Lectures*, pp. 56–70. Third World Studies Center: University of the Philippines.
Bonner, Raymond. 1988. *Waltzing with a Dictator: The Marcoses and the Making of American Policy*. New York: Times Books, Random House, Inc.
Bormeo, N. 1997. "Myths of Moderation: Confrontation and Conflict During Democratic Transitions." *Comparative Politics* 29: 305–322.
Boudreau, Vincent. 1996. "Northern Theory, Southern Protest. Political Opportunity Structure Analysis in Cross-National Perspective." *Mobilization: An International Journal* 1(2):175–187.

— 2001. *Grassroots and Cadre in the Protest Movement.* Quezon City: Ateneo de Manila University Press.

— 2003. "Methods of Domination and Modes of Resistance: The U.S. Colonial State and Philippine Mobilization in Comparative Perspective." In Julian Go and Anne L. Foster, eds. *The American Colonial State in the Philippines,* pp. 256–290. Durham, NC: Duke University Press.

Bourchier, David. 1984. *The Dynamics of Dissent in Indonesia: Sowito and the Phantom Coup.* Modern Indonesia Project Publication no. 63, Interim Report. Ithaca: Cornell University, Southeast Asia Program Press.

— 1992a. "Pada Masa Liberal, Timbul Semacam Anarki: The 1950s in New Order Ideology." In David Bourchier and John Legge, eds. *Democracy in Indonesia, 1950s and 1990s* pp. 236–248. Clayton: Monash University, Centre of Southeast Asian Studies.

— 1992b. "Crime, Law and State Authority in Indonesia." In Arief Budiman, ed. *State and Civil Society in Indonesia, Papers on Southeast Asia, no. 22,* pp. 177–212. Clayton: Monash University Press.

— 1994. "Solidarity" The New Order's First Free Trade Union." In David Bourchier, ed. *Indonesia's Emerging Proletariat,* pp. 52–63. Clayton: Monash University, Centre of Southeast Asian Studies.

Bourchier, David and John Legge, eds. 1992. *Democracy in Indonesia, 1950s and 1990s.* Clayton: Monash University, Centre of Southeast Asian Studies.

Boyce, James K. 1993. *The Political Economy of Growth and Impoverishment in the Marcos Era.* Quezon City: Ateneo de Manila University Press.

Bratton, Michael and Nicolas van de Walle. 1992. "Popular Protest and Reform in Africa." *Comparative Politics* 25: 419–442.

Bray, John. 1992. "Burma: Resisting the International Community." *Pacific Review* 5(3): 291–296.

Brockett, Charles, D. 1993. "A Protest-Cycle Resolution of the Repression/ Popular-Protest Paradox." *Social Science History* 17 (3): 457–484.

Brooks, Karen. 1995. "The Rustle of Ghosts: Bung Karno in the New Order." *Indonesia* 60: 61–99.

Brown, David. 1996. *Reconstructing Ethnic Politics in Southeast Asia, Working Paper No. 61.* Perth: Murdoch University, Asian Research Centre.

Budiman, Arief. 1967. "Sebuah Pendapat Ttg. Organisasi KAMI: Mahasiswa Seharusnja Djadi Pedjuang Moral", *Sinar Harapan,* September 23, 1967, September 26, 1967, September 27, 1967.

— 1978. "The Student Movement in Indonesia: A Study of the Relationship Between Culture and Structure." *Asian Survey* 18(6): 609–625.

— 1990. "Gerakan Mahasiswa dan LSM: ke Arah Sebuah Reunificasi (Catatan Untuk G. J. A.)." *Kritis* 3(4): 53–59.

— 1992. "From Lower to Middle Class: Political Activities before and after 1988." In David Bourchier and John Legge, eds. 1992. *Democracy in Indonesia, 1950s and 1990s,* pp. 229–235. Clayton: Monash University, Centre of Southeast Asian Studies.

Bunce, Valerie. 1999. *Subversive Institutions: The Design and Destruction of Socialism and the State.* New York: Cambridge University Press.

Bunnell, Fredrick (with assistance from Alice Bunnell) 1996. "Community Participation, Indigenous Ideology, Activist Politics: Indonesian NGOs in the 1990s." In Daniel S. Lev and Ruth McVey, eds. *Making Indonesia? Essays in Honor of George McT. Kahin*, pp. 180–201. Ithaca: Cornell University, Southeast Asia Program Press.

Burma Watcher. 1989. "Burma 1988: There Came a Whirlwind, Part II." *Asian Survey* 29(2): 174–180.

Burton, Sandra. 1989. *The Impossible Dream: The Marcoses, The Aquinos and the Unfinished Revolution.* New York: Warner Books.

Byington, Kyy. 1988. *Bantay ng Bayan: Stories from the NAMFREL Crusade, 1984–1986.* Manila: Bookmark.

Cady, John. 1958. *A History of Modern Burma.* Ithaca: Cornell University Press.

Callahan, Mary.1996. *The Origins of Military Rule in Burma.* Ph.D. dissertation. Department of Government, Cornell University.

— 1998a. "On Time Warps and Warped Time: Lessons from Burma's 'Democratic Era.'" In Robert I. Rotberg's *Burma: Prospects for a Democratic Future*, pp. 49–68. Washington: Brookings Institution Press.

— 1998b. "The Sinking Schooner: Murder and the State in *'Democratic'* Burma." In Carl Troki, ed. *Gangsters, the State and Democracy in Southeast Asia*, pp. 17–37. Ithaca: Cornell University, Southeast Asia Program Press.

— 1999. "Cracks in the Edifice: Military-Society Relations in Burma Since 1988." Burma Update, pp. 22–51. Australian National University.

— 2001. "Civil-Military Relations in Burma: Soldiers as State-Builders in the Postcolonial Era." In Muthiah Alagappa, ed. *Coercion and Governance: The Declining Role of the Military in Asia*, pp. 412–429. Stanford University Press.

Carbonell-Catilo, M. A. de Leon and E. E. Nicholas 1985. *Manipulated Elections.* Manila: Np.

Catilo, Aurora and Prosperpina Tapales. 1988. "The Legislature." In Raul De Guzman and Mila Reforma, eds. *Government and Politics in the Philippines*, pp. 132–163. Singapore: Oxford University Press.

Celoza, Albert F. 1997. *Ferdinand Marcos and the Philippines: The Political Economy of Authoritarianism.* Westport: Praeger.

Chauvel, Richard. 2001. "The Changing Dynamic of Regional Resistance in Indonesia." In Grayson Lloyd and Shannon Smith, eds. *Indonesia Today: Challenges of History*, pp. 146–158. Singapore: Institute of Southeast Asia Studies.

Chipman, John. 1982. *French Power in Africa.* London: Blackwell.

Clarke, Gerard. 1998. *The Politics of NGOs in Southeast Asia: Participation and Protest in the Philippines.* London: Routledge.

Collier, R. and J. Mahoney. 1997. "Adding Collective Actors to Collective Outcomes: Labor and Recent Democratization in South America and South Europe." *Comparative Politics* 29: 285–303.

Consolacion, Strella. 1983. "An Unholy Dialogue: The Alienation of the Church from the State." *Diliman Review* 31(3): 1–45.

Constantino, Renato and Letizia Constantino. 1978. *The Philippines: The Continuing Past.* Quezon City: Foundation for Nationalist Studies.

Coppel, Charles A. 1983. *Indonesian Chinese in Crisis.* Kuala Lumpur: Oxford University Press.

Coronel, Shiela. 1993. "Death on the Tarmac: August 21, 1983." In Shiela Coronel, ed. *Coups, Cults and Cannibals: Reportage on an Archipelago*, pp. 52–59 Manila: Anvil Press.

Coronil, Fernando and Julie Skurski. 1991. "Dismembering and Remembering the Nation: The Semantics of Political Violence in Venezuela." *Comparative Studies in Society and History* **33**(2): 288–337.

Corpuz, O. D. 1989. *The Roots of the Filipino Nation*. Quezon City: Aklahi Foundation.

Cribb, Robert, ed. 1990. "Problems in the Historiography of the Indonesian Killings." In Robert Cribb, ed. *The Indonesian Killings of 1965–66: Studies from Java and Bali, Papers on Southeast Asia, no. 21*, pp. 1–44. Clayton: Monash University Press.

Crouch, Harold. 1971. "The Army, the Parties and Elections." *Indonesia* **11**:177–192.

— 1978. *The Army and Politics in Indonesia*. Ithaca: Cornell University Press.

— 1985. "The Continuing Crisis in the Philippines." ISIS Seminar Paper. Kuala Lumpur: ISIS.

— 1992. "State Control: Introduction." In Arief Budiman, ed. *State and Civil Society in Indonesia, Papers on Southeast Asia, no. 22*, pp. 115–120. Clayton: Monash University Press.

Cutwright, P. 1963. "National Political Development: Measurement and Analysis." *American Sociological Review* **28**: 42–59.

Daroy, Petronila, BN. 1988. "On the Eve of Dictatorship and Revolution." In Aurora Javate De Dios, Petronila BN Daroy and Lorna Kalaw-Tirol, eds. *Dictatorship and Revolution: Roots of People Power*, pp. 1–25. Metro-Manila: Conspectus.

Davenport, Christian. 1995. "Multi-Dimensional Threat Perception and State Repression: An Inquiry into Why States Apply Negative Sanctions." *American Journal of Political Science* **39**(3): 683–713.

— 1996. "The Weight of the Past: Exploring Lagged Determinants of Political Repression." *Political Research Quarterly* **49**(2): 377–403.

— 1999. "Human Rights and the Democratic Proposition." *Journal of Conflict Resolution* **43**(1): 377–403.

David, Stephan. 1991. "Explaining Third World Alignments." *World Politics* **43**(2): 233–257.

De Dios, Emmanuel. 1988. "The Erosion of the Dictatorship." In Aurora Javate De Dios, Petronila BN Daroy and Lorna Kalaw-Tirol, eds. *Dictatorship and Revolution: Roots of People Power*, pp. 70–131. Metro-Manila: Conspectus.

De Dios, Emmanuel, ed. 1984. *An Analysis of the Philippine Economic Crisis: A Workshop Report*. Quezon City: University of the Philippines Press.

Dejillas, Leopoldo. 1994. *Trade Union Behavior in the Philippines 1946–1990*. Quezon City: Ateneo de Manila University Press.

De la Torre, Edicio. 1986. *Touching Ground, Taking Root: Theological and Political Reflections in the Philippine Struggle*. Manila: Socio-Pastoral Institute.

Della Porta, Donatella. 1997. "The Policing of Protest: Repression, Bargaining and the Fate of Social Movements." *African Studies* **56**(1): 97–127.

Della Porta, Donatella and Robert Reiter. 1998. "The Policing of Protest in Western Democracies." In Donatella della Porta and Robert Reiter, eds. *Policing Protest: The Control of Mass Demonstrations in Western Democracies,* pp. 1–32. Minneapolis and London: University of Minnesota Press.

DeNardo, James. 1985. *Power in Numbers: The Political Strategy of Protest and Rebellion.* Princeton University Press.

Denny, J. A. 1989. "Column." *Tempo* (April 4).

— 1990. *Gerakan Mahasiswa dan Politik Kaum Muda, Era 80-an.* Jakarta: Jalan Percetakan Neg.

Dhakidae, Daniel. 1991. *The State, the Rise of Capital and the Fall of Political Journalism: Political Economy of Indonesian News Industry.* Ithaca: Department of Government, Ph.D. dissertation, Cornell University.

Diamond, Larry. 1999. *Developing Democracy Toward Consolidation.* Baltimore: Johns Hopkins University Press.

Dinnen, Sinclair. 1999. "Militaristic Solutions in a Weak State: Internal Security, Private Contractors, and Political Leadership in Papua New Guinea." *The Contemporary Pacific* 11(2): 279–301.

Diokno, Jose. 1982. "U.S. Interventionism, The Nuclear Menace and U.S. Bases." *Diliman Review* 30(1): 18–23.

Diokno, Ma. Serena, I. 1988. "Unity and Struggle." In Aurora Javate De Dios, Petronila BN Daroy and Lorna Kalaw-Tirol, eds. *Dictatorship and Revolution: Roots of People Power,* pp. 132–175, Metro-Manila: Conspectus.

DiPalma, G. 1990. *To Craft Democracies: An Essay on Democratic Transitions.* Berkeley: University of California Press.

Doeppers, Daniel F. 1984. *Manila, 1900–1940: Social Change in a Late Colonial Metropolis.* Quezon City: Ateneo de Manila University Press.

Donnison, Frank S. V. 1970. *Burma.* New York: Praeger.

Doronila, Amando. 1992. *The State, Economic Transformation and Political Change in the Philippines, 1942–1972.* New York and Singapore: Oxford University Press.

Duff, Ernest A. and John F. McCamant. 1976. *Violence and Repression in Latin America: A Quantitative and Historical Analysis.* New York: Free Press.

Dupuy, Trevor. 1961. "Burma and its Army: Contrast in Motivations and Characteristics." *Antioch Review* 20(4): 428–440.

— 1985. *Military History of World War II: Asian and Axis Resistance Movements.* New York: Trevor Dupuy.

Duvall, Raymond and Michael Shamir. 1980. "Indicators from Errors: Cross-National Time-Serial Measures of the Repressive Disposition of Governments." In Charles Taylor, ed. *Indicator Systems for Political, Economic and Social Analysis,* pp. 155–182. Cambridge, MA: Oelgeschlager, Gunn and Hain.

The Economist. 1991. "A Whisper of Democracy." *The Economist* (April 20).

— 1996. "Indonesia: All the President's Henchmen." *The Economist* (July 26).

Earl, Jennifer. 2003. "Tanks, Tear Gas and Taxes: Toward a Theory of Movement Repression." *Sociological Theory* 21(1): 44–68.

Ekiert, G. 1996. *The State Against Society: Political Crises and their Aftermath in East Central Europe.* Princeton University Press.

Eklöf, Stefan. 1999. *Indonesian Politics in Crisis: The Long Fall of Suharto, 1996–98.* Copenhagen: The Nordic Institute of Asian Studies.

Eisinger, Peter. 1973. "The Conditions of Protest Behavior in American Cities." *American Political Science Review* **67**: 11–28.

Escobar, Edward, J. 1993. "The Dialectics of Repression: The Los Angeles Police Department and the Chicano movement, 1968–1971." *The Journal of American History* **79**(4): 1483–1514.

Eldridge, Philip. 1989. *NGOs in Indonesia: Popular Movement or Arm of Government?* Clayton: Monash University: Centre for Southeast Asian Studies Working Paper no. 55.

— 1995. *Non-Government Organizations and Democratic Participation in Indonesia.* Oxford University Press.

Evers, Hans-Dieter. 1995. "The Growth of an Industrial Labor Force and the Decline of Poverty in Indonesia." *Southeast Asian Affairs* 164–174.

Fact-Finding Commission. 1990. *The Final Report of the Fact-Finding Commission (pursuant to R.A. No. 6832).* Metro Manila: Bookmark.

Fagan, David. 2000. "The Left and the Future of the Marcos Regime in the Philippines." (Reprint of Article by Renato Constantino, circulated under the pseudonym David Fagan, 1977.) *Journal of Contemporary Asia* **30**(3): 444–459.

Fanon, Frantz. 1963. *The Wretched of the Earth.* New York: Grove Press.

Fatton, Robert, J. 1991. "Democracy and Civil Society in Africa." *Mediterranean Quarterly* **2**(4): 83–95.

Far Eastern Economic Review. 1982. "A Little Vietnam." (March 12).

Fein, Helen. 1993. "Revolutionary and Anti-Revolutionary Genocides: Murders in Democratic Kampuchea, 1975 to 1979, and in Indonesia, 1965 to 1966." *Comparative Studies of Society and History* 35: 796–823.

Feith, Herbert. 1962. *The Decline of Constitutional Democracy in Indonesia.* Ithaca: Cornell University Press.

— 1963. "Dynamics of Guided Democracy." In Ruth McVey, ed. *Indonesia,* pp. 309–409. New Haven: Human Relations Area Files.

Feith, Herbert and Daniel Lev. 1963. "The End of the Indonesian Rebellion." *Pacific Affairs* **36**(1): 32–46.

Foulcher, Keith. 1992. "The Construction of an Indonesian National Culture: Patterns of Hegemony and Resistance." In Arief Budiman, ed. *State and Civil Society in Indonesia, Papers on Southeast Asia, no. 22,* pp. 301–320. Clayton: Monash University Press.

Franck, Thomas. 1992. "The Emerging Right to Democratic Governance." *American Journal of International Law* **86**(46): 46–91.

Francisco, Ron. 1996. "Coercion and Protest: An Empirical Test of Two Democratic States." *American Journal of Political Science* **40**(4): 1179–1204.

Franco, Jennifer Conroy. 2000. *Campaigning for Democracy: Grassroots Citizenship Movements, Less-than Democratic Elections and Regime Transition in the Philippines.* Quezon City: Institute for Popular Democracy.

Friend, Theodore. 1965. *Between Two Empires.* New Haven: Yale University Press.

Furnivall, John. 1941. *Progress and Welfare in Southeast Asia: A Comparison of Colonial Policy and Practice.* New York: Secretariat, Institute of Pacific Relations.
— 1949. "Twilight in Burma: Independence and After." *Pacific Affairs* 22(2): 155–172.
— 1956. *Colonial Policy and Practice: A Comparative Study of Burma and Netherlands India.* New York University Press.
Gamson, William and David Meyer. 1996. "Framing Political Opportunity." In Doug McAdam, John McCarthy and Meyer Zald, eds. *Opportunities, Mobilizing Structures and Framing: Comparative Applications of Contemporary Movement Theory,* pp. 46–91. New York: Cambridge University Press.
Garcia, Robert Francis B. 2001. *To Suffer Thy Comrades: How the Revolution Decimated its Own.* Manila: Anvil Publishing Company.
Garreton, M. and Manuel Antonio. 1996. "Social Movements and the Process of Democratization: A General Framework." In *Revue Internationale de Sociologie/International Review of Sociology* 6(1): 41–49.
Gartner, Scott and Pat Regan. 1996. "Threat and Repression: The Non-Linear Relationship Between Government and Opposition Violence." *Journal of Peace Research* 33(3): 273–287.
Gayatri, Irine H. 1999. "Arah Baru Perlawanan: Gerakan Mahasiswa 1989–1993." In Muridan S. Widjojo, ed. *Penakluk Rezim Orde Baru: Gerakan Mahasiswa 98,* pp. 64–125. Jakarta: Pustaka Sinar Harapan.
Geddes, Barbera. 1999. "What do we Really Know About Democratization After Twenty Years?" *Annual Review of Political Science* 2: 115–144.
George, T. J. S. 1988. *Revolt in Mindanao: The Rise of Islam in Philippine Politics.* Singapore: Oxford University Press.
Gerakan Pemuda Ansor. 1996. *Kerusuhan Situbono. Draft Buku Puti.* Unpublished manuscript: Gerakan Pemuda Ansor.
Gibson, James L. 1989. "The Policy Consequences of Political Intolerance Political Repression during the Vietnam War Era." *Journal of Politics* 51(1): 13–35.
Giugni, Marco, Doug McAdam and Charles Tilly. 1998. *From Contention to Democracy.* Lanham: Rowman & Littlefield.
Glenn, John K. 1999. "Competing Challengers and Contested Outcomes to State Breakdown: The Velvet Revolution in Czechoslovakia." *Social Forces* 78(1): 181–203.
Golay, Frank. 1971. "The Philippine Economy." In George M. Guthrie, ed. *Six Perspectives on the Philippines,* pp. 113–129. Manila: Bookmark.
Goodno, James. 1991. *The Philippines: Land of Broken Promises.* London and New Jersey: Zed Books.
Goodwin, Jeff. 2001. *No Other Way Out: States and Revolutionary Movements, 1945–1991.* New York: Cambridge University Press.
Guerrerro, Amado. 1979. *Philippine Society and Revolution.* Oakland: International Association of Filipino Patriots.
Gunn, Geoffrey. 1979. "Ideology and the Concept of Government in the Indonesian New Order." *Asian Survey* 19(8): 751–769.

Guyod, Dorothy. 1966. "The Political Inpact of the Japanese Occupation of Burma." Ph.D. dissertation, Yale University.

Hadiz, Vedi R. 1994. "Challenging State Corporatism on the Labour Front: Working Class Politics in the 1990s." In David Bourchier and John Legge, eds. *Democracy in Indonesia, 1950s and 1990s*, pp. 190–203. Monash Papers on Southeast Asia No. 31. Clayton: Monash University, Centre of Southeast Asian Studies.

Haggard, S. and R. R. Kaufman. 1997. "The Political Economy of Democratic Transitions." *Comparative Politics* **29**: 263–283.

Hansen, Gary. 1975. "Indonesia 1974: A Momentus Year." *Asian Survey* **15**(2): 148–156.

Hardy, Richard P. 1984. *The Philippine Bishops Speak (1968–1983)*. Quezon City: Maryknoll School of Theology.

Harvey, Barbara. 1998. "Diplomacy and Armed Struggle in the Indonesian National Revolution: Choice and Constraint in a Comparative Perspective." in Daniel S. Lev and Ruth McVey, eds. *Making Indonesia: Essays on Modern Indonesia in Honor of George McT. Kahin*, pp. 66–80. Ithaca: Cornell University, Southeast Asia Program Press.

Hari, Syamsuddin. 1990. "PPP and Politics Under the New Order." *Prisma* **49**(June): 31–51.

Hariyadhie. 1997. *Perspectif Gerakan Mahasiswa 1978: Dalamn Pacaturan Politik Nasional.* Jakarta: Golden Terayon Press.

Hawes, Gary. 1992. "Marcos, His Cronies, and the Philippines' Failure to Develop." In Ruth McVey, ed. *Southeast Asian Capitalists*, pp. 145–160. Ithaca: Cornell University, Southeast Asia Program Press.

Heidhues, Mary Somers. 1996. "When we Were Young: The Exile of the Republic's Leaders in Bangka, 1949." In Daniel S. Lev and Ruth McVey, eds. *Making Indonesia: Essays on Modern Indonesia in Honor of George McT. Kahin*, pp. 81–95. Ithaca: Cornell University Southeast Asia Press.

Hein, Gordon R. 1990. "Indonesia in 1989: A Question of Openness, Part II." *Asian Survey* **30**(2): 221–230.

Henderson, Conway W. 1991. "Conditions Affecting the Use of Political Repression." *The Journal of Conflict Resolution* **35**(1): 120–142.

Herbert, Patricia. 1982. *The Hsaya San Rebellion (1930–1932) Reappraised.* Clayton: Monash University Press.

Heryanto, Ariel. 1988. "The Development of 'Development.'" *Indonesia* **46**(October): 1–48.

— 1996. "Indonesian Middle Class Opposition in the 1990s." In G. Rodan, ed. *Political Opposition in Industrialising Asia*, pp. 242–260. London. Routledge.

— 1999. "Where Communism Never Dies: Violence, Trauma and Narration in the Last Cold War, Capitalist Authoritarian State." *International Journal of Cultural Studies* **2**(2): 147–177.

Higley, J., and R. Gunther. 1992. *Elites and Democratic Consolidation in Latin America and Southern Europe*. Baltimore: Johns Hopkins University Press.

Hill, Helen. 1978. "Fretelin: The Origins, Ideologies and Strategies of the Nationalist Movement in East Timor." MA thesis, Clayton: Monash University Press.

Hill, Stuart and Donald Rothchild. 1986. "The Contagion of Political Conflict in Africa and the World." *Journal of Conflict Resolution* **30**: 716–735.

Hipscher, Patricia. 1996. "Democratization and the Decline of Urban Social Movements in Chile and Spain." *Comparative Politics* **28**: 273–297.

— 1998. "Democratic Transitions as Protest Cycles: Social Movement Dynamics in Democratizing Latin America." In David S. Meyer and Sidney Tarrow, eds. *The Social Movement Society: Contentious Politics for a New Century*, pp. 153–172. Boulder: Rowman and Littlefield Publishers, Inc.

Honna, Jun. 2001. "Military Ideology in Response to Democratic Pressure in the Late Suharto Era: Political and Institutional Context." In Benedict Anderson, ed. *Violence and the State in Suharto's Indonesia*, pp. 54–89. Ithaca: Cornell University Southeast, Asia Program Press.

Hoover, Dean and David Kowalewski. 1991. "Dynamic Models of Dissent and Repression." *The Journal of Conflict Resolution* **36**(1): 150–182.

Htun Aung Kyaw. 1997. "Student Movements and Civil Society in Burma." MA thesis, Ithaca: Cornell University Press.

Human Rights Watch. 1997. "Human Rights Watch World Report 1998: Indonesia and East Timor." New York: Human Rights Watch.

Huntington, Samuel. 1968. *Political Order in Changing Societies*. New Haven: Yale University Press.

— 1991. *The Third Wave: Democratization in the Late 20th Century*. Norman: University of Oklahoma Press.

Hutchcroft, Paul. 1993. *Predatory Oligarchy, Patrimonial State: The Politics of Private Domestic Commercial Banking in the Philippines*. Ph.D. dissertation, Yale University Department of Political Science.

— 1998. *Booty Capitalism: The Politics of Banking in the Philippines*. Ithaca: Cornell University Press.

Inkeles, Alex and David H. Smith. 1974. *Becoming Modern*. New York: Cambridge University Press.

Ingleson, John. 1979. *Road To Exile: The Indonesian Nationalist Movement, 1927–1934*. Singapore: Asian Studies Association of Australia and Heinemann Educational Books.

Integrated Bar of the Philippines. 1983. "Report to the Commission on Human Rights and Due Process, Integrated Bar of the Philippines." Manila: Integrated Bar of the Philippines.

Jacobs, David. 1979. "Inequality and Police Strength: Conflict Theory and Coercive Control in Metropolitan Areas." *American Political Sociological Review* **44**(6): 913–925.

Jenkins, David. 1983. "The Evolution of Indonesian Army Doctrinal Thinking: The Concept of *Dwifungsi*." *Southeast Asian Journal of Social Science* **11**(2): 15–30.

— 1984. *Suharto and His Generals: Indonesian Military Politics 1975–1983*. Ithaca: Modern Indonesia Project, Cornell University, Southeast Asia Program Press.

Jenkins, J. C. 1985. *Politics of Insurgency*. New York: Columbia University Press.

Johnson, Bryan. 1987. *The Four Days of Courage: The Untold Story of the People Who Brought Marcos Down.* New York: Free Press.

Jones, Greg. 1989. *Red Revolution: Inside the Philippine Guerilla Movement.* Boulder: Westview Press.

Jose, Ricardo Trota. 1992. *The Philippine Army, 1935–1942.* Quezon City: Ateneo De Manila University Press.

Kahin, George McT. 1952. *Nationalism and Revolution in Indonesia.* Ithaca: Cornell University Press.

Kammen, Douglas. 1997. "A Time to Strike: Industrial Strikes and Changing Class Relations in New Order Indonesia." Ithaca: Department of Government, Ph.D. dissertation, Cornell University.

Karl, Terry Lynn. 1990. "Dilemmas of Democratization in Latin America." *Comparative Politics* **23**: 1–21.

Kell, Tom. 1995. *The Roots of the Acehenese Rebellion, 1989–1992.* Ithaca: Modern Indonesia Project, Cornell University, Southeast Asia Program Press. .

Kerkvliet, Benedict. 1974. "Land Reform in the Philippines Since the Marcos Coup." *Pacific Affairs* **47**(3): 286–304.

— 1986. *The Huk Rebellion: A Study of Peasant Revolt in the Philippines.* Berkeley: University of California Press.

Kerkvliet, Melinda Tria. 1982. *Mutual Aid and Manila Unions.* Madison. University of Wisconsin, Wisconsin Papers on Southeast Asia, no. 7.

— 1992. *Manila Workers' Unions, 1900–1950.* Quezon City: New Day.

Kessler, Richard J. 1984. "Politics, Philippine Style, Circa 1984." *Asian Survey* **24**(12): 1209–1228.

— 1989. *Rebellion and Repression in the Philippines.* New Haven: Yale University Press.

Khawaja, Marwan. 1993. "Repression and Popular Collective Action: Evidence from the West Bank." *Sociological Forum* **8**: 47–71.

Khin Nyunt, Brigadier General 1988a. *Burma Communist Party's Conspiracy to Take Over State Power.* Rangoon: Guardian Press.

— 1988b. *The Conspiracy of Treasonous Minions within the Myanmar Naingngan, and Traitorous Cohorts Abroad.* Rangoon: Guardian Press.

Khin Yi. 1988. *The Dobama Movement in Burma (1930–1938).* Ithaca: Cornell University Southeast Asia Program Press.

Kimura Masataka. 1997. *Elections and Politics Philippine Style: A Case in Lipa.* Manila: De La Salle University Press.

King, Dwight. 1982. "Indonesia's New Order as a Bureaucratic Polity, a Neopatrimonial Regime or a Bureaucratic-Authoritarian Regime: What difference does it Make?" In Benedict Anderson, Audrey Kahin, eds. *Interpreting Indonesian Politics: 13 Contributions to the Debate*, pp. 104–116. Ithaca: Modern Indonesia Project, Cornell University, Southeast Asia Program Press.

Kitschelt, Herbert. 1986. "Political Opportunity Structures and Political Protest: Anti-Nuclear Movements in Four Countries." *British Journal of Political Science* **165**: 57–85.

Kitley, Philip. 2001. "After the Bans: Modeling Indonesian Communications for the Future." In Grayson Lloyd and Shannon Smith, eds. *Indonesia Today:*

Challenges of History, pp. 256–269. Singapore: Institute of Southeast Asia Studies.

Komisar, Lucy. 1987. *Corazon Aquino: The Untold Story of a Revolution.* New York: George Braziller.

Koopmans, Ruud. 1997. "Dynamics of Repression and Mobilization: The German Extreme Right in the 1990s." *Mobilization: An International Journal of Research and Theory About Social Movements and Collective Behavior* 2(2): 149–164.

Kropotkin, Petr Alekseevich. 1995. *The Conquest of Bread and Other Writings.* New York: Cambridge University Press.

Kriesi, Hanspeter, Ruud Koopmans, Jan W. Duyvendak, and Marco Giugni. 1992. "New Social Movements and Political Opportunities in Western Europe." *European Journal of Political Research* 22(2): 219–244.

KSP 1984. "Overview of Opposition Forces in the Philippines." Utrecht: Mimeograph (February 28).

Kunio, Yoshihara. 1985. *Philippine Industrialization: Foreign and Domestic Capital.* Quezon City: Ateneo de Manila University Press.

Kyaw Kyaw Htut. 1992. "Refugee Student Interviews: Kyaw Kyaw Htut." *Deadly Enterprises: A Burma–India Situation Report* (December): 10–12.

Kyaw Yin Hlaing. 1996. "The Mobilization Process in the 'Four Eights' Democratic Movement in Burma." Paper presented at the 1996 Association of Asian Studies Annual Meeting, Honolulu, Hawaii.

— 2001. *The Politics of State-Business Relations in Post-Colonial Burma.* Ithaca: Department of Political Science, Ph.D. dissertation, Cornell University.

Lacaba, Jose. 1970. "Rain and the Rhetoric of Revolution." *Philippine Free Press* June 20.

Lane, Max. 1990. *The Urban Mass Movement in the Philippines.* Canberra, Australia. Monograph 10, Department of Political and Social Change, Australian National University.

Lawyers' Committee for International Human Rights. 1983. *The Philippines: A Country in Crisis.* Washington: The Lawyers Committee for International Human Rights.

Lande, Carl. 1978. "The April 7th Election in Manila: A Brief Report." *Philippine Studies Newsletter* (June).

Leary, Virginia, *et al.* 1984. *The Philippines: Human Rights After Martial Law.* Geneva: International Commission of Jurists.

Lebra, Joyce. 1969. "Japanese Policy and the Indian National Army." *Asian Studies (Manila)* 7(1).

Lee, Jungyeon. 1998. "Democratization and Social Movements in South Korea: Comparative Analysis of Authoritarian and Democratic Periods." American Sociology Association, Association Paper.

Lee, Junhan. 2001. "Political Protest and Democratization in South Korea." *Democratization* 7(3): 181–203.

Legge, J. D. 1972. *Sukarno: A Political Biography.* New York: Prager.

— 1988. *Intellectuals and Nationalism in Indonesia: A Study of the Following Recruited by Sultan Sjahrir in Occupation Indonesia.* Ithaca: Modern Indonesia Project, Cornell University, Southeast Asia Program Press.

Lev, Daniel. 1963–1964. "The Political Role of the Army in Indonesia." *Pacific Affairs* **36**: 349–364.

— 1966a. "Indonesia 1965: The Year of the Coup." *Asian Survey* **6**(2): 103–110.

— 1966b. *The Transition to Guided Democracy: Indonesian Politics, 1957–1959.* Ithaca: Modern Indonesia Project, Cornell University, Southeast Asia Program Press.

— 1987. *Legal Aid in Indonesia. Working Paper no. 44.* Clayton: Monash University, Centre of Southeast Asian Studies.

— 1994. "On the Fall of the Parliamentary System." In David Bourchier and John Legge, eds. *Democracy in Indonesia, 1950s and 1990s*, pp. 96–113. Clayton: Monash University, Centre of Southeast Asian Studies.

— 1996. "Between State and Society: Professional Lawyers and Reform in Indonesia." In Daniel Lev and Ruth McVey, eds., *Making Indonesia: Essays on Modern Indonesia in Honor of George McT. Kahin*, pp. 144–163. Ithaca: Cornell University, South East Asia Program Press.

Lichbach, Mark I. 1987. "Deterrence or Escalation? The Puzzle of Aggregate Studies of Repression and Dissent." *Journal of Conflict Resolution* **31**: 266–297.

— 1995. *The Rebel's Dilemma.* Ann Arbor: University of Michigan Press.

Liddle, William. 1973. "Evolution from Above: National Leadership and Local Development in Indonesia." *Journal of Asian Studies* **32**(2): 287–309.

— 1985. "Suharto's Indonesia: Personal Rule and Political Institutions." *Pacific Affairs* **58**(1): 68–90.

— 1992. "Indonesia's Democratic Past and Future." *Comparative Politics* **24**(4): 423–462.

— 1996a. "The Islamic Turn in Indonesia: A Political Explanation." *Journal of Asian Studies* (**55**): 3. 613–634.

— 1996b. "Indonesia: Suharto's Tightening Grip." *Journal of Democracy* **7**(4): 58–72.

— 1996c. "A Useful Fiction: Democratic Legitimation in New Order Indonesia." In R. H. Taylor, ed. *The Politics of Elections in Southeast Asia*, pp. 34–60. New York: Cambridge University Press.

Lindsey, Charles. 1984. "Economic Crisis in the Philippines." *Asian Survey* **24**(12): 1185–1208.

Lintner, Bertil. 1989. *Outrage: Burma's Struggle for Democracy.* London: Review Publishing Company, Ltd.

— 1990 *The Rise and Fall of the Communist Party of Burma (CPB).* Ithaca: Cornell University, Southeast Asia Program Press.

— 1994. *Burma in Revolt: Opium and Insurgency since 1948.* Boulder and Bangkok: Westview and Lotus Press.

Linz, J. J. and H. E. Chahabi, eds. 1998. *Sultanistic Regimes.* Baltimore: Johns Hopkins University Press.

Lipset, Seymour M. 1959. "Some Social Requisites of Democracy: Economic Development and Political Legitimacy." *American Political Science Review* **53**: 245–256.

Lipset, Seymour M. and Kyoung R. Seong and John C. Torres. 1993. "A Comparative Analysis of the Social Requisites for Democracy." *International Social Science Journal* **136**: 155–175.

Lockman, Zachary. 1988. "The Social Roots of Nationalism: Workers and the National Movement in Egypt, 1908–19." *Middle Eastern Studies* **24** (4): 445–459.

Loveman, Mara. 1998. "High-Risk Collective Action: Defending Human Rights in Chile, Uruguay, and Argentina." *American Journal of Sociology* **104**(2): 477–525.

Lucas, Anton. 1992. "Land Disputes in Indonesia: Some Current Perspectives." *Indonesia* **56**(1): 79–92.

— 1997. "Land Disputes, the Bureaucracy, and Local Disputes in Indonesia." In Jim Schiller and Barbera Martin-Shiller, eds. *Imagining Indonesia: Cultural Politics and Political Culture*, pp. 229–260. Ohio University Center for International Studies, Monograph on International Studies, Southeast Asia Series, no. 97. Ohio: Athens.

Luwarso, Lukas (ed.). 1997. *Jakarta Crackdown*. Jakarta: Alliance of Independent Journalists.

Macaranza, Bach. 1988. *Workers Participation in the Philippine People Power Revolution: An Examination of the Roles Played by Trade Unions in the Philippine People Power Revolution*. Manila: Friedrich Ebert Stiftung.

MacDougall, John James. 1976. "The Technocratic Model of Modernization: The Case of Indonesia's New Order." *Asian Survey* **16**(12): 1166–1183.

Machado, Kit. 1971. "Leadership and Organization in Philippine Local Politics." Ph.D. dissertation, University of Washington.

— 1979. "The Philippines 1978: Authoritarian Consolidation Continues." *Asian Survey* **19**(2): 131–140.

MacIntyre, Andrew. 1990. *Business and Politics in Indonesia*. Sydney, Australia: Allen and Unwin.

Magno, Alex. 1986. "The Anatomy of Political Collapse." In Alex Magno, Conrad De Quiros and Rene Ofreneo, eds. *The February Revolution: Three Views*, pp. 27–42. Quezon City: Kerrel.

Malay, Armando, Jr. 1988. "Dialectics of *Kaluwangan:* Echoes of a 1978 Debate." In *Marxism in the Philippines, Second Series*, pp. 1–21. Quezon City: Third World Studies Center, University of the Philippines.

Mallarangen, Rizal and William Liddle. 1995. "Indonesia in 1995: The Struggle for Power and Policy." *Asian Survey* **36**(2): 109–116.

Manapat, Ricardo. 1991. *Some Are Smarter than Others: The History of Marcos' Crony Capitalism*. New York: Aletheia Publications.

Manning, Robert. 1984–1985. "The Philippines in Crisis." *Foreign Affairs* **63** (Winter): 392–410.

Marcos, Ferdinand. 1978. *Revolution from Above: How the Philippines is using Martial Law to Build a New Society*. Raya Books: Hong Kong.

Mason, T. David and Dale A. Krane. 1989. "The Political Economy of Death Squads: Toward a Theory of the Impact of State-Sanctioned Terror." *International Studies Quarterly* **33**:175–198.

Maung Maung (Dr.). 1958. "Burma at the Crossroads." *Indian Quarterly* **14**(4).

— 1969. *Burma and General Ne Win*. Rangoon: Self-published.

— 1999. *The 1998 Uprising in Burma*. New Haven: Yale University, Southeast Asian Studies Program Press.

Maung Maung, former Brigadier General. 1953. *Grim War Against the KMT.* Rangoon: Maung Maung.

— 1990. *Burmese Nationalist Movements.* Honolulu: University of Hawaii Press.

Maung, Mya. 1991. *The Burmese Way to Poverty.* New York: Praeger Press.

Maung, Shwe Lu. 1989. *Burma: Nationalism and Ideology.* Dhaka University Press.

Mayo, Manuel. 1984. "Businessmen's Hopes Falling Like Confetti." *Diliman Review* 32(1): 6–9.

McAdam, Doug. 1982. *The Political Process and the Development of the Black Insurgency, 1930–1970.* University of Chicago Press.

— 1983. "Tactical Innovation and the Pace of Insurgency." *American Sociological Review* 48(6): 735–754.

McAdam, Doug, Sidney Tarrow and Charles Tilly. 2001. *Dynamics of Contention.* Cambridge, MA: Cambridge University Press.

McCammon, Holly. 2003. "Out of the Parlors and Into the Streets: The Changing Tactical Repertoire of the U.S. Women's Suffrage Movements." *Social Forces* 81(3): 787–818.

McCoy, Alfred. 1988. "Quezon's Commonwealth: The Emergence of Philippine Authoritarianism." In R. Paredes, ed. *Philippine Colonial Democracy,* pp. 123–154. New Haven: Yale Southeast Asian Monograph Series, no. 32.

— 1994. "An Anarchy of Families: A Historiography of State and Family in the Philippines." In Al McCoy, ed. *An Anarchy of Families: State and Family in the Philippines,* pp. 1–32. Quezon City: Ateneo de Manila University Press.

— 1999. *Closer Than Brothers: Manhood at the Philippine Military Academy.* New Haven: Yale University Press.

McDonald, Hamish. 1980. *Suharto's Indonesia.* Australia: Fontana Books.

McRae, Dave. 2001. "The 1998 Indonesian Student Movement, Working Paper 170." Clayton: Monash University, Monash Asian Institute.

McVey, Ruth. 1965. *The Rise of Indonesian Communism.* Ithaca: Cornell University Press.

— 1971. "The Post-Revolutionary Transformation of the Indonesian Army," Part 1. *Indonesia* 11: 131–176.

— 1972. "The Post-Revolutionary Transformation of the Indonesian Army," Part 1. *Indonesia* 13: 147–181.

— 1996. "Nationalism, Revolution and Organization in Indonesian Communism." In Ruth McVey and Daniel Lev, eds. *Making Indonesia: Essays in Modern Indonesian in Honor of George McT. Kahin,* pp. 96–117. Ithaca: Cornell University, Southeast Asia Program Press.

Meyer, David, Nancy Whittier and Belinda Robnet. 2002. *Social Movements: Identity, Culture and the State.* New York: Oxford University Press.

Meyer, John. 2000. "The Changing Cultural Context of Nation-State: A World Society Perspective." In G. Steinmetz, ed. *State and Culture,* pp. 1–43. Ithaca: Cornell University Press.

Migdal, Joel. 1988. *Strong States and Weak States: State–Society Relations and State Capabilities in the Third World.* Princeton University Press.

Migdal, Joel, Atol Kohli and Vivian Shue, eds. 1994. *State Power and Social Forces.* Cambridge University Press.

Ministry of Education and Culture (Indonesia). 1980. *NKK: "Reaksi dan Tanggapan."* Jakarta: Ministry of Education and Culture.

Miranda, Felipe. 1990. *The Final Report of the Fact-Finding Commission (pursuant to R.A.no. 6382)*. Manila: Bookmark.

Mijares, Primitivo. 1976. *The Conjugal Dictatorship of Ferdinand and Imelda Marcos.* San Francisco: Union Square Publications.

Mitchell, Neil and John McCormick. 1988. "Economic and Political Explanations for Human Rights Violations." *World Politics* 49: 510–525.

Molloy, Ivan. 1985. "Revolution in the Philippines: The Question of an Alliance Between Islam and Communism." *Asian Survey* 25(8): 822–833.

Moodie, T. Dunbar. 2003. "Mobilization on the South African Goldmines." In David S. Meyer, Nancy Whittier and Belinda Robnett, eds. *Social Movements: Identity, Culture and the State*, pp. 47–65. New York: Oxford University Press.

Moore, Barrington. 1966. *Social Origins of Dictatorship and Democracy: Lord and Peasant in the Making of the Modern World.* Boston: Beacon Press.

Mortimer, Rex. 1974. *Indonesian Communism Under Sukarno: Ideology and Politics 1959–1965.* Ithaca: Cornell University Press.

Moscotti, Albert D. 1974. *British Policy and the Nationalist Movement in Burma.* Honolulu: University of Hawaii, Asian Studies Program.

Mrazek, Rudolf. 1996. "Sjahrir at Boven Digoel: Reflections on Exile in the Dutch East Indies." In Daniel S. Lev and Ruth McVey, eds. *Making Indonesia: Essays on Modern Indonesia in Honor of George McT. Kahin*, pp. 41–65. Ithaca: Cornell University, Southeast Asia Program Press.

Muego, Benjamin. 1982. "Testimony of Professor Benjamin Muego. The Hearing before the Subcommittee on Asian and Pacific Affairs and on Human Rights and International Organizations of the House Committee on Foreign Affairs." Washington. 97th Congress, 2nd Session.

— 1983. "The Executive Committee in the Philippines: Successors, Power Brokers, and Dark Horses." *Asian Survey* 26(11): 1159–1170.

Mya Maung. 1990. "The Burma Road from the Union of Burma to Myanmar." *Asian Survey* 30(6): 602–624.

— 1992. *Totalitarianism in Burma: Prospects for Economic Development.* New York: Paragon House.

Nagazumi, Akira. 1972. *The Dawn of Indonesian Nationalism: The Early Years of Budi Utomo.* Tokyo: Institute of Developing Economies, Occasional Paper Series no. 10.

Naipospos, Coki Tigor. 2000. "East Timor in the Dynamics of Indonesian Politics." *Bulletin of Concerned Asian Scholars* 32(1&2): 87–90.

Nasution, Adnan-Buyung. 1994. "Defending Human Rights in Indonesia." *Journal of Democracy* 5(3): 114–123.

National Committee on Human Rights (Komisi Nasional Hak Asasi Manusia). 1996. *Laporan Final Fact-Finding Komnas HAM (Final Report of the Fact-Finding Committee of the National Committee on Human Rights)*. Jakarta: Komisi Nasional Hak Asasi Manusia. October 11.

Neher Clark, D. 1980. "The Philippines in 1980: The Gathering Storm." *Asian Survey* 21(2): 261–273.

Nemenzo, Francisco. 1987. "A Season of Coups: Reflections in the Military in Politics." *Kasarinlan* 2(4): 17–35.

Ng Chin-Kaong. 1976. "The Stormy Months Between 5th August and 15th January, 1974 in Indonesia: The Issues and Agitations." Singapore: Institute for the Humanities and Social Sciences, Nantang University Occasional Paper Series No. 36.

Noonan, Rita K. 1995. "Women Against the State: Political Opportunities and Collective Action Frames in Chile's Transition to Democracy." *Sociological Forum* 10(1): 81–111.

Nowak, Thomas C. and Kay A. Snyder. 1974. "Clientalist Politics in the Philippines: Integration or Instability?" *American Political Science Review* 68(3): 1147–1170.

Nu, U. 1975. *Saturday's Son*. Translated by U Law Yone. New Haven: Yale University Press.

Nusantara, Ariobimo A., R. Masri Sareb Putra and Y. B. Sudarmento. 2001. *Aksi Mahasiswa Menuju Gerbang Reformasi*. Jakarta: Gramedia Widiasarana Indonesia.

Nyi Nyi Lwin. 1992. "Refugee Student Interviews: Kyaw Kyaw Htut." *Deadly Enterprises: A Burma–India Situation Report* (December): 16–17.

Oberschall, Anthony. 1973. *Social Conflict and Social Movements*. Englewood Cliffs: Prentice-Hall.

O'Donnell, Guillermo. 1989. "Transitions to Democracy: Some Navigation Instruments." In R. Pastor, ed. *Democracy in the Americas: Stopping the Pendulum*, pp. 87–104. New York: Holms and Meier.

O'Donnell, Guillermo and Philippe C. Schmitter. 1986. *Transitions from Authoritarian Rule: Tentative Conclusions about Uncertain Democracies*. Baltimore: Johns Hopkins University Press.

Ofreneo, Rene E. 1984. "Contradictions in Export-Led Industrialization: The Philippine Experience." *Journal of Contemporary Asia* 14(4).

Opp, Karl-Dieter. 1989. "Repression and Revolutionary Action: East Germany in 1989." *Rationality and Society* 6(1): 101–138.

Osborne, Bobin. 1985. *Indonesia's Secret War: The Guerilla Struggle in Irian Jaya*. Sydney, London and Boston: Allen and Unwin.

Overholt, William H. 1986. "The Rise and Fall of Ferdinand Marcos." *Asian Survey* 26(11): 1137–1163.

Pasquale, Giordano T. 1988. *Awakening to Mission: The Philippine Catholic Church, 1965–1981*. Quezon City: New Day Publishers.

Pattiradjawane, René L. 1999. *Trisakti Mendobrak Tirani Orde Baru. Fakta dan Kesaksian Tragedi Berdarah 12 Mei 1998*. Jakarta: Gramedia Widiasarana Indonesia.

Pauker, Guy J. 1962. "The Role of the Military in Indonesia." In John J. Johnson, ed. *The Role of the Military in Underdeveloped Countries*, pp. 185–230. Princeton University Press.

Peltzer, Karl J. 1979. *Planter and Peasant: Colonial Policy and the Agrarian Struggle in East Sumatra, 1863–1947*.

Petition of 50. 1984. "White Paper: The September 1984 Incident at Tanjung Priok." Unpublished typescript, reproduced in *Indonesia Reports* (November 15): 5–8.

Pimentel, Benjamin. 1989. *Edjop: The Unusual Journey of Edgar Jopson.* Quezon City: Ken Inc.

Pineda-Ofreneo, Rosalinda. 1988. *The Manipulated Press: A History of Philippine Journalism Since 1945.* Manila: Solar Publishing Corporation.

Pion-Berlin, David. 1997. *Through Corridors of Power: Institutions and Civil-Military Relations in Argentina.* University Park: Pennsylvania State University Press.

Poe, Steven and C. Neal Tate. 1994. "Repression and Personal Integrity in the 1980s: A Global Analysis." *American Political Science Review* **88**: 853–872.

Polletta, Francesca. 2002. *Freedom is an Endless Meeting: Democracy in American Social Movements.* University of Chicago Press.

Ponna, Wignaraja, ed. 1993. *New Social Movements in the South: Empowering the People.* London; Atlantic Highlands, NJ: Zed Books.

Porter, Donald. 2002. "Citizen Participation Through Mass Mobilization and the Rise of Political Islam in Indonesia." *The Pacific Review* **15**(2): 201–224.

Porter, Gareth. 1989. "Strategic Debates and Dilemmas in the Philippine Communist Movement." In Steven R. Dorr and Lt. Deborah J Mitchell, eds. *The Philippines in a Changing Southeast Asia*, pp. 13–32. Washington: Defense Academic Research Support Program.

PPBI – *Pusat Perjuangan Buruh Indonesia.* 1997. "Profile of Mass Organisations Affiliated to the PRD." Jakarta: unpublished document.

Przeworski, Adam. 1986. "Some Problems in the Study of Transitions to Democracy." In Guillermo O'Donnell, Philippe C. Schmitter and Laurence Whitehead, eds. *Transitions from Authoritarian Rule: Prospects for Democracy*, pp. 47–63. Baltimore: Johns Hopkins University Press.

— 1991. *Democracy and the Market: Political and Economic Reforms in Eastern Europe and Latin America.* Cambridge, MA: Harvard University Press.

Psnakis, Steve. 1981. *Two "Terrorists" Meet.* San Francisco: Alchemy Books.

Pusat Perjuangan Buruh Indonesia (Indonesian Center for Labor Struggles). 1998. Profile of Mass Organizations Affiliated to the PRD. Unpublished document.

Pye, Lucien. 1990. "Political Science and the Crisis of Authoritarianism." *American Political Science Review* **84**: 3–19.

Rafael, Vincent. 1990. "Patronage and Pornography: Ideology and Spectatorship in the Early Marcos Years." *Comparative Studies in Society and History* **32**(2): 282–304.

Ramage, Douglas Edward. 1995. *Politics in Indonesia: Democracy, Islam and the Ideology of Tolerance.* London and New York: Routledge.

Randall, Vicky. 1998. *Political Change and Underdevelopment: A Critical Introduction to Third World Politics.* Durham, NC: Duke University Press.

Raquiza, Antoinette. 1997. "Philippine Feminist Politics: Disunity in Diversity." In Miriam Coronel Ferrer, ed. *Civil Society Making Civil Society*, pp. 171–185. Quezon City: Third World Studies Center, University of the Philippines.

Reeve, David. 1992. "The Corporatist State: The Case of Golkar." In Arief Budiman, ed. *State and Civil Society in Indonesia*, pp. 151–176. Clayton: Monash University, Monash Papers in Southeast Asia. No. 22.

Reid, Anthony. 1974. *The Indonesian National Revolution, 1945–1950*. Westport: Greenwood Press.

— 1980. "Indonesia: From Briefcase to Samurai Sword." In Alfred McCoy, ed. *Southeast Asia under Japanese Occupation, 1942–1945*, pp. 13–26. New Haven: Yale University South Asian Studies.

Rianto, Gatoto.1996. "Petani Badega Memperjhuangkan Maknya atas Tanah." In Boy Fidro and Noer Fauzi, eds. *Pembangunan Berbuah Sengketa:29 Tulisan Pengalaman Advokasi Tanah*, pp. 35–44. Jahafta: Yayasan Sentesa *et al.*

Rivera, Temario C. 1985. "Political Opposition in the Philippines: Contestation and Cooperation." Wisconsin Papers in Southeast Asia. Madison: University of Wisconsin Center for Southeast Asian Studies.

— 1994. *Landlords and Capitalists: Class, Family and State in Philippine Manufacturing*. Quezon City: The University of the Philippines Press.

Robinson, Geoffrey. 1984. "Some Arguments Concerning US Influence and Complicity in the Indonesian 'Coup' of October 1, 1965." Manuscript.

— 1995. *The Dark Side of Paradise: Political Violence in Bali*. Ithaca: Cornell University Press.

Robison, Richard. 1988. "Authoritarian States, Capital-Owning Class, and the Politics of Newly Industrializing Countries: The Case of Indonesia." *World Politics* 41(1): 52–74.

— 1993. "Indonesia: Tensions in State and Regime." In K. Hewison, R. Robison and G. Rodan, eds. *Southeast Asia in the 1990s: Authoritarianism, Democracy and Capitalism*, pp. 39–74. St. Leonards, Australia: Allen and Unwin.

Rocamora, Joel. 1994. *Breaking Through: The Struggle Within the Communist Party of the Philippines*. Manila: Anvil.

Rose, Mavis. 1987. *Indonesia Free: A Political Biography of Mohammad Hatta*. Ithaca: Modern Indonesia Project, Cornell University, Southeast Asia Program Press.

Rosenberg, David A. 1974–1975. "Civil Liberties and the Mass Media Under Martial Law in the Philippines." *Pacific Affairs* 47(4): 472–484.

Rudebeck, Lars and Olle Tornquist. 1998. "Introduction." In Lars Rudebeck, Olle Tornquist and Virgilio Rojas, eds. *Democratization in the Third World: Concrete Cases in Comparative and Theoretical Perspective*, pp. 1–24. New York: Macmillan Press, St. Martin's Press.

Rummel, Rudolph J. 1984. "Libertarianism, Violence within States and the Polarity Principle." *Comparative Politics* 16(4): 443–462.

Sadikan, Ali. 1985. "Testimony of Ali Sadikin at the October 31, 1985 Session of Lt. General Dharsono's Subversion Trial." Reprinted in *Indonesia Reports – Politics Supplement* 15(April): 1–8.

Saidi, Ridawan. 1989. *Mahasiswa dan Lingkaran Politik*. Ridawan Saidi. Jakarta: Lembaga Pers Mahasiswa Mapussy Indonesia (LPMI).

Santoso (editor). 1997. *Peristiwa 27 Juli*. Jakarta: Institut Studi Arus Informasi and Aliansi Jurnalis Independen.

Saunders, Joseph. 1998. "Academic Freedom in Indonesia." New York. Human Rights Watch Report.

Sawyers, Traci M. and David S. Meyer. 1999. "Missed Opportunities: Social Movement Abeyence and Public Policy." *Social Problems* **46**(2): 187–206.

Schulte-Nordholdt, N. G. 1987. *State–Citizen Relations in Suharto's Indonesia. Occasional Papers no. 26.* Queensland: James Cook University Centre for Southeast Asian Studies.

Scipes, Kim. 1996. *KMU: Building Genuine Trade Unionism in the Philippines, 1980–1994.* Quezon City: New Day.

Scott, Peter Dale. 1985. "The United States and the Overthrow of Sukarno, 1965–1967." *Pacific Affairs* **57**(Summer): 239–264.

Scott, William Henry. 1983. "The Union Obrera Democracia, First Filipino Labor Union." *Philippine Social Sciences and Humanities Review.* **47** (1–4).

Sein Win. 1988. AP Wire Report from Burma. March 22.

Selth, Andrew. 1986. "Race and Resistance in Burma, 1942–1945." *Modern Asian Studies* **26**(3): 483–507.

— 1989. "Death of a Hero: The U Thant Disturbances in Burma, December 1974." Nathan, Queensland: Centre for the Study of Australian–Asian Relations, Division of Asian and International Studies, Griffith University.

Sembiring, Ita. 1998. *Catatan dan Refleksi Tragedi Jakarta 13 & 14 Mei 1998.* Jakarta: Elex Media Komputindo.

Setsuho, Ikahata, 1999. "The Japanese Occupation Period in Philippine History." In Ikahata Setsuho and Ricardo T. Jose, eds. *The Philippines Under Japan: Occupation Policy and Reaction*, pp. 1–20. Quezon City: Ateneo de Manila University Press.

Sheo. 1992. "Refugee Student Interviews: Kyaw Kyaw Htut." *Deadly Enterprises: A Burma–India Situation Report* (December): 19–20.

Shiraishi, Takashi. 1990. *An Age in Motion: Popular Radicalism in Java, 1912–1926.* Ithaca: Cornell University Press.

— 2003. "A New Regime of Order: Surveillance Politics in Indonesia." In James Siegel and Audrey Kahin, eds. *Southeast Asia Over Three Generations: Essays presented to Benedict R. O' G. Anderson*, pp. 47–74. Ithaca: Cornell University, Southeast Asia Program Press.

Shwe Lu Maung. 1989. *Burma: Nationalism and Ideology.* Dhaka: University Press.

Siegel, James. 2001. "Thoughts on the Violence of May 13 and 14, 1998." In Benedict Anderson, ed. *Violence and the State in Suharto's Indonesia*, pp. 90–123. Ithaca: Cornell University, Southeast Asia Program Press.

Silverstein, Josef. 1964. "From Democracy to Dictatorship." *Current History* **46**: 83–88.

— 1977. *Burma: Military Rule and the Politics of Stagnation.* Ithaca: Cornell University Press.

Silverstein, Josef and Julian Wohl. 1964. "University Students and Politics in Burma." *Pacific Affairs* **37**(1): 50–65.

Simmons, Geoff. 2000. *Indonesia: The Long Repression.* New York: St. Martin's Press.

Singh, Balawart. 1993. *Independence and Democracy in Burma, 1945–52: The Turbulent Years.* Ann Arbor: Center for South and Southeast Asian Studies.

Slim, Field Marshall the Viscount William. 1961. *Defeat into Victory.* New York: David McKay Company.

Skocpol, Theda. 1979. *States and Social Revolutions: A Comparative Analysis of France Russia and China.* New York: Cambridge University Press.

Smith, Christian, and Liesl Ann Haas. 1997. "Revolutionary Evangelicals in Nicaragua: Political Opportunity, Class Interests, and Religious Identity." *The Journal for the Scientific Study of Religion* 36(3): 440–455.

Smith, Martin. 1999 *Burma: Insurgency and the Politics of Ethnicity.* London: Zed Books.

Snyder, Richard. 1992. "Explaining Transitions from Neopatrimonial Dictatorships." *Comparative Politics* 24(4, July): 379–399.

Soe Lwin. 1992. "Refugee Student Interviews: Kyaw Kyaw Htut." *Deadly Enterprises: A Burma–India Situation Report* (December): 18–19.

Soewarsono. 1999a. "Dari 'OTB' ke 'OTB:' Catatan-Catatan 'Resmi' Mengenai Gerakan Mahasiswa Indonesia, 1993–1996." In Muridan S. Widjojo, ed. *Penakluk Rezim Orde Baru: Gerakan Mahahsiswa '98,* pp. 126–140. Jakarta: Pustaka Sinar Harapan.

— 1999b. "Dari 'Prolog: Gerakan Mahasiswa 1998." In Muridan S. Widjojo, ed. *Penakluk Rezim Orde Baru: Gerakan Mahahsiswa '98,* pp. 1–16. Jakarta: Pustaka Sinar Harapan.

Soriano, Vic. 1984. "Lakbayan, Boycott and Civil Disobedience: A Reading of the Political Events Before May 14, and some Projections." *Diliman Review* 32(3–4): 3–7.

Southeast Asia Advisory Group to the Asia Society. 1975. "Rural Development Panel Seminar on Land Reform in the Philippines." New York: Southeast Asia Advisory Group Reports, Asia Society.

Southeast Asia Chronicle (editors). 1978. "Preparing for the Revolution: The United Front in the Philippines." *Southeast Asia Chronicle* 62(May–June): 6–7.

Southeast Asia Chronicle (editors). 1982. "Turning Point: The NDF Takes the Lead." *Southeast Asia Chronicle* 83 (April): 2–7.

Southwood, Julie and Patrick Flanagan. 1983. *Indonesian Law, Propaganda and Terror.* London: Zed Press.

Staff Report Prepared for the use of the Senate Select Committee in Intelligence, US Senate. 1985. *The Philippines: A Situation Report.* Committee Print, 99th Congress. November 11.

Staff Report Prepared for the use of U.S. Senate Committee on Foreign Relations. 1973. *Korea and the Philippines, November 1972.* Committee Print, 93rd Congress. 1st Session, February 18.

Stauffer, Robert. 1977. "Philippine Corporatism: A Note on the 'New Society.'" *Asian Survey* 17(4): 393–407.

Stepan, Alfred. 2001. *Arguing Comparative Politics.* Oxford and New York: Oxford University Press.

Steinberg, David. 1960. "The Philippine 'Collaborators': Survival of an Oligarchy." In Josef Silverstein, ed. *Southeast Asia in World War II: Two*

Essays, pp. 67-86. New Haven. Southeast Asia Studies Monograph Series, Yale University, no. 7.

— 1982. *Burma: A Socialist Nation of Southeast Asia*. Boulder: Westview Press.

Stohl, M. and G. A. Lopez. 1984. "Introduction." In M. Stohl and G. A. Lopez, eds. *The State as Terrorist*, pp. 3-10. Westport: Greenwood Publishing Company.

Stoler, Ann Laura. 1985. *Capitalism and Confrontation in Sumatra's Plantation Belt*. New Haven: Yale University Press.

Sudjatmiko, Budiman. 1996a. "Exceptie of Budiman Sudjatmiko." Jakarta Court Document, circulated via internet. December 19, 1996.

— 1996b. *People's Democratic Party and its Standpoints Surrounding the 27 July 1996 Turbulence*. Jakarta August 9, 1996. Unpublished internet posting.

Sumardi, I. Sandyawan, SJ. 1998. "Condition of Our Shared Life: The May 1998 Tragedy in Indonesia." Jakarta: *Tim Relawan untuk Kemanusiaan* (Team of Volunteers for Humanitarian Causes), unpublished report (July 28).

Sumitro, (Lieutenant General, Retired). 1989. "Aspiring to Normal Politics." *Far Eastern Economic Review* (April 6).

Sundhaussen, Ulf. 1982. *The Road to Power: Indonesian Military Politics 1945–1967*. Kuala Lumpur and Oxford: Oxford University Press.

Suryadinata, Leo. 1989. *Military Ascendancy and Political Culture: A Study of Indonesia's GOLKAR*. Athens: Ohio University Center for International Studies, Southeast Asia Series, no. 85.

— 1997. "Democratization and Political Succession in Suharto's Indonesia." *Asian Survey* 37(3): 269–280.

Sutherland, Heather. 1979. *The Making of the Bureaucratic Elite*. Singapore: Heinemann Educational Books.

Swift, Ann. 1989. *The Road to Madiun: The Indonesian Communist Uprising of 1948*. Ithaca: Modern Indonesia Project, Cornell University, Southeast Asia Program Press.

Tanter, Richard. 1992 "The Totalitarian Ambition: Intelligence Organizations in the Indonesian State." In Arief Budiman, ed. *State and Civil Society in Indonesia, Papers on Southeast Asia, no. 22*, pp. 213–284. Clayton: Monash University Press.

Tarling, Nicholas. 1982. "A New and Better Cunning: British Wartime Planning for Postwar Burma, 1942–1943." *Journal of Southeast Asian Studies* 13(1): 33–59.

— 1998. *Nations and States in Southeast Asia*. Cambridge University Press.

Tarrow, Sidney. 1998. *Power in Movement: Social Movements, Collective Action and Politics*. New York: Cambridge University Press.

Taylor, Robert H. 1973. *Foreign and Domestic Consequences of the KMT Intervention in Burma*. Ithaca: Cornell University, Southeast Asia Studies Program Press.

— 1974. *The Relationship Between Burmese Social Classes and British–Indian Policy on the Behavior of the Burmese Political Elite, 1937–1942*. Ph.D. dissertation, Cornell University.

— 1981. "Party, Class and Power in British Burma." *Journal of Commonwealth and Comparative Politics* 19(11): 44–62.

— 1983. "The Burmese Communist Movement and its Indian Connection: Formation and Factionalism." *Journal of Southeast Asian Studies* **14**(1): 95–108.

— 1987. *The State in Burma*. Honolulu: University of Hawaii Press.

Taylor, Robert H., ed. 1984. *Marxism and Resistance in Burma, 1942–1945*. Athens: Ohio University Press.

Thaung, U. 1995. *A Journalist, A General, and an Army in Burma*. Bangkok: White Lotus.

Thomas, R. Murray and Soedijarto. 1980. *Political Style and Education Law in Indonesia*. Hong Kong: Asian Research Service.

Thompson, Mark. 1995. *The Anti-Marcos Struggle*. New Haven: Yale University Press.

"Thursday Night Club." 1998 (March). "Kelompok Profesional Ingin Perubahan." Unpublished group statement.

Tiglao, Robert. 1988. "The Consolidation of the Dictatorship." In Aurora Javate De Dios, Petronila BN Daroy and Lorna Kalaw-Tirol, eds. *Dictatorship and Revolution: Roots of People Power*, pp. 86-131. Metro-Manila: Conspectus.

Tilly, Charles. 1978. *From Mobilization to Revolution*. Reading, MA: Addison-Wesley Publishing Co.

— 1986. *The Contentious French*. Cambridge, MA: Harvard University Press.

— 1995. *Popular Contention in Great Britain*. Cambridge, MA: Harvard University Press.

— 1999. "Regimes and Contention." Unpublished paper.

— 2000. "Processes and Mechanisms of Democratization." *Sociological Theory* **18**: 1–16.

Timberman, David. 1991. *A Changeless Land: Continuity and Change in Philippine Politics*. Manila and Singapore: Bookmark and the Institute for Southeast Asian Studies.

Tinker, Hugh. 1967. *The Union of Burma: A Study of the First Years of Independence*, 4th edn. London: Oxford University Press.

— 1986. "Burma's Struggle for Indpendence: The Transfer of Power Thesis Re-examined." *Modern Asian Studies* **20**(3): 461–481.

Tolentino, Arturo. 1990. *Voice of Dissent*. Quezon City: Phoenix Publishing House.

Toye, Jeremy. 1980. "Subversion Trial Opens." *The Asia Record* (July): 7–14.

Trager, Frank. 1959. "Political Divorce in Burma." *Foreign Affairs* **37**(1): 317–327.

— 1966. *From Kingdom to Republic*. London: Pall Mall Press.

Uhlin, Anders. 1995. *Democracy and Diffusion: Transnational Lesson Drawing Among Indonesian Democracy Actors*. Lund University Press.

— 1997. *Indonesia and the "Third Wave of Democratization": The Indonesian Pro-Democracy Movement in a Changing World*. Surrey, England: Curzon.

United States State Department. 1988. *Country Reports on Human Rights Practices for 1988: Burma*. Washington: US State Department.

University of the Philippines, School of Economics. 1984. *An Analysis of the Philippine Economic Crisis*. Quezon City: University of the Philippines, School of Economics.

Valdepenas, Vicente Jr. 1970. *The Protection and Development of Philippine Manufacturing*. Manila: Ateneo University Press.

Van Aelst, Peter and Stefaan Walgrave. 2000. "Who Is That (Wo)man in the Street? From the Normalisation of Protest to the Normalisation of the Protester." American Sociological Association, Association Paper.

Van der Kroef, Justus M. 1970. "Indonesian Communism Since the 1965 Coup." *Pacific Affairs* 43(1): 34–60.

— 1973a. "Sukarno's Indonesia." *Pacific Affairs* 46(2): 268–288.

— 1973b. "Communism and Reform in the Philippines." *Pacific Affairs*, 46(1): 29–58.

Van der Veur, Paul W. 1969. *Education and Social Change in Colonial Indonesia*.

Van Dijk, C. 1985. "Survey of Political Developments in Indonesia in the Second Half of 1984: The National Congress of the PPP and the Pancasila Principle." *Review of Indonesian and Malaysian Affairs* 19(1): 177–202.

— 1989. "Political Development, Stability and Democracy: Indonesia in the 1980s." Occasional Paper no. 17. Centre for South-East Asian Studies.

Van Langenberg, Michael. 1990. "Gestapu and State Power in Indonesia." In Robert Cribb, ed. *The Indonesian Killings of 1965–66: Studies from Java and Bali, Papers on Southeast Asia, no 21*, pp. 45–65. Clayton: Monash University Press.

— 1992."The New Order State: Language, Ideology and Hegemony." In Arief Budiman, ed. *State and Civil Society in Indonesia, Papers on Southeast Asia, no. 22*, pp. 121–149. Clayton: Monash University Press.

Van Niel, Robert. 1950. *The Emergence of the Modern Indonesian Elite*. The Hague: Van Hoeve.

Vatikiotis, Michael. 1993. *Indonesian Politics Under Suharto: Development and Pressure for Change*. London and New York: Routledge.

Villegas, Bernardo. 1985. "The Philippines in 1985: Rolling with the Political Punches, Part II." *Asian Survey* 26(2): 127–140.

Wardhana, Veven, S. P. 1997. *Kemelut PDI di Layar Televisi: Survei Pemberitaan PDI di Lima Stasiun TV*. Jakarta: Institut Studi Arus Informasi.

Weekley, Kathleen. 1996. "From Vanguard to Rearguard: The Theoretical Roots of the Crisis of the Communist Party of the Philippines." In P. N. Abinales, ed. *The Revolution Falters: The Left in Philippine Politics after 1986*, pp. 28–59. Ithaca: Cornell University, Southeast Asia Program Press.

Wertheim, W. F. 1979a. "Whose Plot – New Light on the 1965 Events." *Journal of Contemporary Asia* 9(2): 197–215.

— 1979b. "The Latief Case: Suharto's Involvement Revealed." *Journal of Contemporary Asia* 9(2): 197–215.

— 1987. "Indonesian Muslims Under Sukarno and Suharto: Majority with Minority Mentality." In Christine Doran, ed *Indonesian Politics: A Reader*, pp. 31–52. Townsville, Australia: Centre for Southeast Asian Politics. James Cook University of North Queensland.

Werz, Nikolaus 1989. "Democratic Forms of Government in Latin America." In *Law and State* 39: 58–78.

Wessel, Ingrid. 2001. "The Politics of Violence in New Order Indonesia in the Last Decade of the 20th Century." In Ingrid Wessel and Georgia Winhofer, eds. *Violence in Indonesia*, pp. 64–81. Hamburg: Abra.

White, Gordon 1998. "Civil Society, Democratization and Development." In Lars Rudebeck, Olle Tornquist and Virgilio Rojas, eds. *Democratization in the Third World : Concrete Cases in Comparative and Theoretical Perspective.* New York: Macmillan Press; St. Martin's Press.

White, Robert W. 1989. "From Peaceful Protest to Guerilla War: Micromobilization and the Provisional Irish Republican Army." *American Journal of Sociology* 94(6): 1277–1302.

Widjojo, Muridan, S. and Moch., and Nurhasim 1998. "Organisasi Gerakan Mahasiswa 1998: Upaya Rekonstruksi." In Muridan S. Widjojo, ed. *Penakluk Rezim Orde Baru: Gerakan Mahasiswa '98*, pp. 290–376. Jakarta: Pustaka Sinar Harapan.

Williams, Michael. 1982. *Sickle and Crescent: The Communist Revolt in 1926 in Banten.* Ithaca: Modern Indonesia Project, Cornell University, Southeast Asia Program Press.

Wood, Elizabeth J. 2000. *Forging Democracy From Below: Insurgent Transitions in South Africa and El Salvador.* New York: Cambridge University Press.

Worby, Eric. 1998. "Tyranny, Parody and Ethnic Polarity: Ritual Engagements with the State in North Zimbabwe." *Journal of African Studies* 24(3): 561–578.

Wurfel, David. 1977. "Martial Law in the Philippines: The Methods of Regime Survival." *Pacific Affairs* 50(1): 5–30.

— 1988. *Filipino Politics: Development and Decay.* Quezon City: Ateneo de Manila University Press.

Yawnghwe, Chao-Tzang. 1995. "Burma: The Depoliticization of the Political." In Muthiah Alagappa, ed. *Political Legitimacy in Southeast Asia*, pp. 170–192. Stanford University Press.

Yayasan Lembaga Bantuan Hukum Indonesia (YLBHI). 1997a. *1996: Tahun Kekerasan: Potret Pelanggaran HAM di Indonesia.* Made Tony Supriatma, ed. Jakarta: Yayasan Lembaga Bantuan Hukum Indonesia.

— 1997b. *Amuk Banjarmasin.* Harius Salim HS and Andi Achdian, eds. Jakarta: Yayasan Lembaga Bantuan Hukum Indonesia.

Yitri, Moksha. 1989 "The Crisis in Burma: Back from the Heart of Darkness?" *Asian Survey* 29(6): 543-558. .

Younes, Mona M. 2000. *Liberation and Democratization: The South African and Palestinian National Movements.* Minneapolis: University of Minnesota Press.

Young, Crawford. 1994. *The African Colonial State in Comparative Perspective.* New Haven and London: Yale University Press.

Youngblood, Robert. 1981. "The Philippines in 1981: From 'New Society' to 'New Republic.'" *Asian Survey* 22(6): 222–235.

— 1990. *Marcos Against the Church: Economic Development and Political Repression in the Philippines.* Ithaca: Cornell University Press.

Zald, Mayer. 1988. "The Trajectory of Social Movements in America." In L. Kriesberg and B. Misztal, eds. *Social Movement as a Factor of Change in the*

Modern World: Research in Social Movements, Conflicts and Change, pp. 19–42. Greenwitch: JAI Press.

Zimmermann, Ekkart. (1998). "On the Readiness to Use Protest and Violence in East Germany." International Sociological Association, Association Paper.

Zulkifli, Arif. 1996. *PDI Di Mata Golongan Menengah Indonesia: Studi, Komunikasi, Politik.* Jakarta: Grafiti.

Index

Lightning Source UK Ltd.
Milton Keynes UK
UKHW040220250519
343311UK00001B/10/P